CONTOURS OF CHRISTOLOGY
IN THE NEW TESTAMENT

McMaster New Testament Studies

The McMaster New Testament Studies series, edited by Stanley E. Porter, is designed to address particular themes in the New Testament that are of concern to Christians today. Written in a style easily accessible to ministers, students, and laypeople by contributors who are proven experts in their fields of study, the volumes in this series reflect the best of current biblical scholarship while also speaking directly to the pastoral needs of people in the church today.

Contours of Christology in the New Testament

Edited by

Richard N. Longenecker

WILLIAM B. EERDMANS PUBLISHING COMPANY

GRAND RAPIDS, MICHIGAN / CAMBRIDGE, U.K.

© 2005 Wm. B. Eerdmans Publishing Co.

Wm. B. Eerdmans Publishing Co.
255 Jefferson Ave. S.E., Grand Rapids, Michigan 49503 /
P.O. Box 163, Cambridge CB3 9PU U.K.

Printed in the United States of America

10 09 08 07 06 05   7 6 5 4 3 2 1

Library of Congress Cataloging-in-Publication Data

Contours of christology in the New Testament / edited by Richard N. Longenecker.
p.   cm.   — (McMaster New Testament studies)
Includes bibliographical references and index.
ISBN 0-8028-1014-4
1. Jesus Christ — History of doctrines — Early church, ca. 30-600 — Congresses.
2. Bible. N.T. — Theology — Congresses.
I. Longenecker, Richard N.   II. Series.

BT198.C6126   2005
232′09′015 — dc22

2005040484

www.eerdmans.com

Contents

CONTENTS

Preface

This is the seventh volume in the McMaster New Testament Studies series, sponsored by McMaster Divinity College, Hamilton, Ontario, Canada. The series is designed to address particular themes in the New Testament that are (or should be) of crucial concern to Christians today. The contributors are selected because of their proven expertise in the areas assigned and their known ability to write intelligibly for readers who are not necessarily academics. Each article included in these symposium volumes, therefore, will evidence first-class biblical scholarship, but will also be written in a manner capable of capturing the interest of intelligent lay people, theological students, and ministers. In purpose, the articles will be both scholarly and pastoral. In format, they will be styled to reflect the best of contemporary, constructive scholarship, but in a way that is able to be understood by and that speaks to the needs of alert and intelligent people in the church today.

This seventh volume in the MNTS series focuses on christology in the New Testament. It is a topic that has been treated extensively in monographs, commentaries, systematic theologies, and devotional writings of the Christian church. Nonetheless, we believe it deserves a better critical, historical, exegetical, and "biblical theology" treatment than is usually received in either the scholarly or the popular press. So we have prepared this volume with the hope that a more responsible treatment of christology in the New Testament will prove to be of help to many earnest Christians who seek to think and live in a more Christian fashion, and thereby that it will have a positive impact on the church at large.

Our thanks are expressed to the family of Herbert Henry Bingham,

B.A., B.Th., D.D., a noted Canadian Baptist minister and administrator of the previous generation, which generously funded the "H. H. Bingham Colloquium in New Testament" at McMaster Divinity College during June 25-26, 2001. It was at that colloquium that the authors of the present volume presented their papers and received criticism from one another, from the editor, and from others in attendance before then reworking and polishing their papers, as necessary, prior to final editing and the normal publication process. Most heartily, however, we thank those who have written articles for this volume, for they have taken time out of busy academic schedules to write in a more popular fashion — in many cases, distilling from their previous academic publications material of pertinence for the Christian church generally. And we thank Bill Eerdmans and the Wm. B. Eerdmans Publishing Company for their continued support and expertise in publishing this series.

THE EDITOR

Abbreviations

BJRL	*Bulletin of the John Rylands Library*
CBQ	*Catholic Biblical Quarterly*
HBT	*Horizons in Biblical Theology*
JB	Jerusalem Bible
JBL	*Journal of Biblical Literature*
JSNT	*Journal for the Study of the New Testament*
JTS	*Journal of Theological Studies*
LXX	Septuagint
MT	Masoretic Text
MTZ	*Münchener theologische Zeitschrift*
NEB	New English Bible
NIV	New International Version
NRSV	New Revised Standard Version
NTS	*New Testament Studies*
par.	and parallels
RB	*Revue Biblique*
TDNT	*Theological Dictionary of the New Testament*
TZ	*Theologische Zeitschrift*
ZNW	*Zeitschrift für die neutestamentliche Wissenschaft*
ZTK	*Zeitschrift für Theologie und Kirche*

Contributors

David E. Aune, Ph.D. (Chicago). Professor of New Testament and Christian Origins, University of Notre Dame, Notre Dame, Indiana

Richard Bauckham, Ph.D. (Cambridge), F.B.A. Professor of New Testament Studies and Bishop Wardlaw Professor, St. Mary's College, University of St. Andrews, St. Andrews, Scotland

Terence L. Donaldson, Th.D. (Wycliffe-Toronto), D.Cn.L. (Emmanuel, Saskatoon). Lord and Lady Coggan Professor of New Testament Studies, Wycliffe College, University of Toronto, Toronto, Ontario

Donald A. Hagner, Ph.D. (Manchester). George Eldon Ladd Professor of New Testament, Fuller Theological Seminary, Pasadena, California

Morna D. Hooker, Ph.D. (Manchester), D.D. (Cambridge), D.Litt. (Bristol), D.D. (Edinburgh). The Lady Margaret Professor of Divinity Emerita, University of Cambridge; Fellow of Robinson College, Cambridge, England

William Horbury, Ph.D. (Cambridge), D.D. (Cambridge), F.B.A. Professor of Jewish and Early Christian Studies, University of Cambridge; Fellow of Corpus Christi College, Cambridge, England

Richard N. Longenecker, Ph.D. (Edinburgh), D.D. (Wycliffe). Professor Emeritus of New Testament, Wycliffe College, University of Toronto, Toronto, Ontario

Contributors

I. Howard Marshall, Ph.D. (Aberdeen), D.D. (Asbury). Honorary Research Professor of New Testament, King's College, University of Aberdeen, Aberdeen, Scotland

Ralph P. Martin, Ph.D. (London). Distinguished Scholar in Residence, Fuller Theological Seminary, Pasadena, California; Azusa Pacific University, Azusa, California; Logos Evangelical Seminary, Los Angeles, California

J. Ramsey Michaels, Th.D. (Harvard). Professor Emeritus of Religious Studies, Southwest Missouri State University, Springfield, Missouri; Adjunct Professor of New Testament, Bangor Theological Seminary, Portland, Maine

Douglas J. Moo, Ph.D. (St. Andrews). Blanchard Professor of New Testament, Wheaton College Graduate School, Wheaton, Illinois

Philip H. Towner, Ph.D. (Aberdeen). Associate Professor of New Testament, Denver Seminary, Denver, Colorado; Director of Translation Services, United Bible Societies, UBS World Service Center, Reading, England

Ben Witherington III, Ph.D. (Durham). Professor of New Testament Interpretation, Asbury Theological Seminary, Wilmore, Kentucky

Introduction

Christology, which may generally be defined as theological interpretation of the person and work of Jesus of Nazareth, was the focus of early Christian proclamation and is at the heart of the New Testament witness. Primitive Christian theology, in fact, as Oscar Cullmann (*Die Christologie des Neuen Testaments* [1957] = *The Christology of the New Testament* [²1963]) and Vincent Taylor (*The Person of Christ in New Testament Teaching* [1963]) long ago argued, was almost exclusively christology. And that is a judgment with which the post-apostolic church generally agreed, as witness its vigorous and extensive christological debates, and with which scholarship today widely concurs.

In the determination of the nature of New Testament christology, however, questions regarding method are always with us. Should our approach be dominantly critical, historical, literary, exegetical, theological, developmental, circumstantial, or devotional? How can we both responsibly and constructively use such disciplines as text criticism, source criticism, redaction criticism, form criticism, tradition criticism, narrative criticism, epistolary analysis, and rhetorical criticism in the study of New Testament christology? What significance is to be assigned to comparative and contextual studies in our analyses of the New Testament portrayals, statements and representations?

The endeavor of the present volume is to treat New Testament christology in a "biblical theology" fashion — that is, (1) with sensitivity to the concerns and circumstances within which the authors of the New Testament wrote, (2) attempting to use the best critical-historical-literary-exegetical tools available in analyzing what they wrote, (3) allowing each of them to speak in his own way, in line with his own purposes and emphases, and (4) desiring to be true to the various contingencies present within the materials and to discern what is at the heart of matters, with a recognition of both "contingency" and "coherence" in the New Testament witness. The stance taken is that there is a certain "sense of center" in the various representations and statements about Jesus of Nazareth by the different writers of the New Testament, but also that there are distinctive features in each of their respective christological portrayals — and that both what is common and what is distinctive must be appreciated for a proper understanding of the New Testament presentation. The differing features may, to some extent, be described as different christologies. More appropriately, however, they should probably be seen as contours in the overall christology of the New Testament, with the term "contours" suggesting undulations in the terrain or somewhat differing emphases of the respective authors within a basic commonality of conviction.

What follows in this book, therefore, are thirteen articles written by thirteen first-class biblical scholars that attempt to portray the christology of the New Testament in terms of a "biblical theology" approach and to use the tools of contemporary biblical scholarship in a responsible and constructive manner. The articles build on the scholarly expertise of their respective authors, but they are presented in a manner intended to be understood by intelligent lay people, theological students, and ministers. Each article has a "Selected Bibliography" for further study, with many of the entries being foundational for that article itself. All of the articles, however, are devoid of footnotes that interact with competing positions or bring in subsidiary materials. Documentation is held to a minimum and, where it is absolutely necessary, is set in abbreviated form in parentheses in the text.

The focus of this volume is on the portrayals, statements and presentations of the New Testament writers themselves. There is no attempt to analyze the self-consciousness or self-understanding of Jesus, which would require at least another volume of comparable size. Rather, the focus is entirely on the understandings of the various writers of the New Testament *about* Jesus. Section I deals with certain important features in "The Setting" of their understanding — that is, with Jewish messianism of the day, Jesus as the basis for and focus of the writers' thought, and christological materials that circulated within the early Christian communities. Sections

II-IV bring the reader to the heart of the volume in analyzing the writings of ten or more New Testament authors — with those materials treated in more-or-less canonical order, though with the Gospels and the Pauline letters arranged according to their most probable historical order.

Unabashedly, the authors of these articles have reflected their own confessional perspectives, expressed their own scholarly and critical stances, and used a variety of interpretive methods in their respective treatments. Uniformity of perspective, stance, or method has not been called for and should not be expected. The only criterion the authors have followed is that of greatest compatibility with the material being studied. Each author is an expert in his or her respective area, and it is expected that their expertise will be readily evident in what they write. More than that, however, it is hoped that through their efforts the christological portrayals, statements, and representations of the New Testament will be better presented than is usually the case. And what is ultimately prayed for is that by such a truer and abler presentation, Christians will be instructed and challenged to live more genuine lives as Jesus' followers and the Christian church will be benefited in carrying out its God-given mission.

THE EDITOR

I. THE SETTING

CHAPTER 1

Jewish Messianism and Early Christology

WILLIAM HORBURY

Modern scholarly discussion of the significance of Jewish messianism at the time of Christ has extended over two hundred years or more. On at least one occasion it touched the course of world history. This occurred in connection with two famous skeptical writers on the historical Jesus, David Friedrich Strauss and Bruno Bauer. When Strauss published his two-volume *The Life of Jesus* in 1835-36, Bauer asserted that the book was not radical enough. Strauss had argued that Christ was presented by the evangelists along the lines of already existing Jewish mythical narratives of the coming Messiah's advent and work. Bauer mockingly replied that Strauss was arguing like a traditionally-minded member of the church, for his argument presupposed that there was, indeed, a highly developed messianic expectation among the Jews before the birth of Christ — whereas, in fact, so Bauer maintained, there was little or no evidence for a pre-Christian messianic hope, and the best-attested Jewish messianism appeared only after the rise of Christianity.

These comments on Strauss appeared in Bauer's *Critique of the Gospel History of the Synoptics,* which was issued in 1841. The publication of this book led to Bauer's dismissal by the Prussian government from his position at the University of Bonn, and so to much reduced prospects for his academic friends and protégés. One of these was the young Karl Marx, who through Bauer's encouragement had won his doctorate with a dissertation on Democritus and Epicureanism. Marx had had hopes of a university post and further work on later Greek philosophy under Bauer's wing. Now, however, Marx turned to journalism and fatefully immersed himself in politics.

The controversy between Bauer and Strauss — which led to this change of direction for Marx — turned, in part, on the question: Was messianic hope, in the sense of the expectation of a coming king or ruler, a significant element in Judaism at the time of Christian origins — and did it have any importance for the origins of New Testament christology? This question has been discussed ever since, and it concerns us now.

1. The Earlier Dossier of Texts and Earlier Arguments

Bauer's argument that pre-Christian messianic hope was insignificant has been substantially repeated down to the present day and forms the background for modern discussion of New Testament christology. In evaluating that argument, the literary evidence on which it was built and Bauer's own position vis-à-vis more traditional stances need to be set out first.

The Earlier Dossier of Texts

In the first part of the nineteenth century, those who argued for the existence of a pre-Christian messianic hope among Jews could point to the Hebrew Bible (the Old Testament) and to a certain amount of textual evidence outside it. The church from earliest times had treated the Old Testament as messianic prophecy, which could, of course, be disputed, and this had occurred extensively in the long history of medieval and later Jewish-Christian debate. So from the Middle Ages on, the Christian side of the argument also appealed for support to rabbinic interpretation. This appeal — made, of course, not without rebuttal — included messianic passages in the Targums, which are Aramaic biblical paraphrases that took their present form after the rise of Christianity, perhaps from the second century CE on. It also embraced Jewish mystical writings, which were used to show that ancient Jewish monotheism came close to specifically Christian doctrine — an argument that has come to the fore again in more recent study.

In the early nineteenth century, however, this Christian messianic interpretation of the Hebrew Bible and of post-biblical Jewish exegesis was encountering a new intellectual climate. The older objections to the traditional Christian interpretation were being strengthened by ever-increasing scholarly efforts to connect the Old Testament with the history of Israel and the neighboring peoples.

It was in this setting that a vast defense of the messianic interpretation of the Hebrew Bible was issued from 1829 onward by E. W. Hengstenberg, under the title *Christology of the Old Testament.* This work reviewed the newer historical exegesis, but retained many of the older traditional arguments. Hengstenberg based himself not only on rabbinic interpretation, but also on later Jewish mystical writings. The most important of these is the *Zohar* — a long Aramaic text composed in the thirteenth century, but which represents itself as issuing from Simeon ben Yohai and his circle in the second century CE. In Hengstenberg's time it was often used to defend a messianic interpretation of Old Testament prophecy.

A general aim in early-nineteenth-century Christian apologetics, as in the Christian interpretation of prophecy from medieval and earlier times, was to show (1) that a Messiah was expected in Israel, (2) that the prophecies of his person and work were fulfilled by the church's Christ, and (3) that, correspondingly, the Old Testament foretold a divine Christ and, perhaps, also hinted at a doctrine of the trinity. Yet the strongly historical tendency of biblical study, coupled with a concomitant recognition of the medieval setting of the *Zohar,* meant that conclusions such as those defended by Hengstenberg could not be taken for granted.

Those who argued for pre-Christian messianism in this situation might, therefore, tend to put less emphasis on the Old Testament, the rabbinic literature, and the *Zohar.* They could, however, still urge that pre-Christian messianic hope was discernible in the Jewish Greek translation of the Pentateuch and the other Old Testament books known as the Septuagint (LXX), which dated in its earliest parts from the third century BCE. Moreover, much further attestation of messianism was found in the Targums, which had been handed down within the Jewish communities, as well as in various Jewish apocalypses from the time of Christian origins, which had been transmitted through the church.

Two such apocalypses were particularly important in the 1840s. One was familiar, whereas the other was new to most western readers. The familiar work was the book called *2 Esdras* in the Apocrypha of the English Bible and *4 Ezra* in the appendix of the Vulgate. It had been known since ancient times through its Latin version. It seemed in its oldest part (chs. 3–14) to reflect the years soon after the destruction of Jerusalem in 70 CE.

This section of the book included clear references to messianic victory and reign.

The other work was *1 Enoch*, which is most fully preserved in Ethiopic. The Ethiopic text was first translated in 1821 and edited in 1838 by Richard Laurence, Archbishop of Cashel and formerly Regius Professor of Hebrew in Oxford. In the section of the book called the "Parables of Enoch" (chs. 37–71) there are striking references, as Laurence observed, to a preexistent Messiah, together with historical allusions that suggest that this section was composed in the early Herodian age. The claims for Jewish anticipations of trinitarian belief, which some had made on the basis of the *Zohar,* could now be founded more securely, so Laurence suggested, on the *Book of Enoch.*

Bruno Bauer's Own Position

Bauer himself argued — against claims for a pre-Christian messianic hope based on the Septuagint, the Targums, *2 Esdras (4 Ezra),* and *1* (Ethiopic) *Enoch* — that in pre-Christian Jewish sources a silence on messianism was more obvious than its attestation. Messianic hope left no clear traces, he asserted, in the Septuagint, the Old Testament Apocrypha, or Philo. He allowed its presence in Daniel, a book that would later be thought ambiguous in this regard. He insisted, however, that otherwise it appeared only in apocalypses like *1 Enoch* and *2 Esdras,* which in his view were post-Christian or perhaps added to by Christians, and in the Targums, which were not so early as to give clear attestation of pre-Christian views. Bauer was inclined to set the efflorescence of Jewish messianic hope in the late first century CE — and to see it, at least in part, as a result of the rise of Christianity. Christian christological thought, then, could not have drawn on a Jewish messianic hope. Rather, Jewish messianism would have arisen, in part, as a result of the influence of nascent Christianity within Judaism.

Although this final suggestion of Christian influence on Jewish messianism has not been widely followed, the view that pre-Christian messianism was insignificant has affected later study up to the present. This emerges, for instance, when the sparseness of non-Christian witness to Jewish messianic hope in New Testament times is underlined by Marinus de Jonge (*Christology in Context: The Earliest Christian Response to Jesus* [Philadelphia: Westminster, 1988], pp. 65, 110) and Raymond

Brown (*An Introduction to New Testament Chistology* [New York/Toronto: Paulist, 1994], p. 73).

2. The Modern Recovery of Ancient Jewish Literature

The dossier of texts on Jewish messianism, however, has changed considerably since Bauer's time. The nineteenth and twentieth centuries formed a period of reassessment, reconsideration, and fresh discovery of ancient Jewish literature. Lost works were found again and hitherto unknown works came to light. For this reason the present-day discussion of messianic hope, influenced as it is by observations that Bauer brought to the fore, should be approached first of all through consideration of the changes that have occurred in the dossier of literary evidence.

Nineteenth-Century Reassessment and Recovery of Texts

Already in the 1840s attention was being given again to the *Psalms of Solomon,* which had been preserved in Greek and were first printed in the seventeenth century. These poems, which were grouped and transmitted in the ancient church together with the Septuagint, reflect Judean history during the period between about 63 and 40 BCE and express the desire for a God-given anointed Davidic king. Furthermore, it was also noticed that the long-familiar Jewish *Sibylline Oracles* included messianic passages — although the clearest instance comes from book 5, which reflects the period after the destruction of Jerusalem by Titus.

Reassessment of *1 Enoch,* especially in light of seeming allusions to the Maccabean age in the "Dream Visions" of chs. 83–90, led not only to the recognition of the "Parables" in chs. 37–71 as the latest section of the writing, but also to the identification of a second-century BCE messianic prophecy in 90:37, which speaks of a white bull with great horns (cf. Deut 33:17; see J. Schaper, *Eschatology in the Greek Psalter,* 111-12, 124-25, and n. 444). Likewise, the *Assumption of Moses,* which was first published in 1861 and dates from the period of the tetrarchs after the death of Herod the Great, was found to speak in 10:1-2 of the revelation of God's kingdom and the consecration of a messenger in heaven.

Renewed consideration was also given to Philo of Alexandria, who

7

was writing in the period to which the *Assumption of Moses* belongs. National hope is important in Philo's treatise *De Praemiis et Poenis* ("On Rewards and Punishments"). In *De Praemiis* 95 he envisages a glorious return of Jewish exiles, led by the great Man of Balaam's prophecy in Num 24:7 (LXX): "There shall come forth a man." Then the *Syriac Apocalypse of Baruch,* or *2 Baruch,* which was first translated and edited in 1866 and 1871, respectively, proved itself to be close to *2 Esdras* 3–14, not only in date and outlook but also in kindred predictions of messianic victory and reign.

Finally, fresh notice was taken of messianic features in ancient Jewish prayers — especially in the *Eighteen Benedictions,* which form the thrice-daily petition known as the *Tefillah* ("the prayer") or *Amidah* ("standing prayer"). Mentioned repeatedly in the Mishnah (*Berakoth* 4:1–5:5) and transmitted among the liturgical texts of the Jewish community, these benedictions probably reflect prayer themes that were customary at the end of the first century CE. Most significant for our discussion is the fact that they include petitions for the coming of the anointed Davidic king (cf. E. Schürer, *History of the Jewish People,* 2.455-63; also P. S. Alexander, "The King Messiah," 471-72).

When these texts were considered together, as was done by Emil Schürer in 1873 (and later by his revisers), messianic hope was found to be attested in Jewish sources from before the beginning of the Herodian period to its end. These non-Christian Jewish texts ranged from the "Dream Visions" of *1 Enoch,* the *Psalms of Solomon,* and the "Parables" of *1 Enoch,* to *2 Esdras* (*4 Ezra*), *2 Baruch,* book 5 of the *Sibylline Oracles,* and the *Eighteen Benedictions.* They therefore spanned the time during which the New Testament books were written. By the same token, however, a good part of them came from the period just after the emergence of Christianity and so recalled Bauer's assertion that Jewish messianic hope arose only in the wake of the earlier Christian messianism.

Moreover, the ambiguity of the *Assumption of Moses* (e.g., is the messenger in heaven angelic or messianic, or possibly both?) raised questions regarding the coherence of the materials in this body of texts. Furthermore, although these writings mention a messianic figure, other eschatological texts do not. This suggested that the revelation of the divine kingdom could be envisaged in ancient Judaism without any clear reference to a Messiah. Nineteenth-century reassessment of these texts, therefore, made it harder to deny a pre-Christian Jewish messianic hope altogether, but by no means did it preclude the view that such a hope was either insignificant or incoherent.

Reconsideration of Jubilees *and* the Testaments of the Twelve Patriarchs

Two other writings that received fresh attention in the mid-nineteenth century were *Jubilees* and the *Testaments of the Twelve Patriarchs*. These works seemed, at first, rather unimportant or ambiguous as evidence for a Jewish messianic hope. In the twentieth century, however, they gained more significance through the publication of hitherto unknown Hebrew texts from the Second Temple period.

Jubilees was edited in full from Ethiopic manuscripts in 1859. This work, which was probably written in Hebrew in the second century BCE, was familiar in Greek to the early Christians as the "Little Genesis" (*Leptogenesis* or *Microgenesis*), but was later known mainly through quotations. In *Jubilees*, when Jacob goes to visit his father Isaac before he dies (Gen 35:27-29), he takes with him two of his twelve sons, Levi and Judah. Isaac blesses Levi and Judah in terms appropriate to the high-priesthood (in the blessing of Levi) and to the kingship (in the blessing of Judah). He foretells in *Jubilees* 31:18 that Judah and one of his sons will each be a prince over the children of Jacob. This promise seems to anticipate the famous blessing of Gen 49:10 that Isaac's son Jacob will, in his turn, give to Judah: "The scepter shall not depart from Judah, nor the ruler's staff from between his feet, until he shall come whose it is." Isaac's saying, therefore, suggests the expectation of a Messiah from Judah, perhaps side by side with one of the glorious priestly descendants who are promised to Levi. This portentous blessing of Isaac is said in *Jubilees* 31:32 to be inscribed on the heavenly tablets.

The blessings of Levi and Judah in *Jubilees* were seen to resemble the messianic promises made to Levi and Judah in the *Testaments of the Twelve Patriarchs*. This book had been known in the west since the thirteenth century. By the end of the eighteenth century some accepted it as Jewish, but others took it to be an early Christian writing, at least in its final form. This latter view, which is strongly maintained today by Marinus de Jonge, predominated in the early nineteenth century. In late-nineteenth-century reconsiderations, however, the book was judged to be — as seems most probable to me — a Jewish work from the Hasmonean period with some Christian interpolations (cf. G. Vermes in Schürer, *History of the Jewish People*, 3.2.767-81).

Then in 1910 the Hebrew *Damascus Document* was published from two medieval manuscripts that had been preserved in the Cairo Genizah. The *Damascus Document* was found to mention *Jubilees* under the title "The Book of the Divisions of the Times into Their Jubilees and Weeks" (CD 16.3-4). It spoke also of "the anointed of Aaron and Israel" (CD 12.23–13.1; 14.19; 20.1), which recalls the blessing of Levi and Judah in *Jubilees*. The *Damascus Document* is probably referring to two anointed rulers, a priestly Messiah and a kingly Messiah. When the Qumran texts were discovered in the mid-twentieth century, this interpretation of the phrase in the *Damascus Document* was supported by other hitherto unknown sectarian writings, including the *Community Rule* according to the text from Cave 1 (1QS = 1Q28) and the *Messianic Rule* and the *Blessings* (1QSa-b = 1Q28a-b), which successively follow the *Community Rule* in this copy. Furthermore, many fragments of the Hebrew text of *Jubilees* were found in the Qumran caves.

It became clear that *Jubilees* and the *Damascus Document*, which depends on *Jubilees*, and probably also the *Testaments of the Twelve Patriarchs*, envisage two messianic personages, a priestly Messiah and a royal Messiah, and that this view goes back to at least the second century BCE. The background of this dual messianic expectation was the theory of a dual constitution in which high priest and king ruled together, but in which the king defers to the high priest. This theory is reflected in the pentateuchal narrative of the ordination of Joshua as "a man over the congregation" who was subject to the oracular direction of Eleazar the priest (cf. Num 27:15-23). It also surfaces in the prophecy of Zechariah concerning the two sons of oil enthroned, the Branch and the priest (cf. Zech 3:8; 4:14; 6:12-13). Later on it probably reappears in the coinage of the Bar Kokhba revolt (132-35 CE), where, beside coins bearing the Hebrew name and title "Simeon Prince of Israel," are others naming "Eleazar the Priest" (see texts and translations in Schürer, *History of the Jewish People*, 1.606).

This material from *Jubilees* and elsewhere, therefore, supplied a relatively early pre-Christian attestation of Jewish messianic hope. On the other hand, its reflection of a dual constitution, rather than a unitary Davidic hope, also strengthened the impression that pre-Christian messianic hope was marked where it did appear by variety and even incoherence.

Twentieth-Century Discovery of Texts

The twentieth century, however, has been repeatedly marked by the discovery of hitherto unknown ancient Jewish writings. The *Damascus Document* from the Cairo Genizah and the sectarian texts from Qumran have already been mentioned in connection with the book of *Jubilees*. Newly-identified targumic manuscripts have also greatly enriched the study of Jewish messianism. For the discussion of pre-Christian messianism, however, perhaps the Qumran texts are the most important. The whole group of messianic, or possibly messianic, texts has been vigorously discussed (see especially Knibb, "Eschatology and Messianism in the Dead Sea Scrolls"). Of particular importance for our consideration here is the question of date.

The relatively strong attestation of messianic themes in the Dead Sea Scrolls occurs in writings that seem to reflect, in the main, the Hasmonean period (from about 167 BCE, when Judas the Maccabee became leader of the Jewish uprising after his father Mattathias's death, to 40 BCE, when Herod the Great was appointed king). Some historical figures of this period are mentioned in the Qumran texts by name. The latest of them is the commander Peitholaus, who is named in fragment 4Q468g. He was active in Judea and Galilee during the 50s BCE.

Similarly, a number of writings from the Old Testament Apocrypha and Pseudepigrapha are attested in the Qumran finds. All of them, however, are works usually dated well before the Herodian age. There are no attestations of comparable Herodian works like the *Assumption of Moses*. In accord with this phenomenon, *1 Enoch* is attested in Aramaic in all the parts usually regarded as Hasmonean or earlier, with the addition of the hitherto lost "Book of Giants" — but not chapters 37–71 (the "Parables"), which are usually ascribed to the Herodian age.

The Qumran texts known to date, therefore, attest personages and writings of the Hasmonean period, but not of the Herodian period that followed. The suggestion has accordingly been made that these texts were deposited in their caves in late Hasmonean times rather than during the first Judean revolt against Rome, which occurred over a century later in 66-70 CE (cf. I. Hutchesson and G. L. Doudna in *The Qumran Chronicle* 8 [1999], numbers 3 and 4). This proposal is noted here only because it underlines the strikingly Hasmonean character of the internal evidence for dating the texts. Recognition of the Hasmonean character of the texts does not depend on when they were deposited, whether at the end of the Hasmonean age or during the Herodian period. Irrespective of the actual date of their deposit, the important point for the history of Jewish messianism is that, as presently known, the Qumran texts reflect the Hasmonean era rather than the Herodian age — both in their personal and literary Hasmonean references and in their lack of Herodian references.

It is therefore not at all surprising that the Qumran texts do not attest the *Psalms of Solomon* or any of the Herodian apocalypses cited above with regard to a Jewish messianic hope, such as chapters 37–71 of *1 Enoch* (the "Parables"), chapters 3–14 of *2 Esdras,* or *2 Baruch.* By the same token, they strengthen the dossier for an earlier period. For these texts, like *Jubilees,* help to fill the gap in the witness to Jewish messianic hope between the Septuagint Pentateuch, from as early as the third century BCE, to the *Psalms of Solomon,* in the middle of the first century BCE.

Summation

To look back now over this survey of reconsidered and newly discovered literary attestations of Jewish messianism, it emerges that, although the argument proposed by Bauer in 1841 is still influential, the shape of the evidence to which it can appeal has changed considerably. In Bauer's time and for much of the nineteenth century, the clearest evidence for a messianic hope (if one discounted the Septuagint) came from the first century BCE onward — with the weight of the evidence coming toward the end of the first century CE, just after the emergence of Christianity.

An important feature in the nineteenth-century understanding of these texts was the tendency to put the "Parables" of *1 Enoch* (chs. 37–71) much later than the early Herodian date suggested by Laurence and to regard them as a Christian work (see Schürer, *History of the Jewish People 3/* 1.256 and n. 13). This tendency to date the Parables late was strengthened again in the twentieth century by the absence of the Parables from the rich Qumran attestation of *Enoch* in Aramaic (G. Vermes opts for the last quarter of the first Christian century in Schürer 2.520-22; 3/1.259). But this absence, as noted above, can now be seen as entirely consistent with an early Herodian date, given the Hasmonean references in the Qumran texts and their general silence on Herodian personages and writings.

Moreover, in the twentieth century the messianic allusion in *Jubilees,* which was written in the second century BCE, has gained in significance through the discovery of the *Damascus Document* among the Cairo Genizah manuscripts and then of other hitherto unknown sectarian works — together with fragments of *Jubilees* in Hebrew in the Qumran finds.

Now it is possible to trace a continuous line in the attestation of Jewish messianic hope from the Septuagint Pentateuch onward. It begins in the third century BCE, not long after Alexander the Great — and not so long after the probably fifth- or early-fourth-century date of the biblical books of Chronicles. In the second and early first centuries BCE it is represented especially by *Jubilees*, the *Damascus Document*, and many of the Qumran texts. From the mid-first century, after 63 BCE and toward the end of the Hasmonean period, come the *Psalms of Solomon*. The Herodian age is represented by the "Parables of Enoch," which were composed probably in the late first century BCE, and by *2 Esdras*, *2 Baruch*, and Book 5 of the *Sibylline Oracles*, which all seem to have been written sometime about 100 CE, when the Herodian age came to an end with the death of King Agrippa II. The *Eighteen Benedictions* likewise reproduce prayer themes of the late Herodian age; while the Targums and rabbinic literature reflect later Jewish messianic expectations, mainly from the second century CE onward.

Christian messianism as attested in the New Testament, therefore, must now be seen to have arisen in the context of a Jewish messianic hope that can be traced continuously in Jewish writings from the third century BCE onward.

3. Messianic Hope as Tradition

It is very hard today to claim, as did Bruno Bauer, that there was little or no messianic expectation before the rise of Christianity. The silences that Bauer and others emphasized have become less striking. It no longer seems possible to point to long periods after Alexander the Great in which there was no trace of a Jewish messianic expectation. Yet it is still possible to debate the dating and interpretation of particular texts. It also remains possible to suggest that pre-Christian Jewish messianic expectations were too varied or incoherent to be regarded as important during the Second Temple period.

Signs of a Tradition of Messianic Interpretation

Interpretation of the Jewish messianic texts surveyed above, however, should not be guided solely by a recognition of their variety. Other features of the texts indicate that, for all their variation, they attest a continuous tradition of messianic biblical interpretation.

The first such feature is the regular messianic interpretation of a number of biblical passages. Among these passages are Gen 49:10 ("The scepter shall not depart from Judah, nor the ruler's staff from between his feet . . ."); Num 24:17 ("A star shall come out of Jacob, and a scepter shall rise out of Israel . . ."); and Isa 11:1-4 ("A shoot shall come out from the stump of Jesse, and a branch shall grow out of his roots . . ."). These passages already formed important items of messianic prophecy in the Septuagint (cf. Horbury, *Jewish Messianism*, 50, 129-30; *Messianism among Jews and Christians*, ch. 4; see also J. Lust, *Messianism and the Septuagint*). They are also interpreted messianically in the Qumran texts: Gen 49:10 in 4Q252, which is a pesher on Genesis; Num 24:17 in the *War Scroll* and the *Damascus Document*; and Isa 11:1-4 in a pesher on Isaiah attested in 4Q161 and in a composition on eschatological war attested in 4Q285 and 11Q14. To pick out only one or two more instances, Gen 49:8-10 is echoed in *Jubilees* 31:18 and *2 Esdras (4 Ezra)* 12:31-34, and Num 24:17 and Isa 11:1-4 in *Psalms of Solomon* 17:21-25, 35-37. Likewise, all these passages receive messianic interpretation in the Targums (see Horbury, *Jewish Messianism*, 66, 93).

New psalms, oracles, and visions, as well as translations and interpretations of Scripture, are, therefore, indebted to existing messianic interpretation of these and other biblical texts on the Israelite king. When allowance is made for the variation to be expected in any living tradition, it seems permissible to relate the dossier of texts attesting a messianic hope to a continuous tradition of messianic biblical interpretation.

A second feature to be noted is that the texts often imply the existence of what may be called a "messianic myth." D. F. Strauss assumed this to be the case in his *The Life of Jesus* (1835-36), from which we began. Perhaps, however, he associated this insight too closely with his Gospel criticism for it to be appreciated independently. Sixty years later Hermann Gunkel developed the same insight in a different atmosphere (cf. Horbury, *Jewish Messianism*, 15 and n. 25). He compared the vision in Revelation 12 of the woman clothed with the sun, who is saved with her man-child from the great red dragon, with a story of a child born to be Messiah but snatched away by the wind, which is preserved in Aramaic in the midrash on Lamentations (1.51) and in the Jerusalem Talmud (*Berakoth* 5a). And he suggested that existing messianic legend helped form both the vision described in Revelation 12 and the narrative preserved in rabbinic tradition.

The material of the passages cited above hints at several kindred mythical narratives. Particularly vivid is the depiction of the Messiah's victory over his adversary. It is developed from Isa 11:4 and envisaged as a solemn public execution in the Dead Sea fragment 4Q285 (where the prince of the congregation puts the adversary to death) and in *2 Baruch* 40 (where the Messiah, after conducting a war crimes trial, puts his adversary to death on Mount Zion). Many further signs of wide-ranging and relatively detailed messianic expectations have been collected by John O'Neill (see his "What Would the Messiah Be Like?"). These traces of myth are, like the recurrent biblical echoes, signs of a living tradition.

A third indication of continuous tradition lies in the connection between messianic hope and Jewish prayer. Some of the messianic passages in the texts surveyed above have their context in hymnody and prayer. This is the case with the *Psalms of Solomon,* the Qumran *Blessings,* and the *Eighteen Benedictions.* This context suggests that the messianic expectations reflected in these passages were communal, not simply idiosyncratic.

These features of the dossier of Jewish messianic texts attest a tradition that not only proliferates, but is also unified (1) by a common biblical inheritance of royal oracles and praises, (2) by myth-making on a common theme, and (3) by a tradition of prayer. One should, therefore, avoid too atomistic a treatment of individual texts and passages.

Questions regarding the Coherence of Messianic Tradition

The signs of continuity that have just been noted imply that messianic tradition had some coherence. Great stress is often laid, however, on the variety of messianic hopes. I have discussed the coherence of messianism more fully elsewhere (cf. Horbury, *Jewish Messianism,* 64-108; *Messianism among Jews and Christians,* 53-64). Here, however, two or three questions that might be raised by such a claim for coherence are briefly considered.

The first is this: Should the Greek Septuagint (LXX), which has its own special characteristics, be viewed together with other sources for messianism, such as the Qumran texts cited above on page 14? Johan Lust warns against overestimating the septuagintal witness to messianism, referring, for example, to the texts from the prophecies of Balaam, Num 24:7, 17, which I cited above. His questions are stimulating, but they should not lead to a total dissociation of LXX renderings of the relevant passages from the often comparable interpretations evinced elsewhere. His discussion of the individuality of the prophecies of Balaam in the Septuagint Pentateuch, for example, can be complemented by C. T. R. Hayward's consideration of similarities between the treatment of the same passages in Philo and the targums (cf. his "Balaam's Prophecies").

A second and similar question is: Should one segregate the Qumran texts, and perhaps also *Jubilees,* from other texts on messianism, since they possibly attest a special sectarian interpretation? Links with non-sectarian texts, however, as we have noted earlier, discourage a wholly separate treatment.

A third question is: Do not developments in the various Jewish sources of pre-Christian times differ to the point of inconsistency? Perhaps this is so. Yet inconsistency is usually in the eye of the beholder, and differing developments need not have been regarded as being incompatible. The Qumran material suggests that this consideration applies to the unified Davidic messianic tradition, on the one hand, and expressions of dual messianism, on the other. Thus in the Qumran texts the "Prince of the Congregation," who cooperates deferentially with the priest, is, nonetheless, "the Branch of David," as in 4Q285. Somewhat comparably, in the biblical tradition itself the oracles in Zech 3:8 and 6:12, which reflect a dual constitution, appear to pick up the existing Davidic appellation "Branch" (cf. Jer 23:5; 33:15).

Summation

The theory sponsored by Bruno Bauer, despite its continuing vigor among many students of christology, does less than justice to the relevant Jewish literature as it has been reconsidered and recovered in the nineteenth and twentieth centuries. By the time Christianity arose, Jewish messianic expectations were attested not only widely but also in a way that suggests they had considerable influence. There was, in fact, what can properly be called a tradition of messianic expectation among Jews. Its variety did not nullify its coherence. Its expression was, of course, strongly influenced by political circumstances (cf. Oegema, *The Anointed and His People*). Yet its links with biblical interpretation and prayer gave it an independent life.

4. Messianism and Christology

Christian interpretation of messianic prophecy in the early nineteenth century appealed, as I have noted earlier, to Jewish mystical literature in an argument for kinship between Jewish and Christian theology. Yet this appeal soon began to seem misguided, for scholars increasingly recognized the medieval date of the *Zohar* and the very different historical setting of the Old Testament. Later developments in the study of messianism, however, have shown that the whole argument merits fresh consideration.

Jewish Mysticism and Christian Origins

Further study of Jewish mysticism in the twentieth century, particularly by Gershom Scholem (see his *Major Trends in Jewish Mysticism* [New York: Schocken, 1941]) and his successors, illuminated the ancient antecedents of medieval Jewish mysticism. It could now be seen not only that the *Zohar* took up mystical traditions from earlier rabbinic literature but also that rabbinic mysticism was itself continuous with still earlier traces of ancient Jewish mysticism. These traces could be found in the apocalypses of the Hasmonean and Herodian eras — that is, in those apocalyptic writings that often also attested a messianic hope, as noted above. Moreover, discernment of a continuity between earlier Jewish apocalyptic texts and later Jewish mystical texts served to underline observations that had been independently made on the broadly mystical character of other Jewish writings from the Second Temple period — notably, wisdom literature and Philo's writings. Thus *Sirach (Ecclesiasticus)* and the *Wisdom of Solomon*, different as they are, both focus on divine-human intercommunion.

This development has formed part of the background for the return of an appeal to ancient Jewish mystical theology in the modern study of both Jewish messianism and Christian christology. In the case of Jewish messianism, this return has been manifest especially in discussions of a superhuman, heavenly, and angel-like messianic figure, notably with regard to the Parables of Enoch (*1 Enoch* 37–71) and other texts that interpret the

Danielic Son of Man. Here developments recall Richard Laurence's comment that the Enochian Parables give a surer indication of Jewish theological anticipations of Christianity. In the case of christology, the appeal to mystical trends in ancient Jewish theology has been particularly strong in the realm of so-called "angel christology," as represented by Christopher Rowland, Jarl Fossum, and others.

It can be said, therefore, that the traditional Christian argument for the Old Testament and other ancient Jewish literature as anticipating Christianity was not altogether misguided. The Christian interpretation of the Old Testament, as expressed in its classical form from Justin Martyr and Eusebius down to Hengstenberg, could not prove all that its representatives wished. Nonetheless, it did succeed in indicating a real continuity between ancient Judaism and early Christianity. Against this background it can be argued, as I seek to show, that Christian "angel christology" or "spirit christology" should be related more closely to Jewish "angel messianism" or "spiritual messianism."

Spiritual Messianism and Spirit Christology

What can be called "spiritual messianism" is widely evinced in the Jewish interpretations of the Old Testament toward the end of the Second Temple period. It tended to envisage the messianic figure above all as an embodied spirit. Its background was in the biblically rooted conception of the deity as lord of angels and spirits. These had developed in ways that overlapped with Greek and Roman conceptions of intermingled divine and human spirits. In this setting Jewish messianism — building especially on the honoring of the king in the royal psalms and oracles of the Old Testament — portrayed the messianic figure as a godlike spiritual being and evinced a kinship with the Greek and Roman ruler cults. Such a "spiritual messianism" was in many ways continuous with a Christian christology, which can often be described as "spirit christology" (for a fuller exposition, see Horbury, *Jewish Messianism*, 86-127; *Messianism among Jews and Christians*, 59-64).

A superhuman and spiritual messianic figure is generally recognized in the Parables of Enoch, 2 Esdras *(4 Ezra),* and Book 5 of the *Sibylline Oracles.* All these works belong to the Herodian period and incorporate an interpretation of Daniel 7, which speaks of "one like a son of man," into existing interpretations of messianic prophecy. They have often been regarded as attesting a separate category of messianic expectation, which is to be distinguished sharply, at least in principle, from the expectation of a human rather than a superhuman figure. In fact, however, as the remarks already made on the general coherence of messianic expectation might suggest, this distinction is hard to maintain in practice. Both human and superhuman traits are present in Old Testament depictions of the king. Likewise, both appear again in the interpretation of these Old Testament passages at the time of Christian origins.

Furthermore, it needs to be noted that superhuman and spiritual messianic traits are to be found not only in the three texts just mentioned. They appear more widely in the depictions of messianic figures that stem from the Second Temple period including *Psalms of Solomon* 17:23, 47; 18:8 and pseudo-Philo, *Biblical Antiquities* 51.5 (cf. Laato, *A Star Is Rising*, 283-84; Horbury, *Messianism among Jews and Christians*, 59-64, see also 55-56).

Fundamental to this development, as Emil Schürer long ago observed (*History of the Jewish People*, 2.522), are the royal oracles and psalms of the Old Testament, which in Hebrew suggest a godlike and preexistent king "whose goings forth are from of old, from everlasting" (Mic 5:2). Among the passages noted above as important in Second Temple Judaism, Isa 11:1-4 presents the Davidic king from the stem of Jesse as endued with the divine spirit, and Balaam's oracle in Num 24:17 aligns the "scepter" from Israel with a "star" from Jacob. This latter designation became prominent in the Jewish revolt during the reign of Hadrian, which was mentioned above in connection with the Old Testament theory of a dual Israelite constitution. Simeon ben Kosebah, the leader who used the title "Prince of Israel," was also nicknamed "Bar Kokhba," that is, "son of the star."

The spiritual and astral associations of the messianic figure are strengthened in a series of septuagintal presentations of messianic texts. These LXX renderings include (1) the association of the king as "angel of great counsel" with "a great light" in Isa 9:2-6, (2) the interpretation "star from Jacob and man from Israel" in Num 24:17, (3) the translation *anatolē*, "rising" or "dayspring," in Zech 3:8 and 6:12 (cf. "the dayspring from on high" in Luke 1:78), and (4) the depiction of a lord begotten "from the womb before the daystar" in Ps 110:3 (cf. Horbury, *Jewish Messianism*, 90-96). Biblical interpretation along these lines from the third and second centuries BCE, as attested in the LXX, was not without basis, for it picked out features already present in the Hebrew text.

Such interpretation forms the counterpart and background to depictions of a glorious, preexistent spiritual Messiah in the Parables of Enoch (1 Enoch 37–71) and 2 Esdras (4 Ezra), as well as in such other writings as the *Psalms of Solomon*. It leaves later traces in the biblical exegesis that is preserved in rabbinic midrash — as, for example, in explanations of the primordial spirit moving over the face of the waters as the spirit of Adam and of the Messiah (*Bereshith Rabbah* 1.4, on Gen 1:2; *Tanhuma Buber, Leviticus,* 16b, *Tazria* 2, on Lev 12:1-2) — with both explanations attributed to Simeon ben Laqish, who taught in Tiberias in the third century CE. Philo had comparably identified the heavenly "man according to the image" of Gen 1:26-27 with the "dayspring man" of Zech 6:12 (cf. Horbury, *Jewish Messianism,* 101).

This portrayal of the messianic figure as a glorious embodied spirit had its background not simply in the biblical depiction of the king as a godlike being, but also in the broader Old Testament view of the God of Israel as master of the divine assembly (Ps 82:1) and "a great king above all gods" (Ps 95:3). In Second Temple Judaism this ancient view developed into a conception of the deity as the lord of a great company of lesser divinities, both angels and spirits, who were known collectively as "gods" (Hebrew *elohim, elim;* Greek *theoi*). Hence, in both Semitic and Greek sources alike, the supreme deity was "king of gods" (in Hebrew hymnody, with *elohim,* in 4Q400 2, 5; also in Esther's prayer in Greek in Septuagint Esther 14:12) and "lord of spirits," to quote the divine title often used in the Parables of Enoch (e.g., 1 Enoch 37:4, and *passim*). This can be compared to the address to God in Qumran hymnody as "lord of every spirit" (1QH 18.8 [formerly 10.8]) and the Christian divine title "father of the spirits" (Heb 12:9).

Characteristic of this period and outlook is the Septuagint rendering of Num 16:22, which in Hebrew reads "God of the spirits of all flesh" but in the Greek reads "God of the spirits and of all flesh." The influence that was exercised on Hebrew as well as Greek literature by this understanding of the biblical phrase can be seen in a well-known passage of the Dead Sea War Scroll, with the term "gods" in the place of "spirits": "to raise up among the gods *(elim)* the princedom of Michael, and the dominion of Israel among all flesh" (1QM 17.7). In this context of thought, therefore, the angelic or spiritual Messiah also had a place with these divine spiritual beings — that is, "among the gods."

A Complementary Spiritual Conception of Human Beings

A strongly spiritual conception of human beings as "souls" or "spirits" relatively independent of the body also developed among Jews during this same Second Temple period. This is especially clear in Wisdom of Solomon. The phenomenon, however, is also found elsewhere, as can be seen in the wide currency of the phrase "souls of the righteous" (e.g., *1 Enoch* 22:9; Dan 3:86 LXX; Wisdom of Solomon 3:1; Heb 12:23; 2 Esdras/*4 Ezra* 7:99; *Sifre Deuteronomy* 344). Philo understands angels to be disembodied souls who can also enter into mortals (*De Gigantibus* 6-18; *De Confusione Linguarum* 174). Philo, of course, speaks in Platonic fashion. He is probably not far, however, from a widespread interpretation of the biblical tradition, as is suggested by Josephus on the transmigration of souls (*War* 2.263; 3.374), by the canonical Gospels on the return of past figures under new names (Mark 6:14-16; Luke 9:7-8), and by the *Prayer of Joseph* regarding Jacob as an embodied archangel (cf. Horbury, *Jewish Messianism,* 89).

Here the mystical tendency of ancient Jewish theology is clearly visible. In conceiving of human beings as "souls" or "spirits," this theology was influential in at least two ways: (1) it discouraged an absolute distinction between the human and the divine, and (2) it fostered aspirations toward communion with God. In such a setting, mediatorial figures could be envisaged in such a way that it became hard either to identify them with God or to describe them simply as divine agents (cf. Chester, "Jewish Messianic Expectations," 63-65). These characteristics of ancient Judaism should be recalled as a complement to the emphasis often placed on the importance of a transcendental monotheism in Jewish theology (cf. Horbury, *Messianism among Jews and Christians,* for a fuller discussion in connection with R. J. Bauckham's presentation of Jewish monotheism). It is against this background that the preexistence and the glory of the messianic figure need not have seemed incompatible with mortality. They are combined in striking fashion in 2 Esdras 7:28-29 (cf. also 12:32 and 13:26), where the preexistent Messiah is revealed to reign gloriously — but ultimately dies.

Spiritual Messianism, Spirit Christology, and Ancient Kingship

Messianism expressed in terms such as these resembles the ruler cults of the Greco-Roman world (cf. Horbury, *Jewish Messianism,* 68-77, 127-40).

Such ruler cults were central features in the life of the Greek world after Alexander the Great, and they attracted attention and emulation as a focus of power. Jewish messianic expectation formed in many ways a counterpart to them. The oracles and psalms of the Old Testament that are taken up in messianic hope reflect more ancient, but still comparable, understandings of kingship. Similarly, the astral and spiritual associations of the messianic figure in Jewish writings during the Greek and early Roman periods recall the contemporary association of kings with stars and divinities. The epiphany of the enthroned Elect One in *1 Enoch* 62, for example, where the Elect One receives worship and supplication and gives judgment, echoes Psalm 72, which is a royal psalm. It also, however, corresponds to contemporary royal public appearances in the Greco-Roman world, including those of the Herodian kings.

Expressions of messianic hope within Second Temple Judaism that drew on the royal oracles and psalms of the Old Testament thus also incorporated language and imagery that was characteristic of the Greek and Roman ruler cults, including association with the world of divine spiritual beings and emphasis on obeisance and petition. Messianism is then likely to have been a major factor in creating the cult of Christ among Christians and their corresponding christological affirmations. Recognition of Christ as the messianic king, which began during the period of Jesus' ministry and pervaded the early Christian community, would lead to titles, acclamations, and hymnody reflected in the New Testament. The development of Christian christology can accordingly be envisaged as part of a contemporary proliferation of the Jewish messianic tradition.

An approach to the origins of christology along these lines can do justice to the perception of the Gentile as well as the Jewish aspects of Christian language. This point is illustrated by several of the major New Testament titles of Christ — in particular, "Lord," "Son of God," "Savior," and "God" — which would have recalled language of the ruler cult to Gentile hearers, but were also connected with the Jewish messianic tradition (see further Horbury, *Jewish Messianism*, 140-50). Two other important titles, "Christ" and "Son of Man," are clearly rooted in the messianism of the Hasmonean and Herodian periods.

Finally, it should be noted that "spiritual messianism," as outlined above, has sometimes linked hands with the study of "angel christology" (see the discussion in Horbury, *Jewish Messianism*, 89-90, 106-8, 119-27). Such study goes back at least to the late nineteenth century, when Wilhelm

Bousset rightly urged that the title "angel of great counsel" in the Septuagint was only one of many indications that the Messiah was envisaged as a preexistent spiritual figure. This spiritual Messiah seems to reappear almost unchanged in second-century expressions of "spirit christology," as when Justin Martyr speaks of Christ as the "holy spirit" and "power of the highest" who overshadowed the Virgin (Justin, *Apology I* 33; *Dialogue* 110.1, commenting on Luke 1:35). In the New Testament, such a conception of the Messiah can help to explain the insistence of Hebrews on the superiority of the Son to the angels and the Johannine assertion that the preexistent Christ appeared before his birth.

Conclusion

The main point to be made at the end of this study, concentrated as it is on relations between Jewish messianism and Christian christology, is that early Christian conceptions of a crucified but spiritual and glorious Messiah are best interpreted by Jewish representations of the Messiah as a glorious king embodying a superhuman spirit. The royal praises and oracles of the Hebrew Scriptures, as understood at the time of Christian origins, did not anticipate a developed Christian doctrine with all the fullness claimed in the classical patristic writings and the later defenses of messianic prophecy. Nevertheless, they did speak of a godlike and spiritual messianic king — and Christian christology was continuous with this Jewish tradition of messianic biblical interpretation.

SELECTED BIBLIOGRAPHY

Alexander, Philip S. "The King Messiah in Rabbinic Judaism," in Day, ed., *King and Messiah in Israel and the Ancient Near East*, 456-73.

Charlesworth, James H., ed. *The Messiah: Developments in Earliest Judaism and Christianity*. Minneapolis: Fortress, 1992.

Chester, Andrew. "Jewish Messianic Expectations and Mediatorial Figures and Pauline Christology," in *Paulus und das antike Judentum*, ed. M. Hengel and U. Heckel. Tübingen: Mohr-Siebeck, 1991, 17-89.

Day, John, ed. *King and Messiah in Israel and the Ancient Near East: Proceedings of the Oxford Old Testament Seminar*. Sheffield: Sheffield Academic, 1998.

de Jonge, Marinus. *Jewish Eschatology: Early Christian Christology and the Testaments of the Twelve Patriarchs. Collected Essays*. Leiden: Brill, 1991.

Hayward, C. T. R. "Balaam's Prophecies as Interpreted by Philo and the Aramaic Targums of the Pentateuch," in *New Heaven and New Earth, Prophecy and the Millennium: Essays in Honour of Anthony Gelston*, ed. P. J. Harland and C. T. R. Hayward. Leiden: Brill, 1999, 19-36.

Horbury, William. *Jewish Messianism and the Cult of Christ*. London: SCM, 1998.

————. *Messianism among Jews and Christians: Twelve Biblical and Historical Studies*. Edinburgh: Clark, 2003.

Knibb, Michael A. "Eschatology and Messianism in the Dead Sea Scrolls," in *The Dead Sea Scrolls after Fifty Years: A Comprehensive Assessment*, ed. P. W. Flint and J. C. VanderKam, 2 vols. Leiden: Brill, 1999.

Laato, Antti. *A Star Is Rising: The Historical Development of the Old Testament Royal Ideology and the Rise of the Jewish Messianic Expectations*. Atlanta: Scholars, 1997.

Lust, Johan. *Messianism and Septuagint: Collected Essays*. Leuven: Peeters, 2004.

Neusner, Jacob, William Scott Green, and Ernest S. Frerichs, eds. *Judaisms and Their Messiahs at the Turn of the Christian Era*. Cambridge: Cambridge University Press, 1987.

Oegema, Gerbern S. *The Anointed and His People: Messianic Expectations from the Maccabees to Bar Kochba*. Sheffield: Sheffield Academic, 1999.

O'Neill, John C. "What Would the Messiah Be Like?" and "Jesus' Messianic Awareness," in *The Point of It All: Essays on Jesus Christ*. Leiden: Deo, 2000, 27-72, 73-96.

Schaper, Joachim. *Eschatology in the Greek Psalter*. Tübingen: Mohr-Siebeck, 1995.

Schürer, Emil. *The History of the Jewish People in the Age of Jesus Christ*, Eng. trans., 4 vols., ed. and rev. by G. Vermes, F. Millar, M. Black, M. Goodman, and P. Vermes. Edinburgh: Clark, 1973 (vol. 1), 1981 (vol. 2), 1986 (vol. 3/1), and 1987 (vol. 3/2), especially 2.488-554.

CHAPTER 2

Jesus as the Alpha and Omega
of New Testament Thought

BEN WITHERINGTON III

The study of the historical Jesus in his original social and religious context has led to a number of remarkable and distinctive findings. First, even taking into account recent revelations from a closer examination of early Jewish sources, including the texts discovered at Qumran, it is fair to say that messianism is hardly the dominant focus in much, if any, of the writings that stem from Second Temple Judaism. This stands in dramatic contrast to what we find in the New Testament, where Christ and christology appear as subjects on almost every page. Obviously, some historical explanation is required for this fact, given that all the New Testament documents, with the possible exception of Luke-Acts, were written by Jews.

Second, there is the more particular point made by the late Raymond Brown that "in all of Jewish history before A.D. 30 . . . we have no evidence that any living Jew was ever referred to as the Messiah except Jesus of Nazareth" (*Introduction to New Testament Christology,* 73). To this fact one may add the point of John Collins, a very careful scholar, that no living Jew of the period, other than Jesus, was ever identified with the Danielic Son of Man figure (*The Scepter and the Star,* 208-9).

These facts require some explanation, and they drive us to the very nub of the matter. What do we make of the fact that Jesus is both the basis for and focus of New Testament thought? Should we conclude that this is yet another example of the enthusiasm of a group of religious zealots who were overly-impressed with, and so over-exegeted, the importance of their founder? Or is there some sort of historical warrant and explanation for their convictions, portrayals, and activities?

In what follows, we will survey a representative sampling of material from the Gospels and Paul's letters that highlights the fact that Jesus is both the basis for and focus of New Testament thought (sections 1 and 2). Then we will concentrate on Paul's letters in a fuller explication of our thesis (sections 3 through 6), since they provide us with the earliest literary witness to how early Christian thinking functioned and was focused on the person and work of Christ. Finally, we will speak of the revolution that "the Christ event" brought about in the orientation, reflection, and worship of the earliest Christians — and that needs to be brought about in the thought and life of Christians today (section 7).

1. Jesus as the Basis for New Testament Thought

Insofar as we can talk about New Testament thought, and not merely the thoughts (plural) of the New Testament writers, there is very little reason to object to the proposition that Jesus is the basis for much of the worldview projected and reflected by the New Testament writers. Even more skeptical New Testament scholars like Rudolf Bultmann have been well aware of the enormous impact of Jesus on the theologizing of the New Testament writers. Whether one examines the way the New Testament writers talk about God the Father or about the Spirit or about soteriology or about eschatology or about ecclesiology, the impact of Jesus is clear. I have shown in another context that it is inadequate to argue that "Father" language used for God in the New Testament is simply a development of such language in early Judaism (cf. my critique of Marianne Meye Thompson's *The Promise of the Father* in B. Witherington and L. Ice, *The Shadow of the Almighty* [Grand Rapids: Eerdmans, 2001]). To the contrary, God is called the Father of Jesus Christ and *Abba* in the New Testament in ways that are not seen in other early Jewish literature.

To put it another way, patrology is viewed through christological spectacles in various parts of the New Testament. And the same can be said in regard to pneumatology. The Spirit is either the one promised by Christ or by God through Christ — or the one sent by Christ, who is even called the Spirit of Jesus Christ. There is no analogy to this in the writings of Second Temple Judaism or, for that matter, in the Hebrew Scriptures. The writers of the New Testament apparently felt it incumbent on them to speak in new and fresh ways.

When we consider the issue of soteriology, the focus is not merely on the person of Jesus but on a specific event in his life, namely his death. So much is this the case that one can hardly speak of alternative theories of salvation in the New Testament, if by that one means theories that do not in some way involve Christ and his death. Even if we were tempted to be skeptical about finding pieces of the meteor called "the Christ event" at this great a remove in history, we can certainly examine the enormous impact crater made by the Christ event on these early Jews' thinking about God, the Spirit, salvation, and a host of other important matters.

Consider for a moment the issue of eschatology. It is very doubtful that Jews before Jesus were conjuring with the possibility of a crucified Messiah. (I have discussed the texts found at Qumran that might be thought to point in this direction in my *The Many Faces of the Christ*. The evidence from *4 Ezra* is too late in the first century to be germane to a discussion about Jesus and his setting.) Likewise, it is implausible that Jews expected a resurrected Messiah. Yet Paul, our earliest New Testament writer, speaks of Jesus' resurrection as "the firstfruits" of the general resurrection. In other words, eschatology, which formerly spoke about the resurrection of the righteous, or perhaps of all, is now modified to speak in a "firstfruits" vis-à-vis "latter fruits" way — with the resurrection of one particular historical individual, Jesus of Nazareth, claimed to be the firstfruits. One could also point to the way that final judgment, whether as presented in Revelation, Mark 14:62, or 2 Cor 5:10, is now seen as focusing on or involving Christ as the judge or implementer of judgment.

Ecclesiological language has also been altered under the impact of the Christ event. This is so not only in obvious ways, such as Paul's use of "body of Christ" language or the reference in Matt 16:18 to Jesus' community, but in (1) the elaborate conversations about Israel in Romans 9–11, (2) passing references to the twelve tribes in the Diaspora (Jas 1:1) or exiles in the Diaspora (1 Pet 1:1) who have been affected by the Christ event, and (3) the new vision that appears throughout the New Testament of God's people being now Jews and Gentiles united in Christ. This is not just a matter of transferring language from one group of people to another, but a transfiguration of the language itself — with, it needs always to be recognized, Christ defining the terms. In all these instances and many more, Christ or the Christ event is the catalyst for new ways of expressing one's faith about matters pertaining to deity, soteriology, eschatology, and ecclesiology. We will return to these four areas in speaking particularly of Paul's letters.

2. Christ as the Focus of New Testament Thought

It goes almost without saying that Christ is the focus of the Gospels. Even a cursory examination of word usage reveals this fact. For example, Jesus is the subject of 24.4 percent of all the verbs in the Gospel of Mark — with another fifth of the verbs in this earliest Gospel occurring on Jesus' lips. The next closest figure in Mark's Gospel is one-eighth of all verbs, with reference to the disciples individually or corporately. In the Gospel of Matthew and the Gospel of Luke, Jesus also dominates the narrative, being the subject of 17.2 percent of the verbs in Matthew and 17.9 percent in Luke. It is also interesting that while 20.2 percent of Mark's verbs focus on Jesus' teaching, in Matthew it is 42.5 percent and in Luke it is 36.8 percent. In the Gospel of John 20.2 percent of the verbs have Jesus as the subject. In addition, over a third of the Johannine verbs, or 34 percent, occur in the teaching of Jesus. Of this material, almost 10 percent is self-referential. "All together then," as Richard Burridge has pointed out, "over half the verbs are taken up with Jesus' deeds or words, performed by him or spoken by him (55.3 percent). . . . Thus the Fourth Gospel occupies a middle position between Mark and Matthew/Luke: despite all John's different 'feel' and discourse material, he places less teaching on Jesus' lips than Matthew and Luke do, and gives Jesus more prominence in his narrative than they have" (*What Are the Gospels?* 223; the statistics given above are all from this same volume, pp. 196-97).

But it is not just the Gospels where Christ is so evidently the focus of thought. Using a different way of measuring things, we discover, for example, that the Greek term *Christos* ("Christ," "Messiah," "Anointed") is used in Paul's letters some 270 times, or on average at least once on each page of these letters. To this we may add the nearly 200 times that Paul uses the term *kyrios* ("lord") in these same documents. But there are even more effective ways to demonstrate the centrality of Christ throughout the Pauline corpus — chiefly by considering such matters as (1) how Paul's storied world is reshaped around the Christ event and (2) how Paul's hermeneutic in handling the Old Testament, the Mosaic Law, God, eschatology, Adam, and a plethora of other subjects changed once he began to look at these topics through the eyes of Christ.

Paul's thought revolved around "the Son," whom he called with great regularity "Jesus Christ" — in fact, some 270 of 531 total uses of *Christos* in the New Testament occur in the Pauline corpus. Furthermore, there are particularly important landmark human figures in the story of God's people with whom Paul chose to compare and contrast Christ — especially such epochal figures as Adam, Abraham, and Moses. He also says quite a lot, however, about Christ's relationship to the Father and to the Holy Spirit, without fully articulating a description of the Trinity. The former comparisons are only natural, since Paul thought of Christ as a truly human figure. But the latter are equally important, for Paul thought of Christ as divine, as part of the story of God, without violating his own vision of monotheism. In other words, christology was a form of theology for Paul, without his thought being "christomonistic" — yet it had much to do, as well, with anthropology.

3. The Narratological Shape of Paul's Christology

We may speak of a fourfold narrative that gives Paul's christology its essential shape and contours. The individual features of this narrative can be identified as (1) the story of Christ himself, (2) the story of Israel, (3) the story of a world gone wrong, and (4) the story of God — with the first inextricably intertwined with the other three stories, but the other three, most significantly, informed by the story of Christ (cf. my *The Many Faces of the Christ,* where another form of this material appears).

The Story of Christ Himself

The first of these, the story of Christ himself, tells about the one who was in the very form of God (Phil 2:6) but set aside his divine prerogatives and status in order to take the status of a human (even becoming a slave among humans), died a slave's death on a cross, and was highly exalted by God because of this. Much of this story Paul seems to have derived from his reflection on and elaboration of early Christian hymns, including notions of the Christ as God's wisdom. But for Paul, the story of Christ does not end with exaltation to God's right hand, for he goes on to relate how Christ has an ongoing role in heaven and will come again as judge and triumphant Lord.

Furthermore, Christ's exalted state, for Paul, does not merely recapitulate his status when preexistent.

The christological hymn of Phil 2:6-11 indicates that it was the career of Christ that determined, for Paul, how Christ should be confessed (cf. my article on "Christology," where another form of this argument appears). Jesus was given the throne name of God — that is, the name "Lord" — precisely because God exalted him as a result of his finished work on earth. We must take seriously the "therefore" *(dio kai)* in Phil 2:9, which indicates that since his death — though, more importantly, *because of* his prior life and death as God's and humankind's servant — this happened to Jesus. The end result of this process is that Christ has now assumed lordship and is functioning as Lord over all. In other words, the acclamation of Christ as Lord means that Jesus, since his resurrection, is the risen Lord.

Paul regularly uses the phrase "the Lord Jesus Christ" in speaking of Jesus. If we compare this to the Roman emperor's throne name "Imperator Caesar Augustus," it suggests (1) that Paul could use "Christ" not only as a name but also as a title and (2) that Jesus' name and titles rival and surpass those of the emperor. Significantly, however, Paul never simply combines the two titles "Lord" and "Christ" (i.e., "Lord Christ"). Rather, he places them before and after the name "Jesus," as did the Roman emperors in their use of names and titles (cf. Richard, *Jesus, One and Many,* 326).

In Paul's view, Christ is now functioning as Lord reigning from heaven. But it would appear from a text like 1 Cor 15:28 that after Christ's work is completed — which involves finally placing everything under the divine dominion at and after the *parousia* — Paul believes that lordship over everything and everyone (even the Son) will be returned to the Father. Thus Christ's lordship looks to the ultimate Lordship and reign of God the Father (cf. Richard, *Jesus, One and Many,* 330). In all of this it is clear that one must ask what point on the timeline of the career of the Christ one is talking about if one is to discover which titles are then appropriate to predicate of Christ. For christological titles are predicated to a significant degree on the basis of the function or task being undertaken at the time.

A good example of what we have just discussed can be seen in the few times that Paul uses *Christos* as something other than a mere second name of Jesus. As a title, "Christ" describes the roles assumed during the Son's earthly career, which climaxed in the cross. This is why Paul can resolve to know nothing but Christ and him crucified (cf. 1 Cor 1:23). This striking and paradoxical affirmation "Christ crucified" is crucial for Paul in various ways. For one, it shows that he, like other early Jews, saw the Christ as a human being — one who could be killed. Yet also it shows that the actual story of Jesus has caused Paul to reevaluate what it meant to be the Jewish Messiah, for it is probable that Paul was not different from other early Jews in that he did not expect a crucified Messiah.

As Werner Kremer has pointed out, Paul is not content to use *Christos* simply in the ways he found it used in his sources; rather, he also puts it to new and sometimes paradoxical uses (see Kremer, *Christ, Lord, Son of God,* 150; also the fuller discussion in 133-50). For most early Jews, the phrase "Christ crucified" would be not merely a paradox but a contradiction in terms. How could the Anointed One of God, God's most blessed one, at the same time be cursed by God, as would be apparent from such a hideous death (cf. Deut 21:23)? If the story of Jesus were read merely in the light of Scripture, it would certainly be possible to conclude that Jesus was not the Christ. But if the starting point is God's action through Jesus, and one then reads the Old Testament in light of the recent events in the life of Jesus, another conclusion is possible.

In short, the primary story for Paul was the story of the historical figure Jesus. It is, in fact, this story that was seen by Paul and the earliest believers in Jesus to be the key to all other stories — including all those found in the Hebrew Scriptures. Paul, of course, did not always use the term "Christ" in a purely historical manner. This can be seen in the way he used the term to speak of the Son during his preexistence — as in 1 Cor 10:4, where "the rock was Christ" should not be taken to suggest an earlier incarnation of Christ on earth as a rock, but that the Son acted on behalf of his people in the same fashion as God the Father did, from heaven — or after his death and resurrection. All this makes clear that it is crucial to understand the Pauline titles for Christ within the storyline and narrative framework that Paul presents to us.

The Story of Israel

A second larger story, the story of Israel, also informs Paul's discussion of the Christ. For example, we are told in Gal 4:4 that Jesus was not only "born of a woman," but also that he was "born under the Law" — which probably goes beyond simply saying he was a Jew, but includes that notion. For Paul this entailed God's sending of the Son to be the human Jesus, sending him to re-

31

deem those under the Mosaic Law. In other words, Jesus was specifically sent to redeem Israel, which, of course, presupposes the lostness of Israel.

It was to Israel that the Messiah had been promised in the first place (cf. Rom 9:4-5), and it was through Israel that the Messiah would spread his benefits to others. One must take very seriously Rom 1:16 and the whole discussion in Romans 9-11. Salvation and the Messiah who brings it are first of all for Israel. But they are also for Gentiles. Messiah, in Paul's view, brings the story of Israel to its proper conclusion and climax. It is also well to keep in mind that, for Paul, sonship was another way of speaking of the Jewish royal character of Jesus, who Paul is happy to affirm was born in the line of David (Rom 1:3-4) — even though this is not a major emphasis in Paul's letters and seems rather to be a quotation of a confessional statement of early Jewish Christians. Paul's use of "Son" also shows that he understands the relational significance of the term, implying, as it does, a special relationship with the Father (cf. Kremer, *Christ, Lord, Son of God*, 189). All the same, Paul uses "Son" far less often than "Christ" or "Lord."

The Story of a World Gone Wrong

A further and even larger story into which the story of Christ and the story of Israel fit is the story of a world gone wrong. For Paul, the world is clearly a fallen place (cf. Rom 1:18-32). It is, in fact, living on borrowed time, for "the current form of this world is passing away" (1 Cor 7:31; cf. Gal 1:4). The world is hell-bent, headed for destruction, but longs for liberation. This is true not just of human beings, but, in Paul's view, of creation as a whole (cf. Rom 8:20-22).

But it is not just that the world has fallen, is unable to get up, and so is gradually decaying. The problem is that there is also active personal evil abroad in the universe. In other words, there are demons and Satan to reckon with, who are part of the present evil age (cf. 1 Cor 10:21; 2 Cor 2:11; 4:4). This is the dark backdrop against which the stories of Christ and of God's people, both old and new, are played out.

The Story of God

Transcending the stories of Christ, of Israel, of the world — yet involved in them all — is the story of God. This is the story of the interrelationships of

Father, Son, and Holy Sprit. It is the story that informs Paul's christology in important ways. But it must also be seen to have been informed by Paul's understanding of the story of Christ as well.

In the christological hymn of Col 1:15-20, for example, we are informed that the Son played an important role in the creation of all things and all beings — even human beings — and that the role the Son plays in redemption is part of the story of God's attempt to win back what he had created in the first place. Creation, redemption, and re-creation, therefore, are not undertaken by different actors in the drama but by the same One, though in multiple personal forms.

The incarnation of Christ, in fact, is seen by Paul as part of the story of God. And the story of subduing and reconciling "every ruler and every authority and power" — destroying even "the last enemy" death itself — is also part of this larger story of God (cf. 1 Cor 15:24-26; Col 2:15). But it is Christ who undertakes these tasks for the Father and in the service of redeeming humankind (1 Cor 15:24). So the big picture involves not just "in the beginning God" but also "in the end God." Only for Paul the eschatological action is to be undertaken by "God in Christ" (cf. 2 Cor 5:19) — or, perhaps better said, "God as Christ."

4. Christ as God *(Theos)* in Paul's Letters

The story of God — that is, the story of the interrelationships of Father, Son, and Holy Spirit — leads us to comment more specifically about Christ's divinity in Pauline thinking. This issue, however, while it includes the question whether Paul called Jesus "God" *(theos)* or not, cannot be narrowed down to that linguistic question alone. A broader database and greater implications are involved.

Early Christian Hymns

In the christological hymn of Phil 2:6-11, as we noted earlier, Christ is called "Lord," which was one of God's names or titles in the Greek Old Testament (the Septuagint). So even if we were to confine ourselves to titles, there are other titles that Paul uses of Jesus that suggest he saw him as divine in some sense.

One must assume that the hymn Paul adopted and adapted he also endorsed, and thus that his inclusion of it tells us something about his own views as well as those of the early Christians from whom he borrowed this material. Eduard Schweizer has said that to a large extent Paul's importance lies in the way he brought together a wide variety of materials — hymns, creeds, confessions, Old Testament formulas and catenae, doxologies, and his own formulations — and focused them by his understanding of Christ's death and resurrection (*Jesus Christ,* 27). There is a large measure of truth in this. Nonetheless, it needs also to be recognized that Paul's letters are not just repositories of earlier Christian fragments that have been refocused by the apostle.

Paul's narratological approach to christology provided him with a large framework in which many truths could be expressed and understood. But through it all Paul has made his source material his own so that we can rightly speak of Pauline christology.

Wisdom Materials

Our evidence regarding Christ's divinity in Paul's thought is augmented when we look at the instances in his letters where Jesus is explicitly called God's wisdom or God's agent in creation (1 Cor 1:24, 30; 8:6; Col 1:15-17). Furthermore, the role that wisdom plays in Wis 11:4 in providing water in the wilderness to God's people is said in 1 Cor 10:4 to have been undertaken by the preexistent Christ. Here Paul is grounding the story of Christ not so much in the story of Israel but in the archetypal story of God's wisdom. And it seems likely that the sapiential ideas found in 1 Cor 1:24, 30; 8:6 blossomed into Paul's concept of the cosmic Christ — not only as Lord over land and universe, but also as involved in its creation.

The full flower of this sort of thinking is seen in texts such as Col 1:15-20, where Christ is said to be the image of the invisible God, the firstborn of creation, and the means and goal of creation — as is wisdom in Wis 7:25-26. The point is that Paul is very happy to attribute divine attributes to Christ. So one must actually ask whether or not he would have gone so far as to call him "God."

We have already suggested that Phil 2:6-7 says as much in affirming that Christ had the status of being equal to God and that he could have taken advantage of the divine prerogatives. Such "divine" language would have been striking in Paul's day, for it was also being used of the Roman emperor — that is, that the emperor was divine but humbled himself to be a public servant. The deity that Paul has in mind, however, performs his public service by dying on a cross, thereby producing peace with God and among humans, while a deified Roman emperor performs his public service by erecting a few more crosses, thereby creating a very different sort of peace — the so-called *pax Romana.*

Romans 9:5

A crucial text in any consideration of the divinity of Christ in Pauline thought is, of course, Rom 9:5. But before dealing with the particulars of this much-debated text, it is important to set the discussion in the larger context of the use of *theos* in the New Testament generally. Murray Harris has shown that the term reflects early Jewish Christian ways of thinking. In particular, *theos* is customarily used in the New Testament for the One the Jews and Jewish Christians called Yahweh — who was also called "Father" by some early Jews and early Jewish Christians. Indeed, *theos* is virtually a proper name for the Father in some Second Temple and New Testament texts. Occasionally, however, *theos* is used in the New Testament as a generic title of Christ in his pre-incarnate, incarnate, or post-resurrection state (cf. Harris, *Jesus as God,* 298-99). The texts Harris has in mind are Rom 9:5; Titus 2:13; Heb 1:8; John 1:1; 20:28; and 2 Pet 1:1. We must now examine the first of these.

Rom 9:5 comes at the beginning of Paul's discussion of the advantages the nation Israel has. The sentence poses a problem in regard to its proper punctuation. The argument turns on whether the verse should be read "the Messiah, who is over all, God blessed forever" (as the NRSV has it), or "the Messiah, who is God over all, blessed forever" (as JB, NIV, and the marginal reading of NRSV have it). NEB's ". . . the Messiah. May God supreme over all be blessed forever" unjustifiably fragments things by starting an invocation with the noun *theos* and the participle *eulogētos.* Why should a participle agreeing with "the Messiah" *(ho Christos)* first be separated from that term and then be given the form of a wish with a *different* person — that is, "God" rather than "Christ" — as the subject?

Rom 9:5a, in speaking of "the Christ" or "the Messiah" *(ho Christos)* has the phrase "according to the flesh" *(to kata sarka).* As the parallel in

Rom 1:3-4 suggests, we would expect a following clause that says something also about what Christ was according to some other category. The language "according to the flesh," therefore, implies an attempt to disclose one aspect of the truth — and it sets up the anticipation that more will be said. Otherwise the phrase is unnatural. Furthermore, the Greek phrase *ho ōn,* which is translated "who is," is normally a way to introduce a relative clause and not a further sentence. And here the parallel with 2 Cor 11:31 seems clear, where we also find "who is" *(ho ōn)* introducing the relative clause "blessed forever" *(eulogētos eis tous aiōnas).*

Paul is offering a doxology of sorts here, but elsewhere his doxologies are always attached to some antecedent subject. Likewise, the doxologies of the Hebrew Bible, Second Temple Jewish writings, and the Septuagint tend in their form and word order to read "Blessed be God," not "God blessed." There is, then, a high probability that here in Rom 9:5 Paul calls Christ "God" in a doxological statement. And, furthermore, such a doxology in attribution to Christ indicates the degree to which Paul is willing to qualify his monotheistic remarks — something that is already evident in 1 Cor 8:6, "For us there is one God, the Father, from whom are all things and for whom we exist, and one Lord, Jesus Christ, through whom are all things and through whom we exist." Indeed, there is a certain naturalness in speaking of the Messiah as one who is "blessed forever" (by the Father), since he is the Anointed One.

As for the meaning of *theos* when attributed to Christ, Murray Harris draws attention to an important distinction in usage between *theos* with and without the article: "When this title is anarthrous (John 1:1, 18; Rom. 9:5), the generic element is emphasized. When it is articular (John 20:28; Titus 2:13; Heb. 1:8; 2 Pet 1:1), the titular aspect is prominent" (*Jesus as God,* 298). So here in Rom 9:5, *theos* is to be seen as "an appellation descriptive of Christ's *genus* as one who inherently belongs to the category of Deity."

Christological Language as God Language

Thus far we have noticed that Paul predicates both divine attributes and divine titles or names to Christ — notably, "Wisdom," "Lord," and "God." But there is other language he uses that makes equally clear that he sees christological language as God language. For example, one of the most common phrases in the Pauline letters is *en Christō* ("in Christ"). As

C. F. D. Moule long ago observed, though some uses of "in Christ" may mean no more than that one is a Christian, there are also numerous other instances where the expression is used to say something about the Christian's condition or religious location (*Origin of Christology,* 62-65). And only an omnipresent one can be spoken of as being, in some sense, the place where and in whom believers dwell.

This picture can be further enlarged by examining Paul's language about Christ's relationship to the Spirit. It is, of course, old news that Paul closely identifies Christ and the Spirit. Beyond that, however, Christ in 1 Cor 15:45 is said to be "a life-giving Spirit." And in Rom 1:3-4 it is made clear (1) that it was through the Spirit's power that Jesus was enabled to be the Son of God in power and (2) that without Jesus' resurrection the Spirit would never have come to believers. Being "in Christ," in fact, is often simply another way in Paul's christological language of speaking about being "in the Spirit," as can be seen by the following coordinate statements: (1) believers are righteous in Christ (Phil 3:8-9), but also in the Spirit (Rom 14:17); (2) believers have life in Christ (Col 3:4), but also in the Spirit (Rom 8:11); (3) believers have hope in Christ for the life to come (1 Cor 15:19), as well as the power of the Spirit to give them eternal life (Gal 6:8); (4) believers are sanctified in Christ (1 Cor 1:2), but also in the Spirit (Rom 15:16); and (5) believers are sealed both in Christ (Eph 1:13) and in the Spirit (Eph 4:30).

The statement "the Lord is the Spirit" in 2 Cor 3:17 — while it likely does not mean that Paul is simply equating the Lord and the Spirit but rather that in the text he is dealing with (Exodus 34) "the Lord" means the Spirit — evidences the close connection that existed in Paul's mind between "the Lord" and "the Spirit." And in Rom 8:8-9 "the Spirit of Christ" equals "the Spirit of God" equals "the Spirit of the Lord." Paul, of course, also distinguishes between Christ and the Spirit. Only Christ came in the flesh, died on the cross, and rose again. And it was Christ who sent the Spirit to believers on earth while he in his resurrected body remained in heaven.

The point of all the above, however, is that this identity in function and effect between Christ and the Spirit surely, at least, implies the deity of Christ. From an Old Testament perspective, it is only God who is a life-giving Spirit and can send the Spirit. So in the church, Christ and the Spirit are not one but two in identity, yet they are often one in function and effect because the Spirit is Christ's agent on earth.

5. The Human Face of Christ

Pauline christology has not only to do with the divinity of Christ but also with his humanity. The identification of Jesus as "Son of David," "last Adam," or simply as "man" all have to do with aspects of Jesus' tasks on earth as a human being, as does the term "Messiah." It must, however, be remembered that Paul does not use "Son of Man" at all. And "Son of God" is relational in character and seems to have been kept for exceptional use at the climax of certain key statements about Christ's work both as a human being and as more than human.

The Jewishness of Jesus

It is not an accident that when Paul discusses Jesus' humanity he stresses, in various ways, his Jewishness. For example, in Gal 4:4 Jesus is not merely said to be "born of a woman," but also "born under the Law." His appearance in this world came in the form of a normal birth from a Jewish mother. "Born of a woman" suggests nothing peculiar or unusual about his birth. But in saying that Jesus was "born under the Law, in order to redeem those who were under the Law," Paul highlights the fact that Jesus' ministry was directed to Israel. This fact, parenthetically, coupled with the fact that Paul was called to be a missionary to the Gentiles, may go some way in explaining why Paul does not say more about Jesus' earthly ministry — for Jesus' ministry was to a people who were largely different from those to whom Paul's ministry was directed.

In Paul's thought there is an interesting paradox: Salvation is of God, but it could come to human beings only in and through a human being, the man Jesus Christ, who was a particular sort of human being — that is, a Jew. For Paul, the heart of the matter is that salvation comes in the form of "Christ crucified," which, in turn, means that the humanness of the Savior is a necessity, as well as his being more than human.

There are a number of Pauline texts that stress that the Son was born in human form and likeness — that is, was truly human. Phil 2:7 says that "he took the form of a slave, being born in human likeness," and was "found in human form." Probably the carefully worded phrase "in the likeness of sinful flesh" of Rom 8:3 is meant to indicate that Jesus did not look any different from any other human being, as well as to avoid saying that he was a sinner or was born with a sinful nature. This comports with the metaphorical statement of 1 Cor 5:7 that Jesus was "our Passover lamb," who had to be unblemished and spotless to be an appropriate sacrificial offering to God. In other words, like Adam, Jesus was born with an unfallen nature that had a capacity to sin, but unlike Adam he was "obedient [to God] even unto death" (Phil 2:8) and so became an unblemished sacrifice.

The only event of Jesus' life other than his birth and death that Paul mentions is the Last Supper. Jesus was one who broke bread, poured wine, and shared in fellowship with his disciples. But though such an occasion reflects something of "the human face of Christ," Paul is not interested just in these mundane facts, but in their soteriological import. The use of events in the life of Jesus is only with an eye to their theological significance.

Jesus' Human Messiahship

By far the most common term Paul uses for Jesus is "Christ" — usually as a name, but occasionally as a title (so especially Rom 9:5). For most Jews, Hebrew *māšîaḥ* was a term referring to an especially anointed and singled out human being, usually a king and sometimes a priest. So it is not surprising that in Rom 1:3-4, where Paul speaks of Jesus' messianic character, there is stress on his humanity — that is, he was "descended from David according to the flesh." The use of the term Christ for Jesus in Paul's letters, therefore, should probably be seen as laying stress on the humanness of the Messiah. This also is clearly implied in the phrase "Christ crucified" in 1 Cor 1:23. The "story of Jesus," as noted earlier, certainly brought about a redefinition of Paul's understanding of the Davidic Messiah in various ways. But it did not cause Paul to drop the Davidic terminology or category altogether.

The Last Adam as a Human Being

Paul says very little about Jesus' humanity in general. The subject of anthropology does not intrigue him when applied to Christ — except insofar as it has christological significance. This is especially to be noted in Paul's understanding of Christ as the last Adam, which surfaces in more than one Pauline letter and so was obviously of some importance to him. When Paul thought of Jesus' true humanness, he thought in terms of a comparison with the first human being. And when he thought of Adam and Christ, he thought typologically.

In the midst of his comparison and contrast between Adam and Christ in Rom 5:12-21, Paul says that just as death came by "the one" Adam, so God's grace and the gift that accompanied it (i.e., "righteousness") came by "the one" Jesus Christ (vv. 15, 17). This same comparison and contrast is reiterated in 1 Cor 15:21, though with the additional reference to the resurrection as coming "through a human being" *(di' anthrōpou)*. In the later and disputed Pauline letters, in particular 1 Tim 2:5, these notions are further developed when we hear about Christ as the one mediator between God and human beings — where, again, he is said to be "the man *(anthrōpos)* Christ Jesus." But there is more emphasis here on Jesus being both divine and human, and so standing at once on both sides of the fence in order to know, experience, and represent both sides of things.

Summation

Why all this stress on grace, righteousness, reconciliation, and even resurrection coming by a human being? Presumably part of the answer is that sin was a human problem that had to be resolved for humankind by and through a human being. While it has sometimes been stressed that the efficacy of salvation was due to Jesus' divinity, Paul, in fact, emphasizes the opposite. If Jesus had not been human, humans would not have ever received God's grace. God is immortal (cf. 1 Tim 6:16) and, apart from the Son's incarnation, is not subject to death. Thus for Paul and the early Christians to proclaim "Christ crucified," there must also be an emphasis on Christ's humanity.

6. Christ, the Center of Pauline Thought

One way to demonstrate the importance and centrality of christology for Paul is to examine the impact that it had on other areas of his thinking. For the encounter of Christ on the Damascus road caused a Copernican revolution in Paul's thinking (cf. Kim, *The Origin of Paul's Gospel*). Four such areas are especially important for our consideration here: eschatology, soteriology, ecclesiology, and theology proper.

Eschatology

Paul's eschatological outlook most certainly changed when he encountered Christ on the Damascus road. There is little or no evidence that Jews expected two comings of a Messiah — contrary to James Charlesworth's argument that *Psalms of Solomon* 18:5 should be read "to bring back the Messiah" ("From Jewish Messianology to Christian Christology," 30), which I find unconvincing. Yet that is precisely what Paul and other early Jewish Christians who prayed "Our Lord, come!" (*Marana tha,* 1 Cor 16:22) believed.

This bifurcation of the Christ event affected how Paul viewed the future and the life of believers. Because in "the fullness of time" Christ had already come, the eschatological age could be said to have already dawned. Redemption was already available, though not yet completed. Redemption was now in the spirit, but later, when Christ returned, it would be accomplished in the body as well.

The coming of the eschatological age had relativized everything. So while the forms and institutions of this world were still extant, they were nonetheless already passing away (1 Cor 7:31) and should not be adhered or clung to in some sort of ultimate fashion. And while powers and principalities still existed and menaced the world, they could not separate believers from God's love. Col 2:15, in fact, makes clear that Christ had disarmed the powers and principalities insofar as their being able to dominate or rule believers was concerned.

Furthermore, lives of believers had changed. A believer was now a new creature, part of a new creation begun by the last Adam (2 Cor 5:17) — a new creature, who experiences righteousness, joy, and peace in the Holy Spirit. This was a major part of what it meant for Paul to say that "the kingdom of God" had already come (Rom 14:17). The full redemption of the body at the resurrection, however, was yet to come. So not only the world but also the believer's very existence was in "an already" and "not yet" state of eschatological affairs, which had been initiated by Christ's coming and would be brought to consummation only when he returned.

There is no early Jewish evidence that a resurrection of the Messiah, much less an isolated resurrection of the Messiah apart from other believers, was expected in the midst of history. Yet on the basis of the story of Jesus, this is precisely what Paul proclaimed. What happened to Jesus made Paul rethink and reshape his eschatology, for the clearest piece of evidence that the eschaton had arrived for a Pharisee like Paul was the resurrection of Jesus. Or as Earl Richard points out: "Paul sees the Christian reality from the perspective of the risen Lord, the one whom God raised from the dead" (*Jesus, One and Many*, 326). Yet Paul also continued to see resurrection as a unified thing, by using the concept of Christ being "the firstfruits" of a future resurrection of all believers.

Soteriology

Paul's concept of salvation was equally reshaped because of what he came to believe about Christ — in particular, about Christ's death and resurrection. There is no evidence to date that a crucified Messiah was expected in the Judaism of Paul's day. In fact, Paul tells us that his message of a crucified Messiah was scandalous to Jews (1 Cor 1:23). The message of 1 Corinthians 1–4 is deliberately paradoxical. For to the factionalized Corinthians, Paul depicts a Christ who on the surface appears to create more division than healing, being a stumbling block to Jews and a scandal to Gentiles. Deut 21:23 does not speak directly to the matter of crucifixion — much less the crucifixion of God's Anointed One — and it could not have generated such a belief. Nor is there any early-first-century evidence that Isaiah 53 was understood to refer to a crucified Messiah (though see the later targum on Isaiah 53).

Because of the bifurcation of the Christ event, salvation also came in more than one stage or part. Paul speaks of large numbers of Gentiles already being saved, but also says that God has not as yet completed his plan for saving Jews (cf. Rom 11:11-32). Already a believer has a right standing with God and even peace (Rom 5:1), but that same believer is not yet fully sanctified and glorified — as is clear from the ongoing tension between "the flesh" and the Holy Spirit in the believer's life (Gal 5:16-26).

Ecclesiology

Paul's thinking about God's people was also changed because of the coming of Jesus. This is especially so with regard to the issue of the basis for inclusion in God's people. In Paul's view, God's people were Jews and Gentiles united in Christ (Gal 3:28) and could even be called "the Israel of God" (Gal 6:16). Neither heredity nor obedience to Torah could secure one a place in true Israel or God's coming kingdom (cf. Rom 3:23–4:8). In Christ, the Law — at least as a basis of obtaining or maintaining a right standing with God — was at an end (Rom 10:4). Paul also asserts that it was no longer necessary for him or for other Jewish or Gentile Christians to continue to keep the laws of clean and unclean (Rom 14:14). This means that in Paul's mind the Christ event had changed the very basis of fellowship among God's people. It had changed the badges or markers of identity that singled God's people out.

Torah, temple, and territory were three of the great pillars or landmarks of early Judaism. "In Christ" these landmarks had undergone a remarkable transformation. We have already said a bit about Paul's view of the Law. But when we examine what he says about sacrifice and temple, things are also radically different. For one thing, Christ is seen as the paschal lamb who was sacrificed once for all, thereby making any further literal sacrifices unnecessary and not even useful (1 Cor 5:7). Henceforth, only the sacrifice of presenting oneself wholly to God in devotion and for service was required (Rom 12:1-2). It is also Paul's belief that the new temple is, on the one hand, comprised of Jews and Gentiles united in Christ and indwelt by the Holy Spirit (1 Cor 6:19), and, on the other hand, the individual believer's body (1 Cor 3:16-17).

It is also notable that the territorial doctrine of Israel nowhere comes up for real discussion in the Pauline letters, even though Paul wrote when such a doctrine was still a critical part of Israel's hope — that is, before 70 CE. It is possible that Paul made room for such a doctrine as being feasible when Christ returns and "all Israel" will be saved (Rom 11:23-26). Nonetheless, it is remarkable that in the list of things that Paul says God promised Israel according to the flesh, nowhere is land mentioned (cf. Rom 9:4-5, unless the vague reference to the promises involves such an idea). It would appear, therefore, that a Jewish territorial doctrine was also transformed by Paul's understanding of the Christ event, and so he could speak of an inheritance — possibly even a commonwealth or citizenship — in heaven (Col 1:12; Phil 3:20).

Theology Proper

We have already seen evidence of how Paul's christological monotheism changed his thinking about God, but further evidence can certainly be produced. Notice, for instance, that in 2 Cor 5:10 and 1 Thess 5:4-10 it is not Yahweh but Christ who will come to judge the world — and this is not because the Father decided to send someone less than divine to accomplish this task. Paul is quite happy to speak about Christ assuming a variety of functions previously predicated only of Yahweh in the Old Testament. Though Paul did not articulate a full trinitarian theology, the raw stuff of trinitarian thinking surfaces again and again in his letters, especially in doxological texts, where Paul is thinking about whom he worships, or in prayer texts (cf. 1 Thess 1:2-5; 2 Cor 13:14). Paul had previously invoked blessing only in God's name, but now God had three names by which the Lord could be called.

7. And So?

More could be said regarding Christ as the basis for and focus of such diverse New Testament writings as Hebrews, 1 Peter, Revelation, and even the Acts of the Apostles. The speeches in Acts are full of narrative christology explaining how Jesus came, was a man mighty in word and deed, was crucified and raised, and was made both Lord and Christ, being vindicated by God. The high priestly christology of Hebrews provides a focus for the work, as do the images of Christ as the Lion and the Lamb and the one who unseals the seals in Revelation. In 1 Peter, Christ as Shepherd and Suffering Servant provides both comfort and a paradigm for living for the letter's audience. So how, at the end of the day, do we explain this preoccupation with Jesus the Christ in the Gospels, in Paul's letters, and throughout the rest of the New Testament, especially in light of the dearth of similar discussions in Early Judaism?

It is my thesis that though we have been speaking about Christ as the basis for and focus of New Testament thought, we need to keep steadily in view that early Christianity did not solely — perhaps even not primarily — involve an intellectual revolution. There is something not quite right with treating the subject of this article as just a matter of abstract thought. The earliest Christians were not, by and large, philosophers or highly educated people. Nor were most of them wealthy persons of leisure who had time for contemplation or dialogue with the great minds of the age. It is a mistake to see the authors of the New Testament as persons with doctoral degrees devoted to the life of the mind and the flexing of their intellectual muscles.

What we are dealing with here is a group of people who had had profound religious experiences that they interpreted as encounters with the living Lord — that is, with Jesus the Christ. To be sure, some of their leaders, such as Paul or the author of Hebrews or the Beloved Disciple, could match wits with many of the great minds of their age. But it was their religious experiences with Christ that they had in common. And it was their communities of worship and fellowship, which came into being because of those experiences, that provided the matrix for reflection about the meaning of the Christ event.

Even more to the point, it must always be remembered that these communities were worshiping communities. So probably all the New Testament writers derived much of their orientation about these matters from the context of worship — which generated hymns, creeds, confessions, and other source materials that were often christologically focused. More attention needs to be paid to the social setting, namely to worship in the early house churches, which produced the orientation and reflection on the One seen as their living Lord. Perhaps it would even be in order to reflect on household worship in the Greco-Roman world in general, but that is a subject for another essay.

Here it must suffice to say that Christ is, indeed, the basis for and focus of New Testament thought because he was believed and experienced to be the basis for and focus of early Christian life — both in corporate worship and in daily living. At the bottom of the christological well there lie deep waters of religious experience, which we have by no means plumbed the depths of — even 2,000 years after the ministry, death, and resurrection of Jesus Christ.

SELECTED BIBLIOGRAPHY

Brown, Raymond E. *An Introduction to New Testament Christology.* New York: Paulist, 1994.

Burridge, Richard A. *What Are the Gospels?* Cambridge: Cambridge University Press, 1992.

————. *Four Gospels, One Jesus? A Symbolic Reading.* Grand Rapids: Eerdmans, 1994.

Charlesworth, James H. "From Jewish Messianology to Christian Christology: Some Caveats and Perspectives," in *Judaisms and Their Messiahs at the Turn of the Christian Era,* ed. J. Neusner, W. S. Green, and E. S. Frerichs. Cambridge: Cambridge University Press, 1987, 225-64.

Collins, John J. *The Scepter and the Star: The Messiahs of the Dead Sea Scrolls and Other Ancient Literature.* New York: Doubleday, 1995.

Harris, Murray J. *Jesus as God: The New Testament Use of "Theos" in Reference to Jesus.* Grand Rapids: Baker, 1992.

Kim, Seyoon. *The Origin of Paul's Gospel.* Tübingen: Mohr-Siebeck, 1981; Grand Rapids: Eerdmans, 1982.

Kramer, Werner. *Christ, Lord, Son of God,* trans. B. Hardy. Naperville: Allenson, 1966.

Moule, C. F. D. *The Origin of Christology.* Cambridge: Cambridge University Press, 1977.

Richard, Earl J. *Jesus, One and Many: The Christological Concept of New Testament Authors.* Wilmington: Glazier, 1988.

Schweizer, Eduard. *Jesus Christ: The Man from Nazareth and the Exalted Lord.* Macon: Mercer University Press, 1987.

Witherington, Ben, III. *The Christology of Jesus.* Philadelphia: Fortress, 1990.

———. "Christology," in *The Dictionary of Paul and His Letters,* ed. G. F. Hawthorne, R. P. Martin, and D. G. Reid. Downers Grove: InterVarsity, 1993, 100-15.

———. *Paul's Narrative Thought World: The Tapestry of Tragedy and Triumph.* Louisville: Westminster/John Knox, 1994.

———. *The Jesus Quest: The Third Search for the Jew of Nazareth.* Downers Grove: InterVarsity, 1995, 1997[2].

———. *Friendship and Finances in Philippi: A Socio-Rhetorical Commentary on Philippians.* Philadelphia: Trinity Press International, 1997.

———. *The Paul Quest.* Downers Grove: InterVarsity, 1998.

———. *Jesus the Seer: The Progress of Prophecy.* Peabody: Hendrickson, 1999.

———. *The Many Faces of the Christ: The Christologies of the New Testament.* New York: Crossroad, 1999.

CHAPTER 3

Christological Materials in the Early Christian Communities

RICHARD N. LONGENECKER

Christology, or what may be defined as theological interpretation of the person and work of Jesus of Nazareth, did not arise in a vacuum. It was, Christians believe, rooted in the Jewish Scriptures, developed by prophets and seers in the Religion of Israel and Second Temple Judaism, expressed in the ministry of a rather obscure Jewish prophet, teacher, and miracle worker of Galilee, and held in the memory of that prophet's earliest followers, who proclaimed him to be Israel's promised and long-expected Messiah. But its central features seem also to have been incorporated into certain materials that circulated — whether orally or in written form, or both — within the early Christian communities. And it was from these materials that Paul in his letters, the evangelists in their Gospels, and the other writers of the New Testament drew in formulating their respective portrayals and presentations of Jesus.

The identity and reconstruction of these early christological materials is, of course, highly conjectural. We do not have any independent access to them. Their existence, nature and contents — in fact, everything about them — must be inferred by means of form-critical and tradition-critical analyses of the New Testament, into which, it is believed, they have been incorporated. Nevertheless, most scholars are convinced (1) that there existed among early believers in Jesus various oral and written christological materials, (2) that these materials were first formed and used in the contexts of worship, preaching, and teaching, (3) that these materials gave guidance to the authors of the New Testament in their presentations and arguments, and (4) that it is possible to identify some of these early materials and to describe some of their essential features.

This is not to deny the impact of Jesus' teaching and ministry on his earliest disciples, nor to minimize the significance of eyewitness reports and the church's memory of such reports. Nor is it to devalue the importance of either oral tradition or the work of God's Spirit in the nascent church. But these are matters not easily accessible to literary analysis or historical investigation and so must be left to the domains of informed speculation and personal faith.

Our thesis in this article is that — in addition to personal remembrances, eyewitness reports, the communal memory of the early church, and the work of God's Spirit in the retention and interpretation of all these recollections about Jesus of Nazareth — it needs also to be recognized that there circulated within the early Christian communities various christological materials, both written and oral, which brought much of that earlier testimony together and were used by the writers of the New Testament in their portrayals and presentations. Four such bodies of material we want to highlight here: (1) passion narratives and reports, (2) an eschatological tractate and traditions, (3) a Logia or Sayings collection, and (4) confessional portions — with, undoubtedly, other related materials also existing within the early Christian communities.

1. Passion Narratives and Reports

An emphasis on the death of Jesus on a cross is prominent throughout the New Testament and a major feature in all of its various strands and strata. A number of early Christian hymns and confessions quoted in the New Testament attest to the centrality of Jesus' death on a cross in early Christian thought — as, for example, the reference to Christ being "obedient unto death, even death on a cross" in Phil 2:8, which serves as the focal point of the hymn of 2:6-11; and the statement "Christ died for our sins" in 1 Cor 15:3b, which stands at the head of the material quoted in 15:3b-5 and is buttressed by the affirmation that this was "according to the Scriptures" (cf. also such portions as quoted in Gal 3:13; Rom 3:25; and Col 1:20). And Paul repeatedly declares that the focus of his preaching in his mission to Gentiles was "the cross" and "Christ crucified" (e.g., 1 Cor 1:17-18, 23; 2:2; Gal 3:1).

Further, while the canonical Gospels must certainly be seen as more than just "passion narratives with extended introductions," as Martin Kähler once called them (*The So-Called Historical Jesus and the Historic, Biblical Christ*, trans. C. E. Braaten [Philadelphia: Fortress, 1964; first German ed., 1892], 80, n. 11), there can be no doubt that Jesus' death on a cross is a major emphasis of all four of the canonical evangelists. Its depiction, in fact, constitutes the climax of each of their Gospels. About fifteen percent of the total amount of material in the four New Testament Gospels is made up of passion narratives. So prominent was Jesus' death on a cross in the consciousness of the early Christians that at many places in the New Testament the terms "death" and "cross" appear as metonymies for all that Christ did in accomplishing human redemption.

Such a focus of concern and frequency of emphasis have raised a number of critical questions. Three, in particular, call for consideration here: (1) What was the rationale for emphasizing Jesus' death on a cross? (2) Was there a connected passion narrative (or narratives) within the early church? and (3) In what context (or contexts) were these early passion materials formed and used?

What Was the Rationale for Emphasizing Jesus' Death on the Cross?

Ultimately, of course, the rationale for the death of Jesus on a cross is rooted in the sovereign will and purposes of God — which are matters that I must leave to the realm of mystery and the greater expertise of theologians. Historically, however, the rationale for Jesus' death on a cross among the earliest Jewish believers in Jesus seems to have been, largely, apologetically and biblically based.

The greatest problem that faced Jews who believed in Jesus as God's Messiah was the declaration of Deut 21:23: "Anyone who is hung on a tree is under God's curse." The statement originally had reference to the exposure of a criminal executed for a capital offense, whose lifeless body was to be hung on a tree for public ridicule. But it came to be understood among Jews as referring also to the impalement or crucifixion of a living person on a pole or cross (with, of course, the pole or cross viewed as parts of a tree). Paul reflects the general Jewish repugnance of the idea of a crucified

Messiah when he speaks in Gal 5:11 and 1 Cor 1:23 of the "scandal" of Christ having been put to death by crucifixion.

The earliest believers in Jesus, however, seem to have resolved this problem of a crucified Messiah by viewing God's curse of Christ on the cross as his sharing in humanity's curse — that is, as an "interchange" wherein Christ participated in our life and bore God's judgment on sin in order that we might participate in his life and death (i.e., his "active" and "passive" obedience) and thereby receive righteousness before God. Morna Hooker has aptly and amply explicated this New Testament understanding (see her "Interchange in Christ," *JTS* 22 [1971] 349-61; "Interchange and Atonement," *BJRL* 60 [1976] 462-81; "Interchange and Suffering," in *Suffering and Martyrdom in the New Testament,* ed. W. Horbury and B. McNeil [Cambridge: Cambridge University Press, 1981], 70-83; and "Interchange in Christ and Ethics," *JSNT* 25 [1985] 3-17; cf. also K. Berger's use of the expression *ein Tauschgeschäft* in "Abraham in der paulinischen Hauptbriefen," *MTZ* 17 [1966] 52). In what is probably an early Christian confessional portion, Gal 4:4-5, for example, speaks of God's Son as having been "born under the Law" so that he could redeem those who are under the Law and make them God's sons and daughters. Thus Christ's death on a cross was interpreted as being not punitive but redemptive (cf. Gal 3:13; see also 2 Cor 5:21).

In addition, early Jewish believers in Jesus looked to their sacred Scriptures, that is, to what Christians later called the Old Testament, for biblical justification for the death of Jesus on a cross. C. H. Dodd has shown how certain *testimonia* passages drawn from the Old Testament — particularly Isa 52:13–53:12, Psalm 22, and Zechariah 9–14 — served as an apology for Jesus' passion and provided the substructure for all of early Christian theology (*According to the Scriptures,* especially 72, 92-93, 127).

Joachim Jeremias and Christian Maurer have also noted the many allusions to Isa 52:13–53:12 in the passion narratives of the Gospels and argued that the figure of the suffering Servant depicted in Isaiah was applied by the early Christians to Jesus (cf. Jeremias, "παῖς θεοῦ," 700-12; Maurer, "Knecht Gottes und Sohn Gottes"). And Barnabas Lindars, while recognizing that the focus of early Christian proclamation was on the resurrection (in his second chapter), has insisted that it was impossible to speak of the resurrection of Jesus without attaching, as well, some positive significance to Jesus' death (*New Testament Apologetic,* 75). So Lindars set out what he called the "passion apologetic" of the early church (in his third chapter), laying particular emphasis on allusions to Isaiah 53, quotations from the "Passion Psalms" (Psalms 22, 31, 34, 41, 69, and 109), and references to Zechariah 9–14 that can be found in the passion narratives of the canonical Gospels (*New Testament Apologetic,* 75-137).

The exact nature of the passion apologetic found in the four Gospels can be legitimately debated. Morna Hooker is quite right to point out the precariousness of building too much on allusions to the Isaian Servant passages in the passion narratives and to object to differentiating too sharply between the Servant of the Lord and known figures of messianic expectation in Second Temple Judaism (cf. *Jesus and the Servant;* see also her *Son of Man in Mark*). And Douglas Moo has done scholarship a service in clarifying many matters regarding the use of Scripture in Judaism and early Christianity, highlighting the "remarkably unified interpretation" of the Old Testament passages used by the evangelists in their passion narratives, and directing us back to the teaching of Jesus himself for an ultimate explanation of the interpretations found in those passion narratives (cf. *Old Testament in the Gospel Passion Narratives*). But that passion materials of some type existed before the writing of our New Testament — and, further, that their formulations were motivated in large part by apologetic and biblical concerns — seems to be an axiom that deserves credence.

Was There a Connected Passion Narrative (or Narratives) within the Early Church?

Accepting the presence of passion materials within the early church, the further question arises: Was there a connected passion narrative (or narratives) within the early church?

Resemblances between the Synoptic Gospels and the Fourth Gospel in their portrayals of Jesus' final week in Jerusalem are impressive. One might have expected a certain similarity among the three synoptic evangelists, for their portrayals of Jesus' ministry before that final week are similar. But the fourth evangelist's passion narrative is also remarkably similar to those of the other three — even though his portrayal of Jesus' pre-passion ministry is in many ways quite different from theirs. In fact, of the approximately six percent of material in John's Gospel that is paralleled in the Synoptic Gospels, almost all of it occurs in the fourth evangelist's account of Jesus' sufferings and death in Jerusalem. And it is this coming together of the four Gospels in their respective passion narratives that has often suggested to interpreters that all four of the evangelists were drawing on either an earlier stereotyped oral tradition or an earlier connected written account in their portrayals of Jesus' passion — or, perhaps, on earlier connected accounts, whether oral or written, that overlapped extensively.

Further, it needs to be noted that, while somewhat differing traditions of Jesus' pre-passion ministry are reflected in the Synoptic Gospels and John's Gospel, there are a number of rather surprising agreements between the Synoptics and John in the passion narratives. This suggests something of a common tradition or similar source materials being used by all four evangelists for their respective passion narratives.

For example, both Mark and John (though not Matthew or Luke) agree on such relatively minor linguistic matters as (1) Jesus being anointed with "pure nard" (Mark 14:3; John 12:3), (2) the "300 denarii" (Mark 14:5; John 12:5), (3) Peter going "into" the courtyard of the high priest (Mark 14:54; John 18:15) and (4) "warming" himself at the fire there (Mark 14:54, 67; John 18:18, 25), (5) the cry "crucify him" in the imperative (Mark 15:14; John 19:15), and (6) mention of the "Day of Preparation" (Mark 15:42; John 19:31). And both Luke and John (though not Matthew or Mark) include material regarding (1) Joseph of Arimathea taking Jesus' body down from the cross, wrapping it in linen cloth, and burying it in a new tomb (Luke 23:53; John 19:38-41), and (2) the risen Jesus appearing to his disciples in Jerusalem, where he teaches and commissions them (Luke 24:36-49; John 20:19-29) — the latter passage in Luke's Gospel being frequently referred to as "a bolt out of the Johannine sky."

Agreements and disagreements among the passion narratives have been set out rather generally by Joachim Jeremias in his *Eucharistic Words of Jesus* (see pages 89-96). On the basis of his observations, Jeremias has posited a four-stage development of the passion narrative: (1) an early kerygmatic confession, as now appears in 1 Cor 15:3b-5; (2) a "short account," which began with the arrest of Jesus; (3) a "long account," which included "the triumphal entry, the cleansing of the temple, the question about Jesus' authority, the Last Supper with the announcement of betrayal, Gethsemane, arrest of Jesus, trial before the Sanhedrin, denial of Peter, the condemnation by Pilate, the crucifixion, the empty grave"; and (4) expansions of the then existing narrative "by the addition of particular incidents and blocks of traditional material into the forms which we now have in the four gospels" (*Eucharistic Words*, 96). In a sentence that concludes the scenario as set out above, Jeremias added the following caveat: "It goes without saying that these four stages are only milestones in a much more colourful and complicated development."

There has been a rather general consensus among scholars (1) that some sort of connected passion narrative existed in the early church and (2) that this connected narrative became one of the chief sources for the writing of our Synoptic Gospels and Fourth Gospel. In 1970, for example, Raymond Brown, expressing what he believed to be a "centrist" view of the matter, stated: "Critical scholars of diverse tendencies (Bultmann, Jeremias, and Taylor, to name a few) agree that the Marcan Passion Narrative is composite and that one of Mark's chief sources was an earlier consecutive account of the passion" (*The Gospel According to John* [Garden City: Doubleday, 1970], 787 and 789). And Brown went on to say that this "earlier consecutive account of the passion" was not only the basic source for the three synoptic passion accounts but also the primary source for the fourth evangelist's passion account.

Several studies since the early 1970s, however, have tended to cast doubt on the hypothesis of a connected passion narrative that all the canonical evangelists used. Eta Linnemann, for example, argued that we must distinguish between "independent reports" *(Berichte)* and a "connected account" *(Erzählung),* and concluded from her analysis of the passion narratives that the four evangelists worked from a collection of "independent reports" rather than a "connected account" (*Studien zur Passionsgeschichte* [Göttingen: Vandenhoeck und Ruprecht, 1970). Ludgar Schenke highlighted the need for scholars to distinguish more carefully between tradition and redaction in the evangelists' passion portrayals (*Der Passionsbericht nach Markus* [Gütersloh: Mohn, 1974]; see also his *Der gekreuzigte Christus* [Stuttgart: Katholisches Bibelwerk, 1974], which builds on his earlier, more extensive *Auferstehungsverkündigung und leeres Grab* [Stuttgart: Katholisches Bibelwerk, 1969]). Detlev Dormeyer developed a "redactional vocabulary" for the passion narratives of the Gospels by studying statistical relationships between the terms used in them and terms used elsewhere in early tradition and the evangelists' pre-passion portrayals, and so proposed a more exact linguistic method for distinguishing between tradition and redaction (cf. his *Die Passion Jesu als Verhaltensmodell* [Münster: Aschendorff, 1974]). And many recent studies of the passion narratives have followed the lead of these scholars.

The problem, of course, is how to evaluate relations between tradition and redaction in the canonical passion narratives. Distinctive redactional features in the four individual portrayals seem to negate the view that they are to be understood as simply the product of a stereotyped oral tradition — or, as "the Papias tradition" has often been understood, simply the preaching of Peter, which was recorded verbatim by Mark and then followed by Matthew and Luke (perhaps also John). Yet agreements (or, at least, resemblances) between the passion accounts of the four evangelists, which are extensive and often quite precise, provide a solid foundation for postulating that some form (or forms) of a connected passion narrative (or narratives) existed within the early Christian communities and that it was used by the evangelists in their accounts of Jesus' final ministry in Jerusalem and death on a cross.

It may be (1) that there existed more than one form or version of the passion narrative, as well as various other passion reports, among the early Christians — with each of those narratives possessing a certain "sense of center," but also being somewhat different (as seems to be the case for the portrayals of Jesus' pre-passion ministry given by Mark, Matthew, and Luke vis-à-vis that presented by John) — and (2) that the synoptic evangelists depended heavily on one of these forms and the fourth evangelist on another, though with all four knowing of other materials as well. It is some such thesis that I believe the evidence suggests.

We may never, however, be able to spell out the exact nature of the passion materials that were extant among the earliest believers in Jesus. Nonetheless, we can still feel confident in assuming that the New Testament authors had various source materials at their disposal, which circulated within the Christian communities of their day, and that one important set of such materials was made up of (1) a connected passion narrative or narratives and, perhaps, (2) various other individual passion reports.

In What Context (or Contexts) Were These Passion Materials Formed and First Used?

The earliest Christians viewed themselves as (1) witnesses to the resurrection of Jesus (Acts 1:22b) and (2) proclaimers of all that that most startling event in human history involved (cf. Acts 2:24-36; 3:13-15; 4:2, 10-11, 33; 5:30-32; 10:39-41; 13:30-37; 17:18, 31b-32; 23:6; 24:21; see also 1 Corinthians 15). But "one of the first tasks which the Church had to undertake in defence of its claims," as Barnabas Lindars has pointed out, "was to explain the suffering and death of Jesus the Messiah" (*New Testament Apologetic*, 75).

Where did the early believers look for such a passion apologetic? Obviously, they turned to their ancient Scriptures. But their understanding of their sacred Scriptures had been revolutionized by the ministry and teaching of Jesus. So, as Lindars went on to argue, (1) while actual quotations from Isaiah 53 are not numerous in the New Testament, "allusions to it are embedded so deeply in the work of all the principal [New Testament] writers that it is certain that it belongs to the earliest thought of the primitive Church" (*New Testament Apologetic*, 77; though for better nuancing, see Hooker, *Jesus and the Servant*), and (2) while Jesus is not recorded as having used the Isaian title "Servant of the Lord" with reference to himself, "the enigmatic Son of Man seems to include this idea in certain contexts" (*New Testament Apologetic*, 78; though for a better explication of Son of Man imagery, see Hooker, *Son of Man in Mark*). And thus as Lindars concludes: Jesus' "instruction to the disciples about his coming Passion is likely to have made use of this prophecy," that is, generally Isaiah 53, but more particularly "the enigmatic Son of Man" imagery "at least sufficiently to give it a secure place in their thought. When a Passion apologetic was required, it was there ready-made in the teaching which they had received" (*New Testament Apologetic*, 78).

Such a passion apologetic would have been necessary for both (1) those within the early Christian communities, in affirmation of their new self-identity, and (2) those outside the Christian communities, in proclamation to them of the "good news" of the gospel — which would necessarily have included a biblically-based apologetic that was calculated to overcome their obstacles to belief. We may, therefore, rather confidently assume that the early passion narrative(s) and reports — which were developed within the early Christian communities and used by the evangelists in their respective passion narratives — were formed in the contexts of (1) the affirmation of believers, who needed support for their new self-identity and understanding, and (2) the proclamation of Jesus' resurrection, ministry, and person to non-believers, who required a biblical apologetic for the death of Jesus on a cross.

2. An Eschatological Tractate and Traditions

Another set of materials that evidently circulated among the earliest believers in Jesus and was used by the writers of the New Testament in their christological presentations has to do with futuristic eschatology. These materials come to focus particularly in the Olivet Discourse of Mark 13, Matthew 24–25, and Luke 21.

Critical questions regarding the Olivet Discourse and its auxiliary eschatological traditions are legion, with hardly any passage in the New Testament more controversial than this one. Only three matters of a source-critical and tradition-critical nature, however, are directly relevant to our purposes here — with these three questions being somewhat parallel to those three asked earlier regarding the passion narrative(s) and passion reports: (1) What was the rationale for these eschatological materials? (2) Was there a connected Olivet Discourse circulating in the early church? and (3) In what context (or contexts) were these early eschatological materials formed and first used?

What Was the Rationale for These Eschatological Materials?

There is no doubt that the New Testament lays heavy emphasis on "realized eschatology" — that is, on the eschatological age of redemption as having dawned or been "inaugurated" in the ministry and person of Jesus of Nazareth. This is declared quite straightforwardly in an early Christian confession incorporated by Paul in Gal 4:4-5, which begins with the declaration "When the time had fully come, God sent his Son" and ends with the affirmation "in order that we might receive the full rights of sons" (or "adoption as God's children"). But realized eschatology is not the whole story. "Futuristic eschatology" also has an important place in all of the portrayals and presentations of the New Testament.

C. H. Dodd, even while emphasizing realized eschatology, has shown how the catechetical tradition of the early church as reflected in the New Testament included not only "theological dogmas" and "ethical precepts" but also a number of futurist statements given as "eschatological motives," with these eschatological motivational materials tending "to gravitate to the close of the *catechesis*" (cf. "The 'Primitive Catechism' and the Sayings of Jesus," especially 11-14 and 18-24). Included in these eschatological hortatory materials are such matters as (1) warnings about future false christs and false prophets (cf. Matt 7:22ff.; 1 Thess 5:3; 2 Thess 2:2ff.; 1 Tim 4:1ff.; 2 Tim 4:1ff.; 2 Pet 3:3ff.; Rev 13; 16:12ff.; 17:1ff.); (2) references to future persecutions and sufferings of God's people (1 Thess 1:6; 3:1-4; 2 Thess 1:4-7; 1 Pet 4:12-19; Rev 11:3-13; 13:11-13); (3) statements about future judgments on Jerusalem and its people (Matt 23:34-36; Luke 11:49-51; 13:1-5; 19:41-44; 23:27-31; 1 Thess 2:16; 2 Thess 2:4ff.); and (4) calls to watchfulness in the light of Christ's near but incalculable *parousia* (1 Thess 5:1-11; 2 Thess 2:1-5; 1 Pet 1:13; 4:7; 5:8; Rev 3:2ff.; 16:15). And it is just such futuristic and hortatory statements that appear in the Olivet Discourse.

The basic rationale for these eschatological materials in the early church was not to spell out some sort of eschatological timetable, as can be found in the writings of various apocalyptic authors of Second Temple Judaism. Rather, it was to call believers in Jesus to discernment and watchfulness in the midst of adverse situations (cf. M. D. Hooker's emphasis on Mark 13 as prophetic in content and apocalyptic in form, or as "prophetic-apocalyptic," in *Son of Man in Mark* and "Trial and Tribulation in Mark XIII," *BJRL* 65 [1982] 78-99; see also G. E. Ladd's earlier article, "Why Not Prophetic-Apocalyptic?" *JBL* 76 [1957] 192-200). Futuristic eschatology in these passages functions much as it does in the Old Testament — that is, as a prophetic summons to a seriousness of purpose, a life lived in holiness and justice, and a watchful expectation that awaits God's future actions. The only real difference in the New Testament eschatological passages is that the prophetic call is christologically oriented, with a focus on the parousia or "coming" of Christ.

Was There a Connected Olivet Discourse in the Early Church?

Scholarly study of the Olivet Discourse over the past couple centuries has been both extensive and intensive. During the last half century, however, there have been a number of important source-critical and tradition-critical treatments of this eschatological unit of material. Notable among the more recent treatments has been that of George Beasley-Murray, who in 1954 (and continuing on through 1993) has done scholarship a service in charting the course of the debate and critiquing various arguments used to deny the discourse to Jesus (cf. his *Jesus and the Last Days* of 1993, which incorporates in revised form his *Jesus and the Future* of 1954 and his *Commentary on Mark Thirteen* of 1957).

Significant critical studies of the Olivet Discourse have also been produced by Lars Hartman, who in 1966 noted that the Olivet Discourse may appropriately be identified as a midrash on the book of Daniel (see his *Prophecy Interpreted*), though he did not pay much attention to its parabolic and hortatory materials, and Jacques Dupont, who from 1968 through 1978 explicated a number of the source-critical and tradition-critical issues of pertinence to the discourse's parables and exhortations (see his "Parabole du figuier qui bourgeonne," "Parabole du maître qui rentre dans la nuit," "Ruine du temple et la fin des temps dans de discours de Marc 13," and "Persécution comme situation missionnaire"). Likewise of significance are the treatments of Desmond Ford, who in 1979 investigated the origin and significance of the expression "the abomination of desolation" in Mark 13:14 and Matt 24:15 and spelled out its relation to similar references in 1 and 2 Thessalonians and the Johannine Apocalypse *(Abomination of Desolation in Biblical Eschatology)*, and David Wenham, who in 1984 argued that the Olivet Discourse reflects "an elaborate and substantial pre-synoptic tradition," which, as the title of his book suggests *(Rediscovery of Jesus' Eschatological Discourse)*, must be seen to have been ultimately rooted in the circumstances and teaching of Jesus himself.

There have also been a number of important exegetical and redaction-critical studies of the Olivet Discourse in various commentaries on the Synoptic Gospels, as well as significant comments in various interpretive treatments of the Thessalonian letters and the Johannine Apocalypse. On the source-critical and tradition-critical issues that are involved, however, the works by Beasley-Murray, Hartman, Dupont, Ford, and Wenham have, each in its own way, been high points in the contemporary discussion. And what has seemed most significant to the majority of source-critical and tradition-critical scholars in answering the question "Was there a connected Olivet Discourse in the early church?" is the fact that the contents of the discourse are attested widely and at various places in the New Testament — not only in the Synoptic Gospels, but also in 1 and 2 Thessalonians and the Johannine Apocalypse.

Assuming Markan priority, Matthew 24 follows Mark 13 more closely than does Luke 21. The differences in the accounts may only be redactional in nature. It may be, however, that one tradition of the discourse lies behind Mark and Matthew and another behind Luke — or, perhaps, separate traditions are to be seen as lying behind all three Gospels. Nonetheless, the three presentations are in substantial agreement, and that agreement suggests that there existed in the early church a body of eschatological teaching.

Likewise, similarities between Paul's words in 1 and 2 Thessalonians about what is to precede the End and the evangelists' statements regarding the same in the Olivet Discourse are considerable and suggest that their traditions must in some way be related. Admittedly, verbal similarities — such as the use of *throeisthai*, "to be disturbed" or "frightened" (2 Thess 2:2; cf. Mark 13:7; Matt 24:6) and *sēmeia kai terata*, "signs and wonders" (2 Thess 2:9; cf. Mark 13:22; Matt 24:24); also the expressions *ho anthrōpos tēs anomias*, "the man of lawlessness," and *ho huios tēs apōleias*, "the son of destruction" (2 Thess 2:3), which have frequently been seen as synonymous with *to bdelugma tēs erēmōseōs*, "the abomination of desolation" (Mark 13:14; Matt 24:15) — are, of themselves, rather slight and may be variously ascribed. But the parallels of ideas and structure are strong, with such parallelism being especially evident when comparing 2 Thess 2:1-12 with the first part of the Olivet Discourse, Mark 13:5-22. Further, the portraits of the varied manifestations of the Antichrist in Revelation 11, 13, 14, 16, 17 and 20 embody many of the characteristic features found in Daniel, the Olivet Discourse of the Synoptic Gospels (especially Mark 13), and Paul's Thessalonian letters (especially 2 Thessalonians 2).

This phenomenon of multiple attestation certainly points to a source or sources in the early Christian community on which the three Synoptic evangelists, Paul (and/or his followers), and John the Seer drew. In its earliest form that source (or sources) was undoubtedly oral, with Jesus' teaching about the End having made a deep impression on his disciples, and so retained in their memory and often repeated. A written account (or accounts), however, probably also came about at an early time in the church's existence. For not only would the early believers in Jesus, when facing persecution, have wanted a more tangible record on which they could rely, but also would have desired to preserve in rather fixed form Jesus' teaching that was foundational for their new eschatological existence and orientation. So it may be assumed that they cherished not only accounts about Jesus' passion and resurrection, but also records about what he taught with regard to his coming *parousia*.

In What Context (or Contexts) Were These Eschatological Materials Formed and First Used?

It is impossible to read the Olivet Discourse in the Synoptic Gospels without being impressed by both (1) the remarkable similarities among the three accounts and (2) the different inclusions, recastings, and emphases of each of the evangelists. Nor is it possible to read the related eschatological materials of the Thessalonians letters and the Johannine Apocalypse without being impressed by both commonalities and differences.

The basic interpretive features of the Olivet Discourse suggest a highly creative mind as its originator. The church's witness is that it was Jesus who first interpreted Daniel and the other Old Testament prophets in such a way as to produce the distinctive elements of early Christian eschatology. C. H. Dodd once pertinently observed, "Creative thinking is rarely done by committees, useful as they may be for systematizing the fresh ideas of individual thinkers, and for stimulating them to further thought. It is individual minds that originate" (*According to the Scriptures*, 109-10). And he concluded his observation in words that cannot be improved on: "To account for the beginning of this most original and fruitful process of re-thinking the Old Testament we found need to postulate a creative mind. The Gospels offer us one. Are we compelled to reject the offer?"

On the one hand, therefore, we are compelled to affirm, in the words of Bruce Vawter:

> That Jesus actually made such a prophecy, in view of his consistent es-chatological teaching on the soonness of a divine visitation on Jerusalem and Judea, his conviction of the decisiveness of his own role in the work-ings of salvation history, and his reading of the temper of the times, there is absolutely no reason to question. His words are in the tradition of Israel's prophecy (cf. Jer. 7:1-15; Ezek. 24:15-23) and have not been sim-ply made up by Christian writers in the light of later events. (*The Four Gospels: An Introduction* [Garden City: Doubleday, 1967], 322)

On the other hand, however, it needs also to be recognized that the early church went beyond merely remembering Jesus' words and creatively ap-plied his teaching in the Olivet Discourse to its own circumstances in vari-ous ways.

One particularly illuminating observation, which has often been made, is that the Olivet Discourse in all three of its versions forms both a conclusion to the teaching ministry of Jesus and an introduction to the passion narratives. So it seems proper to believe that the Olivet Discourse, together with various other auxiliary traditions, was used by the early church in contexts having to do with both catechetical instruction and evangelistic proclamation.

3. A Logia or Sayings Collection

A third set of materials that seems to have circulated within the early Christian communities, and which appears to have been used by the authors of the New Testament in their various christological presentations, is a collection of Logia (i.e., "words") or Sayings of Jesus — material that has been designated "Q" (from the German word "Quelle," which means simply "source"). This is a collection of sayings of Jesus that has been compiled by scholars in one of three ways: (1) from the sayings that comprise about one-sixth of Matthew's Gospel and, verbatim or nearly so, one-sixth of Luke's Gospel, but do not appear in Mark — that is, the so-called "double tradition" (which is a "minimalist" definition of "Q"), (2) from such verbal agreements in the double tradition *plus* other sayings in Matthew and Luke that display a general agreement of sense to those with explicit verbal agreements (which is the "generally accepted" definition of "Q"), or (3) from both the verbal and the general agreements in the double tradition *plus* a few sayings that appear in "the triple tradition," which would include some that appear in Mark or that are included only by Matthew or only by Luke — assuming that for some reason the other Gospel omitted them (which is a "maximalist" definition of "Q").

The contents of such a postulated "Q" or Sayings source are usually estimated to have been about 220 to 235 verses, depending on which of the models described above it is reconstructed according to. Most scholars, however, acknowledge that such a source may have been larger than any of our contemporary reconstructions. For Matthew and Luke, who seem to have independently omitted a few passages found in their principal narrative source, namely Mark's Gospel, may also have independently omitted some of the material that appeared in their Sayings source, that is, in the Logia or "Q."

All sorts of critical issues could be raised regarding such a hypothetical Sayings source. Four, however, are directly relevant to our purposes here: (1) Were teachings of Jesus preserved by his early followers? (2) Was there a Logia or Sayings collection that circulated among Christians prior to the writing of our canonical New Testament? (3) What was the nature of this postulated Sayings collection? and (4) In what context (or contexts) was this Sayings collection formed and first used?

Were Teachings of Jesus Preserved by His Early Followers?

It can hardly be doubted that the teachings of Jesus were preserved in some form by his early followers. Jews during the periods of Second Temple Judaism (ca. 200 BCE–120 CE) and early Rabbinic Judaism (ca. 120–500 CE) commonly preserved teachings of their rabbis. This is what the Mishnah and the Babylonian Gemaras (i.e., the Talmud) are all about, as well as the materials found in the Tosephta ("the Additions"), the Palestinian Gemaras, and many of the Midrashim. It may also be the basis for many of the central writings of the Dead Sea Scrolls — in particular, the Thanksgiving Psalms or *Hodayot,* which are preserved in two copies from cave 1 (1QH^a and 1QH^b) and six copies from cave 4 (4Q427–432), and the pesher commentaries on such biblical books as Genesis (4QpGen), Isaiah (4QpIsa), Hosea (4QpHos), Nahum (4QpNah), and the Psalms (4QPs), most of which appear in multiple copies. Many scholars, in fact, posit that the *Hodayot* and pesher commentaries at Qumran stemmed, at least ultimately, from the "Teacher of Righteousness" himself (whoever he was).

Paul's letters evidence a lively retention of the teachings of Jesus among the early Christians. In 1 Thess 4:1-12, for example, when giving ethical instruction to his Gentile converts at Thessalonica, Paul speaks in words that sound very much like the ethical teaching of Jesus as later recorded in the Synoptic Gospels. In 4:13–5:11 he speaks about the future coming of Jesus using expressions that are reminiscent of many of Jesus' eschatological statements, as also later recorded in the Synoptic Gospels — once even, in 4:15-17, including a further "word of the Lord," which evidently here means a teaching of Jesus that was known to Paul (and, presumably, to many in the early church) but was not incorporated by the canonical evangelists into their writings (i.e., an *agraphon* or "unwritten saying"). And in 2 Thess 2:1-12, as we noted above, there are significant parallels of ideas and structure with the first part of the Olivet Discourse as later recorded in Mark 13:5-22.

Further, in 1 Cor 7:10, when speaking to his Gentile converts at Corinth about marriage, Paul gives the general Christian maxim that "a wife should not separate from her husband" — which, he insists, is not just his opinion (cf. v. 12), but a command that stems from the Lord Jesus: "I give this command, not I but the Lord" *(paraggellō, ouk egō alla ho kyrios).* In 1 Cor 9:14, when speaking about the right of Christian apostles to receive remuneration, he cites a teaching of Jesus: "In the same way, the Lord commanded *(houtōs kai ho kyrios dietaxen)* that those who preach the gospel should receive their living from the gospel." And throughout the ethical exhortations of Rom 12:1–15:13 there appear numerous reminiscences of Jesus' teaching.

Matthew and Luke also testify to a lively interest in the preservation of Jesus' teachings within the early church, for one-sixth of each of their Gospels is given over to sayings of Jesus that go beyond what appears in Mark — in addition, of course, to the Olivet Discourse, which appears in all three Gospels, and a few other sayings that Matthew and Luke share with Mark. Likewise, the *Gospel of Thomas* and the *Gospel of Philip,* which are collections of Jesus' sayings found at Nag Hammadi (or Chenoboskin, as the village was called earlier) in Egypt, evidence a continuing interest in Jesus' teachings among certain sectarian Christians of the second century. There has, of course, been extensive debate regarding the dating of the Nag Hammadi "Gospels" and their relation to the canonical Gospels. But however these matters are finally resolved, it should at least be noted that both canonical and sectarian Gospels demonstrate an interest among early Christians in the preservation of Jesus' teachings.

The statement of Eusebius (ca. 260-339), who was bishop of Caesarea and an eminent church historian, regarding Papias of Hierapolis (who flourished about 130 CE), whom Eusebius identified as "John's hearer" (whether John the disciple or John the Elder, if, indeed, they are to be distinguished) and "an associate of Polycarp," offers further testimony to a continuing interest in Jesus' teaching within the early church. Eusebius says that Papias was the author of "five books" entitled *Expositions of the Logia* (i.e., "Sayings," "Declarations," or "Oracles") *of the Lord,* which volumes, Eusebius says, existed in his day (*Ecclesiastical History* 3.39.1) — though, sadly, they evidently became extinct sometime after Eusebius wrote in the first part of the fourth century.

Was There a Sayings Collection That Circulated among Early Christians?

Given that early believers in Jesus preserved in some fashion the teachings of their Lord, the question, however, still persists: Was there a Logia or Sayings collection that circulated among early Christians prior to the writing of our canonical New Testament? All that can really be said to such a query is that the New Testament writers themselves seem to suggest such a collection as then existing within the early Christian communities — whether written or transmitted orally — and that such a hypothesis makes sense historically.

The major evidence in favor of an early Sayings collection stems from the study of literary relations among the three Synoptic Gospels. Most Christians up through the nineteenth century generally assumed that there was some sort of primitive oral gospel circulating among the early Christians and used by the four evangelists in the writing of their respective Gospels. In the nineteenth century, however, attention was focused on the remarkable parallels of language and structure among the Synoptics, as well as on their distinctive differences. Explanations for the composition of these Gospels were proposed in terms of literary interdependence and the sources that they used. Thus there developed a twofold explanation of, first, the common *narrative* of the Synoptic Gospels ("the triple tradition") and then of the extensive number of verbatim and near-verbatim *sayings* of Jesus that appear in Matthew and Luke but not in Mark ("the double tradition"): (1) for the common narrative material, Mark's Gospel was not only "medial" (so Karl Lachmann in 1835) but also "prior" (so C. H. Weisse in 1838); (2) for the many sayings found in Matthew and Luke but not in Mark, we must postulate a Sayings source (so H. J. Holtzmann in 1863), which can be designated "Q" (so Johannes Weiss in 1890).

These literary analyses and conclusions were first undertaken and drawn up by liberal scholars, so many conservative Christians have viewed them with suspicion. But the hypothesis of an early Sayings collection, whether written or orally stereotyped, has become accepted by most conservative New Testament scholars as well. For as Raymond Brown concisely puts it (assuming, of course, the basic validity of the "two-source theory"), "the existence of Q . . . remains the best way of explaining the agreements between Matt and Luke in material they did not borrow from Mark" (*An Introduction to the New Testament* [New York: Doubleday, 1997], 122).

The hypothesis of an early Sayings collection is further supported by Paul's repeated distinctions in 1 Corinthians between what Jesus commanded and his own statements as an apostle. These distinctions are most evident in 7:10 ("I give this command, not I but the Lord") and 9:14 ("in the same way, the Lord commanded"), where Paul quotes in an *ad sensum* manner the teachings of Jesus on particular problems within the Corinthian church, and in 7:12 ("I say, not the Lord") and 7:25 ("I have no command of the Lord, but I give my opinion as one who by the Lord's mercy is trustworthy"), where he acknowledges that he has no express teaching of

Jesus on a particular matter but tells his converts that what he is writing them is his own opinion — which, of course, he believes to be trustworthy. Such distinctions, however explained, suggest not only that Paul knew of a collection of Jesus' sayings but also that his Gentile converts at Corinth knew of such a collection as well. More to the point, they suggest that both he and they knew what that Sayings collection contained (where he quotes Jesus' teaching) and what it did not contain (where he goes beyond the recorded teaching of Jesus and attempts to contextualize the Christian gospel with respect to the problems faced by his converts).

Mention should also be made of the numerous parallels in the ethical teaching that appear particularly in Romans, 1 and 2 Thessalonians, Ephesians, 1 Peter, and James. These parallels suggest the existence of a common body of catechetical material within the early church from which their respective writers drew. To spell out these parallels and to argue for a common source would take far more space than the constraints of this chapter allow. E. G. Selwyn did that with respect to parallels between 1 Peter and 1 and 2 Thessalonians, which he believed can also be found in Romans, Ephesians, and James, and on the basis of his investigation has argued that they evidence "a high degree of interdependence . . . on a common stock of teaching" (*The First Epistle of St. Peter* [London: Macmillan, 1947], 19). His argument, in fact, is that the ethical teaching of 1 Peter — as well as that of 1 and 2 Thessalonians, Romans, Ephesians, and James — builds on the *verba Christi* ("the words of Christ"), "which were collected at an early date explicitly as words of the Lord, and therefore inspired," and which "lie below the surface of the Epistle [of 1 Peter], and usually not far below it" (p. 23; see the extensive treatments in his "Introduction," Section 3: "Sources Underlying the Epistles," pp. 17-24, and his Essay II: "On the Inter-Relation of 1 Peter and other N.T. Epistles," pp. 365-466).

What Was the Nature of This Postulated Sayings Collection?

This postulated Sayings collection, as reconstructed from materials in the Synoptic Gospels, seems to have consisted almost entirely of sayings of Jesus and a few short parables. It probably had very little narrative material. Only three narrative portions can be claimed to have been included: the temptation of Jesus, the healing of the centurion's servant, and the visit of the disciples of John the Baptist with Jesus. Its content may have been essentially what was referred to by Eusebius, quoting Papias with reference to Matthew: "Matthew compiled the Logia," that is, the "sayings" or "oracles," which, however, the early church usually assumed to be Matthew's Gospel, "in the Hebrew language [i.e., Aramaic], and everyone interpreted [or 'translated'] them as he was able" (*Ecclesiastical History* 3.39.16). Nevertheless, most reconstructions of "Q" today follow Luke's order and use the traditional chapter and verse designations of Luke's Gospel — since Luke's version of any particular saying of Jesus is usually shorter and more terse, whereas Matthew's, while at times more Palestinian in its imagery, is often more expansive and interpretive, with most of the sayings of Jesus in Matthew's Gospel worked into larger sermonic sections of the Evangelist's presentation.

There is a strong sapiential (i.e., "wisdom") tone to Q. For as reconstructed from the Synoptic Gospels, the Jesus of "the non-Markan sayings found in Matthew and Luke" is primarily a Jewish sage who taught wisdom and gave ethical instruction. This need not imply that the earliest Christian message was only ethical — without any eschatological or christological features — as those who speak of Q as a "Q Gospel" or "The First Gospel" usually assume. The Old Testament has a wide variety of content and literary genres (historical narrative, prophecy, psalms, wisdom literature, etc.) and cannot be judged on the basis of only one type of writing. Likewise, the Dead Sea Scrolls exhibit diverse materials (organizational codes, pesher commentaries, testimonia collections, psalms of thanksgiving, the Temple Scroll, the War Scroll, the Copper Scroll, etc.), as does also the later rabbinic literature (halakah or "ethical rules for living" being dominant in the Mishnah, Tosephta, and Gemaras, with haggadah or "expositions, sermons and everything else," prominent in the Midrashim). So the early believers in Jesus seem to have possessed not only a Logia or Sayings collection, but also, as we have argued above, (1) passion narrative(s) and reports and (2) eschatological tractate(s) and traditions. And each of these bodies of material, it may be postulated, served to enhance the fullness of the gospel within the early Christian congregations.

But even if, for the sake of argument, one accepts Q as something of a "Gospel," it needs to be recognized that such a reconstructed group of sayings is not entirely devoid of either eschatology or christology. "There is," as Raymond Brown points out with respect to postulated Q, "a strongly eschatological thrust in the warnings, woes, and some of the parables" (*An Introduction to the New Testament* [New York: Doubleday, 1997], 120). More pertinent for our purposes, however, are Brown's observations regarding Q's christology:

Many would attribute to Q a low christology since in it Jesus emerges simply as a Sophist or Cynic wisdom teacher. Yet the Q Jesus is to come and baptize with the Holy Spirit, as proclaimed by JBap (3:16-17; 7:18-23). He is greater than Solomon and greater than Jonah the prophet (11:31-32). He is portrayed as the Son of Man who will come in judgment (17:23-27, 30, 37) and as the Son of Man who is rejected and suffers in his lifetime (7:31-35; 9:57-60). He is the Son to whom all has been given; he is known only by the Father, and only he knows the Father (10:22). It is insufficient simply to call Jesus Lord; one must hear his words and do them if one is to survive (6:46-49). Jerusalem must bless him (13:34-35), and one must prefer him over family (14:26-27). He can proclaim with assurance that in the kingdom those who follow him will sit on thrones, judging the twelve tribes of Israel [evidently alluding to 22:29-30]. Such a Jesus is far more than a wisdom teacher. (120)

In What Context (or Contexts) Was This Sayings Collection Formed and First Used?

We need not get involved with trying to trace out stages of growth in Q. Nor need we try our hand at attempting to discern diversity among the various Christian groups where such a Sayings collection was used — nor to posit some original locality for its formation, whether at Jerusalem, Antioch, or elsewhere. These are matters that reflect a high degree of speculation and probably depend more on a particular scholar's propensities than the data itself. They may, in fact, be no better than Papias's statement that "Matthew compiled the Logia . . . and everyone interpreted them as he was able."

It is possible that some of the differences of wording in Q sayings between Matthew and Luke are attributable to variant copies of an original Sayings source. Or it may be that there were somewhat different Greek translations of an original Aramaic version — as would, of course, be inevitable among translations. This latter understanding seems to be suggested by Papias's statement that "everyone interpreted [or 'translated'] them as he was able."

But however matters of provenance may eventually (if ever) be resolved, it seems necessary to postulate (1) that there existed within the early church a collection of the sayings of Jesus, (2) that this Sayings collection was principally ethical in nature, (3) that it was first formed in catechetical and/or teaching contexts, and (4) that it was known and used widely in various Christian communities. Such a Sayings collection seems to have been known and used even in Gentile churches, such as those at Thessalonica, Corinth, and Rome. In fact, to judge by statements in 1 Cor 7:10, 12, 25; 9:14, both Paul and his Gentile converts seem to have known not only what was included in that Sayings collection but also what was not included.

4. Confessional Portions

A further body of material to be highlighted here consists of what may generally be called "confessional portions," which appear to have been widely known within the early Christian communities and were incorporated by the authors of the New Testament into their writings. The verb "confess" and the noun "confession" are commonly used today in a legal sense to refer to the admission of guilt. In the New Testament, however, as well as in the church's language drawn from the New Testament, "confess" and "confession" most often signal statements of belief that express basic theological and christological convictions — with those statements taking various forms (e.g., hymns, formulaic prose, single-statement affirmations) depending on the circumstances in which they come about (e.g., worship, prayer, preaching, liturgy, teaching, catechism, apologetic discourse).

Eduard Norden's analyses of "artistic prose" in the ancient world (*Die antike Kunstprosa vom VI. Jahrhunderts vor Christus in die Zeit der Renaissance,* 2 vols. [Leipzig: Teubner, 1898; reprint 1983]) inaugurated modern form-critical study of ancient writings. Building on his analyses, Johannes Weiss began the study of hymnodic materials in Paul's letters ("Beiträge zum paulinischer Rhetorik," in *Theologische Studien* [*Festschrift* B. Weiss], ed. C. R. Gregory et al. [Göttingen: Vandenhoeck und Ruprecht, 1897], 165-247), Eduard von der Goltz took up the study of prayer among the earliest Christians (*Das Gebet in der ältesten Christenheit* [Leipzig: Hinrichs, 1901), Alfred Seeberg attempted to reconstruct the earliest Christian catechism (*Der Katechismus der Urchristenheit* [Leipzig: Deichertschen, 1903; reprint Munich: Kaiser, 1966]), and Norden himself went further to apply his own form-critical principles to further analyses of New Testament prayers and hymns (*Agnostos Theos. Untersuchungen zur Formengeschichte religiöser*

Rede [Leipzig: Teubner, 1913; reprint 1956]). And throughout the twentieth century the study of early Christian confessional materials has been widely and vigorously pursued (for details, see my *New Wine into Fresh Wineskins*, chapter 1).

Discussion of these early Christian confessional materials has frequently been carried on under such rubrics as "hymns," "prayers," "formulas of faith," "catechetical teachings," "liturgical formulations," "ecclesial traditions," and/or "narrative stories" — with the transliterated Greek terms *kerygma* ("proclamation"), *paradosis* ("tradition"), *didachē* ("teaching"), and *homologia* ("confession") often used as descriptive titles. But as Ethelbert Stauffer long ago observed: "Many confessions were hymn-like and many hymns were creed-like" (*New Testament Theology,* trans. J. Marsh [London: SCM, 1955], 237). Contemporary scholars tend to speak of all these materials as simply "confessions."

A number of matters having to do with these confessional materials call for both scholarly and pastoral treatment, and I have attempted to do that, at least to an extent, in *New Wine into Fresh Wineskins.* Three questions, however, are directly relevant to our purposes here: (1) Were these confessional portions circulating among the early Christian communities prior to the writing of our canonical New Testament? (2) What was the nature of these early Christian confessions? (3) In what context or contexts were these confessional materials formed and first used?

Were Confessional Portions Circulating among the Early Christian Communities?

The writers of the New Testament did not use quotation marks or indentations to mark off confessional material quoted or used in their compositions. The identification of early Christian hymns (i.e., poetic portions of worship and praise) and *homologiai* (i.e., formulaic prose statements and affirmations) which have been incorporated into the New Testament depends almost entirely on form-critical and tradition-critical analyses of the writings of the New Testament authors.

Scholars over the past century have had their own variations and refinements with respect to method. Nonetheless, despite some differences, there is widespread critical agreement with regard to the legitimacy of the following criteria for the identification of early Christian hymns:

1. the presence of parallel structures *(parallelismus membrorum)* that reflect either Jewish or Hellenistic poetic conventions or both,
2. the presence of words and phrases not characteristic of a particular New Testament author (i.e., *hapax legomena*) — or, if appearing elsewhere in that author's writings, not with the meaning or in the manner found elsewhere in his other writings — suggesting that the material in question was probably composed by someone else,
3. a preference for participles over finite verbs, suggesting an original oral provenance for the material rather than the literary setting in which it now appears,
4. frequent use of the relative pronoun *hos* ("who") to begin passages,
5. contextual dislocations, which may be either poetic material breaking into a prose section or doctrinal material breaking into an ethical section or both,
6. continuance of a portion after its content has ceased to be relevant to its immediate context, and
7. affirmation of a basic Christian conviction, which usually has to do with the work or person of Jesus Christ.

Many of the form-critical criteria used to identify early Christian hymns in the New Testament are, of course, also used to identify early Christian *homologiai*. In particular, the following are usually considered indicators of the presence of formulaic, but non-poetic, confessional materials:

1. the presence of parallel structures *(parallelismus membrorum)*, even though the material is not poetry,
2. the presence of an expression that does not appear elsewhere in an author's writings *(hapax legomena)* or words or phrases not used in the author's manner elsewhere,
3. a preference for participles over finite verbs, and
4. an affirmation regarding the work or person of Jesus Christ.

Added to this list have been linguistic indicators such as

5. use of the noun "confession" *(homologia)* to signal the content of such early Christian material, either expressed or implied,
6. use of the verb "confess" *(homologeō)* with a double accusative or an infinitive to introduce a direct or an indirect quotation,

7. use of *hoti* (the "so-called" *hoti recitativum*) to introduce a direct or indirect quotation,

8. use of verbs having to do with preaching *(euaggelizō, kērussō,* or *kataggellō),* teaching *(didaskō),* or witnessing *(martureō* or *marturomai)* to introduce confessional material, and

9. use of a participial construction or a relative clause to introduce the material in question.

The most obvious early Christian hymns in praise of God are those found in Rom 11:33-36 and Rev 15:3b-4. The most commonly accepted early Christian hymns extolling Christ are Phil 2:6-11; 1 Tim 3:16b; and 1 Pet 2:22-23. The most widely acknowledged *homologiai,* or formulaic prose confessional statements are 1 Cor 15:3b-5; Rom 1:3b-4; 3:24-26; Gal 3:26-28; 4:4-5; and Heb 1:3. The material in Col 1:15-20 is also considered by most New Testament scholars to be an early christological hymn. It could, however, just as well be seen as a *homologia* or formulaic prose confessional portion since its lyrical quality and strophic structure are not readily identifiable.

We modern readers seem to have difficulty in identifying the confessional materials that have been incorporated by the New Testament authors into their writings. That is possibly because we have lost the thread of the narrative structure of early Christian proclamation. More likely, however, it is because we have never heard the hymns sung, the confessions repeated, or the affirmations made in the context of corporate worship, and so cannot recognize them when we come across them on the pages of the New Testament. Nonetheless, even though it may be possible to identify only some of these early Christian hymns, *homologiai,* and single-statement affirmations — perhaps, one might venture to say, as many as forty or fifty, with others still remaining to be identified — scholars are reasonably convinced that such materials were incorporated by the writers of the New Testament into their compositions.

What Was the Nature of These Early Christian Confessions?

The hymns and formulaic prose statements that are incorporated within the New Testament appear to have been originally devotional in nature, expressing the early believers' praise to God and adoration of Christ in the context of corporate worship. This may seem hardly surprising. For confessions in the biblical sense are faith expressions, and memorable faith expressions take form most commonly in the context of corporate worship — whether that worship is planned or spontaneous.

Further, the christological confessional materials of the New Testament, as differentiated from the purely theocentric confessional materials, reflect a narrative substructure or story line in which Jesus Christ is the main character. Each confession, whether in the form of poetry or prose, narrates a portion of the story about Jesus as God's redemptive agent. We cannot, of course, say whether or not all of the addressees of the New Testament writings already knew each of the confessional portions quoted. What can be affirmed, however, is that these confessions, whether cited in whole or in part, were meant to remind readers of the basic story about Jesus — a story that they already knew and that was foundational for their new lives "in Christ."

It needs also to be noted that the early Christian hymns and formulaic prose confessional statements of the New Testament are dominantly functional — that is, that they affirm what "God in Christ" has done and is doing redemptively, rather than speculate about ontology. This functional emphasis is particularly prominent in the confessions found in Paul's earlier letters (e.g., Gal 1:4; 3:13; 4:4-5; 1 Cor 15:3b-5; Rom 3:24-26), which, as the earliest writings of the New Testament, presumably incorporate some of the earliest Christian confessional materials. Very soon, however, ontological categories that were inchoate in the earlier confessional affirmations seem also to have come to the fore (e.g., Heb 1:3; John 1:1-14).

Finally, and perhaps more obviously, it needs to be constantly kept in mind that the confessional portions that appear in the New Testament use the language and metaphors of their day in speaking about the work of Christ and its significance (e.g., to cite only the most obvious, Rom 3:24-26; Col 1:15-20; Heb 1:3; John 1:1-14). Some of this language and some of these expressions may seem a bit out of place in the context of the respective writings in which they appear. And they often require considerable translation to be understood today. Nonetheless, they were important as foundation stones, building blocks, and points of contact for the writers of the New Testament in their presentations and for their addressees in their understanding (for further on the nature and contents of these early Christian confessional materials, see my *New Wine into Fresh Wineskins*, chapter 2).

In What Context (or Contexts) Were These Confessional Materials Formed and First Used?

Observations regarding the nature of early Christian confessional materials in the New Testament — that is, their devotional nuances, their reflections of a narrative story line that focused on Jesus, their functional affirmations, and their use of the language and metaphors of the day — all seem to locate their original formation and first use in the corporate worship of the early believers in Jesus, whenever and wherever that took place.

Paul's letters indicate that some of this confessional material was cast into poetic form and sung as hymns in corporate worship. In 1 Cor 14:26 he alludes to the singing of hymns in corporate worship ("When you come together, everyone has a hymn . . ."); in Col 3:16-17 and Eph 5:19-20 there are explicit exhortations to include in the church's worship "psalms, hymns, and spiritual songs," which are to be directed in christocentric fashion ("in the name of the Lord Jesus" and "through him") to God the Father. Outside the Pauline corpus, the existence of such confessional materials is suggested by references in Hebrews to confessing Jesus (3:1), confessing the faith (4:14), and confessing one's Christian hope (10:23) — perhaps also in Jude to "the faith" (v. 3) and "the most holy faith" (v. 20).

More important, however, are the early hymns and prayers within the New Testament that both reflect various Jewish nuances and express distinctively Christian ideas. The most obvious of these hymnic prayers or prayerful hymns are the canticles of Mary, Zechariah, and Simeon in the infancy narrative of Luke 1–2 and the songs of praise to God and the victorious Lamb in Revelation 4, 5, 7, and 15. These New Testament hymns are comparable to the hymns of praise directed to God in the Jewish Scriptures (cf. the "Song of Moses" in Exod 15:1-18, which is echoed in the "Song of Miriam" in Exod 15:21; the "Song of Deborah" in Judg 5:1-31; and the "hymns" of Psalms 8–9, 29, 33, 65, 67–68, 96, 98, 100, 103–105, 111, 113–14, 117, 135–136, 145–150), as well as in some of the writings of Second Temple Judaism (cf. Judith 16:1-17; Sirach 1:1-12) and many of the hymns contained in the Qumran texts (especially in 1QH, the *Hodayot* or Thanksgiving Psalms/Hymns).

It may be postulated with some confidence, therefore, that the early Christian confessional materials incorporated within the New Testament were first formed and used within the context (or contexts) of corporate worship within the early church. Their use by the various writers of the

New Testament may have varied (see *New Wine into Fresh Wineskins,* chapters 3-5). And their use certainly needs to be revived today (see *New Wine,* chapters 6-7). But originally, it seems, these confessions were formed and used as formulaic statements, whether as hymns or *homologiai,* in the corporate worship of the early church.

5. Conclusion

Luke tells us that in writing his Gospel he (1) had the precedents of "many others" *(polloi)* who had written accounts of God's redemptive work in the ministry of Jesus, (2) took the opportunity to investigate the various traditions that had been "handed on to us" *(paredosan hēmin),* and (3) used sources that depended ultimately on eyewitness reports (Luke 1:1-4). John tells us that his Gospel should not be taken as a complete account, but that "Jesus did many other signs in the presence of his disciples, which are not written in this book" (John 20:30).

Paul indicates that both he and his Gentile converts at Corinth knew not only what Jesus taught, but also what was not included in the collection of sayings from which they both seemed to have worked (cf. 1 Cor 7:10 and 9:14 vis-à-vis 7:12 and 7:25) — though, in all likelihood, that collection contained more teachings of Jesus than were later recorded in the Synoptic Gospels (as witness the *agraphon* that Paul quotes in 1 Thess 4:15-17). The various parallels of ethical teaching that exist between Romans, 1 and 2 Thessalonians, Ephesians, 1 Peter, and James, together with resemblances of this material with what we know from the canonical Gospels of the teaching of Jesus, suggest the existence of a common body of catechetical material within the early church from which the respective New Testament writers drew. And there are many places in the New Testament where we are alerted to the fact that the early Christians in their corporate worship sang hymns (e.g., 1 Cor 14:26; Col 3:16-17; Eph 5:19-20; cf. also the canticles of Luke 1–2 and the hymns to God and the Lamb of the Johannine Apocalypse) and confessed their faith (e.g., Heb 3:1; 4:14; 10:23; perhaps Jude 3 and 20).

We may not be able to identify or spell out the nature of all of the sources alluded to by the evangelists and the other writers of the New Testament. But we can still feel confident in assuming (1) that there circulated within the early Christian communities various christological materials, (2) that these materials brought together much of the church's early testimony, as based on eyewitness reports, personal remembrances, and oral tradition, and (3) that these materials were used by the writers of the New Testament in their portrayals of and arguments about Jesus of Nazareth, who was acclaimed to be the Messiah or "the Christ." We need to focus our attention redactionally, exegetically, and theologically on the christological presentations of the New Testament (as will take place in the chapters that follow). But we also, by means of form-critical and tradition-critical analyses, need to be cognizant (1) that there existed prior to the writing of our New Testament various christological source materials, such as have been set out in rather elemental fashion above, and (2) that the writers of the New Testament used these materials as building blocks in their portrayals and presentations.

SELECTED BIBLIOGRAPHY

Allison, Dale C., Jr. *The Jesus Tradition in Q.* Harrisburg: Trinity Press International, 1997.

Beasley-Murray, George R. *Jesus and the Future: An Examination of the Criticism of the Eschatological Discourse, Mark 13, with Special Reference to the Little Apocalypse Theory.* London: Macmillan, 1954.

―――. *Jesus and the Last Days: The Interpretation of the Olivet Discourse.* Peabody: Hendrickson, 1993 (incorporates in revised form *Jesus and the Future* [London: Macmillan, 1954] and *A Commentary on Mark Thirteen* [London: Macmillan, 1957]).

Deichgräber, Reinhard. *Gotteshymnus und Christushymnus in der frühen Christenheit. Untersuchungen zu Form, Sprache und Stil der frühchristlichen Hymnen.* Göttingen: Vandenhoeck und Ruprecht, 1967.

Dodd, C. H. *The Apostolic Preaching and Its Developments.* London: Hodder and Stoughton, 1936.

―――. *According to the Scriptures: The Sub-Structure of New Testament Theology.* London: Nisbet, 1952; New York: Scribner, 1953.

―――. "The 'Primitive Catechism' and the Sayings of Jesus," in his *More New Testament Studies.* Manchester: Manchester University Press, 1968, 11-29 (an article "partly re-written, with additional matter" from one originally published in *New Testament Essays: Studies in Memory of T. W. Manson* [Manchester: Manchester University Press, 1959]).

Donahue, John R. "From Passion Tradition to Passion Narrative," in *The Passion in Mark: Studies on Mark 14-16*, ed. W. H. Kelber. Philadelphia: Fortress, 1976, 1-20.

Dupont, Jacques. "La Parabole du figuier qui bourgeonne (Mc, XIII,28-29)," *RB* 75 (1968) 526-48.

————. "La Parabole du maître qui rentre dans la nuit [Mc 13,34-36]," in *Mélanges Béda Rigaux*. Gembloux: Duculot, 1970, 89-116.

————. "La ruine du temple et la fin des temps dans de discours de Marc 13," in *Apocalypses et Théologie de l'Espérance*, ed. L. Monloubou. Paris: Cerf, 1977, 207-69.

————. "La Persécution comme situation missionnaire (Marc 13,9-11)," in *Die Kirche des Anfangs. Festschrift für H. Schürmann*. Freiburg: Herder, 1978, 97-114.

Ford, Desmond. *The Abomination of Desolation in Biblical Eschatology*. Washington: University Press of America, 1979.

Hartman, Lars. *Prophecy Interpreted: The Formation of Some Jewish Apocalyptic Texts and of the Eschatological Discourse Mark 13 par*. Uppsala: Gleerup, 1966.

Hooker, Morna D. *Jesus and the Servant*. London: SPCK, 1959.

————. *The Son of Man in Mark*. London: SPCK; Montreal: McGill University Press, 1967.

Jeremias, Joachim. *The Eucharistic Words of Jesus*, trans. N. Perrin, 3rd ed. rev. New York: Scribner, 1966.

————, and Walther Zimmerli, "παῖς θεοῦ," *TDNT* 5.654-717 (pp. 654-77 by Zimmerli, pp. 677-717 by Jeremias).

Karris, Robert J. *A Symphony of New Testament Hymns: Commentary on Phil 2:5-11, Col 1:15-20, Eph 2:14-16, 1 Tim 3:16, Tit 3:4-7, 1 Pet 3:18-22, and 2 Tim 2:11-13*. Collegeville: Liturgical, 1966.

Kloppenborg, John S. *Q Parallels: Synopsis, Critical Notes, and Concordance*. Sonoma: Polebridge, 1988.

————. *The Formation of Q*. Philadelphia: Fortress, 1987; Harrisburg: Trinity Press International, 2nd ed., 1999 (with new Preface).

Lindars, Barnabas. *New Testament Apologetic: The Doctrinal Significance of the Old Testament Quotations*. London: SCM; Philadelphia: Westminster, 1961.

Longenecker, Richard N. *The Christology of Early Jewish Christianity*. London: SCM, 1970; Grand Rapids: Baker, 1981; Vancouver: Regent Publishing, 2001.

————. *New Wine into Fresh Wineskins: Contextualizing the Early Christian Confessions*. Peabody: Hendrickson, 1999.

Maurer, Christian. "Knecht Gottes und Sohn Gottes in Passionsbericht des Markusevangeliums," *ZTK* 50 (1953) 1-38.

Moo, Douglas J. *The Old Testament in the Gospel Passion Narratives*. Sheffield: Almond, 1983.

Wenham, David. *The Rediscovery of Jesus' Eschatological Discourse*. Sheffield: JSOT, 1984.

II. GOSPELS AND ACTS

CHAPTER 4

"Who Can This Be?"
The Christology of Mark's Gospel

MORNA D. HOOKER

In 1973 Etienne Trocmé, a well-known Markan scholar, wrote an essay entitled "Is There a Markan Christology?" His question sounds, at first, like the echo of a view of Mark belonging to an earlier generation, which saw Mark as a mere collector and recorder of traditions rather than as a creative writer. Trocmé's purpose, however, was to underline the problem of distinguishing Mark's christology from that of his predecessors. Few would deny that Mark used earlier traditions in writing his Gospel. But to what extent did he adapt them or change them? Did he simply take them over? If Mark's was the first Gospel, then clearly he was doing something new. But did his creative genius lie simply in producing a new format, or was his understanding of the gospel different from that of his contemporaries? In other words, is the christology he presents his own or was it shared by others in the early church? Or was he, as some have suggested, perhaps deliberately opposing someone else's understanding of Jesus by putting a different "spin" on the materials?

The problem, of course, arises from the fact that the only evidence we have in making any kind of judgment is Mark's Gospel itself. His Gospel, however, does not lend itself to serious redaction-critical study (unless, of course, we believe that it was written *after* Matthew's Gospel and/or Luke's Gospel). Though commentators have endeavored to sort out "pre-Markan traditions" from Mark's editing, the arguments are inevitably circular. Thus the summaries of Jesus' activities *may* be traditional and have come down to Mark, or they could be the result of his own editing — a necessary reminder of "the story so far" in a lengthy narrative. The collection of "conflict stories" in Mark 2:1–3:6 *may* be pre-Markan, but it is more likely that the stories have been brought together by Mark himself. The strange overlap of material in 6:30–7:37 and 8:1-26 *may* be the result of Mark using "blocks" of material already in circulation, but could just as well be due to Mark's own deliberate editing.

Trying to separate Markan terms from non-Markan material is a dangerous procedure. For while we may confidently say that some words and phrases are typically Markan (e.g., the recurring expression *kai euthys,* "and immediately"), we cannot dub words "non-Markan" simply because they occur only once in the Gospel. The most reliable indication of Mark's viewpoint is probably to be found in the so-called "Markan seams" that link the various portions of the material together (see E. Best, *The Temptation and the Passion*). Analyzing the stories that they join, however, is more problematic, since one cannot profitably discuss an author's redaction of his materials without access to his sources. And while there may or may not have been some kind of *Ur-Markus* before Mark's Gospel, any attempt to reconstruct it is inevitably hypothetical.

To discover Mark's christology, therefore, we can only consider the Gospel as it stands today — ending at 16:8, as witnessed by the best-attested texts. Mark has chosen to present "the gospel of Jesus Christ" in the form of a narrative. And if we want to understand his Gospel, we must study the story that he tells.

This sounds deceptively easy, but it is not, for the way in which we hear Mark's story will be determined by our own context, circumstances, and prejudices. We may very well misunderstand what Mark intended to say because we do not know the context in which he was writing or the way in which he would have been heard in his own day. Some would even say that we should not try to discover Mark's own beliefs. But since the present volume is concerned with the christologies of the individual New Testament writers, we are clearly being invited to consider authorial intention.

Traditionally, of course, christological studies have frequently concentrated on the so-called christological "titles." There are obvious advantages in this method, since such titles are often used in confessional statements and occur at significant points in the narrative. But the very fact that they *are* used at significant points in the narrative indicates that it is best to consider them in the context of that narrative. Titles are, after all, simply shorthand expressions of what is held to be true. To understand what is meant by the use of a title, it is necessary to look at the way in which it is used within the story.

Mark may be our shortest Gospel, but the task of examining the evangelist's narrative is a daunting one that calls for a book rather than a chapter. Fortunately, however, Mark has provided a guide to his narrative in the form of a prologue that provides the information we need to read the rest of his Gospel, and so gives us a succinct summary of his christology.

1. The Prologue

Mark's Gospel begins with the words "The gospel of Jesus Christ" (1:1), which can mean either "the gospel proclaimed *by* Jesus Christ" or "the gospel *about* Jesus Christ" — or both. In 1:14-15, after the prologue in 1:1-13, Mark will begin to spell out the gospel proclaimed *by* Jesus. For Mark, however, the gospel is more than the message that Jesus preached. It is, in fact, Jesus himself — that is, the gospel *about* Jesus Christ. So from 1:9 onward — with the exceptions of 6:14-29 and 14:66-72 — Jesus is the central figure in the narrative. Yet even those passages in chs. 6 and 14 are included, as we will see, because of what they tell us about Jesus.

But while the central issue concerns the identity of Jesus, this is interwoven with the related theme of the reaction of various groups of people *to* Jesus and the different answers that they give to the question "Who is he?" The different responses of the various characters in the narrative to Jesus continually emphasize the importance of this question. And this is the major question that confronts Mark's readers as well.

Vital Information about Jesus

The fact that Mark describes Jesus as "Christ" *(Christos)* in 1:1 is highly significant, even though Jesus is not openly proclaimed as "the Christ" *(ho Christos)* during his ministry (cf. 8:29-30). For the recognition that he is the Christ, that is, "the Messiah," is clearly an essential part of the Gospel. The identification of Jesus as "Son of God" *(huios theou)* is probably an addition to 1:1, but this belief is central to Mark's Gospel and so the words are entirely appropriate here. Mark himself, perhaps, did not feel the need to include the phrase at this point, since the identification is made so clearly at 1:11.

The "beginning" *(archē)* of Mark's Gospel lies in the purpose of God, which is spelled out in Scripture: "Look, I am sending my messenger ahead of you to prepare your way; a voice crying out in the wilderness: 'Prepare the way of the Lord, make his paths straight'" (1:2-3). Mark attributes his quotation, which is a mixed one from Exod 23:20; Mal 3:1; and Isa 40:3, to "the prophet Isaiah." An early scribe, however, corrected this to the more accurate "the prophets." But perhaps Mark's mistake was deliberate. Certainly Mark shows a particular interest in the hopes expressed in the book of Isaiah (see Watts, *Isaiah's New Exodus*). This interest in Isaiah tells us something significant about the christology of Mark — namely, that the evangelist sees Jesus as the fulfillment of Old Testament hopes and as the one who brings a redemption that is, in effect, a new exodus.

The Baptist is identified in the quotations as a "voice" who cries in the wilderness and prepares "the way of the Lord" (1:3). John's function is to call the nation to repentance (1:4-5) and, even though unknowingly, to witness to the identity of the one whose coming he announces (1:7-8). Everything he does serves this purpose. His clothing and food identify him as a prophet (1:6), and his baptism with water is a prophetic action pointing to the coming baptism with the Spirit (1:8-9; see Stacey, *Prophetic Drama*; Hooker, *Signs of a Prophet*). Mark's succinct three-point account of John's teaching in vv. 7-8 concentrates on his witness to his successor, who is far stronger than he, for whom he is unworthy to perform the most menial of tasks, and who will baptize the people with the Holy Spirit, not water.

Although Mark gives no hint that John recognized Jesus as the one whose coming he has proclaimed, the narrative makes the identification clear. Jesus responds to John's call and is himself baptized, whereupon he is baptized with the Spirit (1:9-10). We are left in no doubt that this is the one who will baptize his people with the Spirit. Moreover, he is addressed directly by a voice from heaven as "My beloved Son, with whom I am well pleased" (1:11). We have had the words of Scripture and the witness of John, but now we have an unambiguous identification of Jesus by the highest authority. Whatever answers are given to the question "Who is Jesus?" in the rest of the narrative will certainly have to be judged against this one.

"And immediately," says Mark, "the Spirit drove Jesus into the wilderness" (1:12). There Satan tested him (1:13). Unlike Matthew and Luke, Mark does not tell us the nature of this test or its outcome. But from ensuing events it is clear that Jesus was victorious. His future actions and words would be governed by the Spirit, not by Satan. The work of the Holy Spirit is clearly another key element in Mark's christology, for it is mentioned in each of the three paragraphs in 1:1-13 (vv. 8, 10, and 12).

The Prologue as the Key to the Gospel

Mark's prologue functions as the key to his Gospel, for it provides readers with essential information as to how his Gospel should be read (see my *Beginnings: Keys That Open the Gospels*). This does not mean that it is a summary of the contents of the Gospel. Notably, the prologue does not use the term "the Son of man" and does not mention specifically that "the Son of man must suffer," as emphasized later in the Gospel. Since, however, "the Son of man" is found throughout the Synoptic Gospels only in the mouth of Jesus, we could hardly expect to find it here.

What we do find in Mark's prologue is the reason that Jesus, *as* "the Son of man," can claim authority — namely, because he is also "the Son of God," who is pleasing to God because he is obedient to God's will and so fulfills Israel's vocation. That very obedience, however, may lead to suffering. There is, perhaps, also a hint of this coming suffering in Jesus' baptism, a hint that is made plain when we come to 10:38-39. His self-identification with his countrymen, who are in need of "the forgiveness of sins," means sharing their "baptism of repentance" — and will involve him in a baptism of a more traumatic kind. The struggle with Satan suggests, as well, a future conflict and possible suffering. These verses, with their hints of suffering, are not intended, however, to provide a summary of the Gospel, but a guide to reading it.

Since all the evangelists follow Mark's example by "laying their cards on the table" at the beginning of their accounts, it is worth comparing Mark's prologue with those of the other evangelists. In format, of course, the four canonical prologues are very different — though each is appropriate to its particular Gospel. John's prologue, couched in theological language and interspersed with narrative fragments in 1:6-8 and 15, presents the kind of statement that we might expect from the Fourth Evangelist. More importantly, however, despite theories that it is an addition to the Gospel, the Johannine prologue provides material that is essential to an understanding of the Johannine Jesus. Luke 1–2, which has also been dismissed as an addition by commentators who fail to see its purpose, and Matthew 1–2 both provide christological information in narrative form, as does Mark, but their stories concern the birth of Jesus.

Each of our four evangelists uses themes in their respective prologues that are of particular concern to them. Nonetheless, certain themes are common to them all: (1) the Gospel had its origins long ago in the purpose of God (Mark 1:1-3; Matt 1:1-17, 23; 2:6, 15, 18, 23; Luke 1:68-79; 2:29-32, 38; John 1:1), (2) Jesus is the Messiah (Mark 1:1; Matt 1:18; 2:1-6; Luke 1:69; 2:11, 26; John 1:17) and the Son of God (Mark 1:11; Matt 2:15; Luke 1:35; John 1:18), and (3) in him the Holy Spirit is at work (Mark 1:8, 10, 12; Matt 1:20; Luke 1:35; John 1:15, also 30-34). If, as we suppose, Mark was the first of the four evangelists to write, this common christological core cannot help us to determine what contribution Mark himself made to the development of christology. But since these elements are all central in Paul's writings, we may properly conclude that our key witnesses to New Testament theology are in basic agreement. What is *distinctive* about Mark — as also about *each* of the evangelists — is the way in which he tells his story, and so presents his christology.

2. God's Kingdom

Mark's story proper begins at 1:14. Some scholars think that the Prologue continues to the end of 1:15, principally because of what appears to be an *inclusio* formed by use of *euangelion* in vv. 1 and 14-15 (for a summary of the arguments, see Marcus, *Mark 1–8*, 137-38). There is, however, an important difference between 1:1-13 and 1:14-15. In 1:1-13, Mark shares information concerning Jesus' identity with his readers, knowledge hidden from Jesus' contemporaries, even from John, whereas in 1:14-15, Jesus' proclamation of the kingdom of God is in the public domain in the story. So 1:14, we believe, should be seen as beginning a new section.

The Announcement of God's Kingdom

Jesus returns to Galilee and announces that God's rule has drawn near: "The time has come, and the kingdom of God is at hand. Repent and believe the good news" (1:14-15). His authority for doing so is not explained, but readers of 1:1-13 will understand what this is. As the beloved Son who is obedient to God's will, the one with whom God is well pleased, Jesus embodies the kingdom of God — that is, the rule of God — both in his person and in his teaching. With his coming, God's rule has drawn near. This is the first announcement of the coming kingdom, an announcement that is addressed primarily to Jesus' followers. And it is followed immediately by Jesus' summons to Simon, Andrew, James, and John to become his disciples (1:16-20). Response to the proclamation of the kingdom, therefore, implies response to Jesus himself.

The second announcement, which is also addressed primarily to Jesus' followers, occurs in 9:1, where he declares that some of his hearers will see the kingdom of God "come with power" before they die. This announcement follows Peter's recognition of Jesus as "the Messiah" (8:29) and Jesus' warning about his own future suffering (8:31-33) — together with his demand that his disciples take up their cross and follow him (8:34-37). Then, immediately before the announcement of the kingdom's coming we are told that when the Son of man comes in "the glory of his Father with the holy angels," he will be ashamed of those who have been ashamed of him (8:38).

Following this second announcement, we have the story of the Transfiguration (9:2-13) in which the heavenly voice again declares Jesus to be God's beloved Son — though on this occasion the voice addresses three disciples, who are commanded to "hear" Jesus (9:7). The parallel between 1:11 and 9:7 is obvious. At this point in the narrative the disciples share, to a limited extent, in the knowledge about Jesus that we, the readers of Mark's Gospel, have already been given in the prologue. They recognize Jesus as Messiah and as Son of God, but are unable to grasp the significance of this knowledge — as Peter's reactions indicate (cf. 8:32-33; 9:5-6, 10-11). In 8:27–9:13, as in 1:1-20, there is a close link between (1) the identity of Jesus, (2) the disciples' response to Jesus, and (3) the coming of God's kingdom. In 8:27–9:13, however, the cost of obedience to God's will is emphasized (see especially 8:31, 34-38).

A quick glance at other references to God's kingdom shows that they, too, link entry into the kingdom with response to Jesus. Thus the words of 4:11, "to you has been given the secret of God's kingdom," are spoken to "those around him, together with the Twelve" (4:10) — that is, Jesus' followers. To this group, Jesus explained the meaning of the parables about the kingdom of God (4:26, 30, 34).

Most of the references to the kingdom occur in the section that spells out the meaning of discipleship in 8:34–10:45. Disciples of Jesus should be prepared to sacrifice anything that will prevent them from entering the kingdom (9:47). They must be prepared to renounce wealth (10:23-25). Those to whom the kingdom belong are those who, like children, have nothing (10:14-15) and are prepared to give away everything and follow Jesus (10:21) and to leave everything they have in order to be his disciples (10:28-31). The scribe who approves Jesus' teaching that what God demands can be summed up in the commands to love God and one's neighbor as oneself is, in turn, commended by Jesus, and told that he is not far from the kingdom of God (12:34). Once again, God's rule implies radical obedience to his will. For this man, however, personal commitment to Jesus is absent: Jesus is seen as a teacher (12:32), but nothing more.

Two references to the kingdom of God remain, both of them in the passion narrative in chs. 14–15. In the first, Jesus declares that he will not drink of the fruit of the vine again until the day he drinks it new in the kingdom of God (14:25). This is, in effect, a third, though somewhat muted, announcement that the kingdom is at hand. Its coming now seems to be linked with Jesus' own imminent death. Paradoxically, it is that death that proclaims Jesus' identity to the world. For Mark tells us (1) that Jesus himself, when asked by the high priest whether he is "the Christ, the Son of the Blessed One" (14:61), declared plainly "I am" (14:62), (2) that Jesus was crucified as "king of the Jews" (15:2, 9, 12, 18, 26, 32), and (3) that when Jesus died, the centurion in charge of the crucifixion acknowledged him to be "Son of God" (15:39). The second reference to God's kingdom in the Markan passion narrative appears at the end of that narrative, where Mark remarks, with typical irony, that Joseph of Arimathea, who buried Jesus, was waiting for the kingdom of God (15:43).

The Kingdom and the Son

It is not clear whether Mark believes that with Jesus' resurrection the kingdom of God has arrived in power or is himself still waiting for the kingdom's coming. What *is* clear, however, is that all three announcements of the coming kingdom are linked in Mark's Gospel with revelations of Jesus' identity as God's Son. The first and second come from heaven, and the third is from the Roman centurion in charge of Jesus' crucifixion. And while all three revelations occur in passages that refer to Jesus as Messiah

(1:1; 8:29; 14:61-62; 15:2, 18, 26, 32), it is clear that, for the evangelist, Jesus is supremely the *Son of God.*

3. Mark's Story

Mark's story about Jesus is full of christological significance — a significance sometimes expressed clearly but more often only suggested by allusions, hints, and the juxtaposition of his materials. To understand what the evangelist believes about Jesus, we need to examine the way in which he tells that story.

Scenes of Authority

Jesus' initial announcement of the kingdom's coming in 1:14-15 introduces a series of short scenes in which he acts with impressive authority. He calls disciples and they leave home and livelihood to follow him (1:16-20; 2:13-14); he teaches with authority (1:21-22, 27); and he exercises authority over unclean spirits (1:27, 34). He heals diseases (1:29-34), cleanses a leper (1:40-45), demonstrates his authority to forgive sins (2:1-12), and declares that he has come to call sinners (2:17). He claims authority over the Sabbath (2:23–3:6). And his authority is recognized by the unclean spirits, who acknowledge him to be "the Holy One of God" (1:24) and "the Son of God" (3:11).

In 3:13-19 Jesus appoints twelve disciples — a clear sign that he is gathering a restored Israel around him, in fulfillment of the promises found in deutero-Isaiah. In the next scene in 3:20-30 he is involved in a clash with the religious authorities. The issue is the nature of his authority — whether it is from God or from Satan. For Jesus' opponents, the answer is plain: "He is possessed by Beelzebul, and he drives out demons by the prince of demons" (3:22). With our knowledge of 1:12-13, however, we are aware of the *correct* explanation: Jesus is empowered by the Holy Spirit (3:29).

Jesus' Teaching

In spite of Mark's references to Jesus' teaching, the only summary of that teaching in the first three chapters — apart from Jesus' responses to criticisms — is that given in 1:15: "The time has come, and the kingdom of God is at hand. Repent and believe the good news." For Mark, the good news — that is, the gospel — concerns Jesus himself, and response to the gospel means response to Jesus. So at the end of ch. 3, in vv. 20-35, we see the division that is taking place between the disciples of Jesus, together with those who are around him (3:34), and those who oppose him, that is, the Pharisees and the Herodians (3:6), together with their scribes — and even his own family, who remain "outside" (3:21, 31, 33).

In ch. 4 we have Mark's first block of Jesus' teaching, beginning with the parable of the sower. It is a parable about parables (4:13). And though it is not specifically said to be about God's kingdom, it is clear from 4:11-12 that Mark understands the parables to proclaim the kingdom to those who have eyes and ears to understand. Those to whom the secret of the kingdom of God is given are Jesus' disciples and companions, and they correspond to the abundant harvest. Those who reject the message, on the other hand, produce nothing. The kingdom itself, however, will not be seen until the time of harvest arrives (4:26-32).

Whatever its original meaning, it is clear that for Mark this parable concerns the response of men and women to Jesus himself, for it is Jesus' followers who are given the secret of God's kingdom. Moreover, the material that frames this section concerns the nature of Jesus' authority, for it follows 3:20-35 and is, in turn, followed by the story of the stilling of the storm in 4:35-41, which ends with the unanswered question: "Who can this be? Even the wind and the sea obey him." For Mark, this is the all-important question. It is the question with which he confronts his readers, both then and now.

Miracle Stories

The stilling of the storm is the first of several miracle stories that present us once again with examples of Jesus' extraordinary authority. He controls not only the wind and the waves (4:35-41), but also a whole legion of unclean spirits (5:1-20) who address him as "Son of the Most High God" (5:7). Here is evidence for Jesus' claim that he has bound Satan and is plundering his goods (cf. 3:27). He then restores life to a woman who has been hemorrhaging for twelve years and to a dead child, who is twelve years old (5:21-43).

These events affect those who observe them with terror (4:41; 5:15), amazement (5:20), and astonishment (5:42), for they can find no answer to the question posed in 4:41, "Who can this be?" In his home town, on the other hand, his former neighbors think that they know exactly who Jesus is, and so reject him (6:1-6) — as did his family earlier (cf. 3:31-32).

John the Baptist and Jesus

In 6:7-13 there is the beginning of a new section, as Jesus hands over to his disciples the authority to teach and to exorcise evil spirits. Then there follows in 6:14-29 the story of the beheading of John the Baptist.

The link between John and Jesus is stressed in this story, for Herod, hearing rumors of Jesus' activities, assumes that he is none other than John himself raised from the dead. The account of how John met his death has ominous hints of what lies in store for Jesus. John dies because a weak ruler is trapped into killing someone whom he considers to be "righteous and holy" — trapped by those who object to John's teaching and are determined to destroy him. In his death, as in his life, John points forward to the one who follows him.

The account ends with the comment that John's disciples "came and took his body away and laid it in a tomb" (6:29). In spite of Herod's fears, there was, in fact, no resurrection for John.

Further Miracle Stories

Mark returns to the story of Jesus, setting out the accounts of the first feeding miracle (6:30-44) and the crossing of the lake (6:45-52). Clearly these are christologically significant stories. But what precisely is their meaning? Jesus had compassion on the people "because they were like sheep without a shepherd" (6:34). Are we meant to see him as a new David? Or is it rather as a new Moses, providing food in the wilderness (cf. Exodus 16 and Numbers 11)? Or maybe he is a new Elisha, feeding the people with a few loaves (cf. 2 Kgs 4:42-44)? But it was God who gave the manna, not Moses; and it was God who walked on the waves (cf. Job 9:8) and who made a path through the sea at the exodus (cf. Isa 43:16; 51:10; Ps 77:19).

When, therefore, Jesus identifies himself with the words *ego eimi* in 6:50, are we, perhaps, intended to understand them to mean "I am" — that is, God's own self-identification — rather than simply "It is I"? Certainly these stories are telling us something about Jesus' identity — something that the disciples failed to understand.

They were "astounded," says Mark, "because they had not understood about the loaves" (6:51-52). This comment is picked up in the conversation between Jesus and his disciples following the *second* feeding (8:1-9). Once again they are crossing the lake, and Jesus is with them (8:10, 13). They have only one loaf with them (8:14). In the light of past events, however, they should have known that this would be sufficient! Jesus reminds them of what they have witnessed at the feeding miracles, and asks, "Do you still not understand?" (8:21). But even though they have eyes and ears, they fail to see and hear (8:18).

Like the Pharisees and like Herod, their hearts are hardened (8:15, 17). Herod did, at least, regard Jesus as a prophet — as John the Baptist, who he believed had returned from the dead. But the Pharisees have been opposed to Jesus from the beginning and demand a sign from him, unable to see the significance of what he has already done (8:11-13). In contrast, a deaf man has been given his hearing and his speech (7:31-37) and a blind man is about to be given his sight (8:22-26). So what is the truth that the disciples are unable to grasp?

The Truth about Jesus

Mark's careful ordering of the material makes it clear that Peter's declaration at Caesarea Philippi marks a breakthrough in the disciples' understanding (8:29). For in contrast to those who, like Herod, think of Jesus as a prophet, Peter now acknowledges Jesus to be "the Messiah" *(ho Christos)*. But like the healing of the blind man immediately before, illumination is not instant. Peter fails to grasp that messiahship involves suffering and refuses to accept Jesus' teaching on that theme (8:32-33).

So even at this point in the story, the disciples are still incapable of grasping the whole truth. Since Mark headed his work "the Gospel of Jesus Christ," we know that Peter has stumbled onto *part* of the truth. We know also that he has *not* understood the necessity for suffering. But what else is still hidden from him? And if it is only at this stage that the disciples began to think of Jesus as Messiah, then what understanding of Jesus is Mark suggesting that they had *before* Caesarea Philippi? Why did they follow Jesus?

Who did they think he might be? Unlike the Fourth Evangelist (cf. John 1:41, 45, 49), Mark gives no answer to these questions — though twentieth-century scholars have tried to do so, as we will see when we return later to their answers.

The next section of Mark's Gospel, from the latter part of ch. 8 through the end of ch. 10, is concerned primarily with the theme of discipleship. But the nature of discipleship depends on the calling of the leader. Jesus now speaks about himself, but only because he is teaching his disciples about the inevitability of suffering. He refers to himself as the Son of man. And though he declares that the Son of man "must" suffer, he also speaks of his resurrection (8:31; 9:9, 31; 10:34) and his coming in glory (8:38; 13:26; 14:62).

The once-popular assumption that first-century Jews were expecting an eschatological "Son of man" from heaven has not been backed up with hard evidence. Nor is there any evidence that Christians ever used the phrase as a christological title. The early confessions were "Jesus is the Christ," "Jesus is Lord," "Jesus is the Son of God," but *not* "Jesus is the Son of man." It is not surprising, then, that there is no indication that the evangelist Mark understood it in this way. Rather, he suggests that it was Jesus' way of talking about his vocation and destiny: the Son of man "has authority on earth to forgive sins" and "is Lord of the Sabbath" (2:10, 28); he must suffer many things and be put to death, but he will be vindicated by God and come in glory (8:31, 38; 9:9, 12, 31; 10:33, 45; 13:26; 14:21, 41, 62).

We have noted already that the reference in 8:38 to the Son of man coming in glory and the declaration in 9:1 that the kingdom of God will shortly be seen in power are followed by the story of the Transfiguration in 9:2-13. Echoes of Moses' experience on Sinai are obvious in the references to the mountain, the glory, the cloud, and the voice from heaven. Moreover, Moses himself appears on the mountain, together with Elijah and Jesus. Earlier stories in Mark's Gospel have indicated that the popular view of Jesus as "Elijah" or "one of the prophets" is inadequate (cf. 6:14-16; 8:27-30). But Peter's response in 9:5 suggests that he is putting Jesus on a par with Moses and Elijah. In contrast, the heavenly voice singles out Jesus and identifies him as "my beloved Son," urging the disciples to obey him (see Hooker, "What Doest Thou Here, Elijah?"). And here, once again, we must assume that the words attributed to this voice represent what Mark believes to be the truth about Jesus.

The conversation on the way down the mountain explains that the truth about Jesus can be known only after "the Son of man has risen from the dead." His coming death is now firmly linked with that of "Elijah." Mark, of course, does not explicitly *tell* us that "Elijah" must be understood to mean John the Baptist. But with Mark 6:14-29 in our minds, we can hardly miss his meaning. A modern writer might put a footnote here, something like "see 6:14-29 above," or even spell out the identification. Not so Mark. His method is to allude to important connections. And so we need to be on the lookout for significant juxtapositions, repetitions, and echoes within the text.

If we are looking for links of this kind, then we will do well to pay attention to the fact that this section of Mark's Gospel is "introduced" (I use that term to avoid the problem of deciding where exactly it begins) and concludes with the healing of two blind men (8:22-26; 10:46-52). Bartimaeus, the second of these two blind men, addresses Jesus as "Son of David" and appeals for help. Does he call Jesus "Son of David" because he is blind? If so, then "Son of David," like "one of the prophets," is for Mark an inadequate title.

Yet Jesus responds to Bartimaeus. It would be typical of Mark's irony to suggest that the blind see more than do those with eyes. Like several other healing miracles, this one emphasizes the sufferer's faith. Is Mark, then, perhaps hinting that, like the disciples since Caesarea Philippi, Bartimaeus was only *semi*-blind? That he recognized Jesus, to some extent, as "the Messiah" *(ho Christos)?* What is clear is that once his sight was restored, Bartimaeus "followed Jesus on the road" — that is, became a disciple. Mark uses the word *hodos* ("way" or "road") when speaking of "the way of the Lord" in 1:3, and this "way" has now proved to be the road leading to Jerusalem (cf. 9:33-34; 10:32, 46, 52; 11:8).

Further Scenes of Authority

In the next story, that of Jesus' Triumphal Entry into Jerusalem, Mark seems to hint that Jesus was — perhaps unconsciously — welcomed as "Son of David" by the crowd as he rode into Jerusalem (11:1-11). Certainly they hailed him as "the one who comes in the name of the Lord" and were expecting "the coming kingdom of our father David" (11:9-10). In Matthew's account, Jesus is clearly understood to be "Son of David" (Matt 21:9; cf. 1:1-17; 2:1-6). What of Mark? Is he perhaps suggesting that the crowd unknowingly hit upon the truth and so greeted the Son of David without realizing it? Does he expect readers of his Gospel to recognize the truth concealed in their words?

The difficulty arises in 12:35-37, where Jesus is said to ask how "the Christ" can be David's son. We are inclined to assume that the logic of this passage means that Jesus *cannot be* David's son if he is David's lord. But it is clear that the evangelists Matthew and Luke did not understand what is said here as contradicting their birth narratives (Matt 22:41-6; Luke 20:41-4), and we must not assume that Mark thought that Jesus' lordship contradicted belief in Jesus' Davidic descent. It may well be that this passage is intended to make us realize that belief in Jesus as Lord is *more important* than belief that he is the Son of David. The essential point is that a greater than David is here (cf. Mark 2:25-28).

The reference to David in 11:10, "Blessed is the coming kingdom of our father David," is somewhat ambiguous, but Jesus' entry into Jerusalem is clearly significant. Nonetheless, questions regarding his entry arise. Does he enter the city as king? Or is it as Lord *(kyrios),* the term he is said to have used of himself in 11:3? The problem with the term "Lord" is that it is itself somewhat ambiguous, for it could simply signify the polite form of "Master." Or it could mean "owner," in which case Jesus is apparently claiming ownership of the animal. Or it could be used in an honorific and exalted sense of "Lord," in which case Jesus' action is perhaps seen as the fulfillment of Mal 3:1 and Isa 40:3, which were quoted in the prologue at 1:2-3.

Furthermore, instead of walking into Jerusalem as a pilgrim should, Jesus rides into the city (11:7-8) — which, in itself, is a significant claim to authority. He then comes into the temple, looks around, and returns the next day (11:11). His condemnation of the worship in the temple, sandwiched as it is between the two halves of the story of the fig tree (11:12-14, 20-25), is clearly intended as a judgment on Israel's failure to produce the fruit that God expects from his people. The implication may well be that Jesus is the Messiah (see Telford, *Barren Temple*). Certainly he is God's representative who makes God's final appeal to his people — for in the parable of the vineyard in 12:1-12, Mark portrays Jesus as the "beloved son" who follows many "servants," the prophets. It is noteworthy that this parable immediately follows the challenge to Jesus by "the chief priests, scribes and elders," who demand to know who gave him authority "to do these things" (11:27-33). Jesus replies by asking another question concerning the authority of John the Baptist: Was that from God or from humans?

Jesus' opponents once again refuse to acknowledge what should be self-evident (cf. the similar passage about Jesus' authority in 3:20-30). The link with John is this time clearly made, and the implication is plain: If the answer to their question about Jesus' authority depends on the answer to his own question about the authority of John, then he must be the one about whom John spoke. He is the Lord, whose coming John announced and who has now come to his temple (cf. Mal 3:1). But those who refused to acknowledge John's authority will certainly refuse to acknowledge that of Jesus — with inevitable results.

The Passion Narrative

It is in the passion narrative, chs. 14–15, however, that Jesus' true identity is finally revealed — though even here, it is often hinted at rather than clearly spelled out. The anointing at Bethany (14:3-9), for example, is interpreted as preparation for Jesus' burial. But is Jesus at this moment also anointed as king?

Certainly it is in death that he is *proclaimed* as king (cf. 15:2, 9, 12, 18, 26, 32). In 14:27, Jesus is said to have described himself as "the shepherd" of the sheep. But at his trial he affirms, in response to the high priest's question, that he is the Messiah and the Son of the Blessed One (14:61-2). It is for this that he is put to death. The confession that he is "Son of God," which greets his death, is the final comment on his identity in the Gospel.

It is not that Jesus is Messiah and Son of God *in spite of suffering*. Rather, it is (1) *because* he is the Messiah that he will not come down from the cross (15:32) and (2) *because* he is God's Son that he dies in obedience to what he believes to be his Father's will (15:39; cf. 14:36). All that is needed to round off the story is a brief epilogue in 16:1-8, which tells the women that he has been raised and summons his disciples once again to follow him.

4. Mark's Purpose

Mark's Gospel is the Gospel about Jesus Christ, and so it is christological from beginning to end. The greatest puzzle is *why* the evangelist decided to write it! Perhaps he simply felt compelled to preach the gospel. That he did so in this new way, however, suggests that some particular circumstance or situation provoked him into doing so. Did he write his "Gospel" because he was aware of certain difficulties confronting the Christian communities of his day — problems that existed either within the churches or outside them? Did he perhaps write because he wanted to oppose an alternative understanding of the gospel?

Is Mark Countering an Alternative Christology?

This last suggestion has proved popular among many scholars who believe that Mark's Gospel was written in order to attack an alternative christology. It has been argued, for instance, that two entirely opposing christologies are presented in the Gospel: first, one that saw Jesus as a *theios anēr*, a "divine man" who performed mighty acts — a belief expressed by Peter in the scene at Caesarea Philippi; then Mark's own understanding of Jesus as the suffering Son of man (see, e.g., T. J. Weeden, *Mark: Traditions in Conflict*).

In view of the lack of evidence for the thesis that Mark wrote to oppose an alternative understanding of the gospel, it is extraordinary how influential this thesis has been! One is bound to say that if Mark's intention in his early chapters was to *attack* the view of Jesus as one who did mighty deeds, he was a remarkably clumsy author. For Mark uses these miracle stories *positively*. The healings, feedings, and mighty acts of Jesus are not dismissed, but are understood by Mark to be signs that point to the true significance of who Jesus is. They pose the vital question "Who can this be?" (4:41). And for those with eyes to see and ears to hear, they point to the answer. If, as is argued, the disciples are "attacked" in Mark's Gospel, it is only because they are unable to grasp the truth — both before and after their declaration of Jesus as Messiah at Caesarea Philippi. What Peter confesses in 8:29, therefore, must be true, since it agrees with Mark's own viewpoint. The irony is that Peter does not understand the significance of what he proclaims.

Another proposal suggests that the christology under attack held Jesus to be "the Son of David" (e.g., Tyson, "The Blindness of the Disciples"). We have already noted, however, that the material referring to this title in Mark's Gospel is ambiguous. It certainly does not suggest that Mark was trying to undermine such a belief. Rather, it would seem that "Son of

95

David," like the ascription "prophet," indicates a positive — but still inadequate — response to Jesus.

The Meaning of Discipleship

One view that certainly does come under attack in Mark's Gospel, however, is that which assumes that suffering and death are incompatible with messiahship. This view is linked with the attitude that refuses to see that discipleship, similarly, demands humility and suffering. It is these two features in Jesus' teaching that his disciples are said to have found impossible to accept.

For Christians of Mark's time, Jesus' own death was a given fact and part of the proclamation of the gospel message. The tension in the evangelist's day was between Christians and Jews who continued to find messiahship and ignominious death incompatible. If Mark was seeking to persuade non-Christians of the truth of his Gospel, he would need to stress this point — for the message of "Christ crucified" was "a stumbling block to Jews, and foolishness to Greeks" (1 Cor 1:23; Gal 5:11; cf. Deut 21:23). Is this why Mark portrays Jesus so graphically as saying that "it was necessary for the Son of man to suffer"? If so, one might have expected him to engage more with Old Testament texts supporting the idea that those who are faithful to God are likely to suffer rather than simply affirming the "necessity" of suffering.

Jesus' death was a given fact. The meaning of Christian discipleship, however, was *not* a given fact. Mark's contemporaries might well find the picture of discipleship that he paints unacceptable. Like the Corinthians chided by Paul, they might well think that being disciples of the Messiah meant enjoying status, riches, and glory, and conveniently forget the summons to take up the cross and follow a crucified Lord. Was this the kind of situation that led Mark to write his Gospel? Was his book primarily intended to remind its hearers of the implications of Christian discipleship?

Son of God

It is difficult to know precisely what Mark is attacking. But what exactly is he affirming? Clearly, he is affirming that Jesus is the Son of God. But what does

"Son of God" mean? Was Mark himself perhaps influenced by Hellenistic ideas of what "sonship" meant? Did he intend to portray Jesus in terms of a *theios anēr* or "divine man" as understood in Greek religious thought? For a comprehensive treatment of the so-called *theios anēr* traditions and their possible use by Mark, see Blackburn, *Theios Anêr and the Markan Miracle Traditions*.

It is impossible in the space available to analyze such an understanding of Mark's purpose in any adequate fashion. Suffice it here to point to the pertinent evidence in the Gospel itself — that is, to those places in Mark's Gospel (1) where sonship is clearly linked both with obedience to God's will and suffering, (2) where the power that is at work in Jesus is said to be that of the Holy Spirit, (3) where the whole of Jesus' ministry is seen as the fulfillment of God's purpose set out in the prophets and as the proclamation of God's kingdom, and (4) where Jesus himself speaks of his own vocation as the "Son of man." In considering each of these matters, it is important to remember that the materials used by Mark — as well as his overall understanding of the gospel itself — are demonstrably Jewish rather than Greek.

The Messianic Secret

There is, however, one final piece of the puzzle that we need to consider here — namely, the mystery of the so-called "messianic secret." This issue raises problems at various levels. Was the "secret" part of the tradition as Mark received it? Or was it a way of handling tensions in the material, either at the pre-Markan stage or when Mark shaped it? With these questions we have come, full circle, back to the questions with which we began this chapter.

But our concern is with *Mark*. What, then, is meant by "the messianic secret"? In fact, the secret is not always directly "messianic." Some obvious occasions when it is are when unclean spirits are silenced (1:24-5, 34; 3:11-12) or the disciples are commanded to keep quiet about Jesus' identity (8:29-30; 9:9). Contrast with these, however, the clear — though implicit — claims made by Jesus when he comes to Jerusalem. For he rides into the city, acts with divine authority in the temple, tells a parable about a beloved son (whose meaning is grasped by his enemies), teaches with authority in the temple, and even raises a question about who the Messiah might be. And finally at his trial before the high priest and the Sanhedrin, he openly acknowledges that he is the Messiah, the Son of God.

With healings, too, there is a contrast between those where silence is imposed (1:43-44; 5:35-43; 7:31-37; 8:22-26) and those that are performed openly (2:1-12; 3:1-6; 5:1-20, 25-34; 9:14-29). In the case of the leper, however, the instruction to say nothing is a temporary one — until he reaches the priest and is recognized as clean (1:43-44). The deaf man and the blind man symbolize Israel's failure to hear and see the truth (7:31-37; 8:22-26) — a truth that is not made plain until we get to the end of the story. Nor can the resurrection of a dead child be spoken of until Jesus himself has been raised from the dead (5:35-43).

We find a similar contrast in the accounts of Jesus' teaching, much of which is given in private to his disciples. Sometimes this teaching is concerned particularly with suffering (8:31-33; 9:30-50; 10:23-45). At other times it is laden with meanings that become clear to the disciples only later (4:10-20; 7:17-23; 10:10-12; 13). Yet Jesus also appeals openly to all, demanding that his hearers respond to his message — as in the parables in ch. 4 and the parable, questions, and debate in ch. 12. In effect, Mark presents Jesus as having taught them the word "as they were able to hear it" (4:33).

Within Mark's story, then, "the messianic secret" is the equivalent of the Johannine "My hour has not yet come." During Jesus' ministry many things are hidden — not only from the crowds but also from the disciples. Only with the crucifixion and resurrection does full understanding finally come. For Mark, "the messianic secret" is, perhaps, some explanation for Israel's failure to recognize her Messiah. It is also a pointer to the true meaning of being a disciple.

Above all, however, "the messianic secret" in Mark's Gospel is a pointer to the truth about Jesus — a truth that so many fail to grasp, but which is spelled out for us at the beginning of the Gospel in the prologue, in the middle at the Transfiguration, and at the end in the words of the centurion. It serves to nudge Mark's readers in the ribs, as though to say: "And you, of course, because I have let you into the secret, will understand precisely what this means!" Nearly 2000 years later, we may not understand his meaning precisely, but we grasp enough to comprehend the gospel with which he challenges us.

SELECTED BIBLIOGRAPHY

Best, Ernest. *The Temptation and the Passion.* Cambridge: Cambridge University Press, 1966, 1990[2].

Blackburn, Barry. *Theios Anêr and the Markan Miracle Traditions.* Tübingen: Mohr-Siebeck, 1991.

Hooker, Morna D. *The Message of Mark.* London: Epworth, 1983.

―――. "'What Doest Thou Here, Elijah?' A Look at St Mark's Account of the Transfiguration," in *The Glory of Christ in the New Testament: Studies in Christology in Memory of George Bradford Caird,* ed. L. D. Hurst and N. T. Wright. Oxford: Clarendon, 1987, 59-70.

―――. *The Gospel according to St Mark.* London: Black; Peabody: Hendrickson, 1991.

―――. *Beginnings: Keys That Open the Gospels.* London: SCM; Harrisburg: Trinity Press International, 1997.

―――. *The Signs of a Prophet.* London: SCM; Harrisburg: Trinity Press International, 1997.

Marcus, Joel. *Mark 1–8.* New York: Doubleday, 2000.

Rhoads, David M., Joanna Dewey, and Donald Michie. *Mark as Story: An Introduction to the Narrative of a Gospel.* Minneapolis: Augsburg, 1999[2].

Stacey, W. David. *Prophetic Drama in the Old Testament.* London: Epworth; Harrisburg: Trinity Press International, 1993.

Telford, William R. *The Barren Temple and the Withered Tree.* Sheffield: JSOT, 1980.

―――. *The Theology of the Gospel of Mark.* Cambridge: Cambridge University Press, 1999.

Trocmé, Etienne, "Is There a Markan Christology?" in *Christ and Spirit in the New Testament: Essays in Honour of C. F. D. Moule,* ed. B. Lindars and S. Smalley. Cambridge: Cambridge University Press, 1973, 3-13.

Tyson, Joseph B. "The Blindness of the Disciples in Mark," *JBL* 80 (1961) 261-68.

Watts, Rikki E. *Isaiah's New Exodus and Mark.* Tübingen: Mohr-Siebeck, 1997.

Weeden, Theodore J. *Mark: Traditions in Conflict.* Philadelphia: Fortress, 1971, 1979[2].

CHAPTER 5

The Vindicated Son:
A Narrative Approach to Matthean Christology

TERENCE L. DONALDSON

To ask about the christology of Matthew's Gospel is to seek Matthew's answer to the question, "Who is Jesus and how is he significant?" To do so from a narrative perspective, it is necessary to identify those elements of Matthew's Gospel in which the shape of the story's plot comes most clearly into focus. This means that we will need to direct our attention particularly to the "contract" element of the evangelist's story where the mandate is clarified and accepted, where certain resources are communicated, and where the shape of the story's "topic" begins to come into view. I will argue (1) that this contract element is to be found in the baptism and temptation narratives and (2) that it is from this vantage point that we are able to identify the central thread of Matthew's plot as having to do with the vindication of the humble, obedient Son of God.

1. From Titles to Story

In his *Matthew: Structure, Christology, Kingdom* of 1975, Jack Kingsbury produced a book that stands (as can now be seen in retrospect) at a kind of watershed in the scholarly study of Matthean christology. On the one hand, with respect to content, it shares with earlier scholarship a focus on titles, for Kingsbury attempted to answer the question of Matthew's christology primarily on the basis of titles applied to or used by Jesus in Matthew's Gospel. On the other hand, with respect to methodology, it represents an early attempt to move beyond redaction criticism toward what has come to be called narrative criticism, which is a method of interpretation that both opens up a more comprehensive approach to the question and leads to a more satisfactory kind of answer. Kingsbury's work, therefore, provides us with a convenient point of entry into both the question of Matthew's christology itself and the way in which one can most responsibly and profitably deal with the issues involved.

Let us begin with the backward-oriented part of Kingsbury's study — that is, with his concentration on titles. He begins with a study of the title Son of God and its equivalents ("my Son," "the Son"), arguing that this is "the most fundamental christological category in Matthew's Gospel" (p. 83). He then goes on to survey the other titles that appear in Matthew, which he identifies as follows:

Major Titles	*Minor Titles*
Messiah	Jesus
King	Son of Abraham
Son of David	The Coming One
Lord	Shepherd
Son of Man	Prophet
	Rabbi/teacher
	Servant
	Emmanuel

He argues that these other titles are all related in a subordinate way to the dominant title Son of God, their function being to add depth to and nuance Matthew's presentation of Jesus as God's Son.

As is readily apparent, this approach assumes (1) that Matthew's christology is focused in his christological titles, and (2) that it is possible to focus his christology even further by identifying one of them as primary and as governing the rest. But such an approach is open to significant criticism. For one thing, as Kingsbury himself has shown (pp. 41-42), there has been significant scholarly disagreement about the christological titles in Matthew, with others (e.g., Lord, Son of Man, Messiah) identified, either singly or in combination, as dominant. Of more significance, the material in Matthew's Gospel that has a bearing on the question "Who is Jesus and why is he significant?" is by no means limited to titles. For Matthew contains many christologically significant statements that either contain no title at all or cannot be identified with one particular title in an unambiguous way.

Take, for example, the Sermon on the Mount. Except for "Lord, Lord," addressed to Jesus by false disciples about to be banished from the kingdom at the judgment (7:21-23), the sermon contains no title whatsoever — neither in the discourse proper nor in the introduction and conclusion. Yet it contains material that carries significant christological weight. Jesus' declaration that he has come "not to abolish but to fulfill" the Law and the Prophets (5:17); his authoritative reinterpretation of the Torah ("you have heard that it was said . . . but I say to you," 5:21-48); the amazement of the crowds that "he taught them as one having authority, and not as their scribes" (7:28-29) — such statements have a great bearing on the overall significance of Jesus in Matthew's Gospel, despite the absence of any ascribed title. And many other examples could be adduced from elsewhere in the Gospel — such as attributions of authority to Jesus (8:9; 9:6, 8; 21:23-27; 28:18), descriptions of Jesus as the recipient of reverence or worship (2:11; 14:33; 28:9, 17), and statements indicating his ability to delegate authority over unclean spirits to others (10:1).

The case of Jesus' healing ministry illustrates another aspect of the issue. For while Jesus' role as a healer is of evident christological significance, the role cannot be associated with any one title in particular. In chs. 8-9, for example, a variety of titles appear in connection with Jesus' healing activity — such as Lord, Son of Man, Son of God, and Son of David. The evangelist's own comment in 8:17 on Jesus' healing activity, which is a citation of Isa 53:4, alludes to an additional title, that of Isaiah's Suffering Servant. Similar observations, in fact, could be made about Jesus' teaching activity, his role as interpreter of the Law, and many other aspects of his ministry.

In other words, a focus on titles provides no direct access to many significant aspects of Matthew's christology. What is needed is an approach that will allow the whole of the evidence, and not simply the titles, to be taken into account. Which brings us to the issue of methodology.

2. A Narrative-Critical Approach

A Brief History of the Method's Development

When Kingsbury's work was published, the dominant method for interpreting the Synoptic Gospels was redaction criticism. In this approach, in order to identify the characteristics, themes, and intentions of a Gospel such as Matthew, preference was given to redactional material — that is, to ways in which Matthew reshaped, supplemented, or trimmed his sources, which were assumed to include the Gospel of Mark and a collection of Jesus' sayings (Q), which were also used by Luke. Take, for example, Peter's confession of Jesus in Matt 16:16: "You are the Christ, the Son of the living God." In assessing the christological implications of the statement, a redaction-critical study would place much more emphasis on "the Son of the living God," which Matthew apparently added to Mark 8:29, than on "the Christ," which had been simply taken over from Mark.

But without denying its utility as an interpretive tool, one needs to point out that redaction criticism is subject to several limitations and blind spots. For one thing, to continue with the example just introduced, the presence of "the Christ" in Matt 16:16 is just as much the result of an editorial choice (the choice to retain an aspect of the tradition) as is "the Son of the living God." "Christ" is, after all, the very first descriptive term that Matthew ascribes to Jesus (1:1), which means that its presence in 16:16 should not be devalued simply because it was taken over from Mark. Retained tradition might have just as much evidential value as redactional addition. Another limitation of redaction criticism is that it imposes an unnatural reading strategy on the interpreter. For any competent reader should be able to arrive at a full and proper understanding of the meaning of a narrative by reading it on its own terms. It should not be necessary to read any narrative with one eye constantly on a parallel set of texts.

Considerations such as these have led, of late, to a method of interpretation that attempts to read the Gospels on their own terms as narratives — that is, as stories told by a narrator with a particular point of view and containing a set of characters, a sequence of events, and a plot that moves from beginning, through middle, to the end. Indeed, Kingsbury (see especially his *Matthew as Story*) and his students (especially Powell, *What Is Narrative Criticism?*) have made major contributions to the development of narrative criticism.

As for Kingsbury's earlier *Matthew: Structure, Christology, Kingdom*, while not explicitly a work of narrative criticism, it nevertheless anticipated a narrative approach in several respects. One way it did so was Kingsbury's argument that the main structuring feature of Matthew's Gospel is not the five discourses, which are static, thematic bodies of teaching, but the repeated phrase "From that time Jesus began to" (4:17; 16:21), which effectively divides the Gospel temporally into three successive narrative sections. The other is the virtual absence of redactional considerations in Kingsbury's discussions of christology. For the most part he attempted to describe Matthew's Gospel on its own terms, without privileging one body of evidence (the redactional) over the other body of evidence (the traditional). Still, it was not until the first edition of his *Matthew as Story* in 1986 that we had a full-blown narrative-critical treatment of Matthew's Gospel.

Two Important Preliminary Observations

The purpose of this chapter is to provide insight into Matthew's christology from a narrative-critical perspective. Before turning to the Gospel directly, however, two important preliminary observations are in order. First, it needs to be recognized that the turn to narrative is not simply a scholarly fad. Rather, narrative criticism puts us in touch with something that is fundamental to the New Testament as a whole. For before there were Gospels, there was the gospel — the basic proclamation about the saving significance of the life, death, and resurrection of Jesus (cf. 1 Cor 15:1-8).

This proclamation, which is found at the heart not only of the canonical Gospels but also of all the other writings in the New Testament (James, of course, being a special case), is in its essence a narrative. It is a story that involves a sequence of events in which Jesus of Nazareth is the main character — and which, in turn, functions as the surprising climax to a larger story having to do with God's dealings with the world through the covenant people Israel. The narrative nature of this proclaimed gospel is most clearly seen in the written Gospels themselves, but the gospel proclaimed by Paul and the other apostles (cf. 1 Cor 15:11), as well as by their successors, had just as much a narrative shape (see Hays, *The Faith of Jesus Christ*). A narrative approach to Matthew, therefore, is in keeping not only with its genre as a Gospel but also with its substance as gospel.

Of course, as with any significant narrative, the fundamental gospel narrative invited — indeed, demanded — second-order reflections on its meaning. The basic gospel proclamation raised a number of significant questions for its earliest hearers and proclaimers alike. These included questions about Jesus' identity. Who is this person, that the events of his life should have such far-reaching significance? Second-order reflections on the proclaimed gospel are what we call theology, a component of which is christology. While Paul expressed his theological, second-order reflections in the form of letters, the evangelists wove their reflections back into a retelling of the primary gospel narrative. Thus their particular answers to theological questions (e.g., Who is Jesus?) are provided in the fabric of the narrative itself.

A second observation to highlight here has to do with the nature of personal identity. What are we looking for when we ask "Who is Jesus?" Here we can turn with profit to Hans Frei, whose work has been a major factor in the current emphasis on narrative in both theology and New Testament studies. In "Theological Reflections on the Accounts of Jesus' Death and Resurrection" Frei argues that a person's identity should not be conceived of as an inner essence that exists in some intangible realm separate from the outer world of deed and interaction. Rather, it is constituted by what the person does, which Frei defines more fully as the unified combination of intention and action. In other words, as Frei expresses it, "a person's identity is constituted (not merely illustrated) by the intention which he carries into action" (p. 63), and so is analogous to "the interrelation of character with circumstance that we get in a novel or short story" (p. 64). And bringing these insights to bear on the christology of the Gospels, Frei argues that the identity of Jesus is to be found in the narrative itself: "The identity of Jesus is focused in the circumstances of the action and not in back of them. He is what he does and undergoes" (p. 73).

This means that Jesus' identity is inextricably linked with the story in which he is the central character. The narrative of any one of the Gospels is not merely a convenient receptacle for that Gospel's christology, something that might be discarded once the christological contents have been extracted from it. Rather, christology is narratively constituted. The christology of a Gospel such as Matthew is located precisely in the actions and experiences of Jesus as they contribute to the story as a whole. Thus to ask about the christology of Matthew's Gospel is to inquire about the function of Jesus as a character in the plot of the story Matthew has to tell.

3. The Character of Jesus in Matthew's Narrative

A narrative-critical approach to Matthew's christology proceeds along two lines of investigation: (1) the character of Jesus as it is depicted in the Gospel and (2) the function of Jesus in the Gospel's plot. With respect to the first, I do not believe that a study of character development will take us very far in our quest for Matthew's christology. Rather, a consideration of the function of the portrayal of Jesus in Matthew's plot will be much more determinative. Still, the study of character development is a necessary first step. Moreover, it provides a much more complete inventory of christological material than does an approach that focuses primarily on titles.

Narrative critics have identified a number of literary devices by means of which an author constructs and communicates to the reader an evaluative point of view — that is, a framework of values and meaning essential for a proper understanding of the narrative as a whole (for detailed descriptions see Powell, *What Is Narrative Criticism?* and Culpepper, *Anatomy of the Fourth Gospel*). A thoroughgoing analysis of the presence of these devices in Matthew's Gospel would provide us with a full inventory of pertinent christological material. Space prohibits a complete analysis, but we will attempt to identify the main Matthean literary devices and provide illustrative examples of how those devices are used to highlight the identity and significance of the various characters in the evangelist's narrative.

Explicit Commentary

The most overt device used by an author to construct a framework of meaning for the guidance of the reader is that of explicit commentary. Such commentary consists of statements where the narrator comments directly on some aspect of the story being narrated — "the narrator" understood not as the actual flesh-and-blood author but as "the person whose voice tells the story."

Most of the explicit commentary in Matthew has direct christological significance. The first sentence in the Gospel, where the narrator introduces Jesus as "the Christ" (1:1), is a case in point (cf. also 1:17). The prime example, however, is Matthew's set of "fulfillment formula" quotations — that is, those occasions where the narrator interrupts the flow of the story to identify a text of Scripture as fulfilled in this or that action of Jesus (1:22-23; 2:15, 18, 23; 4:14-16; 8:17; 12:17-21; 13:35; 21:4-5; 27:9-10).

All of the Matthean fulfillment formula quotations have intrinsic christological import, for they identify Jesus as a person whose life somehow brings Scripture to completion. Most of them also ascribe to him some specific element of significance. Some of these elements are titles: Emmanuel (1:22-23), God's Son (2:15), God's Servant (12:17-21), or Zion's King (21:4-5). Others have to do with his activity: his taking up residence in Capernaum as a fulfillment of Isaiah's promise of the coming of light to a darkened Galilee (4:14-16), his healing as a manifestation of his role as Isaiah's Suffering Servant (8:17; 12:17-21), or his speaking in parables as a fulfillment of the psalmist's statement about things hidden from the foundation of the world (13:35).

One of these fulfillment formula quotations contains an additional statement on the part of the narrator — an explicit comment within an explicit comment. In the citation of Isa 7:14 in Matt 1:23, the narrator provides an interpretation of the Hebrew word "Emmanuel," adding to the quotation the explanatory comment: "that is, God [is] with us." The christological force of the comment, however, depends on a decision about its form. Should it be rendered "God with us," in which case the narrator was ascribing some sort of divine status to Jesus? Or, as is more likely, should it be rendered "God is with us," in which case the birth of Jesus is being understood simply as a sign that God is present (for discussion see Davies and Allison, *Matthew*, 1.217-18.)

Implicit Commentary

In addition to explicit commentary, there are several forms of implicit commentary that an author can use in constructing a framework of meaning. Three types of implicit commentary are particularly important for a study of Matthew's christology: (1) value-laden descriptions, (2) reliable statements, and (3) portrayals of contributing events.

Value-Laden Descriptions   While the primary task of a narrator is to describe action and to report speech, this can be done in a way that conveys the author's judgments about the value or significance of the things being described and reported. For example, on a number of occasions the

First Evangelist has chosen to describe people's response to Jesus with the term "worship" (the verb *proskyneō*, 2:2, 11; 8:2; 9:18; 14:33; 15:25; 20:20; 28:9, 17), rather than such more purely descriptive terms as "kneel" (Mark 1:40) or "fall at his feet" (Mark 5:22). To be sure, the term does not always have the full sense of religious devotion as is normally present in our word "worship." It can also be used simply to indicate obeisance before a human master (Matt 18:26). Still, the first instance of the word in Matthew's Gospel does have the sense of that type of devotion that is to be given exclusively to God (4:10), which means that Matthew's use of the word with reference to Jesus adds a christologically significant judgment to his description of people's response to him (especially in 14:33; 28:9, 17).

Such value-laden descriptions are especially effective when they are associated with privileged information — that is, with information that would not have been readily apparent to an outside observer, such as a character's inner thoughts or intentions. The effect of such privileged information on readers is to increase their sense of the narrator's authority and thus to add further weight to the evaluative description. For example, after having indicated the amazement of the crowds at the end of the Sermon on the Mount, Matthew goes on to disclose the reason: "For he taught them as one having authority, and not as their scribes" (7:28-29). Not only does this statement add a judgment as to the nature of the crowd's response to Jesus, it comes with added authority by virtue of the implied fact that the narrator has access to the inner perceptions of the crowd. Similar phenomena are at work in statements that Mary's pregnancy was "from the Holy Spirit" (1:18), that at the baptism what was seen as a dove was perceived by Jesus to be the Holy Spirit descending on him (3:16), that Herod (14:5) or the Pharisees (21:46) feared the crowds because they perceived Jesus to be a prophet, and so on.

Reliable Statements   Another form of implicit commentary are reliable statements made by characters in the story — that is, statements that (1) have a bearing on the meaning of the story, (2) are made by fully reliable characters (e.g., God, Jesus), or (3) are presented in such a way that the reader knows them to be reliable. God speaks directly about Jesus on two occasions: at his baptism ("This is my Son, the beloved, with whom I am well pleased," 3:17) and at his transfiguration (the same statement with the addition "listen to him," 17:5). The words of God are also presumably to be heard in the statement of the "angel of the Lord" to Joseph that he is to "name him Jesus, for he will save his people from their sins" (1:20-21) — a statement that is doubly effective in that, with the narrator having access to the content of Joseph's dream, it is so clearly a case of privileged information.

By far the largest set of christologically significant statements, however, are those made by Jesus himself. Some of these involve titles: Son of man (frequently), Messiah (23:10), King (25:34), Coming One (23:39), Son (of the Father) (11:27; 24:36). Related to the latter are references to "my [or 'the'] Father," which imply a special relationship with God (10:32-33; 11:25-27; 18:19-20; 20:23; 24:36; 26:53; cf. 28:19). Others are explicit statements about Jesus' mission, which appear in several forms: "I have come" (5:17; 9:13; 10:34-35) or "the Son of man has come" (20:28), "I was sent" (15:24), "it is necessary" (16:21; 26:54) or "it is fitting" (3:15), and self-comparisons to a physician (9:12) and a bridegroom (9:15). Jesus also makes a number of statements in which he asserts his superiority over various Jewish institutions or Old Testament saints: the temple (12:6), the temple tax (17:24-26), the Sabbath (12:8), the Law (5:21-48), David (22:41-43), Jonah (12:41), and Solomon (12:42).

Furthermore, Jesus speaks of his own authority (9:6; 21:23-24), equates his healing activity with the presence of the kingdom (12:28), attaches ultimate significance to people's response to him (10:32-39; 11:20-24), and ascribes to himself the role of eschatological ruler and judge (16:27; 19:28; 20:20-23; 25:31; 26:63-65). The sheer number of such statements means that the reader's assessment of Jesus' person and significance will be shaped in significant ways by the voice of Jesus himself.

In addition, various other characters in the story make statements about Jesus that can be taken as reliable, if not always full, indications of Jesus' character. On a number of occasions Jesus is addressed as God's "Son" — by the disciples (14:33), by Peter (16:16), by the centurion at the cross (27:54), and even by demons (8:29). Jesus is identified as "king of the Jews" by the Magi (2:2) and, with readily discernible irony, by the anonymous inscription on the cross (27:37). John the Baptist recognizes Jesus as the "more powerful" one he has been announcing (3:11, 14). The crowds acclaim Jesus as a prophet (21:11; cf. 14:5; 21:46), proclaim him to be the Son of David (12:23; 21:9), are amazed at his authority (7:28-29; 9:8), and praise God for his mighty works (15:31; cf. 9:33).

Portrayals of Contributing Events   Finally, one can include in this inventory of implicit commentary events that have christological significance not so much as elements in a plot but as contributions to the development of Jesus' character. The appearance of angels ministering to Jesus after the departure of the tempter (4:11) is one case in point. Another is the set of apocalyptic signs that accompany Jesus' death (27:51-53). Neither of these events plays a significant role in the unfolding of the story. Rather, their function is to underline the cosmic significance of Jesus and the events associated with him.

Summation

By means of such narrative devices, the author of Matthew's Gospel guides the reader's encounter with Jesus as a character in the story. The cumulative effect of this material, as readers make their way through the Gospel, is the development of a rich and detailed set of characteristics that they carry with them into each new scene of the narrative and that are ultimately incorporated into their final assessment of the significance of Jesus as they come to the end of the narrative. That final assessment, however, is not simply the sum total of the individual bits of christological material. Rather, it is the plot of the narrative, as readers encounter it by following the story from its beginning through its middle to its end, that provides the organizing structure within which the rich and detailed set of characteristics finds its distinctive shape.

4. The Function of Jesus in Matthew's Plot

Plots and Their Structure

A narrative or story is constructed out of these basic elements: (1) a sequence of events (2) involving a group of characters (3) in particular settings. But in order to constitute a story — as distinct from a simple chronicle, logbook, or diary — these elements need to contribute to the emergence of a plot. The emergence of a plot, in turn, requires two additional features.

First, it is of the nature of a story that through the sequence of events readers are presented with a completed process of change impinging on the main character in one way or another. In stories such as we encounter in the Gospels, this change is primarily one of circumstance. The story be-

gins with one set of circumstances, usually involving some state of disequilibrium (i.e., a state of imbalance, some lack or desire), and ends with another in which a new state of equilibrium is achieved. Second, the
completed process of change cannot be arbitrary but must appear as the
necessary result of the sequence of events. In other words, for the set of
events to add up to a plot, it is necessary that they be linked in a causal sequence, with the final state of affairs emerging as the necessary outcome of
the events that preceded it.

Of course, it is important that there be an element of surprise. There
is little enjoyment in a story whose shape and outcome are totally predict-
able from beginning to end. Still, at the end of a good story there is a sense
that the events work together in a unified way to produce an outcome that
is both appropriate and satisfying. A plot, then, can be understood as com-
prising a unified sequence of events whose accumulated causal effects produce a completed process of change in the circumstances surrounding the
main character.

To build on this basic definition of a plot, it will be helpful to refer to
the French structuralist A. J. Greimas, whose work on the structure of narrative has been brought to the attention of biblical scholars by Daniel Patte
(What Is Structural Exegesis?). Greimas's goal is the development of a "narrative grammar." Ordinary grammar allows us to discern, beneath the surface of an infinite number of possible sentences, a much smaller set of
grammatical categories and functions that provide the structure within
which meaning is generated. Analogously, narrative grammar attempts to
discern, beneath the surface of an infinite variety of stories and events that
they comprise, a much smaller set of narrative functions that work together in a structured way to create narrative meaning.

Aristotle was the first to recognize that in order to be a unified whole,
a story needs to have "a beginning and a middle and an end" (*Poetics* 7.3).
Building on this insight, Greimas identifies three narrative "sequences":
(1) the "Initial," in which a lack of equilibrium (as described above) is established, (2) the "Topical," in which the essential substance or "topic" of
the story is developed, and (3) the "Final," in which the process of change is
brought to completion. (In the interests of brevity and clarity, I am simpli-
fying Greimas's structure and terminology.)

The Topical Sequence is further subdivided into three units of narrative grammar, each with its own narrative function. The first unit in a Topical Sequence, the "Contract," is crucially significant in shaping the mean-

ing of the rest of the story. It is that element of the story in which the main character is identified and accepts a mandate to do what needs to be done in order to resolve the situation of disequilibrium. In addition, the protagonist often receives resources of various kinds — such as knowledge, power, helpers, and devices — to assist in the accomplishment of the mandate. The second unit in a Topical Sequence is the "Departure," that aspect of the story in which the main character sets off to carry out the mandate. The third is the "Performance," which usually comprises a number of attempts on the part of the protagonist to carry out the task and accomplish the mandate. These involve confrontation with opponents or with other obstacles standing in the way of success. Here the resources received in the Contract are put into play. The Performance usually occupies a substantial portion of the actual narrative (though Greimas's analysis involves further subdivisions that need not concern us here). The outcome of the Performance unit leads into the Final Sequence, in which the elements of the plot are resolved and a new state of equilibrium is established.

It is, of course, not necessary to be adept in structuralist theory before one can understand and appreciate a narrative, any more than it is necessary to know the names of the various types of subordinate clauses before one can converse intelligibly. Still, by putting names to things of which we are already intuitively aware, we are able to create analytical tools that enable us to see things we may not have been aware of at all. Which brings us back to Matthew's narrative and the question of his christology.

The Contract Unit of Matthew's Gospel

Greimas's analysis allows us to recognize the narrative structure within which Jesus functions as the main character and, consequently, within which the christological meaning of Matthew's Gospel is to be sought. To return to the grammatical analogy, meaning will emerge not simply from a mass of individual christological statements — the narrative equivalent of a collection of individual words — but, rather, from a single narrative "sentence." Just as the meaning of individual words is determined by their function in the structure of the sentence as a whole, so the meaning of individual christological statements will be determined by their place in the structure of the story as a whole. Matthew's christology is to be sought, first of all, in the plot of the story he has to tell.

This is not the place to attempt a full analysis of Matthew on the basis of Greimas's structure. But the structure itself suggests ways of getting quickly to the heart of the matter. Essential to the plot of any story is the change in circumstances effected by the events that link the Initial Sequence and the Final Sequence. And the crucial element in this process of change is the agency of the protagonist, which comes clearly into view in the Contract unit of the Topical Sequence — that element of a narrative in which the protagonist (1) is presented with a mandate having to do with the need or lack that was identified in the Initial Sequence, (2) accepts the mandate, and (3) receives resources of one kind or another (knowledge, power, helpers, devices) that will aid in the fulfilling of the mandate.

In Matthew, the first event in which Jesus appears as an active character is the baptism (3:13-17). Immediately after the temptation (4:1-11) Jesus departs for Galilee, where he begins his ministry of proclaiming the kingdom of heaven (4:17), gathering disciples (4:18-22), healing (4:23-25), and teaching (5:1). This leads us to expect that the Contract unit will be found in the linked events of baptism and temptation (3:13–4:11).

The Baptism of Jesus

By the time we reach the account of Jesus' baptism, we as readers have been given several indications of Jesus' mandate. The most explicit mandating statement comes in the angel's words to Joseph: "You are to name him Jesus, for he will save his people from their sins" (1:21). Less directly, the mandate of the Messiah is given in 2:6: "From you [Bethlehem] shall come a ruler who is to shepherd my people Israel." This statement is made by the religious leaders, already tainted by their association with Herod, which might lead us to see the statement as unreliable. But it is a quotation of Scripture. And, as quickly becomes apparent, it is correct in its identification of Bethlehem as the birthplace of the Messiah (Jesus has already been identified as such in 1:1, 18). Thus, it too can be taken as a reliable statement of the mandate that Jesus is called to fulfill.

From this we can discern the lack or need that Jesus as the main character is to address. It has to do with Israel and its need of a leader (Messiah, Shepherd) to deliver the nation from the consequences of its sin. This is, indeed, hinted at already in the genealogy with which the narrative begins (1:1-17). For in that genealogy the exile — which stands as the primary historical consequence of Israel's sin — marks the beginning of the period of Israel's history that culminates in the arrival of the Messiah (1:11-12, 17).

It is in his baptism that Jesus accepts this mandate and makes it his own. John the Baptist has been presented as the one whose ministry addresses Israel's situation of need. He is Isaiah's voice in the wilderness, calling on exiled Israel to prepare for the Lord's arrival (3:3; cf. Isa 40:3). He announces the nearness of God's reign (3:2) and the coming of "one who is more powerful than" he (3:11). In coming for baptism, then, and even insisting, over John's objections, that baptism is necessary "to fulfill all righteousness" (3:15), Jesus identifies himself with John's program — thereby accepting the mandate that has already been laid out for him.

Jesus' action is met with a heavenly response in (1) the descent of the Holy Spirit, who was already active in his birth (1:18, 20), was central to John's description of Jesus' promised ministry (3:11), and is later identified as an essential "helper" in his ministry (12:28), and (2) a voice from heaven, which commends him in the words: "This is my Son, the Beloved, with whom I am well pleased" (3:17). This is the second time in the narrative that Jesus has been identified as God's Son, the first being the quotation from Hos 11:1 in 2:15 ("Out of Egypt I have called my son"), a passage to which we will return later.

The Temptation of Jesus

The voice from heaven not only commended Jesus but also provided him with essential information about his mandate and the way in which it was to be carried out. In order to see this clearly, however, we need to move on in our reading to the subsequent event — that is, to Matthew's account of the temptation of Jesus in 4:1-11, in which Jesus' calling as God's Son is put to the test.

The tempter's role is complex. For one thing, even though the devil is clearly an adversary, Jesus' encounter with him is brought about by the Spirit, who leads Jesus "into the wilderness to be tempted" (4:1). The encounter with the devil, therefore, is somehow essential to the story. Furthermore, complexity is found in the nature of the temptations themselves. Satan's point of entry is with Jesus' identity as the "Son of God." The tempter does not call this identity into question. Rather, the three testings operate on the assumption that if one is the Son of God, certain things follow just as others are excluded. Specifically, the tempter's assumption is that to be the Son of God is to be a person of power (changing stones into bread), privilege (the recipient of divine protection), and sovereignty (the ruler of all the kingdoms of the world).

What makes the tempter's role complex is that, on the basis of the way Jesus has been presented to this point in the narrative, this assumption seems to be justified. Jesus has been clearly identified as Israel's king (1:1, 17, 18; 2:2, 4), as "son of David" (1:1), "the child who has been born king of the Jews" (2:2), the ruler/shepherd of God's people Israel (2:5-6). All these attributions culminate in the words spoken from heaven at the baptism, "This is my Son," which probably echo Ps 2:7 ("You are my son; today I have begotten you"), in which Israel's king, enthroned on Zion, is addressed by God as "my son" (see Davies and Allison, *Matthew*, 1.336-39). While the echo is not as strong as it is in Mark, where the second person singular is retained ("You are my son"), it is no doubt present in Matthew as well (cf. 2 Sam 7:14, where "son" is also used to refer to Davidic royalty; see also Ps 89:26-27).

In various reliable ways, then, readers have been led to see Jesus as Israel's anointed king — and therefore, it would seem to follow, as a person endowed by God with power, protection, and sovereignty. In other words, readers have been given good reasons to believe that the tempter's premises are correct. Why, then, does Jesus reject the tempter's suggestions? The third temptation might suggest that worship of Satan is the sole reason. But that is only part of it. For to this point in the story there has been a second definition of sonship at work, one that comes clearly into view in the way Jesus responds to the tempter. The important thing to note about Jesus' response is not simply that he rejects the tempter's overtures, but that he does so on the basis of an alternative definition of what it means to be God's Son. Jesus responds to each temptation by quoting Scripture. The choice of texts that Jesus quotes, Deut 8:3; 6:16; 6:13, is anything but random. All three come from a single extended passage, a section of Deuteronomy (chs. 6–8) in which Moses, addressing the people of Israel as they are about to enter the land, surveys the years in the wilderness and identifies the lessons they should have learned.

The central lesson the people should have learned is succinctly stated in Deut 8:2: "And you shall remember all the way which the Lord your God has led you these forty years in the wilderness, that he might humble you, testing you to know what was in your heart, whether you would keep his commandments or not." The texts quoted by Jesus refer to three of the "tests" by which God sought to determine what was in Israel's heart: (1) the provision of manna (Deut 8:3; Exod 16), (2) water from the rock at Massah (Deut 6:16; Exod 17), and, more generally, (3) deliverance from Egypt (Deut 6:13) — with, perhaps, an allusion to the incident in which Israel did indeed "forget the Lord who brought [them] out of the land of Egypt" (Deut 6:12) by worshiping a golden calf that they identified as the god "who brought [them] up out of the land of Egypt" (Exod 32:4). The parallels are readily apparent. For just as Israel was tested (LXX *ekpeirazō*) forty years in the wilderness *(en tē erēmō)*, having been led *(agō)* there by God, so Jesus was tested *(peirazō)* forty days and nights in the wilderness *(en tē erēmō)*, having been led *(anagō)* there by the Spirit. But so too are the contrasts. For where Israel failed the tests — complaining about hunger, demanding drink, and forgetting God — Jesus remains faithful.

The Story of Jesus and the Story of Israel

This is not the first time, of course, that readers of Matthew have encountered a parallel between the story of Jesus and the story of Israel. Matthew has already drawn our attention to the fact that, like Israel, Jesus has been "called out of Egypt" (2:15, citing Hos 11:1). Here, too, the parallel is contrastive, at least implicitly. The text from Hosea is found in a context whose theme has to do with Israel's waywardness and disobedience: "When Israel was a child, I loved him, and out of Egypt I called my son. The more I called them, the more they went from me; they kept sacrificing to the Baals, and offering incense to idols" (Hos 11:1-2). Matthew, therefore, presents Jesus as one who in his experience recapitulates the story of Israel. Like Israel of old, Jesus has been called by God out of Egypt to a life of humble obedience; like Israel, this calling was put to the test in the wilderness. The hope of the story is that, unlike Israel, Jesus will remain faithful where Israel was disobedient.

The most important part of the parallel, however, is that both Jesus and Israel are called God's son: "Out of Egypt I have called my son." Hos 11:1 is not unique in this regard. "Son" is used more often in Israel's biblical tradition of the nation itself (Exod 4:22-23; Jer 31:20; also Sir 36:17; Wis 18:13) than of the nation's king. In fact, the term is present in the context of Jesus' quotations from Deuteronomy, at least in the form of a simile. For in speaking of Israel's experience in the wilderness, Moses says: "Know then in your heart that as a father disciplines a son so the Lord your God disciplines you" (Deut 8:5).

What is going on in the temptation narrative, therefore, is a conflict between two contrasting definitions of what it means to be God's Son, both rooted in Israel's Scriptures. The tempter understands the title in terms of royal sovereignty. So Jesus as God's Son is one who should avoid suffering by using his filial power, depend on divine protection, and claim universal sovereignty. Jesus, on the other, understands the term against the background of Israel's calling. Thus as God's Son, he is called to a life of humble obedience — even if it should lead, as indeed turns out to be the case, to suffering and death.

The Source of Jesus' Understanding of Sonship

But what was the source of Jesus' understanding of sonship? Perhaps we as readers are to take this as something that he innately possessed, something that he came to understand prior to his first appearance as an active, adult character in the story. More plausible, however, is the possibility that this understanding was rooted in the voice from heaven at his baptism. For if the tempter's definition goes back to the royal overtones present in the first half of the declaration from heaven, "This is my son," Jesus' understanding may be seen to have come about — or, at least, to have been confirmed — in the second half of that declaration, "The beloved, with whom I am well pleased."

In the context of Matthew's Gospel, these words clearly echo Isa 42:1. Admittedly, Matthew's phraseology corresponds neither to the Hebrew text ("Here is my servant, whom I uphold, my chosen, in whom my soul delights") nor to the Septuagint ("Jacob is my servant, I will come to his aid; Israel is my chosen, my soul has welcomed him"). But in Matt 12:18-21 where we find a more substantial quotation of Isa 42:1-4, we encounter the same phrase as is spoken by the heavenly voice at the baptism: "Here is my servant, whom I have chosen, *my beloved, with whom my soul is well pleased*" (Matt 12:18). For our present purpose, it does not matter whether Matthew was simply paraphrasing the Septuagint or quoting a Greek version that is unknown to us. The important point is that, for Matthew at least, the second part of the words spoken from heaven at Jesus' baptism alludes to the figure of Isaiah's Servant.

At least by the time they reach ch. 12, Matthew's readers are fully aware of the close correspondences between the Isaian Servant, the nation Israel, and Jesus. What is significant here is not the term "servant," absent in 3:17, but the close connection in Isaiah between the Servant and Israel. The servant is explicitly identified on several occasions with the nation — for example, "But you, Israel my servant, Jacob, whom I have chosen" (41:8; also LXX 42:1; 44:1-2, 21; 45:4; 48:20; 49:3). The second half of the declaration from heaven at Jesus' baptism, then, alludes to the figure of Israel, called to be God's faithful obedient servant. This is the immediate background for Jesus' interpretation of sonship in terms of humble obedience, and therefore for his response to the tempter.

Two Models of Sonship in Tension

The episodes of the baptism and the temptation are linked together by a dual interpretation of Jesus' mandate focused on his identity as God's Son. Sonship can be understood in royal terms: God's Son as the Davidic "king of the Jews," who will "shepherd [God's] people Israel." And it can be understood in terms of the humble, obedient, servant role that was to characterize Israel. In the baptism narrative, specifically in the words of the divine voice, these two aspects are combined and assimilated, implying that they somehow belong together. In the temptation narrative, however, they are put into tension. The tempter plays one off against the other, urging Jesus to act in a manner consistent with royal sonship — in effect, pressing him to choose between the two.

Admittedly, in the third temptation the choice is presented somewhat differently, as a choice between worship of God and worship of Satan. But in the terms of the temptation narrative, perhaps it amounts to the same thing. To choose an aspect of royal sonship — in this case, sovereignty — over humble reliance on God is, in essence, to cease to worship God and to give one's allegiance to God's demonic rival. In any case, faced with such a choice, Jesus chooses the path of humble, obedient sonship.

Returning to Greimas's structural analysis, the baptism and temptation accounts function as the Contract element in the story — that is, the section of the story in which Jesus as the main character accepts the mandate and receives certain resources that will enable him to carry out his task successfully. The most important resource is in the form of knowledge about his mandate as God's Son. Specifically, the received knowledge is that his calling to be Israel's savior and king is to be accomplished in a manner consistent with Israel's calling to be the humble, obedient servant of God. This knowledge is communicated to Jesus by means of the heavenly voice, with its twofold scriptural allusion. And it is clarified for him by the approach of the tempter, who attempts to deflect him from the path of humble obedience by holding out to him the model of royal sovereignty.

The clarification of Jesus' mandate in Matt 3:1–4:11 also serves to set up the "topic" of the story — that is, the complex set of constraints, intentions, actions, and effects that make up the stuff of the story itself. Stated simply, this has to do with a tension between mandate and means, between two models of sonship and how they relate. The tempter assumes that the two are incompatible. He assumes that if Jesus were to fulfill his mandate as Israel's king, he would need to use the resources at his disposal to avoid suffering and claim sovereignty. And this assumption is shared by other characters at subsequent points in the story — for example, by Peter, who refuses to see suffering as compatible with his recognition of Jesus as "Son of the living God" (16:16, 21-23), and by the mockers at the cross, who assume that sonship and crucifixion are mutually exclusive (27:37-44; see my "The Mockers and the Son of God").

Because of this assumption, these characters perceive an irresolvable tension between mandate and means. For if Jesus continues on a path of humble obedience, which would lead inevitably to suffering and death, how will he be able to fulfill his mandate to be the savior and shepherd of God's people Israel? From this perspective, the mandate seems to contain an inner contradiction. Indeed, it seems that if Jesus were to remain faithful to his calling as Son in the sense that Israel was called to fulfill, it would be impossible for him to fulfill his role as Son in the royal and messianic sense. Dead kings are no help at all.

For readers of Matthew's Gospel, of course, the tension between mandate and means is resolved long before the end of the story. No sooner does it become clear that Jesus' path of humble obedience will lead to the cross (16:21) than readers are informed that he will "be raised on the third day." From this point on, the reader's experience is more one of irony than of suspense. Assured of Jesus' ultimate vindication — that is, that the seemingly contradictory dimensions of Jesus' mandate and means belong inextricably together — readers of Matthew's Gospel can appreciate the irony when the mockers at the cross urge Jesus to demonstrate his divine sonship by coming down from the cross, as well as the full truth of the centurion's reaction to Jesus' death, "Truly this man was God's son" (27:54).

At the end of the story the tension is fully resolved. Jesus' apparent defeat turns out to be his victory. Precisely because he followed the path of humble obedience to the end, refusing to use the power at his disposal to extricate himself from the consequences of his obedience (e.g., 26:53-54), Jesus is vindicated in resurrection and endowed with "all authority in heaven and on earth" (28:18). Sovereignty is won through suffering. It is precisely his faithfulness as the humble, obedient Son that makes possible, in the divine scheme of things, his exaltation as the royal, sovereign Son. And as Son, who shares a name with the Father and the Holy Spirit, he is the teacher and baptismal means of identity for a new people drawn not only from Israel but from all nations (28:19-20).

5. Conclusion: From Story to Christology

My contention is that the christology of Matthew's Gospel — or, for that matter, of any of the canonical Gospels — is to be sought not simply in the individual titles or other christological descriptions predicated of Jesus, but in Jesus' role as a character in the story told in the Gospel as a whole. Of course, what I have sketched above is by no means a full description of Matthew's story. A fuller description would require us to take into account, as well, a number of other important elements, such as (1) the shifts in the composition of Jesus' "people" (1:21) from "[God's] people Israel" (2:6), to "the lost sheep of the house of Israel" (10:6; 15:24), to, finally, a band of disciples drawn from all nations (28:19); (2) the significance and role of the disciples, who are a focus of Jesus' activity from the beginning (4:18-22) to the end (28:16-20; see my "Guiding Readers — Making Disciples"); (3) the role of the religious leaders; (4) the ultimate allegiance of the crowds; (5) the mixed character of the church (e.g., 7:15-23; 13:47-50; 22:11-14); and (6) the nature of Jesus' teaching and its relation to Israel's Law.

Still, an understanding of the underlying structure of a story as articulated by Greimas and others allows us to identify those elements of the evangelist's story in which the shape of the story's plot comes most clearly into focus. Of particular importance is the Contract element, where the mandate is clarified and accepted, certain resources are communicated, and the shape of the story's "topic" begins to come into view. In Matthew's Gospel, this element is to be found in the baptism and temptation narratives. From this vantage point we are able to identify the central thread of Matthew's plot as having to do with the vindication of the humble, obedient Son of God. And it is in this plot, as it is worked out in the narrative as a whole, that we find Matthew's answer to the question, Who is Jesus and how is he significant?

SELECTED BIBLIOGRAPHY

Carter, Warren. *Matthew: Storyteller, Interpreter, Evangelist.* Peabody: Hendrickson, 1996.

Culpepper, R. Alan. *Anatomy of the Fourth Gospel: A Study in Literary Design.* Philadelphia: Fortress, 1983.

Davies, W. D., and Dale C. Allison. *A Critical and Exegetical Commentary on the Gospel According to St. Matthew,* International Critical Commentary, 3 vols. Edinburgh: Clark, 1988, 1991, 1997.

Donaldson, Terence L. "Guiding Readers — Making Disciples: Discipleship in Matthew's Narrative Strategy," in *Patterns of Discipleship in the New Testament,* McMaster New Testament Studies 1, ed. R. N. Longenecker. Grand Rapids: Eerdmans, 1996, 30-49.

———. "The Mockers and the Son of God (Matthew 27.37-44): Two Characters in Matthew's Story of Jesus," *JSNT* 41 (1991) 3-18.

Frei, Hans W. "Theological Reflections on the Accounts of Jesus' Death and Resurrection," in Hans W. Frei, *Theology and Narrative: Selected Essays,* ed. G. Hunsinger and W. C. Placher. Oxford: Oxford University Press, 1993, 45-93.

Hays, Richard B. *The Faith of Jesus Christ: An Investigation of the Narrative Substructure of Galatians 3:1–4:11,* Society of Biblical Literature Dissertation Series 56. Chico: Scholars, 1983.

Howell, David B. *Matthew's Inclusive Story: A Study in the Narrative Rhetoric of the First Gospel, JSNT* Supplement 42. Sheffield: Sheffield Academic Press, 1990.

Kingsbury, Jack Dean. *Matthew: Structure, Christology, Kingdom.* Philadelphia: Fortress, 1975.

———. *Jesus Christ in Matthew, Mark and Luke.* Philadelphia: Fortress, 1981.

———. *Matthew as Story,* 2nd ed. Philadelphia: Fortress, 1988.

Matera, Frank J. *New Testament Christology.* Louisville: Westminster/John Knox, 1999.

———. "The Plot of Matthew's Gospel," *CBQ* 49 (1987) 233-53.

Patte, Daniel. *What Is Structural Exegesis?* Philadelphia: Fortress, 1976.

Powell, Mark Allan, *What Is Narrative Criticism?* Minneapolis: Fortress, 1990.

———. "The Plot and Subplots of Matthew's Gospel," *NTS* 38 (1992) 187-204.

CHAPTER 6

The Christology of Luke's Gospel and Acts

I. Howard Marshall

Luke-Acts is the longest contribution by a single writer to the New Testament. It presents the story of what Jesus did and taught — first in his earthly life (the Gospel) and then as the exalted Christ and Lord through his followers (Acts). Our aim in this chapter will be to trace the development of the presentation of Jesus in Luke's two-volume narrative, seeking thereby to comprehend the total picture of who Jesus is that emerges from it.

A number of difficulties arise in attempting to distill theology from a narrative rather than a doctrinal epistle. Moreover, Luke purports to describe the beliefs of various early Christians rather than to develop his own views. It is always a question, therefore, whether Luke has incorporated different, possibly even differing, views within his work or has used the narrative to present his own unified understanding.

We are, of course, confronted with serious space constraints in a single chapter. So while christology proper is closely related to other issues — in particular, to soteriology and pneumatology — and while the history of ideas expressed by Luke in his two volumes is always of great significance, the task of delineating Luke's understanding of Christ will be a full enough agenda for us here. Modern discussions of these matters are seemingly endless, and they cannot be adequately assessed in a short article (cf. Buckwalter, *Character and Purpose of Luke's Christology*, 3-31, for an informed survey of such matters).

1. The Story of Jesus — Part I: Luke's Gospel

The Prologue

Like Matthew, Luke begins his Gospel in chs. 1–2 with an account of the annunciation of the birth of Jesus and the birth itself. The context is one of longing for the intervention of God in the life of Israel to bring back his people to himself and to liberate them from their current plight. The longing is met by the birth of two divine agents: John the Baptist and Jesus of Nazareth.

John the Baptist will prepare the people for the coming of "the Lord" (1:76) — though the question immediately arises, Is this "Lord" God or Jesus? Jesus will be called the Son of the Most High and will be a ruler in the line of David over the house of Jacob forever. His birth will be due to the coming of the Holy Spirit upon the virgin Mary. When he is born he is said by the angels to be "a Savior . . . Christ the Lord." His appearance is the sign that God's salvation is now visible. In the temple incident his consciousness of God as his Father is clearly depicted.

The main christological themes that appear in this introduction are centered on the concept of "the Lord's Christ." By this expression is meant the coming ruler of God's people, who will function as their Savior or deliverer in a comprehensive sense, whose status vis-à-vis human beings is that of a Lord, and who stands in a unique relationship to God expressed in terms of sonship.

The question of whether Jesus was a divine being who existed alongside God before he "came" into the world does not arise explicitly here or anywhere else in Luke-Acts. There is no *logos* language, no "sending" of the Son, no such statement as "Before Abraham was, I am." God's plan is foretold in Scripture, but there is no explicit pushing it back to the borders of time past. This silence, however, need not mean that Luke's understanding is incompatible with the concept of preexistence. For while the virgin birth of Jesus could presumably be understood as the "creation" of God's Son at that point in time, the Son of Man in some texts of Luke's Gospel, as Crispin Fletcher-Louis has aptly argued, suggests a preexistent figure (see his *Luke-Acts*, 225-50). Luke's outlook, it seems, is comparable to that of Paul, who could affirm both the birth of Jesus of a woman (Gal 4:4) and his preexistence (1 Cor 8:6; 2 Cor 8:9; Phil 2:6-8).

All this may be regarded as a prologue or overture that prepares the readers of the story for what is to follow. Letting the audience into the secret of what was to follow was an established practice in the classical Greek theater. As in the other canonical Gospels, the audience is told who Jesus "really is" and what he will "really do" in advance of the story, so that they have the necessary inside information to understand what is going on. The various adult characters in the birth stories play no further significant role in the story. And Mary is explicitly said to have "treasured all these things in her heart" (2:51), with the implication that she did not share them with other people. It can be assumed, therefore, that the people who appear in the subsequent narrative are unaware of what happened at the birth of Jesus.

The Beginning of the Mission

The story proper begins with the preaching and baptizing activity of John. The people wondered whether John was "the Christ," which is the common Greek equivalent of the Hebrew/Aramaic term "Messiah" used throughout the New Testament. Is he the prophesied deliverer? John denies this and foretells the coming of the Stronger One who will baptize with the Holy Spirit and fire, whereas he himself baptizes (only) with water.

Then Jesus comes, is baptized, and prays, and the Holy Spirit descends on him. He is addressed by God as his "Son" and implicitly identified as God's "Servant," with whom he is well-pleased (3:22; an echo of Isa 42:1). Again, however, this is apparently a private experience. By people at large, Jesus continues to be thought of as the son of Joseph (4:22), although the readers learn that it is through Joseph as his stepfather that he is also descended from David (3:23-31).

Yet another private experience follows in which Jesus, described by Luke as full of the Holy Spirit and therefore divinely equipped for spiritual conflict, faces the devil, who encourages him to do various things in his capacity as the Son of God. The devil's aim is evidently to persuade Jesus to disobey, dishonor, and distrust God — and it is important to recognize that this must be what the spiritual conflict is all about. The calling of Jesus is to proclaim the kingship or rule of God (4:43) and to deliver people who were captives under the rule of Satan (13:16). There is, accordingly, an apocalyptic framework to the Gospel: the world is the arena of a conflict between the forces of evil led by the devil, who enslaves people and oppresses them, and the Christ, who has come to set people free from bondage to the devil and the suffering that he causes and to enable them to serve God and enjoy his goodness.

So at last the mission gets under way with Jesus, empowered by the Spirit, proclaiming his appointment by God as a prophet to announce good news to the poor. Clearly, however, this prophet is more than simply a commentator on what God is about to do. He himself is the agent through whom God is going to act. The prophetic element in his role is strongly emphasized in Luke — not least through implicit comparisons with Moses, as well as with Elijah and Elisha, which Luke achieves by his narrative technique.

At the same time, Luke relates how the people who were possessed by demons recognized Jesus as "the Son of God" or "the Christ" (4:41). These two terms may appear to be used synonymously, and hence interchangeably. But it is more accurate to see them as mutually complementary (cf. Radl, *Das Lukas-Evangelium*, 87).

Major Motifs of the Narrative: Advance of the Kingdom and Identity of the Christ

The ensuing narrative combines two major motifs. The first has to do with the advance of the kingdom of God. For just as a conqueror invades a territory, proclaims himself as king to the existing inhabitants, and demands that they now serve him — emphasizing that he is the ruler by various shows of strength, including the defeat of any rebels who oppose him — so Jesus proclaims the arrival of God's rule in what was Satan's territory, sets free Satan's captives, and attacks Satan's allies. The invasion is not of what we might call "new territory." Rather, it effects the deliverance of those who were by virtue of their physical descent God's people, but had succumbed to an alien power. And the enemy's conquest was fundamentally a spiritual matter in that it was the hearts and wills of the people that had been invaded by evil.

Despite the difficulties of drawing precise analogies, the basic comparison stands and expresses a major motif in the story. Its significance for our present purpose is that Jesus is depicted as acting as "the Christ." Admittedly, his activity was not altogether what might have been expected. The people probably anticipated something more like political and military action than preaching and healing — especially by a person who looked more like a prophet or a holy man than a powerful ruler.

Hence we can detect a second motif in the story. This is concerned with the people trying to identify who Jesus is. His claim at Nazareth to be the fulfillment of Isa 61:1-2 was met with some skepticism. The demoniacs might hail him as the Son of God, but they would have been dismissed as deranged. So the question for the people is whether Jesus is "the Christ" or "the Son of God," or whatever, or simply a false claimant to such a role.

The narrative presents a mix of some people who recognized that he was an agent of God with unusual powers and others who were skeptical and opposed him, because it was obviously a wicked thing to claim to be a special agent of God when this was not the case. The identity question plays a significant role in the story at least as far as Luke 9 (see v. 18), and then it reappears in chs. 20 and 22.

Throughout the narrative Jesus says and does things that demonstrate a claim to authority. He refers to himself as "the Son of Man" (5:24; 6:22; *passim*). It is not clear what significance Luke attached to this phrase, which occurs only on the lips of Jesus and is not used by the narrator in telling the story. What did the evangelist expect his readers to understand regarding the significance of this term as those present heard it? Was it simply a circumlocution for "I"? Or was it a kind of title (e.g., "the Man"), presumably drawn from the Old Testament, that Jesus used to refer to himself? Most likely it indicates a person equipped with authority, who was bestowed by God and destined to a special future role as God's agent. But Jesus was rejected by his opponents presumably because they denied that he was such a person.

Unlike the other evangelists, Luke refers to Jesus as "the Lord" when describing the powerful things he did (7:13) and his authoritative teaching (10:39, 41). The same term is used in the vocative by people who address Jesus (5:8, 12; 7:6). As an address, it need not be seen as anything more than an ordinary title of respect. Luke, however, may have meant to imply that some people actually recognized the status of Jesus as God's supreme agent — or that they used a term in addressing Jesus that had deeper implications than they were aware of (cf. Tuckett, "Christology of Luke-Acts," 141-42). Certainly some people must have thought that Jesus was a great prophet (7:16), though others doubted that this was so (7:39).

When John in prison expresses doubt whether Jesus is the Coming One, Jesus sends back a reply in which he asserts that the conditions of the messianic age foretold in Isaiah 35 are being fulfilled — and he invites John to draw the appropriate conclusion (7:21-23). The point would have come home all the more strongly to the close companions of Jesus who found that they shared his capacity to exorcise demons and cure diseases. By ch. 9 of Luke's Gospel, the stage has been set for Jesus to confront these followers and to elicit from Peter the recognition that he was "the Christ of God" (v. 20b).

The "Taking Up" of the Christ

It is with Jesus' response to Peter's confession that a new element enters the story. For in the passion prediction of 9:22-27 Jesus begins for the first time to speak openly about the fact that the Son of Man will have to suffer, be put to death, and be raised from the dead. His words are then underlined for his closest companions by the event that we call the Transfiguration, in which (1) Jesus appeared to shine with heavenly glory and was surrounded by heavenly companions, (2) he and they talked about his "exodus" or departure, and (3) a heavenly voice confirmed to them that Jesus is God's Son.

This experience had the effect of taking away a veil so that the disciples saw, as it were, heaven brought down to earth — or, at least, brought down to a mountain top — and had a temporary vision of what goes on there. It was a vision comparable to Paul's visionary experience of being lifted up to heaven (cf. 2 Cor 12:1-4) or, perhaps closer to reported deathbed experiences of Christians, to Stephen's vision as he was dying of Jesus as the Son of Man in heaven. The effect was to confirm Jesus' prophecy and to stress that this would happen to him, even though he is the Son of God. Perhaps there is also in Luke's portrayal — as compared with Mark's, who might be said to have stressed the suffering of Jesus and God's undoing of it in his resurrection — a more nuanced view of what would lie ahead at the transition of Jesus from his earthly existence to his heavenly glory, though Luke also emphasizes that it was as "the Christ" that Jesus suffered (see Green, *Theology of the Gospel of Luke*, 64-65).

The Travel Narrative

We are still some distance away from the fulfillment of Jesus' prophecy and its confirmation. But from this point on, the travels of the wandering prophet have his *analēmpsis* ("taking up," 9:51) at Jerusalem as their goal — although, it seems, Luke had something of a struggle to impose this theme on all of the events depicted. There is little that is christologically new in this travel narrative. It is more concerned with the teaching of Jesus to his companions and the growth of opposition to him by those who rejected him.

Yet a number of features appear in this section that are also significant elsewhere in Luke's Gospel. One is the way in which the activity of Jesus is done by the power of the Holy Spirit (or, in 11:20, "by the finger of God"). We might have thought that Jesus had the power and authority in himself as "the Christ" and "the Son of God." But Luke stresses that he was empowered by the Spirit (cf. Acts 10:38). Luke sees no tension between the high status of Jesus and his reliance on the Spirit.

A second feature is that Jesus is depicted as being in close relationship with God through prayer (e.g., 11:1), and it is when he prays that God speaks to him by a heavenly voice (cf. 3:21-22; 9:28-35). Yet this experience is not peculiar to Jesus, for in his prayers he is depicted as a model to the disciples. There may be other "ecstatic" experiences recorded in this section of the story. Opinions differ as to whether the sight of Satan falling from heaven is a report of a visionary experience or simply a metaphorical statement about the significance of the exorcisms performed by the disciples (10:18). The significance of Jesus at prayer, however, should not be underrated. For a *praying* Christ is unprecedented (see Crump, *Jesus the Intercessor,* 235).

A third emphasis in this section of the story has to do with the closeness of the relationship of Jesus to his Father. This is adumbrated in 2:49, but comes to full expression in 10:21-22. In Luke's Gospel the term "Father" does not appear as frequently on Jesus' lips as it does in Matthew's Gospel. But the motif in Luke is just as strong. And along with intimacy a fourth point is to be noted: that of subordination. For Jesus does what God's will lays down for him and is obedient. He is present on earth as a servant (cf. Radl, *Das Lukas-Evangelium,* 84).

Luke tells us at the close of this section that "the people thought that the kingdom was going to appear at once" when Jesus reached Jerusalem

(19:11). This was, undoubtedly, a natural expectation, particularly after the gradual spread of the kingdom earlier in the Gospel. There has to come a time when skirmishes are past and the final, big thrust takes place. The ensuing parable of the ten minas (19:12-27) is to be interpreted in this context as signifying that Jesus will go back to God to be appointed as king and then return in that capacity and set up his rule — which, of course, raises the question whether Jesus is an inactive "absentee" during Part II of the story.

Death and Resurrection

The final section of Luke's Gospel relates the story of the death and resurrection of Jesus. The death takes place by divine destiny and in accordance with Scripture, which is seen as foretelling this fate for the Christ. Jesus is depicted in 22:43-44 — if, indeed, the text is authentic — as needing to be strengthened by an angel for his coming ordeal. This could tie in with the motif of angelic help elsewhere in the Gospels (cf. Matt 26:53; Mark 1:13). At the same time, it is as the Christ that he is crucified (23:35). And even in the hour of death there is one participant who believes that he will still have kingly power (the attribution of a future kingdom to Jesus is not affected by the uncertainty regarding the text of 23:42).

Luke uses the accounts of the resurrection appearances in ch. 24 to indicate how the resurrection confirmed the disappointed expectations of the disciples of Jesus. The travelers going to Emmaus, for example, knew that Jesus was a mighty prophet. They had hoped that he was the one to redeem Israel — that is, the Christ. But they were puzzled by it being the third day, since evidently something was expected to happen by then. All that had happened was that Jesus' body had disappeared and nobody had actually seen him alive. Jesus' response is to point to the divinely ordained way for the Christ, who must suffer before entering "his glory." He also sees the Scriptures as prophesying the preaching of repentance and forgiveness that will follow the empowerment of the disciples as his witnesses.

Luke's Gospel concludes in 24:50-53 with Jesus being taken up into heaven. This is not reported in the other Gospels, but the *theologoumenon* that the Christ is exalted to sit at the right hand of God is present (cf. Matt 28:18; John 20:17).

2. The Story of Jesus — Part II: Luke's Acts

The second part of the story in Acts can be understood, in large part, as an account of the developing understanding and proclamation of Jesus. Such an understanding and proclamation takes place mainly in the first half of the book and through the medium of speeches that have common themes (Bock, *Proclamation*).

Resurrection, Exaltation, and Witness

Acts begins with the question of the disciples about the restoration of the kingdom to Israel (1:6). Jesus' reply, in effect, sets this event in the future, as Peter clearly recognizes in 3:21, and establishes the task of the disciples in the intervening period as witness to Jesus in the power of the Holy Spirit. During this period Jesus is "physically" absent and is with God the Father.

A major part of the story in Acts is concerned with the witness of the apostles, together with Paul, to Jesus. More than once Luke sums up this activity in some such manner as: "he reasoned with them from the Scriptures, explaining and proving that the Christ had to suffer and rise from the dead. 'This Jesus I am proclaiming to you is the Christ,' he said" (17:3; cf. also 17:11; 18:5). The various missionary speeches in Acts follow this broad structure, which involved constructing a picture of the Christ from the Scriptures and then arguing that this picture fitted Jesus — and Jesus only. And this is the same line of argument as can be found in Jesus' responses of Luke 24:25-26, 44-45.

Within this context, the life of Jesus is understood as one of telling the good news of peace, doing good, and healing those oppressed by the devil in the power of the Spirit, as in Peter's preaching at Cornelius's home in 10:36-38. This is a perfectly adequate summary of the mission of Jesus as described in the Gospel, though perhaps deliberately tweaked to be meaningful to Gentiles. The kingdom of God is not specifically mentioned. Rather, the message of Jesus is concerned with peace. Yet the connection between God's rule and peace is obvious enough (cf. Luke 1:79; 2:14; 7:50; 10:5-6), and elsewhere in Acts the content of the preaching is the kingdom (8:12; 19:8; 20:25; 28:23, 31). It follows that the Gospel can be seen as the flesh with which these rather bare bones of the summary statements in 10:36-38 would be clothed.

It is important to recognize, however, that what is going on in Paul's Gentile ministry, as portrayed in Luke's Acts, is something of a redefining of Jewish ideas of "Christship" in the light of the Scriptures, which were understood by Christians as messianic. One can persuade people that Jesus is the Christ only if the nature of Christship is redefined in such a way that Jesus fits the picture. Christopher Tuckett objects that such a redefinition would make dialogue with non-Christian Jews virtually impossible ("Christology of Luke-Acts," 163), but I find this objection unpersuasive.

Death and Resurrection

The main focus in Acts is on the death and resurrection of Jesus as the Christ. The death is depicted principally as the effect of the actions of wicked people who murdered Jesus — and yet, at the same time, as an event predetermined by God himself (2:23). What Luke does not bring out so clearly is what the purpose of God in this was. It is probably oversimplistic to say that God's ultimate purpose was the resurrection of Jesus and therefore that a prior death was necessary — with the implication that Jesus' death was nothing more than a stage on the way to his exaltation. Rather, putting Jesus to death can be seen (1) as an action that focuses the wickedness and disobedience of the Jewish leaders and those who supported their action, and so constituted the culmination of a long history of rebellion (cf. 7:52), but also (2) as an event in which Jesus quietly accepts his fate, and so conforms to the pattern of the Servant of Yahweh in Isa 53:7-8 (cf. Acts 8:32-35).

Luke also records the statement of Paul that God purchased the church with the blood of his Son (20:28). But the language found abundantly in Paul, John, Hebrews, and 1 Peter that speaks of Christ dying on behalf of us is conspicuously absent in Luke's writings (apart from Luke 22:19-20), despite its strong claims to being pre-Pauline. David Moessner, however, believes that Luke has picked up this theme of Jesus dying on behalf of the people, and that only through his death is forgiveness possible, in his use of Moses typology (*Lord of the Banquet,* 322-24).

By contrast, the central place is given in Acts to the resurrection of Jesus. In a way, this is hardly surprising. For in the context of the early days of the church that Luke is describing, there was probably little development of a theology of atonement. Rather, there was first a need to overcome the obvious stumbling-block of proclaiming a crucified Christ. Furthermore, there were the absolute uniqueness and sheer wonder of Jesus' resurrection — a stupendous event that, if it could be credibly attested, must have had enormous apologetic force.

The force of the early church's argument from Scripture, as portrayed in Acts, is to show that, although the crucifixion might seem to rule out the Messiahship of Jesus, the converse was true: (1) the crucifixion, in fact, formed part of a series of events that had been foretold or patterned in Scripture, and therefore fell within the deliberate purpose of God, and (2) it was followed by the resurrection and exaltation of Jesus, wherein God reversed what human beings had done to his Servant. As to the credibility of the resurrection itself, the proof offered lay in the personal experience of the witnesses who testified to it and laid claim to having experienced "many convincing proofs that he was alive" (1:3). Whereas the modern western world looks more for convincing arguments, the ancient world looked more for credible witnesses.

Resurrection, Exaltation, and Ascension

Luke is unique among the evangelists in describing an ascension of Jesus, a visible upward movement in which he was taken up into heaven and disappeared from human sight. With this event Luke is able to bring to an end the series of resurrection appearances of a Jesus who was physical as well as spiritual — although his physicality did not exclude his special appearance to Paul. More than that, he distinguishes the resurrection of Jesus from a mere resuscitation to a continuing (temporary) life in this world, by having him ascend to a continued existence in a different sphere. The picture can be thought of as simply that of a two-story universe. It is more accurate, however, to think of a spiritual sphere that is pictured as "above" the physical sphere, but is of a different kind.

This is not the place to discuss the relation of the ascension of Jesus to his resurrection on the third day. But it does need to be said that Luke's dominant vocabulary is that of resurrection and exaltation rather than ascension, and so we should not make the mistake of thinking that ascension is his major emphasis (see Anderson, "The Resurrection of Jesus in Luke-Acts"). On the other hand, the resurrection of Jesus is not to be dissociated from his exaltation. Kevin Anderson has shown how for Jews, the concept of resurrection, as opposed to mere resuscitation or reanimation, would automatically have been understood on the basis of Dan 12:3 in terms of exaltation to heaven and to a glorious position (Anderson). Those resurrected would become like the angels — though not necessarily identical with the angels (see Fletcher-Louis, *Luke-Acts*).

But the exaltation and glorification of Jesus is to the highest level, and so is more than angelic. This is confirmed by Peter's speech to those gathered at Jerusalem on the day of Pentecost (2:14-36). For in that "Pentecost sermon" Peter quotes Psalms 16 and 110, which refer to the resurrected Christ being "at the right hand of God" (vv. 25 and 34). It is further confirmed by the vision of Stephen, in which he sees the Son of Man standing at God's right hand (7:56). This solitary use of "Son of Man" in Acts provides a crucial link with Luke 22:69, and so makes it clear (as in Luke 22:69, unlike Matthew and Mark) that the "heavenly session" of Jesus is "from now on."

What springs a surprise on the readers in Acts 7:56, however, is that Jesus is depicted as *standing* rather than sitting. While sitting emphasizes a place of authority, standing indicates some kind of action. It is most probable that Jesus is standing as advocate to acknowledge his faithful witness (cf. Luke 12:8; see Crump, *Jesus the Intercessor,* 176-203), rather than to condemn Stephen's opponents or in anticipation of the *parousia.*

Implications of Jesus' Exaltation

The significance of the exaltation of Jesus is expressed in various ways. One important implication of his exaltation is that Jesus now has the authority to give the Spirit to others. In the context of Pentecost it is natural that Peter mentions first that Jesus received the Holy Spirit from the Father to pour out on the disciples (2:33). The parallel with the citation of Joel 2:28-32 (MT 3:1-5) in Acts 2:17 is significant. For whereas in Joel it is God himself who pours out the Spirit, in Acts the authority to pour out the Spirit has been handed over to, or is now shared with, Jesus — which is the fulfillment of the prophecy made by John the Baptist in Luke 3:16. Thus from the anointing of Jesus with the Spirit in the Gospel, Luke has moved in Acts to Jesus' new role as the dispenser of the Spirit to others, which is something that had not previously happened.

A distinction can be made between (1) Jesus acting by the power of the Spirit in teaching people, healing them, and exorcising evil spirits (e.g., 1:2; 10:38) and (2) Jesus conferring the power of the Spirit on people. This conferral of the Spirit on others has led Odette Mainville to speak of Jesus' "pneumatic messianism" ("Le Messianisme de Jésus," 318-20). But it should also be noted that in the remainder of Acts the Spirit is linked to Jesus only at 16:7 (possibly also at 5:9; 8:39). Otherwise, the Spirit is given only by God (cf. 5:32; 15:8). It is doubtful, therefore, that the messianism of Jesus is most aptly characterized by this one activity — that is, by his conferral of the Spirit on others.

A second implication of the exaltation of Jesus is that people may now be sure that God has made him both Lord and Christ (2:36). Jesus is exalted as a "Prince and Savior to give repentance and forgiveness of sins to Israel" (5:31). For Luke, it seems, the exaltation of Jesus in itself confers on him the authority to dispense salvation. Yet it is important to remember that already during his earthly mission Jesus had called Israel to repentance and conferred the forgiveness of sins. So these are not new powers. Rather than something new, the force of Peter's statement suggests that God has confirmed what Jesus was already authorized to do. And if there is a difference, it is perhaps that Jesus continues to have this power and that it is now available without his physical presence — with the apostles acting as his agents.

A third implication of his exaltation is that significance now attaches to "the name of Jesus." This phrase is remarkably frequent in Acts. It is used as an authorization formula when the apostles and others carry out healings (3:6) and exorcisms (16:18). In particular, forgiveness of sins is conferred "through his name" to people who believe in Jesus (10:43). And baptism is performed in his name (2:38).

Fourth, it is asserted that the exalted Jesus, who has departed to heaven, will return "in the same way you have seen him go into heaven" (1:11), that his return will be associated with the restoration of all things (3:21, which must include "the restoration of the kingdom to Israel," as asked in 1:6), and that he is appointed to be the judge of all people (10:42). Clearly, a visible return to earth by one who is now in heaven is in mind. The full establishment of the kingdom of God and the appearance of the Christ belong together.

3. The Status and Role of Jesus

What picture of Jesus emerges from all of this? In Acts 2:22 and 17:31 the identity of Jesus as a human being is assumed, if not actually stressed, by Christian speakers. The Jewish Sanhedrin in Acts 5:28 naturally refers to him in this way as well. The overwhelming emphasis in Luke's two volumes, however, is on Jesus' superior status and role, with that status and role frequently indicated by the terms and titles used of him. Despite the obvious limitations of creating a christology on the basis of a study of titles alone, we should not go to the opposite extreme and ignore them.

Major Terms and Titles

The terminology used in Luke's Gospel carries over into Acts. In the Gospel there was a notable use of prophetic categories to describe the activity of Jesus. This is picked up in Acts by seeing in Jesus the fulfillment of the raising up of a prophet like Moses (3:22-23; 7:37). The identification would seem to refer primarily to the earthly Jesus and his role as God's messenger. But it also surely implies that the teaching of Jesus continued to play a role in the early church, despite the conspicuous lack of citation of it in Acts. His teaching continues to be authoritative, and that same authority is now attached to the teaching of Jesus as mediated by his witnesses.

The title or name "Christ" occurs about twenty-five times in Acts (see Strauss, *The Davidic Messiah in Luke-Acts*). Sometimes it is used on its own and refers to the Davidic Messiah, who was expected by some Jews (cf. 2:31; 3:18; 4:26; 8:5; 26:23). Likewise in Acts the witnesses proclaim that "the Christ" is none other than Jesus (cf. 2:36; 5:42; 9:22; 17:3; 18:5, 28). The career of the Christ is understood from the Scriptures to include not only suffering but also resurrection (2:31; 26:23) and the proclamation of light (i.e., salvation) to both Jews and Gentiles (26:23).

Combinations involving Christ and other names or titles — especially "Jesus Christ" and "(our) Lord Jesus Christ" — are used to create compound phrases as names for Jesus. The effect is to express respect. Later manuscripts of Acts tended to elaborate this feature, but its origin goes back to the early church.

Sparsely Used Terms and Titles

The title "king" is used sparsely as an unpacking of "Christ" (cf. Luke 23:2), and appears to be used of Jesus' earthly as well as his exalted role. Other titles occur spasmodically, including "prince," "savior," and "the author of life." The term "servant" *(pais)* is used of Jesus in the speeches of Peter (Acts 3:13, 26; 4:27, 30). It is also used of David (Acts 4:25). Since the servant is God's servant, the description expresses not just subordination to God but also the honor of being appointed by God as his representative — as is reinforced by the adjective "holy" in Acts 4:27, 30.

"Son" or "Son of God" is rare in Acts, being found only twice. In 9:20 the first description of Paul's preaching is summed up in the statement "Jesus is the Son of God" — which is immediately followed by the further statement that Paul proved to the Jews that "Jesus is the Christ" (Acts 9:22). This collocation of titles, which is paralleled in Luke 4:41, strongly suggests that the significance of the two terms was very similar, though not identical. The other occurrence is in Acts 13:33, where the promise in Ps 2:7 is linked with the resurrection of Jesus — or, more probably, with the bringing of Jesus onto the stage of history, as in Acts 3:22.

The Title "Lord"

Whereas preaching to Jews throughout Acts is concerned with the identity of Jesus as the Christ, this is not so with the title "Lord," which is the primary term used by Luke to express Jesus' exalted and authoritative status. The confessional form "Jesus is Lord," however, scarcely figures in Acts, though there is an echo of it in 10:36.

"Lord" occurs over one hundred times in Acts and is used in a variety of ways. In a large number of cases it refers unequivocally to God (e.g., "the Lord your God" in 3:22), as in Old Testament usage (cf. 3:19; 4:26). Jesus is also commonly referred to as "the Lord" or "the Lord Jesus [Christ]." The vocative continues to be used in Acts, as in the Gospel, as an address to Jesus when he is seen and heard in visions (as in Stephen's vision and Paul's conversion). Jesus' status as Lord is given to him by God (2:36). He is the object of faith (cf. 5:14 in the light of 16:31) and he has universal authority (10:36).

There are many cases in Acts where the context makes it clear that the referent must be Jesus rather than God (e.g., 2:21 in the light of 2:36 and 22:18-19). The term, however, also figures in a number of Old Testament quotations or phrases — such as, "the angel of the Lord," "the day of the Lord," and "the name of the Lord." In these and other cases it is sometimes a moot point whether the reference is to God or Jesus. This does not mean that Luke was deliberately ambiguous or consciously intermingling the two referents (as argued by Tuckett, "Christology of Luke-Acts," 156-57). Rather, it can be argued that the proximity of the texts would almost inevitably have suggested to Luke's readers an equivalence between God and Jesus.

The facts that (1) Old Testament language is used of Jesus, (2) he has authority on a par with that of God, and (3) the same title "Lord" is used to refer to both of them — including those passages where it is not possible to be completely sure which is the referent — all contribute to viewing both Jesus and God as vested with equal dignity and entitled to the same reverence from human beings. Prayer may be addressed to both Jesus (Acts 1:24; 7:59-60) and God (Acts 4:24). And the Spirit is bestowed by each of them.

Yet God the Father and Jesus are not simply interchangeable. They have different sets of functions. The Father is the One whose plan is put into effect (Acts 1:7), and Jesus is "the Lord's Christ." He owes his authority to God who makes him Lord and Christ and begets him as his Son.

4. Four Important Questions

Four important questions arise from Luke's christological portrayals in his two volumes. The first is whether there is a particular significance in the subordination of Jesus to God. The second concerns the activity of Jesus between his exaltation and his return. The third has to do with the installation of Jesus as Lord and Christ. And the fourth concerns the appropriateness of the category of "divinity" in respect of Luke's Jesus.

Subordination?

A number of scholars insist that an important characteristic of the christology of Luke-Acts is its "subordinationism," as if this were somehow emphasized or expounded more in Luke's two volumes than elsewhere in the

New Testament. Acts brings out strongly the role of God as the initiator of salvation and the way in which his plan is announced beforehand and put into operation by his will. Furthermore, there are a remarkable number of statements in Acts in which God is the subject and Jesus is the object (see Schneider, *Apostelgeschichte*, 1.334).

Indeed, the soteriology of Luke-Acts may seem to fall into the category of "Redemption confirmed by Christ," as analyzed by Arland Hultgren (*Christ and His Benefits*, 69-89). The subordination of the Son to the Father, however, is a theme that appears throughout the New Testament — and, of course, is inherent in the imagery itself (see my "The Christology of Acts and the Pastoral Epistles"). Jesus, in fact, is no more subordinate to God in Luke's writings than elsewhere in the New Testament. And Acts emphasizes as much as any other New Testament writing the authority shared by Jesus with the Father.

The evidence for the subordination of Jesus to God is balanced by the evidence in Luke-Acts for the co-equality and co-regency of Jesus with God, as has been laid out by Douglas Buckwalter ("Divine Saviour"). The categories proposed by Hultgren are somewhat too neat, and the individual New Testament writings do not fit precisely into any of them. From the point of view of human beings, both God and Jesus are possessed of supreme authority and are to be reverenced.

An Inactive Christ?

Second, there is the question whether Jesus is portrayed by Luke as being genuinely "active" during the period between his exaltation and return. There is a sharp contrast between the views represented by Jacob Jervell, who questions whether the exalted Christ has any real function in Acts (*Theology of the Acts of the Apostles*, 33-34), and Douglas Buckwalter, who can speak of him as "immanent deity" ("Divine Saviour," 115-20). For Jervell, other people act through the name of Jesus, rather than Jesus himself — and if anybody acts from heaven, it is God rather than Jesus. It seems to me, however, that Buckwalter has the better of the debate, for the role of Jesus is depicted as being analogous to that of God.

Jesus works through his agents. The Holy Spirit, described once as "the Spirit of Jesus" (Acts 16:7) and expressly said to be poured out visibly and audibly by Jesus on his followers, is the principal agent. But Jesus also speaks through human agents, as, for example, Ananias (Acts 9:10-17). And he himself can appear in occasional visions — as, for example, at the conversion of Paul (Acts 9:3-5; 22:6-10; 26:12-18; cf. also 18:9).

There is nothing particularly odd about this. The same could be said by the other New Testament writers, for whom Jesus is also exalted to heaven. At the same time, it is God who sends the Spirit (Acts 5:32; 15:8) and who speaks through angels (Acts 10:3; 27:23). The conclusion to be drawn from all of this is that the exalted Jesus is no more inactive than is God himself (see Turner, *Power from on High,* 430-31).

The real difference, if it be a difference, is that in Paul and John there is a spiritual link between believers and Christ that is expressed in terms of life "in Christ" (as with Paul) or of "mutual indwelling" (as with John), and this feature is largely missing from Acts. Similarly, in Acts the work of the Spirit in believers, other than empowering and guiding them for mission, receives little attention. It is not so much, then, that Jesus is inactive in Luke's writings as that the close personal relationships with him found in Paul and John are absent.

Luke, it seems, stands closer to Hebrews in this regard. It is, therefore, inaccurate to say that Jesus is spiritually inactive in Luke's portrayals. Jesus is closely linked with God the Father, to whom he has "returned," rather than being understood as spiritually sent into the world like the Spirit.

A Two-Stage Christology?

A third question that arises from Luke's portrayals concerns the kind of christology to be found in Luke-Acts. If we had only Acts without the Gospel, it would be possible to develop a case that for the author of Acts Jesus was a human being — a prophet empowered by the Spirit of God — who was exalted by God and made Lord and Christ from the time of his resurrection onward, and who was also at that point "begotten" by God as his Son (Acts 2:36; 13:33; see Mainville, "Le Messianisme de Jésus"). On this view there could be different christologies in the Gospel and Acts — that is, Acts could be interpreted as portraying a christology in which Jesus is elevated to be Christ, Lord, and Son of God at his resurrection, in contrast with the Gospel, where he has this status from birth. The christology of Acts could be said to be more "primitive" — or, in C. K. Barrett's word, "unreflecting" (*Acts of the Apostles,* 1.152) — than that of the Gospel. Such an understanding has sometimes been associated with the suggestion that Acts was composed before the Gospel. An alternative position is that Luke incorporated into Acts less developed christological statements that reflect an earlier point of view, although he himself did not necessarily share that point of view.

The thesis that the earliest Christians had a less developed christology has been argued by a number of scholars, who have used the material in Acts as part of the evidence (e.g., Barrett, *Acts of the Apostles,* 1.151-52). Support for a primitive two-stage christology has been detected in Rom 1:3-4, where, it is argued, Jesus was first regarded as a descendant of David during his earthly life and then later seen as having been appointed Messiah and Son of God at his resurrection. The parallel, however, is inexact, since the statement in Romans has Jesus as the Christ already during his earthly life. And there are, in any case, grave doubts as to whether Rom 1:3-4 really is a pre-Pauline "adoptionist" formula.

The interpretation of Acts 2:36 ("Therefore, let all Israel be assured of this: God has made this Jesus whom you crucified both Lord and Christ") and 13:33 ("He [God] has fulfilled for us [what he promised our fathers], their children, by raising Jesus from the dead. As it is written in the second Psalm: 'You are my Son; today I have become your Father'") must take at least two considerations into account. First, a distinction must be made between what the text may have meant in whatever source was used by Luke and how he himself understood it. Our concern here is with the latter, and it is very questionable whether Luke, writing at least thirty years after Pentecost, would have written what can be construed as adoptionism. Second, it must be recognized that the various statements in Acts to the effect that the Christ must suffer and rise from the dead are most naturally taken to mean that the One who is already the Christ undergoes these experiences, not that the person who is destined to be the Christ must first suffer and rise from the dead.

In any case, it is illegitimate to exclude the evidence of the Gospel from consideration. The context provided by the Gospel for the reading of Acts is unavoidable in the light of Acts 1:1. Moreover, it must be remembered that the Gospel precedes Acts in the order of reading.

Odette Mainville's tactic reverses this statement by insisting that what she regards as the plain meaning of Acts 2:36 must determine how the Gospel is read. In effect, she has taken up only one side of the methodologically correct principle that Luke's Gospel and Acts must be read in the light of one another. Consequently, she understands Luke 1:31-35 to mean that the Holy Spirit has nothing to do with the birth of Jesus and that the future tenses used of Jesus — in particular, who *will be called* the Son of God — refer to the time of his exaltation and not his birth. Moreover, "Son of God," in Mainville's view, is to be understood messianically rather than ontologically. Thus Mainville is forced to say that the effect of the Holy Spirit on Mary is really effective on her offspring rather than on herself.

All of this is a very unnatural reading of the text. It plays down the significance of the clear echoes of Isa 7:14 and is embarrassed by Mary's question of Luke 1:34, "How can this be since I am a virgin?" In any case, the comparison of Jesus' birth with the wonder of the birth of John to the aged and childless Elizabeth would not work if Mary was a young woman of marriageable age with a husband.

Furthermore, Peter's summation of Jesus' person and ministry in Acts 10:36-38 agrees with the account of Jesus' baptism and the self-affirmation in Luke 4:18-19, according to which Jesus was extraordinarily empowered by the Spirit — and therefore already at this point the messianic bearer of the Spirit. In the Gospel, as we have seen, Jesus is confessed as "the Christ" and referred to as "Lord" by the narrator. These factors all suggest that in Acts 2:36 Peter is using the fact that God raised Jesus to life, thereby fulfilling what had been prophesied about the Christ, to confirm to his audience that Jesus really was the Christ, despite the crucifixion.

What the resurrection achieved was the entry of Jesus into his glory (cf. Luke 24:26) and enthronement, not his entry into Messiahship or "Christship." It is the equivalent of being appointed Son of God *with power* in Rom 1:4 or being *highly* exalted in Phil 2:9-11. As Ben Witherington put it, Jesus could not fully exercise his roles as Lord over all and universal Christ until his exaltation, and he did not in a full sense assume these roles until that point (*Acts of the Apostles,* 149). The once-popular view that the words "that he [God] may send the Christ, who has been appointed for you" of Acts 3:20 mean — whether for Luke himself or for his source — that Jesus would become the Christ at the *parousia* can be safely dismissed (see Barrett, *Acts of the Apostles,* 1.204-5). Indeed, something new takes place at Jesus' exaltation. But it is not the appointment of Jesus as Messiah and Son of God. Rather, it is the establishment of Jesus as Lord.

The Language of Divinity?

Finally, is the language of divinity justified in regard to Luke's christology? This, as we have seen, is the position of Douglas Buckwalter and Max Turner — that is, that Jesus shares the status and role of God in his exalted state, so much so that on many occasions it almost seems arbitrary which of them acts. Christopher Tuckett ("Christology of Luke-Acts," following M. Casey) criticizes the view of Buckwalter and Turner that being the giver of the Spirit (cf. Acts 2:33) makes the agent somehow divine and compares other divine prerogatives shared by God with agents who are not thereby made divine. But Max Turner's response seems adequate to me (see his "The Spirit of Christ and 'Divine' Christology," 423).

The subordination of Jesus to God is not an argument to the contrary, since in those parts of the New Testament where a preexistence christology is found Jesus remains subordinate to God as a son to a father. The significant controversial element is that of divine "nature." Do Luke's statements about Sonship and divine begetting indicate a relationship with God that is ontological? That is certainly a possible — even a likely — interpretation of the annunciation statements, but it is not strongly focused. Nonetheless, in view of what Luke says about the universal lordship of Jesus, it is perfectly credible.

5. Summing Up: Christ and Lord

We must now draw together the various threads of the material surveyed above. For although we discussed the data of the Gospel and Acts separately, we found that there is a consistent picture in the two parts of Luke's material.

A Review of the Data

According to the prologue of Luke's Gospel, Mary gives birth to a son whose conception is due to the overshadowing by the Spirit rather than to human impregnation. He is God's Son and is destined to be the Jewish Christ and Savior — and already at this stage his status is expressed in the use of the term "Lord."

The story in the Gospel then goes on to show how Jesus already acts as the Christ in bringing about the kingdom of God and its associated blessings. The two terms "prophet" and "Savior" express the character of what he does. Furthermore, Luke takes over the enigmatic "Son of Man" and retains the tradition that it was used only by Jesus as a self-designation.

Jesus is recognized to be the Christ by Peter, and this recognition is shared by other disciples as a hope that apparently had not been fulfilled by the end of his life. From Luke 9 onward, however, the rejection and suffering of the Christ becomes a dominant theme. The resurrection is understood as the confirmation that Jesus is the Christ, since the scriptural pattern for the career of the Christ provided for suffering and then entry into glory.

In Acts the story starts with the proclamation of the risen Christ and Lord by the apostles. Jesus has been exalted by God. Both his resurrection and the pouring out of the Spirit are seen as indications of this. He is thus confirmed in his position as Christ, with the crucial changes in his situation being (1) that he is now enthroned with God the Father and (2) that he proceeds to exercise his role in the same way as does the Father — that is, mainly through agents, but occasionally in a more direct and unmediated manner.

Throughout Acts the demonstration that Jesus is the Christ is at the heart of Christian preaching to the Jews. At the same time, however, the status of Jesus as Lord is increasingly to the fore in preaching to the Gentiles — though with that proclamation of Jesus as Lord not displacing the more narrowly Jewish message of Jesus as the Christ (see Witherington, *Acts of the Apostles*, 147-53).

The title "Savior," however, is rare in Acts, just as it is in the Gospel (Acts 5:31; 13:23; cf. Luke 1:47; 2:11). But it is a crucial term for encapsulating the activity of Jesus. For just as in the Gospel Jesus acts to liberate and forgive by his own authority, so, too, in Acts he acts in the same way through his agents, who work "in his Name," and by virtue of the authority that he possesses.

Elsewhere in the New Testament considerable salutary significance is attached to Jesus' death and what he does "on behalf of" humanity. In Luke's Gospel and Acts, however, Jesus' death is portrayed more as simply the expression of murderous hatred — with sacrificial and vicarious notes marginal, but not totally absent. The concept of divine grace exercised through Christ is certainly present (cf. Luke 4:22; Acts 15:11; 18:27; 20:32). It would seem that the exaltation of Jesus places him in a position from which he can perform cosmically the kind of things that he did during his earthly mission. In particular, as the exalted Lord he can now convey in a special manner the gift of the Spirit to his disciples — although it must also be noted that the substance of that gift, without the explicit mention of the Spirit, was granted to the Twelve and the Seventy-two in the Gospel.

A Synthesis of the Evidence

How is this evidence best synthesized? The prophetic features of Jesus' role have been highlighted by various scholars. David Moessner, for instance, has stressed the deuteronomic "prophet like Moses" motif, which appears especially in the Gospel's travel narrative. Luke Timothy Johnson has also highlighted the role of Jesus as a prophet and argued that this role continues in Acts through the mission of the disciples — noting how other aspects of Luke's presentation fit in with this view, and so asserting that for Luke Jesus was fundamentally a prophetic figure.

I would claim, however, that the evidence presented earlier in this article is adequate to show that an understanding of Jesus principally as a prophet is a skewed presentation. It has, indeed, captured an important aspect of how Jesus exercised his role. But it fails to recognize the way in which the christology of Luke-Acts is much more coherently organized around the twin foci of "Christship" and "Lordship."

It must also be stressed, however, that a christology purely in terms of "Christship" is one-sided as well. Granted that Luke emphasizes the Christship of Jesus, it is dubious whether Christ can be said to be "the most significant title" (*contra* Jervell, *Theology of the Acts of the Apostles,* 27). Frank Matera's title for his section on Luke-Acts, "Christ and Lord of All," resonates more closely to Luke's outlook than many other modern treatments (Matera, *New Testament Christology*).

One possible way of bringing "Christ" and "Lord" together might be to exploit the term "King," which combines these two ideas. But this is not a line that Luke himself has taken to any great distance. Only in Acts 17:7 does the term surface in the preaching of Paul and Silas — where the position of Jesus vis-à-vis Roman ideology emerges, but the contrast is not elaborated. There is, incidentally, no obviously "non-Jewish" element in the christology of Acts, though it is plausible that the concepts of lordship and saviorhood were more transparent to Gentiles.

Christopher Tuckett criticizes Darrell Bock's view that Luke develops a Christ-Servant christology in the Gospel and then proceeds to "correct" this in Acts, where Jesus is presented as Lord (Tuckett, "Christology of Luke-Acts" vis-à-vis Bock, *Proclamation from Prophecy and Pattern*). Tuckett is rightly skeptical of the idea that Luke would spend one book presenting an inadequate view and then correct it in the second. Bock's view, however, is less vulnerable if we take it to be that Luke describes the development of christological views by the early disciples and shows how they moved from the perfectly valid category of Christship during Jesus' earthly life to a fuller realization of the universal lordship of the exalted Christ after the resurrection. On such a scenario, Luke is not correcting views held by his readers, but chronicling a development that is inherently plausible.

Finally, can we say that what we have discovered is Luke's own christology? Tuckett suggests that Luke has preserved a number of different types of christological conceptions and proposes that his own view can be summed up as "exaltationist" ("Christology of Luke-Acts," 148). Tuckett rightly recognizes the importance of Christship and wants to resist any downplaying of it over against Lordship. Nevertheless, he holds that Christship is so redefined that it is doubtful how far it actually mattered to Luke himself. And he finishes up with Luke as little more than a conservative redactor of his sources.

This seems to be an unnecessarily minimalist view of things. I take a more optimistic view of the situation and I believe that a coherent, unified picture emerges from considering the Gospel and Acts together as two parts of one unified story. In contemporary jargon, I have provided a reading that started from a prejudice in favor of the narrative unity of the Gospel and Acts and that can be held to have confirmed that prejudice. The differences between Luke's two volumes are due to the fact that the Gospel presents the earthly mission of Jesus and what the actors thought of him at that time — though, of course, the narrator knows more than the actors, since he writes from a later perspective — and that Acts presents the post-resurrection understanding of Jesus.

SELECTED BIBLIOGRAPHY

Anderson, Kevin L. "The Resurrection of Jesus in Luke-Acts." Unpublished doctoral thesis, Brunel University, 2000.

Barrett, C. Kingsley. *The Acts of the Apostles,* 2 vols. Edinburgh: Clark, 1994, 1998, especially 2.lxxxv-lxxxvii.

Bock, Darrell L. *Proclamation from Prophecy and Pattern: Lucan Old Testament Christology.* Sheffield: JSOT, 1987.

Buckwalter, H. Douglas. *The Character and Purpose of Luke's Christology.* Cambridge: Cambridge University Press, 1996.

————. "The Divine Saviour," in *Witness to the Gospel: The Theology of Acts,* ed. I. H. Marshall and D. Peterson. Grand Rapids: Eerdmans, 1998, 197-23.

Crump, David M. *Jesus the Intercessor: Prayer and Christology in Luke-Acts.* Tübingen: Mohr-Siebeck, 1992.

Fitzmyer, Joseph A. *The Gospel According to Luke (I–IX).* New York: Doubleday, 1981, 192-219.

Fletcher-Louis, Crispin H. T. *Luke-Acts: Angels, Christology and Soteriology.* Tübingen: Mohr-Siebeck, 1997.

Green, Joel B. *The Theology of the Gospel of Luke.* Cambridge: Cambridge University Press, 1995.

Hultgren, Arlan J. *Christ and His Benefits: Christology and Redemption in the New Testament.* Philadelphia: Fortress, 1987.

Jervell, Jacob. *The Theology of the Acts of the Apostles.* Cambridge: Cambridge University Press, 1996.

Johnson, Luke Timothy. "The Christology of Luke-Acts," in *Who Do You Say That I Am? Essays on Christology,* ed. M. A. Powell and D. R. Bauer. Louisville: Westminster/John Knox, 1999, 49-65.

Mainville, Odette. "Le Messianisme de Jésus. Le rapport annonce/accomplissement entre Lc 1,35 et Ac 2,33," in *The Unity of Luke-Acts,* ed. J. Verheyden. Leuven: Leuven University Press, 1999, 313-27.

Marshall, I. Howard. *The Gospel of Luke: A Commentary on the Greek Text.* Exeter: Paternoster; Grand Rapids: Eerdmans, 1978.

————. *Acts.* Leicester: Inter-Varsity; Grand Rapids: Eerdmans, 1980.

————. "The Christology of Acts and the Pastoral Epistles," in *Crossing the Boundaries: Essays in Biblical Interpretation in Honour of Michael D. Goulder,* ed. S. E. Porter, et al. Leiden: Brill, 1994, 167-82.

Matera, Frank J. *New Testament Christology.* Louisville: Westminster/John Knox, 1999.

Moessner, David P. *Lord of the Banquet: The Literary and Theological Significance of the Lucan Travel Narrative.* Minneapolis: Fortress, 1989.

Pokorný, Petr. *Theologie der lukanischen Schriften.* Göttingen: Vandenhoeck und Ruprecht, 1998, especially 110-20.

Radl, Walter. *Das Lukas-Evangelium.* Darmstadt: Wissenschaftliche Buchgesellschaft, 1988.

Schneider, Gerhard. *Die Apostelgeschichte.* Freiburg: Herder, 1980, especially 1:331-35.

Strauss, Mark L. *The Davidic Messiah in Luke-Acts: The Promise and Its Fulfilment in Luke's Christology.* Sheffield: Sheffield Academic, 1995.

Tuckett, Christopher M. "The Christology of Luke-Acts," in *The Unity of Luke-Acts,* ed. J. Verheyden. Leuven: Leuven University Press, 1999, 133-64.

Turner, Max. "The Spirit of Christ and 'Divine' Christology," in *Jesus of Nazareth: Lord and Christ,* ed. J. B. Green and M. Turner. Grand Rapids: Eerdmans; Carlisle: Paternoster, 1994, 413-36.

————. *Power from on High: The Spirit in Israel's Restoration and Witness in Luke-Acts.* Sheffield: Sheffield Academic, 1996.

Witherington, Ben, III. *The Acts of the Apostles: A Socio-Rhetorical Commentary.* Grand Rapids: Eerdmans; Carlisle: Paternoster, 1998, especially 147-53.

————. *The Many Faces of the Christ: The Christologies of the New Testament and Beyond.* New York: Crossroad, 1999, especially 153-68.

CHAPTER 7

Monotheism and Christology
in the Gospel of John

RICHARD BAUCKHAM

For many scholars the christology of the Fourth Gospel is the "highest" in the New Testament. In my view, this is a mistake — not in the sense of exaggerating the extent to which true and full divinity is attributed to Jesus in the Fourth Gospel, but in failing to recognize the extent to which this is also the case in most other parts of the New Testament. In my view, a "christology of divine identity," in which Jesus is understood to be included in the unique divine identity of the one and only God, the God of Israel, is pervasive in the New Testament writings. It is clearly expressed in some ways that are common to all or most of these writings. But it is also developed in distinctive ways in the most theologically reflective and creative of them.

All the New Testament writings make deliberate use of the ways in which Second Temple Judaism expressed and defined the unique and exclusive divinity of the one God Yahweh. They use these well-understood categories of Jewish monotheism in order to apply them also to Jesus, thereby including him in the unique divine identity (for this argument in detail, see my *God Crucified: Monotheism and Christology in the New Testament*). The Fourth Gospel, like Hebrews, Revelation, and some of the Pauline letters, does this in especially full and unambiguous ways.

Many recent scholars have recognized that the relationship between so-called "high" christology, or what I prefer to call "christology of divine identity," and Jewish monotheism is an important theme in the Gospel of

John. They see this in the passages of debate between Jesus and the Jewish leaders — as, for example, where the Jewish leaders accuse Jesus of "making himself equal to God" (5:18), accuse him of making himself God (10:33), or understand certain of his claims as blasphemous claims to divine identity (8:58-59; 10:30-31, 38-39). These debates in John's Gospel are often thought to reflect debates that were going on in the Gospel's context between Christians and non-Christian Jews, who found the Christian claims for Jesus incompatible with Jewish monotheism. There may, to an extent, be something in such an approach. But the passages in question are too integral to the Gospel's developing narrative and its sophisticated narrative revelation of Jesus' identity to be mere reflections of external debates. In any case, this approach to the material runs the risk of explaining Johannine christology in purely apologetic or polemical terms — or even, as a result, in purely sociological terms — and so failing to appreciate the deeply theological roots of the fourth evangelist's concern to integrate "high" christology into Jewish monotheism.

Johannine christology is not the product of some kind of theological drift toward an ever higher christology and the problems that such a movement caused for monotheism. Rather, monotheism and christology were necessarily related to each other in the Christian understanding of Jesus' identity from the beginning. Without belief in the unique and exclusive divinity of the God of Israel, the inclusion of Jesus in that identity could not have meant what it did.

Although there is much else to Johannine christology, its relationship to Jewish monotheism is central to the Fourth Gospel. That relationship, however, has not usually been adequately understood. For this reason, we will focus in this chapter on "monotheism and christology" in the Gospel of John.

1. Monotheism in the Beginning

In the Prologue of his Gospel, especially the first few verses, the Fourth Evangelist establishes that Jesus is fully and truly divine in a way that does not compromise Jewish monotheism — for he is included within the unique divine identity as understood in Jewish monotheism. Any Jewish reader of the Gospel would at once recognize that the opening verses of John 1:1-5 are a retelling or reinterpretation of the beginning of the Genesis creation narrative in Gen 1:1-4. The opening words "In the beginning" *(en archē)* are identical with the opening of Genesis (Hebrew *bᵉrēʾšît*, Greek LXX *en archē)*. And the impression of the retelling of Genesis would be furthered by the repetition of these words in v. 2, the reference to the creation of all things by the Word in v. 3, and the key words "light" and "darkness" in vv. 4-5 (cf. Gen 1:3-5).

Retellings and reinterpretations of the Genesis creation narrative are common in the extant Jewish literature of this period. Some of them are especially concerned with the monotheistic message that Yahweh is the sole Creator of all things, who designed and accomplished his creation entirely by himself. It was, in fact, a key element in a Jewish understanding of God's unique identity that he alone is the Creator of all things. And this was perhaps the simplest way of making, as Jewish monotheism required, an absolute distinction between God and all other reality: God alone is the Creator of all else; all other things were created by God.

John 1:3 echoes emphatically this monotheistic motif: "All things came into being through it [the Word], and without it not one thing came into being." (I am here translating the pronoun as "it" rather than "him," because at this stage there is no clear indication that "the Word" is to be understood as a personal agent — though, of course, this emerges later in the Prologue.) That all things were created by God through the instrumentality of his Word is very commonly said in Jewish statements about the creation — beginning with Ps 33:6, "By the word of the Lord the heavens were made, and all their host by the breath of his mouth." This is simply a concise expression of the fact that in the Genesis creation account each act of creation is effected by God speaking. Although Genesis 1 itself does not use the term "word," it is easily understood as saying that all things were created by God's Word.

When John uses "Word" in the opening verses of his Prologue, he means simply this: the divine Word, which all Jews understood on the basis of Genesis to have been active in the creation of all things. Moreover, there was no question of this Word being something or someone created. As God's own Word, it was intrinsic to God's own unique identity. To say that all things were created by the Word did not compromise the belief that God alone was the Creator of all things, since his Word belonged to his own identity. In fact, to say, as John does, that all things came into being through the Word is precisely to categorize the Word as belonging to the identity of God rather than to the creation.

But John has already taken care in v. 1 to make it clear that, while the Word can be distinguished from God and said to be with him, the Word is also intrinsic to God's own unique identity. This is the only possible meaning a Jewish reader could find in the claim that the Word was already with God in eternity before creation — that is, "in the beginning." We do not need to postulate any background to these verses other than Genesis 1 and the tradition of Jewish creation accounts dependent on it, which speak of God's Word as his instrument or agent in creation.

Nor should we, as is the habit with many scholars writing on the Johannine Prologue, use the term *Logos,* as if John's Greek word means more than simply "word." The term itself carries no particular metaphysical baggage. It refers simply to God's Word as portrayed in Jewish creation accounts — which is why it does not appear in John's Gospel after the Prologue.

In the Prologue the evangelist uses "Word" to identify the preexistent Christ *within the Genesis creation narrative,* and so within the unique identity of God *as already understood by Jewish monotheism.* He therefore confines his use of the term to his retelling of the Genesis creation account (1:1-5) and to the statement that this Word of the creation account entered human history as the man Jesus Christ (1:14). From the perspective of the rest of the Gospel, however, for which the Word has now been revealed as the Son of the Father, the terms in which the incarnate Christ spoke of himself — that is, primarily as "Son" — naturally supersede the term used in Jewish creation accounts.

The opening five verses of John's Prologue, therefore, read in light of the later statement in 1:14 that the Word became flesh and lived among us as Jesus Christ, include Jesus in the unique divine identity by identifying him with the Word that was with God in the beginning and was God's agent in the creation of all things. These statements place Jesus unequivocally on the divine side of the absolute distinction between the one Creator and all other things. By identifying Jesus with an entity intrinsic to the divine identity — that is, with God's Word — they include Jesus in that identity without infringing monotheism. The Word "was with God," but it was not another besides God — for it "was God" (1:1). Thus the Gospel begins by engaging with one of the most important ways in which Jews defined the uniqueness of the one God — that is, as the sole Creator of all things — and uses this way of understanding the unique identity of God in order to include Jesus within it.

2. The Divine Prerogatives

In the Jewish definition of the one God's exclusive divinity, as well as being the sole Creator of all things, God is also understood as the sole sovereign Ruler of all things. One key aspect of this is his sovereignty over life and death (cf. Deut 32:39: "See now that I, even I, am [he]; there is no god besides me. I kill and I make alive; I wound and I heal; and no one can deliver from my hand"). God is the only living one — that is, the only one to whom life belongs eternally and intrinsically. All other life derives from him, is given by him, and is taken back by him. Another key aspect of God's sole sovereignty over creation is his prerogative of judgment: his rule is just, implementing justice, and therefore he judges both nations and individuals. Such divine prerogatives should be understood not as mere functions that God might delegate to others, but as intrinsic to his divine identity. Ruling over all, giving life to all, exercising judgment on all — these prerogatives belong integrally to the Jewish understanding of who God is.

In John 5, which is the first major passage of the Fourth Gospel where Jesus speaks about his own identity in discussion with the Jewish leaders, these divine prerogatives of sovereignty over life and death and exercising judgment come to the fore. Jesus defends his act of healing on the Sabbath by claiming God's unique prerogative of working on the Sabbath: "My Father is still working [i.e., his work did not cease with his creation of all things, but continues in his sovereign rule over all things], and I also am working" (v. 17). Jesus here presupposes a Jewish argument that, since people are born and die on Sabbath days, it is clear that God exercises his sovereignty over life and death and his prerogative of judgment on the Sabbath as well as on other days. And Jesus claims that in his healing of the invalid man at the Pool of Bethzatha he is doing the same.

The Jewish leaders take this to mean that Jesus "was making himself equal to God" (v. 18) — and the lengthy discourse that follows indicates that in one sense they were right, but in another wrong. Jesus stresses that in all he does he is wholly dependent on his Father, and so is in no way setting himself up as a rival to his Father. In his radical dependence on God, he is not equal to God in the sense that the Jewish leaders intended. Nonetheless, he is equal to God in the sense that what the Father gives him to do are the uniquely divine prerogatives. He does not simply act as God's agent in implementing some aspects of God's sovereignty. Rather, he exercises the full divine sovereignty as given him by his Father — but as also fully his own. So he says in answer to the charges of the Jewish leaders: "Just as the Father raises the dead and gives them life, so also the Son gives life to *whomever he wishes*" (v. 21); "The Father judges no one, but has given *all judgment* to the Son" (v. 22); and, "Just as the Father has life in himself, so he has granted the Son to have *life in himself*" (v. 26). Jesus thus shares in the divine identity as the only living one, the only giver of life, the only judge of all. He does so as the Son who is wholly dependent on his Father. But he shares fully and truly in the divine identity. This means that the unique divine identity *includes* the relationship that Jesus here describes between himself as the Son and God his Father.

Finally with regard to John 5 we should note that from the inclusion of Jesus in the unique divine identity follows the worship of Jesus. Thus Jesus declares: "The Father . . . has given all judgment to the Son, so that all may honor the Son just as they honor the Father" (vv. 22-23). In Jewish tradition, worship is intimately connected with monotheism. The only true God must be worshiped and is the only one who may be worshiped because worship is precisely the recognition of God's unique identity. And in Jewish religious practice it is worship that distinguishes the one God from all other beings, who, however exalted, are his creatures and subject to his sovereign rule. In early Christian practice, therefore, the worship of Jesus indicates his inclusion in the identity of this one God.

3. The "I Am" Sayings

The Gospel of John contains two series of sayings of Jesus that include the words "I am" *(egō eimi* — with the pronoun *egō,* which is not always necessary in Greek, used for emphasis along with the verb *eimi).*

The "I Am" Sayings with Predicates

Readers of the Fourth Gospel in English translation easily recognize one of these series, the "I am" sayings with predicates, "I am" followed by a noun or nouns. These sayings are metaphors in which Jesus describes himself in some way as the one who gives salvation:

I am the bread of life (6:35, 41, 48)
I am the light of the world (8:12; cf. 9:5)
I am the gate for the sheep (10:7, 9)
I am the good shepherd (10:11, 14)
I am the resurrection and the life (11:25)
I am the way, the truth, and the life (14:6)
I am the true vine (15:1)

In ancient Jewish literature, the number seven is never insignificant. It is the number of completeness. So the existence of these *seven* sayings scattered throughout the Gospel indicates the completeness of the salvation Jesus brings and gives.

As a series of complementary metaphors, these seven sayings with predicates illuminate the salvation that Jesus brings and gives from various aspects. We could compare them with the seven "signs" (i.e., "miracles" or "miraculous signs") in the Gospel, which also have to be counted before we realize that there are seven. While the "I am" sayings with predicates are verbal descriptions of Jesus as the Savior, the signs he does show him to be the Savior in concrete demonstrations of his power to give life.

Like the sayings, the signs illustrate the nature of the salvation that Jesus gives in a variety of ways. In some cases, the "I am" sayings with predicates correlate with the miraculous signs: Jesus supplies bread to the five thousand and declares himself "the bread of life"; Jesus opens the eyes of a blind man and declares himself "the light of the world"; Jesus raises Lazarus from death and declares himself "the resurrection and the life." In other cases, the signs and the sayings are independent of each other.

The Absolute "I am" Sayings

Our main concern at present, however, is not with the "I am" sayings with predicates, but with the absolute "I am" sayings, "I am" *(egō eimi)* standing by itself without a predicate. These are less easy to identify in English translations because translators have adopted a variety of strategies in order to make intelligible English of them.

In one case, at least, most translations render *egō eimi* literally by "I am." This, the best known of the absolute "I am" sayings, occurs in 8:58: "Truly, truly, I tell you, before Abraham was, I am." On hearing this, the

Jewish leaders take up stones to stone Jesus for blasphemy (8:59). It is clear that here "I am" indicates not only Jesus' claim to have preexisted Abraham, but also some kind of claim to divine identity — which is taken by his hearers to be blasphemous. Precisely why it constitutes a claim to divine identity is less easy to determine.

But before attempting to deal with that matter, we must first identify this absolute "I am" saying as one of a series of seven that are scattered, like the seven with predicates, throughout John's Gospel: 4:26; 6:20; 8:24; 8:28; 8:58; 13:19; 18:5, 6, 8 — treating the three in ch. 18 as a single saying that is first stated (v. 5) and then twice repeated (vv. 6 and 8). In all but 8:58 ("I am") and 6:20 ("It is I"), the NRSV translates *egō eimi* as "I am he," but with the literal translation "I am" in a footnote.

Not all scholars, however, agree that these sayings belong together as a series. This is mainly because in some cases the Greek can be given an ordinary meaning. In 4:26, which is the first of these sayings, Jesus is replying to the Samaritan woman, who has just spoken about the Messiah. His words — which literally read, "I, the one who is speaking to you, am" — can easily be read as having the antecedent reference to the Messiah as its implied predicate: "I am he," meaning "I am the Messiah." This is probably how the evangelist expects us to suppose the Samaritan woman understood Jesus, since she goes on to ask her friends and neighbors whether it can be true that he is the Messiah (4:29).

In 6:20, the second of the sayings, Jesus, walking on the water, approaches the terrified disciples in the boat and to reassure them says: "I am. Do not be afraid." Here "I am," as noted above, can be understood as Jesus simply identifying himself to the disciples, and so saying "It is I." Mark and Matthew use the same phrase in their versions of the story (Mark 6:50; Matt 14:27). A similar meaning can be understood in the last of the sayings, in John 18, where the soldiers come to arrest Jesus in Gethsemane. Jesus asks them, "Whom are you looking for?" When they reply, "Jesus of Nazareth," he responds: "I am" (vv. 5, 6, 8) — which can, again, mean simply "I am he" or "It is I." In this case, however, we may be suspicious as to whether this ordinary meaning is sufficient to explain the phrase, since the reaction of the soldiers was to fall to the ground (v. 6) and since "I am" occurs three times, suggesting that this may be an emphatic climax of the series of such sayings.

While in three of the seven absolute "I am" cases, therefore, an ordinary meaning is possible and may even be superficially the obvious meaning, in the other four cases no such ordinary meaning is available. In these cases the phrase "I am" is as strangely incomplete in the Greek as it is in a literal English translation. In these four cases, there is no plausible antecedent in the context, as though Jesus could be saying "I am that one we have just been speaking about." In one instance, in fact, the puzzlingly incomplete nature of the phrase is clear in the response of Jesus' interlocutors. For in 8:24, addressing the Jewish leaders, Jesus says: "You will die in your sins unless you believe that I am." They respond in 8:25: "*Who* are you?" — in other words, "What do you mean, 'I am'? 'I am' *who?*"

Jesus is equally obscure when he uses the phrase again in 8:28: "When you have lifted up the Son of Man, then you will realize that I am." He can hardly mean "I am the Son of Man," because "Son of Man" is an enigmatic way of referring to himself that his hearers in the Gospel do not understand.

In 8:24 and 8:28, therefore, Jesus is clearly making some remarkable kind of claim about himself that is obscure to his hearers. Only when he uses the phrase a third time in 8:58, saying "Before Abraham was, I am," do they realize that he is claiming divine identity. And they react accordingly.

Since in these cases, as well as in 13:19, "I am" cannot be given an ordinary meaning, it is best to take all seven occurrences as a set — understanding those cases where an ordinary meaning is possible as instances of double entendre. The Fourth Evangelist is fond of double meanings. In many such cases, Jesus' hearers take his words in a superficially obvious sense, and so miss his real meaning. They fail to catch the symbolic or otherwise more profound significance of his words.

First-time readers or hearers of the Gospel will probably, therefore, like the Samaritan woman herself, take Jesus in 4:26 to mean "I am the Messiah you just mentioned." While this is not wrong, readers who study the Fourth Gospel more carefully will find — particularly in light of the later occurrences of the phrase — that there is a deeper meaning: that Jesus is claiming not just messiahship but divine identity. At this stage in the Gospel narrative, however, such a claim is not made explicit on the surface of his words. Similarly in 6:20, first-time readers will probably give the phrase the ordinary meaning "It is I" — though here the context, which is evocative of Old Testament theophanies, might already suggest to well-informed readers that more is implied.

In chs. 7–8, however, the issue of who Jesus really is becomes the central and explicit topic of discussion among Jesus' hearers and between Jesus and his hearers. Here the special significance of "I am" becomes unavoidable. So in 8:58, which serves to cap the whole presentation of Jesus' climactic declaration of his identity, his affirmation "I am" is understood by the Jewish leaders as blasphemous. The fuller meaning implicit in the earlier occurrences can now be recognized by hindsight. And when in ch. 18 this phrase on the lips of Jesus provokes the soldiers to fall prostrate on the ground before him, attentive readers will not, with ch. 8 as background, be surprised.

We may reasonably conclude, therefore, that the Fourth Evangelist has distributed two series of seven "I am" sayings throughout his narrative, those with predicates, which describe who Jesus is for believers, and absolute "I am" sayings, which state more directly who he is in himself and express his divine identity — which forms the basis for his salvific role.

"I am" as an Expression of Divine Identity

But how exactly does the phrase "I am" express divine identity? One suggestion most often made with reference to 8:58, where Jesus' hearers understand the phrase as blasphemous, is that "I am" is a form of the divine name, the tetragrammaton YHWH. In Exod 3:14, when God reveals his name to Moses, he interprets it as meaning "I am who I am" (which is one of several possible translations of the Hebrew), and then uses just the first of the three Hebrew words of the statement as a form of the name: "Thus shall you say to the Israelites, 'I AM has sent me to you.'" A difficulty with understanding this as the background to the absolute "I am" sayings in John's Gospel is that neither the Septuagint nor any other known Greek translation of Exod 3:14 translates "I am" as *egō eimi*, which is the Greek phrase in John's Gospel. The Septuagint has *egō eimi ho ōn* ("I am the one who is") and *ho ōn apestalkē me* ("the one who has sent me"). This may not be an insuperable difficulty. Like most New Testament writers, the Fourth Evangelist not only uses the Septuagint when referring to the Old Testament text; he also knows the Hebrew text. And when the point he is making requires it, he may allude directly to the latter. It is possible, therefore, that the absolute "I am" sayings of John's Gospel are based directly on the Hebrew of Exod 3:14.

There is, however, another explanation of these "I am" sayings, which, at least with respect to their primary meaning, I believe is preferable — because it explains much more about this whole series of seven sayings. The Septuagint uses *egō eimi* in Deut 32:39 and on several occasions in Isaiah 40–55 (41:4; 43:10; 46:4, the last with the phrase repeated) to translate Hebrew *'ănî hû'*, which is usually rendered in English as "I am he." In Isa 43:25 and 51:12, where the Hebrew has the more emphatic form *'ānokî 'ānokî hû'*, the Septuagint has the double expression *egō eimi egō eimi*.

The phrase *'ănî hû'* (in Hebrew) or *egō eimi* (in Greek), usually translated "I am he," is extraordinarily significant. It is a divine self-declaration, which encapsulates Yahweh's claim to unique and exclusive divinity. It occurs first in the Hebrew Bible in what are almost the last words that God himself speaks in the Torah, as an emphatically monotheistic assertion: "Behold, I, even *I am he*; there is no god besides me" (Deut 32:39). This passage was frequently read in New Testament times as an eschatological prophecy of the salvation that God would achieve for his people in the end times. As such, it links closely with the prophecies of deutero-Isaiah (Isaiah 40–55), where this form of divine self-declaration recurs several times — in Hebrew in Isa 41:4; 43:10, 13, 25; 46:4; 48:12; 51:12; and 52:6.

For early Christians, Isaiah 40–55 contained the most important biblical prophecies of eschatological salvation for Israel and the nations. These chapters provided, as has been frequently noted, the source of many of the biblical quotations and allusions found throughout the New Testament — including the Gospel of John. What needs to be noted also, however, is that the proclamation of eschatological salvation in these chapters is intimately linked to their emphatic assertion of the absolute uniqueness of the God of Israel. For in Isaiah 40–55 Israel's God constantly asserts his unique deity, in contrast to the idols of the nations, who are not gods, and defines his uniqueness as that of the eternal Creator of all things and the unique sovereign ruler over all history. His great act of eschatological salvation will demonstrate him to be the one and only God in the sight of all nations, revealing his glory so that all the ends of earth will acknowledge him as God and turn to him for salvation. All this is summed up in the divine self-declaration, "I am he."

The occurrences of the phrase vary somewhat between the Hebrew Bible and the Septuagint, which in one or two places may translate a variant Hebrew original. But whether we suppose that John worked solely from the Septuagint or (as I think likely) also knew and was influenced by the Hebrew text, it is striking that his series of seven absolute "I am" sayings corresponds numerically to its Old Testament source. The Septuagint has *egō eimi* in three instances (Deut 32:39; Isa 41:4; 43:10) and the double *egō eimi egō eimi* in four (Isa 43:25; 45:18; 46:4; 51:12), making seven in all. The Hebrew has the simple *'ănî hû'* seven times (Deut 32:39; Isa 41:4; 43:10, 13; 46:4; 48:12; 52:6) and the emphatic form *'ānokî 'ānokî hû'* twice (Isa 43:25; 51:12), making a total count of either seven or nine instances — just as John's series could be counted either as seven or as nine, since the last saying given in 18:5 is repeated twice in vv. 6 and 8. In the series of seven absolute "I am" sayings of John's Gospel, therefore, the sevenfold — and thus complete — assertion of Yahweh's unique and exclusive divinity made in the Hebrew Bible is repeated by Jesus as the one who achieves the eschatological salvation and the universal recognition of Yahweh's unique divinity that it entails.

The "I am he" declarations of Deuteronomy 32 and deutero-Isaiah are among the most emphatically monotheistic assertions of the Hebrew Bible. If Jesus in the Fourth Gospel repeats them with application to himself, he must be seen as unambiguously identifying himself with the one and only God, Yahweh, the God of Israel. It does not do justice to these sayings to view them, as some scholars do, merely as an expression of an "agent" or "emissary" christology in the Fourth Gospel. This is a label for the notion that (1) Jesus comes into the world as the agent of God who sends him, for in the Fourth Gospel he very often refers to his Father as "the one who sent me," (2) as God's agent he has full powers to act for God, and so (3) in a sense, as God's agent, Jesus stands in for God.

There is, of course, no doubt that "agency" plays an important part in the portrayal of Jesus in John's Gospel — that is, that Jesus acts, in some sense, as God's agent or emissary. But when these ideas of agency are seen in their wider context in the Fourth Gospel, including the absolute "I am" sayings, it is clear that it is not sufficient to suppose that God sends *someone else* to act as his agent in salvation. What this agent does is not something that God can delegate to someone other than God, since it belongs to the uniquely divine prerogatives of the one God. Only one who truly shares the unique divine identity can give eternal life and reveal God's glory in the world. Jesus' absolute "I am" sayings express his unique and exclusive participation in God's unique and exclusive deity. For just as "I am [he]" in the Hebrew Bible sums up what it is to be truly God, so in John the expression identifies Jesus as truly God in the fullest sense.

The Contexts of the Absolute "I Am" Sayings

We can appreciate this better when we attend not only to the phrase "I am [he]" itself, but also to its contexts in both the Old Testament and John's Gospel.

The first Old Testament occurrence of the formula in Deut 32:39 stresses the uniqueness of Yahweh as sovereign over life and death:

> Behold, I, even I am [he];
>> there is no god besides me.
> I kill and I make alive (cf. 1 Sam 2:6).

Similarly, the Jesus who tells the Samaritan woman that "I am [he]" in John 4:26 has already implicitly claimed to be more than a human Messiah by offering the living water from which eternal life springs (cf v. 14). And Jesus' self-declarations "I am [he]" in John 8 are closely connected with his power to deliver from death (cf. vv. 24, 51-53).

In deutero-Isaiah, the divine "I am [he]" is linked closely with the uniqueness of Yahweh's eternal sovereignty as the One who precedes all things and whom none shall succeed (41:4; 43:10; 48:12). And it is this uniquely divine eternity that Jesus claims in John 8:58: "Before Abraham was, I am." Also in the deutero-Isaianic usage, Yahweh's "I am [he]" includes his claim to be the only Savior (43:11-13; 46:4). Yahweh is the only Savior because he is the only true God. And Jesus' identification with Yahweh in the Fourth Gospel is similarly connected with the exclusivity of his salvific role. In fact, Jesus' hearers "will die in your sins unless you believe that I am he" (8:24) — because it is in his unique and exclusive identity with the one God that eschatological salvation is achieved.

In deutero-Isaiah an important feature in the claim to unique divinity is that, unlike the purported gods of the nations, Yahweh announces beforehand the things that are to come about. This is not merely his power of prediction, but his sovereign power to accomplish what he plans. It is associated with the "I am [he]" self-declaration in Isa 43:9-10. And it is this aspect of the unique divine identity that comes to the fore in John 13, where, having predicted Judas's betrayal (v. 18; cf. 6:70), Jesus tells his disciples: "I tell you this now, before it occurs, so that when it does occur, you may believe that I am he" (v. 19).

As in deutero-Isaiah, these words of Jesus in John's Gospel are not a matter of mere prediction. Rather, they speak of Jesus' sovereignty over the events that lead to his death. When Judas goes to do what he must, it is at Jesus' express command (13:27). And when Judas arrives at Gethsemane with the soldiers, Jesus gives himself up to them — identifying himself for them with the words "I am [he]" (18:5), which are repeated for emphasis once by the evangelist and then once again by Jesus (18:6, 8).

The formula of divine identity reminds us that this was Jesus' own sovereign accomplishment of what he had purposed — that is, that his disciples, seeing what he had predicted had occurred, should now believe that he is "I am he" (13:19). We should also notice that this climactic seventh absolute "I am" saying brings Jesus' identity with Yahweh into direct connection with his death. It is as the uniquely divine Savior who fulfills the sovereign divine purpose that Jesus goes voluntarily to his death — thereby completing his salvific work.

Also notable is the contrast between the scene at Gethsemane in 18:1-11, with Jesus' absolute "I am" sayings of vv. 5, 6, and 8, and the dispute between Jesus and the Jewish leaders in John 8, with Jesus' absolute "I am" sayings of vv. 24, 28, and 58. For in John 8 the reaction of the Jewish authorities to Jesus' utterance of divine self-identification is to take up stones to stone him for blasphemy (v. 59), whereas in John 18 the soldiers "stepped back and fell to the ground" (v. 6).

At the literal level of the narrative as ordinary history, no doubt the soldiers hear Jesus' words as nothing more than an identification of himself as Jesus, the man they are seeking to arrest, and so they are taken aback by the open directness of his admission of who he is. But, as in some other passages of the Johannine narrative, there is a further, ironic level at which the characters act much more significantly than they themselves know or understand. At this level, on hearing the claim to unique divine identity, "I am [he]," they fall down in worship — which is the only appropriate response to recognition of the one true God ("fall to the ground" was frequently used in Jewish parlance of obeisance and prostration in worship). At this seventh absolute "I am" saying — which as seventh symbolically completes the revelation of the unique divinity of the one God in Jesus — both Gentiles (the Roman soldiers) and Jews (the temple police) bow in worship and submission.

The scene probably also reflects one of the most significant passages in deutero-Isaiah's prophetic account of the revelation of Yahweh to the world in his eschatological act of salvation for Israel and the nations —

that is, Isa 45:18-24. This passage begins with an "I am he" declaration (though only in the Septuagint; the Hebrew has "I am Yahweh"): "I am he, and there is no other' (v. 18). This declaration is then repeated in other terms in vv. 19, 21, and 22, as Yahweh proclaims to the nations whose idols have failed them that he alone is the only God and the only Savior:

> I am God and there is no other besides me,
>   a righteous one and a Savior, there is none but me.
> Turn to me and be saved, people from the end of the earth.
> I am God and there is no other.
> By myself I swear . . .
>   that to me every knee shall bow,
>   and every tongue shall swear by God (Isa 45:21-24 LXX).

This is the passage to which Phil 2:9-11 alludes, reading it as referring to the final acknowledgment by every creature in creation of the divinity of the one God, who is revealed in Jesus.

The scene at Gethsemane in John's Gospel is, of course, no more than a symbolic anticipation of that eschatological goal. But it is the evangelist's way of indicating that Jesus' passion, which at Gethsemane he undertook irrevocably in its totality, was both the achievement of salvation for all and the revelation of God's glory to all, such that the unique identity of the one God is demonstrated and wins the recognition of all.

Summation

By way of summation, we may return to the connections among the seven signs, the seven "I am" sayings with predicates, and these seven absolute "I am" sayings we have studied. In their different ways, all three series of sevens reveal who Jesus is and the salvation he gives.

Salvation in the Fourth Gospel can be summarized as knowing the true God and receiving eternal life from him. The signs reveal God's glory in Jesus and the salvation that Jesus brings. As acts of evident divine power, the signs demonstrate what the sayings can only say; whereas the two sets of "I am" sayings make fully explicit what the signs signify.

One series, the "I am" sayings with predicates, focuses on Jesus as the only Savior, using a variety of images that instance the inexhaustible fullness of what salvation means. In these sayings, as in the signs, it is implicit that Jesus can be the only Savior only because he is identified with the only God.

To reveal the glory of God's unique identity and to give the eternal life that God alone has in himself, however, Jesus must himself belong to God's own unique identity. This is what the absolute "I am" sayings make fully explicit. They do this in a sevenfold series of progressive clarity — with Jesus uttering the most concise and comprehensive expression of all that it means for God to be uniquely and truly God. They identify Jesus with God, not just abstractly but in a way that the Scriptures associate with the universal revelation of God's unique divinity in his eschatological act of salvation for Israel and the nations. Jesus' identity with God is, therefore, essential and intrinsic to his work of revelation and salvation.

4. Jesus and the Father as the One God

The second occasion in John's Gospel when Jewish leaders take up stones to stone Jesus for blasphemy is in response to his statement, "I and the Father are one" (10:30). Although, so far as I am aware, no one else has ever suggested such a correlation, it seems to me very probable that this saying of Jesus alludes to the Jewish confession of faith in the one God, the *Shema,* which begins with the words of Deut 6:4: "Yahweh our God, Yahweh is one." This was the most familiar of all monotheistic formulas. Devout Jews recited it daily. It is frequently cited in Jewish literature in the abbreviated form "God is One" — a form in which it also appears in the New Testament (cf. Rom 3:30; Gal 3:20; Jas 2:19). The confession says nothing about the unitariness of God's nature, but simply indicates that Yahweh is the one and only God.

In all the Greek echoes of the *Shema* the word for "one" is masculine *(heis),* as we should expect, whereas in John 10:30 it is neuter *(hen).* But this is a necessary adaptation of language. For Jesus is not saying that he and the Father are a single person, but that together they are one God. That the Fourth Evangelist should in this way incorporate Jesus into the affirmation of one God in the *Shema* is not especially surprising. Paul had already done the same thing in a different way in 1 Cor 8:6 ("For us there is one God, the Father, from whom are all things and for whom we exist, and one Lord, Jesus Christ, through whom are all things and through whom we exist").

Jesus' assertion of his oneness with the Father occurs twice more in

John's Gospel, both in Jesus' prayer to the Father in ch. 17. In both cases Jesus prays that his disciples "may be one, as we are one" (vv. 11 and 22). This analogy between the oneness of Jesus and his Father and the oneness of the disciples has been used to argue that the former indicates no more than a closeness of association or concurrence of will. But, again, attention to the background of these words in the context of Jewish monotheism clarifies the issue considerably.

Jewish writers sometimes say that to the one God there corresponds "one" of something else that belongs especially to him in the world: one temple, one altar, one Law, and especially one chosen people (Josephus, *Antiquities* 4.201; *Contra Apionem* 2.193; *2 Baruch* 48:23-24). And they view the service and worship of the one God as that which unites the people of God (Philo, *De Specialibus Legibus* 1.52; 4.159; *De Virtutibus* 35; Josephus, *Antiquities* 5.111). This Jewish *topos* in no way, of course, implied that God was a unity in the same sense as his people are. It meant only that the divine singularity draws the singular people of God together into a relational unity. In a similar way Jesus prays in John 17:11 and 22 that his disciples might be a single community corresponding to the uniqueness of the one God, in which he and his Father are united (cf. also 10:16).

Whereas the absolute "I am" sayings express Jesus' divine identity without explicit reference to the Father, Jesus' statements of his oneness with the Father indicate that it is as Father and Son that God and Jesus relate to each other within the unique divine identity. When in John 10, in the face of the accusation of blasphemy, Jesus goes on to defend his claim that he and the Father are one, he ends his defense by making yet another statement that provokes the Jewish leaders to try to take legal action against him: "The Father is in me and I am in the Father" (v. 38; see also 14:10, 11, 20; 17:20-23). Evidently, this reciprocal indwelling — the closest conceivable intimacy of relationship — is the inner reality of the oneness of Father and Son. Their unity does not erase their difference, but differentiates them in an inseparable relationship.

We should also notice that the terms "Father" and "Son" entail each other. The Father is called Father only because Jesus is his Son, and Jesus is called Son only because he is the Son of his divine Father. Each is essential to the identity of the other. So to say that Jesus and the Father are one is to say that the unique divine identity comprises the relationship in which the Father is who he is only in relation to the Son and the Son is who he is only in relation to the Father.

It is in the portrayal of this intra-divine relationship that John's christology steps outside the categories of a Jewish monotheistic definition of the unique identity of God. It does not deny or contradict a Jewish monotheistic definition of God. Rather, on the basis of Jesus' relationship to God, the portrayal of this intra-divine relationship in the Fourth Gospel serves to redefine the divine identity as one in which Father and Son are inseparably united in differentiation from each other.

Conclusion

The monotheistic theme in the Gospel of John is far from being merely an apologetic or polemical device designed to show, against Jewish objections to christology, that divine christology is not incompatible with Jewish monotheism. For the proclamation that Jesus belongs to the unique identity of the one and only God has theological roots in the deepest theological concerns of this Gospel. Its theme is the eschatological revelation of God's glory to all and his achievement of definitive salvation for all, as foreseen especially in Isaiah 40–55.

The one true God reveals himself savingly only in the Son, who can reveal God and communicate eternal life only because he is one with the Father. The unique and exclusive divinity of the only God can be revealed savingly in Jesus only because Jesus participates uniquely and exclusively in that divinity.

Without contradicting or rejecting any of the existing features of Jewish monotheism, the Fourth Gospel, therefore, redefines Jewish monotheism as christological monotheism. Christological monotheism is a form of monotheism in which the relationship of Jesus the Son to his Father is integral to the definition of who the one true God is.

SELECTED BIBLIOGRAPHY

Appold, Mark L. *The Oneness Motif in the Fourth Gospel.* Tübingen: Mohr-Siebeck, 1976.
Ashton, John. *Understanding the Fourth Gospel.* Oxford: Clarendon, 1991.
Ball, David Mark. *"I Am" in John's Gospel: Literary Function, Background and Theological Implications.* Sheffield: Sheffield Academic, 1996.

Bauckham, Richard. *God Crucified: Monotheism and Christology in the New Testament.* Carlisle: Paternoster, 1998; Grand Rapids: Eerdmans, 1999.

Boismard, Marie-Émile. *Moses or Jesus: An Essay in Johannine Christology,* trans. B. T. Viviano. Leuven: Peeters; Minneapolis: Fortress, 1993.

Dodd, C. H. *The Interpretation of the Fourth Gospel.* Cambridge: Cambridge University Press, 1968.

Evans, Craig A. *Word and Glory: On the Exegetical and Theological Background of John's Prologue.* Sheffield: Sheffield Academic, 1993.

Harris, Murray J. *Jesus as God: The New Testament Use of* Theos *in Reference to Jesus.* Grand Rapids: Baker, 1992.

Lincoln, Andrew T. *Truth on Trial: The Lawsuit Motif in the Fourth Gospel.* Peabody: Hendrickson, 2000.

Moloney, Francis J. *Signs and Shadows: Reading John 5–12.* Minneapolis: Fortress, 1996.

Morris, Leon. *Jesus Is the Christ: Studies in the Theology of John.* Leicester: Inter-Varsity; Grand Rapids: Eerdmans, 1989.

Neyrey, Jerome H. *An Ideology of Revolt: John's Christology in Social Science Perspective.* Philadelphia: Fortress, 1988.

Williams, Catrin H. *I am He: The Interpretation of* 'ani hu' *in Jewish and Early Christian Literature.* Tübingen: Mohr-Siebeck, 2000.

III. PAULINE LETTERS

CHAPTER 8

The Christology of the Early Pauline Letters

Douglas J. Moo

The christology of the early Pauline letters — here taken as Galatians, 1 Thessalonians, 2 Thessalonians, 1 Corinthians, 2 Corinthians, and Romans, in that probable order of writing — presents a striking paradox. For while christology pervades these letters and is basic to virtually everything taught, Paul rarely tackles it as a topic in its own right. He refers directly to Jesus by one name or another almost four hundred fifty times in these letters, or about once every three verses. And all that he teaches, like the spokes of a wheel, radiates out from Jesus Christ — especially from Jesus' death and resurrection. Yet not once is christology the central topic of a passage in these letters. Or to introduce another metaphor, it might be said that Jesus' person and work in Paul's early letters are like the foundation of a building: it might not be seen very often, but everything rests on it.

We may draw two conclusions from this paradox. First, christology must not have been a matter of contention in the churches to which Paul wrote these early letters. Paul and his churches apparently were in basic agreement about who Jesus was and what he had done. Their disagreements arose over the significance of his person and work. Second, Paul must have inherited a good deal of his understanding of Jesus' person and work from Christians who had gone before him. Almost all the titles that he applies to Jesus were established before he wrote. He appears to cite early traditions about Jesus and his work at several key points, but engages in very little creative elaboration of the significance of Jesus.

The paucity of key christological passages in Paul's early letters also creates a challenge for the investigation of his christology. For it is difficult to know just how to get a handle on a christology that is more assumed than taught and that makes its appearances in various scattered references.

Four possible approaches come to mind. One could, following out what might appear to be an obvious approach, simply summarize the evidence as it comes, working through each letter, perhaps in some chronological order, to see if any significant development occurs. But such an approach would be tediously repetitive, since Paul appeals to so many of the same christological points in all these letters. Moreover, significant development in Paul's christology over the course of the decade during which these letters were written does not seem to have taken place. A second possibility would be to follow the lead of James Dunn, who uses Romans as his point of departure *(The Theology of Paul the Apostle)*. But one has to wonder whether this approach might bias the whole conception of Paul's theology in favor of the particular issues confronted in Romans. And, in any case, the approach would not seem to be as helpful for a specific topic such as christology, which is not a major focus of Romans.

A third possible approach would be to summarize Paul's christology by looking, in turn, at each of the titles Paul attributes to Jesus: "Christ," "Lord," "Son of God," "Son of David," and so forth. However, while a time-honored way of studying New Testament christology at various levels, the "title" approach has fallen out of favor in recent years. And if one uses titles as the sole approach to Paul's christology, the disfavor is warranted. Paul is certainly interested in who Jesus is, and a study of the titles that Paul attributes to Jesus can illuminate this feature of his teaching. But the identity of Jesus is wrapped up for Paul in what Jesus has done. Focusing exclusively on titles, therefore, can miss important aspects of Paul's christology.

Yet a fourth approach to Paul's christology grows out of a renewed emphasis on the narrative structures that underlie the teaching of the letters in the New Testament, and so inform the study of New Testament theology generally. Richard Hays has argued that Paul wrote his letters with an implicit narrative of the life of Jesus in mind (see his *The Faith of Jesus Christ: An Investigation of the Narrative Substructure of Galatians 3:1– 4:11* [Chico: Scholars, 1983], especially 139-91). And N. T. Wright and others, building on Hays's narrative understanding, have proposed that Paul's theology grows out of the story of God's dealings with Israel, with Jesus as the hermeneutical key to the meaning of that story (see Wright, *The New Testament and the People of God* [Minneapolis: Fortress, 1992], especially 31-80).

The narrative approach is a fruitful one, rightly recognizing the degree to which Paul operates within the story-centered worldview of first-century Judaism. To be sure, Hays may find more allusions to Jesus' life than the evidence warrants. And Wright may put too much of his own "spin" on Israel's story and fail to do justice to the degree to which Paul moves beyond the story of Israel to the story of humankind. But this is not to minimize the usefulness of the general approach for illuminating Paul's theology.

But none of these approaches is by itself capable of illuminating the full gamut of Jesus' person and work in the early Pauline letters. This chapter, therefore, will use three different approaches to survey the matter. The first two will operate with basic narrative structures. In Part 1 we will focus on Paul's presentation of Christ as the climax of salvation history. In Part 2 we will use the stages of Jesus' life to survey much of Paul's christological teaching. Finally, in Part 3 we will examine the implications of several of the key titles Paul uses to describe Christ.

1. The Climax of Salvation History

Jews in Paul's day disagreed on many theological issues. But all Jews anticipated the day when God would intervene on behalf of his suffering and oppressed people, fulfilling his promises and establishing righteousness. Influenced by the apocalyptic movement, Jews used a scheme of contrasting ages or epochs to describe this transitional point in salvation history. God's intervention, whether it would take place directly or through an intermediary such as a messianic figure, would bring an end to "this age," the old age of Israel's oppression, and introduce "the age to come," a new age of blessing and salvation.

Paul uses such an apocalyptic two-age scheme to understand and describe Jesus Christ (e.g., Gal 1:4; Rom 12:2). Jesus' death and resurrection, along with the pouring out of God's Spirit, mark the transition from the old age to the new. Jesus is the climax of salvation history, and Christians are those "on whom the fulfillment of the ages has come" (1 Cor 10:11).

Paul inherited much of his theology from Christians who had gone before him. Not least is this the case with respect to christology. But Paul himself insists that the epochal significance of Jesus Christ was not passed on to him from someone else. Rather, it came, as he puts it in Gal 1:12, through "a revelation of Jesus Christ." Here Paul refers to the appearance of the risen Jesus to himself on the Damascus Road. Through this event Paul was suddenly confronted with the realization that the man he had scorned as cursed by God (cf. Gal 3:13; see also 1 Cor 1:23 and Gal 5:11) was none other than God's Messiah. Jesus of Nazareth was the turning point of the ages. And this basic fact was for Paul the essence of the gospel (cf. Gal 1:11).

Scholars, therefore, rightly point to Paul's dramatic Damascus Road experience as the seedbed of his theology. Here we will focus specifically on three key facets of Christ that Paul found particularly significant in that Christ-encounter and conversion experience: (1) Jesus as "the seed of Abraham," (2) Jesus as "the climax of the Law," and (3) Jesus as "the last Adam."

The Seed of Abraham

In Galatians 1 Paul insists that he received his gospel directly from the risen Christ. He does this in order to vindicate his right to define the content of that gospel in the face of the false teachers at Galatia, who were seeking to win his converts over to their version of the gospel. Fundamental to their program was the insistence that followers of Jesus the Messiah needed to confirm their identity as God's people by submitting to certain key provisions of the Law of Moses — especially those provisions pertaining to circumcision, food laws, and religious observances.

Paul's main objection to this line of reasoning is what can be called "salvation-historical." For Jesus' appearance on the Damascus Road revealed to him that the turn of the ages had taken place. Paul associates the Law of Moses with that old age and so concludes that Christians should not have to submit to the provisions of the Law anymore. People who insist on adherence to the Law of Moses for a right standing before God are, in fact, alienating themselves from Christ — they are falling away from the grace that marks the new age of redemption (Gal 5:4; cf. 1:4).

Paul's salvation-historical argument and its christological foundation come to expression most clearly in Gal 3:15–4:7, where he focuses on three key events in salvation history: (1) God's promise to Abraham, (2) the giving of the Law at Sinai, and (3) the appearance of Christ. God's promise to Abraham, he insists, initiated a covenant that the subsequent introduction of the Law could not annul (3:17). Moreover, that initial covenant, because it expressed the unconditional promise of God, was a matter of grace. Yet the Law covenant, requiring as it does human obedience for its validity, stands in contrast to the grace of the Abrahamic provision (3:18). Where is christology in all of this? Just here: Jesus brings to an end the era of the Law and introduces the fulfillment of the Abrahamic promise of grace — which is experienced through faith because Jesus is the "seed" to whom the promise was originally made (3:16).

Paul's claim here is notoriously difficult. The "seed" of Abraham, whom God promised to bless in Genesis, includes his many descendants. The word is a generic singular (Gen 12:7; 13:15; 24:7) and was so understood in Jewish tradition. The "seed of Abraham," therefore, was the Jewish people, the inheritors of the blessing God originally promised to Abraham.

Paul's exegesis in Gal 3:15–4:7 is more than a *tour de force*. His proclamation in 3:29, where he insists that everyone who belongs to Christ is "Abraham's seed," reveals that he well understands the collective sense of the noun *sperma*, "seed" (cf. also Rom 4:13-18). The combination in this text, then, of first the singular — *Christ* is the "seed of Abraham" — and then the plural — *Christians* are the "seed of Abraham" — reveals that Paul is viewing Christ as a corporate figure. In a development hinted at in many other New Testament texts, Jesus is viewed as the embodiment of Israel, God's true people. All of God's promises find their fulfillment in him, and the entire plan of God comes to its climax in him. It is, then, by identifying with him in faith that others can experience the blessings of those fulfilled promises and plan. In a somewhat parallel development, Paul in 4:1-7 can proclaim Jesus as God's Son *par excellence* and at the same time include believers as God's sons and daughters through their inclusion in the Son's redemptive work.

So in what is arguably Paul's earliest letter, Jesus Christ is presented as the one to whom God's promises ultimately refer and, therefore, as the one whose appearance marks the turn of the ages. He is the center and climax of salvation history.

The Climax of the Law

The "seed" christology of Galatians 3 is intended to establish the basis for Paul's claim that Gentile Christians need not submit to the Law of Moses in order to maintain their position within the people of God. While the point is debated, it yet remains most probable that all the language expressing Christ's relationship to the Law is temporal in force — that is, as we would paraphrase Gal 3:25, "the law was the custodian of Israel *until* Christ came." Discontinuity between Abraham and the Law in the Old Covenant and between Christ and the Law in the New Covenant dominates Paul's letter to the Galatians. Naturally enough, such a theology supports Paul's plea to the Galatian Christians not to submit to the Law.

Much of this same theology reappears in Paul's letter to the Romans. But the lack of a clearly polemical occasion behind Romans frees Paul to take a more inclusive approach to the matter of Christ and the Law. The same discontinuities between the Law and Christ reappear in Romans (e.g., 3:20, 21; 4:13-16; 6:14, 15). But these discontinuities are embraced in a wider continuity in God's plan. The Law and Christ are separate, representing successive stages in salvation history. But what emerges forcefully in Romans (though it is surely implied in Galatians) is how the Law, and the era it represents, also belong inseparably to the same salvation history. God's righteousness in Christ, though manifested "apart from the Law," is nevertheless witnessed to by the Law and the Prophets (3:21).

Paul's famous claim about Christ and the Law in Rom 10:4 must be interpreted in light of this comprehensive vision of salvation history. The verse is usually rendered in English versions as "Christ is the end of the Law." This translation suggests — though it does not strictly require — a discontinuous emphasis: Christ brings the Law to an end. But the word translated "end" *(telos)* is not so clearly temporal in its meaning as the English "end" tends to be. It can also mean "goal" or "outcome" (e.g., Rom 6:22; 1 Tim 1:5). It is the root from which we get our words "telic" and "teleology." Scholars have, therefore, long debated whether Rom 10:4 means that Christ ends the Law or that he is the hidden meaning or intended goal of the Law. But a growing number of scholars are convinced that Paul intends something of a combination of these nuances.

Exploiting the racetrack imagery that Paul uses in this context (9:30-32), we could compare Christ to the finish line in a race. As the finish line represents both the "end" of the race and its goal, so Christ is both the goal of the Law and its end. He is the point that the Law has all along had in mind, the "end" toward which it is directed. His coming, therefore, brings the Law and the era it stands for to its climax or culmination. In its context, Rom 10:4 explains the failure of the Jews to embrace the righteousness of God in Christ (v. 3). They have become so preoccupied with the race that they have failed to recognize that the finish line has been reached.

Rom 10:4 should be set alongside Matt 5:17 as a key expression of the nuanced early Christian view of salvation history. As the culmination of the Law, Jesus stands at the center of salvation history, inaugurating the age in which he, not Moses, sets forth God's demands for his people (so one understanding of Matt 5:17). Paul can, therefore, claim that Christians are to find authoritative divine guidance in "the law of Christ" (Gal 6:2; cf. 1 Cor 9:20-21).

We have seen that Paul claims to have derived the essence of his gospel, focused in the epochal significance of Christ, from the revelation of Christ to him on the Damascus Road. Scholars have speculated that the same event might have been the impetus in Paul's view of Christ as culmination of the Law. For Jesus' death on a Roman cross would, according to the Law, have marked him as a man cursed by God (cf. Deut 21:23, which, significantly, Paul quotes in Gal 3:13). On the Damascus Road, however, Paul is suddenly and unexpectedly confronted with the indisputable evidence that Jesus is none other than God's Messiah. And this revelation confronted Paul with the choice between Messiah and the Law. For if the Law was the final and definitive expression of God's will, then Jesus could not be the Messiah. But if Jesus was, in fact, the Messiah, then the Law must not have the central place in the plan of God that Saul the Pharisee had been giving it.

The Last Adam

The revelation of Christ to Paul on the Damascus Road may also have figured in another important way that Paul expresses the epochal significance of Jesus — that is, his status as "the last Adam." From whence Paul derived his concept of Christ as a corporate figure, parallel to Adam, is debated. The idea that he might have been influenced by Gnostic-type speculations about a heavenly redeemer figure has now generally given way to attempts to trace the concept to Jewish antecedents. One intriguing possibility is that the appearance of Jesus to him on the Damascus Road led Paul to identify him as the "image of God" and therefore as one comparable to the original man, Adam, who was created in the image of God (see Kim, *The Origin of Paul's Gospel,* especially 162-268). But whatever its origin, Paul's conception of Christ as "the last Adam," which comes to expression in

1 Cor 15:21-22, 45-49 and Rom 5:12-21, is another way in which he proclaims the epochal significance of Christ.

In 1 Corinthians 15 and Romans 5 Paul presents both Adam and Christ as individuals whose actions affect all who belong to them. Adam's sin introduces sin and death into the world (Rom 5:12). In a manner never specified, though endlessly debated by theologians, Adam's sin is at the same time the sin of all human beings (cf. Rom 5:12 with 5:18-19). Therefore, as Paul puts it in 1 Cor 15:22, "In Adam all die."

But Paul's primary focus in these passages is not on Adam, sin, and death, but on Christ and life. The theological debates over Adam's representative significance arise because Paul, who assumes that his readers are familiar with the basic tradition, never spells out the details. He simply alludes to Adam in order to argue that Christ is a figure of similar epochal significance. The powers of the old age, sin and death, were introduced by Adam — and not even God's Law is capable of breaking their hold on human beings (Rom 5:20). But Adam is a "type of the one to come" (Rom 5:14). And that "one to come" is Jesus Christ, whose one act of righteousness, his death on the cross in obedience to the Father's will, introduces the new age of righteousness and life (Rom 5:18, 19).

Romans, unlike 1 Corinthians, emphasizes the present state of righteousness that is available to all who are "in Christ." But both Romans and 1 Corinthians — though 1 Corinthians more explicitly than Romans — emphasize the certainty of future resurrection life through Christ, whose own resurrection is the surety and basis for the resurrection of believers (1 Cor 15:20-23). All people bear the likeness of Adam. But the people of the new age will bear the likeness of Christ, "the man from heaven" and "life-giving spirit" (1 Cor 15:45-49).

If the Damascus Road experience triggered Paul's identification of Christ as the last Adam, the Old Testament would have furnished him with the necessary conceptual categories to develop the corporate dimensions of Christ's person. For in a way quite foreign to most modern western thinking, the Old Testament views the nature and destiny of groups of people in terms of the actions of a key individual. Attention to this more collective way of thinking will help us do justice to two other sets of distinctively Pauline christological passages: those that use the phrase "with Christ" and those that use the phrase "in Christ." Both ideas, "with Christ" and "in Christ," are probably corollaries of Paul's basic conviction that Christ is "the last Adam," a corporate figure.

Paul claims that believers participate "with Christ" in the whole gamut of redemptive events: from Christ's suffering (e.g., Rom 8:17) to his death and burial (e.g., Rom 6:4-8; Col 2:12, 20) to his resurrection (e.g., Col 2:12) to his return in glory (e.g., 1 Thess 4:14). We must avoid a wooden literalism in explaining these passages. But they seem, at minimum, to imply a conception of Christ according to which believers are in God's sight included in the redemptive actions of Christ. What he does, they do. And although it does not use the "with Christ" language, a passage such as 2 Cor 5:14b fits here: "We are convinced that one died for all, and therefore all died."

Paul's notoriously difficult "in Christ" formula should probably be explained along similar lines. Paul uses the phrase almost forty times in the letters with which we are concerned (sometimes with "Jesus" or "Jesus our Lord" added), and he uses the parallel "in the Lord" another twenty-five times. To be sure, some of these phrases may have a merely instrumental force — that is, "through Christ" (e.g., Rom 8:1; 2 Cor 3:14). Others are virtually adjectival — as, for example, "the church in Judea *in Christ*," which may be read simply as "the Judean *Christian* churches" (Gal 1:22). But in the majority of cases, some kind of local idea seems to be clearly expressed — signifying that Christ is the context in which the believer lives, the touchstone for all that the believer says and does.

The concepts of being "with Christ" and being "in Christ," therefore, imply that Paul views Christ as a corporate figure. And the connection with "last Adam" christology is strongly suggested by the wording of 1 Cor 15:22: "As in Adam all die, so in Christ all will be made alive." Jesus Christ is the climax not only of Israel's story but also of humanity's story. Renewed attention to the Jewish matrix of Paul's thinking should not blind us to the fact that Paul's vision of Christ ultimately transcends the story of Israel. Paul may begin with the narrative of Israel, but he does not end there.

2. The Stages of Jesus' Life

As a product of the contemporary narrative turn in theology, Pauline scholars have suggested that the apostle's theology may owe more to an underlying "story" of Jesus' life than had previously been recognized. While some of the specific conclusions drawn from this new approach have been unconvincing, it does appropriately recognize the degree to which Paul's theology is the product of reflection on redemptive events. Indeed, a narrative approach holds particular promise for a study of Paul's christology. So in this section we will use the stages of Jesus' life as they are reflected in Paul's teaching to go more deeply into the christology of his early letters.

Preexistence and Incarnation

Contemporary discussion of Paul's teaching about Jesus' preexistence and incarnation reflects the impact of two developments. One is the claim of James Dunn that Paul does not teach the personal preexistence of Jesus (*Christology in the Making*). The other, closely related to the first, is the suggestion that speculation in Second Temple Judaism about certain intermediary figures, especially Wisdom, might have provided the context for the early Christian ascription of preexistence — and ultimately of deity — to Jesus. The issue of Jesus' deity will have to wait for a later section in this chapter. Furthermore, the texts of greatest relevance for the issue of Jesus' preexistence fall outside the early Pauline letters we are considering. So we will here confine ourselves to two brief points.

First, the possible Wisdom influence on certain key texts in Paul should not be used, as Dunn does, to deny the personal preexistence of Christ in those texts. Paul explicitly identifies Jesus as "the wisdom of God" in 1 Cor 1:24 and may very well imply this identity in several other texts. But the influence of wisdom thought on Paul might be exaggerated. For outside 1 Corinthians 1–4, where Paul apparently adopts the language of the Corinthians, the evidence for wisdom influence on the christology in the early Pauline letters is slight and allusive. Much depends on alleged parallels to Paul's language in the Jewish wisdom texts. But the parallels are not always clear. And where such parallels may be claimed to appear, they are overwhelmed by closer parallels in other material.

But however common or basic such parallels might be, Paul's identification of Christ with Wisdom constitutes no reason to deny personal preexistence in the key texts. In 1 Cor 8:6, for instance, Paul associates Jesus with God in the act of creation: "Yet for us there is but one God, the Father, from whom all things came and for whom we live; and there is but one Lord, Jesus Christ, through whom all things came and through whom we live." Dunn argues that Paul is simply applying Wisdom language to Christ to affirm of him what Jews believed about Wisdom: that it embodied the power of God (*Christology in the Making*, 182). But Paul's focus is not on the power of God generally; rather, it is specifically on the *creative* power of God. The work of creation, which Jews often attributed to Wisdom, Paul now attributes to Christ. And since Christ is a person, his personal preexistence is clearly assumed in this text.

But this is to anticipate our second point: that Paul clearly assumes the preexistence of Jesus in asserting (1) that Christ was involved with God in the creation of the world (1 Cor 8:6) and (2) that he was the "rock" that followed the Israelites in the desert (1 Cor 10:4, which is another alleged Wisdom text). Furthermore, in claiming that Jesus, "though he was rich, yet for your sakes he became poor" (2 Cor 8:9), Paul anticipates the more explicit incarnational language of Phil 2:7. And Paul's references to Jesus being "sent" also imply preexistence (Gal 4:4; Rom 8:3; cf. also Rom 8:32). Nevertheless, it is true, that while Paul in his early letters assumes Christ's preexistence and can use his incarnation as a basis for ethical exhortation, he attributes in these letters very little christological significance to Jesus' preexistence or incarnation.

Earthly Life

Paul refers only rarely to the earthly life of Jesus — apart, of course, from his death, which is critical to Paul's christology. If we limited ourselves to the early letters of Paul, we would know only that Jesus was human (Rom 8:3; Gal 4:4), that he was a Jew (Gal 4:4), that he was from the royal line of David (Rom 1:3), that he instituted a meal to commemorate his death (1 Cor 11:23-26), and that he sought to please others (Rom 15:3; cf. 2 Cor 10:1). Paul explicitly cites the teaching of Jesus on two occasions, in 1 Cor 7:10 (contrast vv. 12 and 25) and 1 Cor 9:14. Probably he does so also in 1 Thess 4:15, where "the word of the Lord" is best taken to refer to Jesus' own teaching on eschatology.

In addition to these explicit references, there are a handful of texts in which verbal resemblances point to Paul's dependence on the teaching of Jesus (see especially Rom 12:14; 14:4; 1 Cor 13:2; and 1 Thess 5:2, 4; 5:13). The teaching of Jesus may, as well, have informed Paul's theology in a number of other ways (see D. Wenham, *Paul: Follower of Jesus or Founder of Christianity?* [Grand Rapids: Eerdmans, 1995]). Scholarly assessments of the degree to which Paul was directly influenced by Jesus' teaching and life vary widely. Dependence is difficult to prove, for some of the similarities could be explained by Paul's reliance on early Christian tradition. And even on the most generous assessment, we still end up with comparatively few references to Jesus' earthly life. How are we to explain this circumstance?

Rudolf Bultmann, following the lead of some other theologians of his day, insisted that the paucity of references indicated Paul's negative attitude toward the earthly life of Jesus. Paul's interest was in the resurrected Lord, not the human Jesus. And 2 Cor 5:16 was sometimes cited as evidence of Paul's disregard. The verse was understood to mean that Paul no longer would have any concern with "Christ in his fleshly state." But this interpretation of the verse is now almost universally rejected. What Paul is claiming is that he no longer regards Christ "from a fleshly point of view." Moreover, just because Paul says little about Jesus' earthly life in his letters does not mean that he did not know or was uninterested in Jesus' life.

Nevertheless, the relative silence in Paul's early letters about Jesus' earthly life suggests that Paul found little of theological importance in these historical details. It was vital to his christology that Jesus was truly human and was subject to the power of the Law and to sin (Rom 6:10). For Paul puts these facts to work in what Morna Hooker has called the "interchange" pattern (see especially "Interchange in Christ," *JTS* 22 [1971] 349-61; "Interchange and Atonement," *BJRL* 60 [1976] 462-81). According to this pattern, Christ becomes what we are so that we might become what he is. In Gal 4:3-5, for instance, Jesus, the Son of God, is "born under the Law" so that he can redeem those who were under the Law and turn them into God's sons and daughters. And in Rom 8:1-3, Jesus assumes our humanity so that he might take on himself the condemnation that we would otherwise have merited. These texts suggest that Paul's references to Jesus earthly life serve especially to validate the reality of his death. For it is here that Paul's christology comes to its chief point.

Death

In 1 Cor 2:2, Paul claims that he "resolved to know nothing while I was with you except Jesus Christ and him crucified." What Paul means by this is that the crucifixion of Christ was for him the focal point of all his theology and preaching. And it is not only among the Corinthians that Paul maintained the centrality of Christ's death. In Romans, after identifying the revelation of God's righteousness as the heart of the gospel, Paul grounds that righteousness in the sacrificial death of Jesus (Rom 3:21-26). The "one act of righteousness," or the "obedience" of Christ, which more than cancels the effects of Adam's sin, probably refers to Jesus' death (Rom 5:18, 19). In 2 Corinthians, Christ's death, his being made sin for us, is the basis for the message of reconciliation (5:14-15, 21). The true gospel, as distinguished from that which Paul's opponents at Galatia were advocating, focuses on the public presentation of Christ crucified (Gal 3:1; cf. 2:21; 3:13). And Paul can encapsulate the message in which he boasts and for which he is being persecuted as "the cross of Christ" (Gal 6:12, 14).

To be sure, Paul says little about the death of Christ in the Thessalonian letters — the only direct references being 1 Thess 4:14, "we believe that Jesus died and rose again," and 5:10, "he died for us so that, whether we are awake or asleep, we may live together with him." But this relative silence indicates not that the death of Christ was unimportant in Paul's interaction with the Thessalonians. Rather, it suggests that the death of Christ was the assumed foundation for all the other issues that he addresses.

This conclusion is strengthened by the fact that the language of 1 Thess 5:10 reflects a standard Pauline formula that speaks of Christ dying or being handed over "for us" or "for our sins" (Rom 4:25; 5:6, 8; 8:32; 14:15; 1 Cor 8:11; Gal 2:20; 3:13) — sometimes, as in 1 Thess 5:10, with a purpose clause added (cf. Gal 1:4; Rom 14:9; 2 Cor 5:15, 21). And it is just this point — "that Christ died for our sins" — that Paul identifies in 1 Cor 15:3 as one of the key components of the gospel message that he inherited from Christians before him. So we are justified in concluding that Christ's death was fundamental to early Christian teaching and to the gospel that Paul proclaimed wherever he went.

The crucified Messiah is, therefore, the center of gravity in Paul's christology. While considered foolishness to the Greeks and a stumbling block to Jews (1 Cor 1:23), Jesus' death on a Roman cross signals the turn of the ages and is the foundation for the new people, drawn from both Jews and Gentiles, that God calls into being. God acted to reconcile the entire world to himself in Christ (2 Cor 5:19).

But why did Jesus' death have such an epochal importance? A satisfactory answer to that question would take us far beyond the bounds of this chapter. We can, however, get a sense of the basic lines of an answer from Rom 3:24-25 — which appears in the midst of a passage that is unparalleled for its theological density. Prior to these two verses, Paul has proclaimed the revelation of God's righteousness as the solution to the problem of human sinfulness (1:18–3:20) and insisted that anyone who believes has the opportunity to experience that righteousness (3:21-22). This faith, as v. 26 will make clear, is christologically oriented — that is, it is "faith in Jesus" (taking *Iēsou* as an objective genitive). Then after a parenthetical reminder of the universality of sin (3:23), Paul resumes his exposition of God's righteousness here in 3:24-25. Since the righteousness of God is his acting to put his people in a right relationship before him, Paul can use the verb "being justified" to pick up the theme of vv. 21-22.

But what is especially relevant for us in Rom 3:24-25 is Paul's explanation of the basis for God's justifying verdict. That basis is Christ's death. And three aspects of that death deserve mention here.

First, Jesus' death accomplishes a "buying back" or "redemption" *(apolytrōsis).* The *lytro-* word group is prominent in New Testament explanations of Jesus' death, although the early letters of Paul use this specific language in only two other places (Rom 8:23; 1 Cor 1:30). The Greeks used this word group to denote the process by which slaves could purchase their freedom. And this imagery fits Rom 3:24 very well, since Paul has earlier described the condition of human beings as being in slavery to sin (3:9). But a more specific background is probably to be found in the Old Testament, where this language was used to describe God's delivery of the Israelites from their slavery in Egypt (e.g., Deut 7:8; Isa 43:1; 44:22-24). Thus God accomplishes a new exodus by sending his Son as the price for setting his people free from sin. And this basic image lies behind other texts in which Paul speaks of God "buying" or "buying back" Christians (Gal 3:13; 4:5; 1 Cor 6:20; 7:23).

A second feature of Jesus' death highlighted in Rom 3:24-25 is that of his death as a sacrifice. Paul makes this clear in v. 25 both by using the cultic language of *hilastērion* (NIV "sacrifice of atonement") and by referring to Jesus' blood. References to "blood" inevitably invoke the idea of sacrifice in a world where the bloody offering of animals was basic to so many religions (cf. also Rom 5:9; 1 Cor 10:16; 11:25, 27). Indeed, sacrifice is the dominant metaphor that Paul uses in his letters to unpack the significance of Jesus' death. The widespread language we noted above of "for us" and "for our sins" connotes the idea of sacrifice. Rom 8:3 probably also refers to Jesus' death as a "sin offering," for the expression it uses, *peri hamartias,* has this sense in the Septuagint. And, as an extension of his new exodus motif, Paul describes Christ as "our Passover lamb," sacrificed for us (1 Cor 5:7).

But if Jesus' death as a sacrifice effects a new and climactic exodus, it also marks a new and climactic Day of Atonement. And here, implied in his reference to Christ as a *hilastērion,* is the third feature to be noted in Paul's treatment of Jesus' death. For though the term *hilastērion* in Rom 3:25 has been interpreted in several ways, recent scholarship has seen a trend, if not a consensus, that maintains a connection with its dominant Septuagintal reference — that is, the "mercy seat," where the sacrificial blood was sprinkled on the Day of Atonement (Lev 16:14, 15). This "mercy seat," or "atonement cover" (NIV), was so dominant in the Day of Atonement ritual that it came to represent that ritual as a whole. So Christ, Paul implies, is the place where God deals with his people's sin. It is only here in his letters that Paul describes Christ in this way, probably signaling his dependence on an early Jewish Christian interpretation of Jesus' death that surfaces more often and more explicitly in the letter to the Hebrews (see especially Heb 9:11-15).

Resurrection

If Jesus' death is the dominant focus in Paul's christology, Jesus' resurrection is a close second. Indeed, the death and resurrection of Jesus are often paired as two intertwined redemptive events (see especially Rom 4:25; 5:10; 6:5, 10; 8:34; 14:9; 2 Cor 4:10; 5:15; 13:4; 1 Thess 4:14). Typical is Rom 14:9: "For this very reason, Christ died and returned to life so that he might be Lord of both the dead and the living." The pairing is, of course, traditional, as the summary of the gospel in 1 Cor 15:3-8 again reveals: "Christ died for our sins . . . he was buried . . . he was raised on the third day."

At the risk of introducing a distinction where none exists, we might suggest that Paul tends to present Jesus' death as backward-looking and his resurrection as forward-looking. Jesus' sacrificial death rescues human beings from their slavery to sin; his resurrection initiates a new age of spiritual power and, ultimately, resurrected life (Rom 6:4; 2 Cor 4:11).

Resurrection is an eschatological event. Jesus' resurrection, therefore, signals that the final age of fulfillment has dawned. And, as Rom 1:4 suggests, Jesus' resurrection also signals a new stage in his own unique relationship to the Father as Son of God. Those who belong to Christ share in the power of that new existence (Rom 6:4, 10-11) — even as they long for the day when the body itself will be raised "with Christ." He is the "firstfruits," whose resurrection provides for the resurrection of all those who belong to him (1 Cor 15:20-23, 45-49; Rom 8:11; 2 Cor 4:14). To deny Jesus' resurrection is to deny the reality of the new age of redemption and to be left in slavery to sin (1 Cor 15:17).

Exaltation

Paul never refers to Jesus' ascension. And the present reign of Christ in heaven is not a prominent motif in the early letters of Paul. Following the lead of other early Christians, he applies the language of Ps 110:1 to Jesus (Rom 8:34) and so speaks of "Christ Jesus" as being "at the right hand" of the Father. And it is probably Ps 110:1 that provides in 1 Cor 15:25 the starting point for Paul's only extensive reflection on Christ's exalted state: "For he must reign until he has put all his enemies under his feet."

Christians interpreted Ps 110:1 as a statement of God the Father addressed to Jesus: "The Lord says to my Lord: 'Sit at my right hand until I make your enemies a footstool for your feet.'" Paul applies the last part of this verse in 1 Cor 15:25 to Christ's current reign in heaven. Only after the last enemy, death, has been destroyed, will Christ "hand over the kingdom to God the Father" (15:24). Until then, Paul makes clear, using the language of Ps 8:6, Christ rules over all things — whether they be people, the forces of nature, or the spiritual realm (cf. Rom 8:35-39).

Many scholars suspect that Paul's use of Psalm 8 in this context reflects an underlying identification of Jesus as Son of Man, which is a title that Paul never uses. But this is far from clear. The phrase "under his feet" would probably have been sufficient to link Ps 110:1 with Ps 8:6 in Paul's mind.

Parousia

Paul identifies Jesus' *parousia* (i.e., "coming," "return") as the event that will trigger the resurrection of believers and bring this age to a close (1 Cor 15:23). References to the *parousia*, however, are spread very unevenly across Paul's early letters. Galatians and 2 Corinthians contain no clear reference to it at all, though "the Day of the Lord" is mentioned in 2 Cor 1:14. Romans probably refers to it in 11:26b and 13:11. 1 Corinthians has several clear allusions (1:7-8; 4:5; 11:26; 15:23; 16:22; cf. also "the Day of the Lord" in 5:5). It is, however, a dominant topic in 1 and 2 Thessalonians.

These statistics should not be taken as signaling a move of Paul away from apocalyptic eschatology. Rather, they simply reflect the occasional nature of the letters. As the Aramaic expression *Marana tha* ("Come, O Lord!") in 1 Cor 16:22 and the probably traditional character of 1 Thess 1:10 reveal, Paul inherited the teaching of the *parousia* from those who came before him.

The theme of Christ's *parousia* appears so prominently in Paul's Thessalonian letters for two reasons. First, Christians at Thessalonica were confused about events associated with it. They worried about the fate of believers who had died before the *parousia,* and, for some reason, they had become convinced that it was to take place at any moment. So Paul assures them that believers who have died will not be at a disadvantage when Christ returns (1 Thess 4:13-18) and seeks to calm them by reminding them of events that must precede the parousia (2 Thess 2:1-12). Second, the persecution that believers at Thessalonica were suffering led Paul to remind them of the comfort they would receive and the punishment their persecutors would suffer when Christ returned (cf. 1 Thess 1:10; 2 Thess 1:5-10).

These emphases in the Thessalonian letters reflect the general importance of the *parousia* for Paul's christology. The fact of the *parousia* highlights again the epochal significance of Christ. For as Christ's resurrection inaugurated the age of redemption, so his return will consummate it by triggering the resurrection and redemption of his people and the end-time judgment.

3. The Titles

Study of New Testament christology has been bedeviled by an insistence on distinguishing between function and ontology. The early Christians, it is said, were interested in what Jesus did and not so much in who he was. There is some truth in the claim, and thus we have focused so far in this chapter on the way in which Paul's christology emerges from his description of Jesus' work. But as Richard Bauckham has recently emphasized, any final separation between the two categories is impossible (*God Crucified,* 40-42). Paul and the other early Christians could hardly have described what Jesus did without reflecting on the implications of those actions for who he was. And it is at this point that the titles that Paul uses for Jesus come into play.

We have briefly mentioned the significance of several titles in our discussions of Jesus' epochal significance and the stages of his life. But some specific attention still needs to be given to four very important titles: "Christ," "Son of God," "Lord," and "God."

Christ

Christ is by far the most common designation of Jesus in Paul's letters, occurring over 270 times in the entire Pauline corpus and 210 times in the early letters we are considering. *Christos* is the Greek equivalent for the Hebrew *māšîaḥ*, which means "anointed one" and is transliterated "Messiah." The word is not applied to human beings in native Greek speech. So its application to Jesus must reflect the early Christian conviction that Jesus was the agent of eschatological deliverance promised in the Old Testament and expected by the Jews. Paul, therefore, inherits the title, but it is questionable how much significance it had for him.

Several considerations suggest that Paul usually uses "Christ" as not much more than a proper name. First, the very number of occurrences tends to diminish the force of the word. Second, Paul never uses "Christ" as a predicate — that is, he never makes claims such as "Jesus is the Christ." And third, Paul exchanges "Christ" with "Jesus" and other names for him in an apparently arbitrary manner. These circumstances have led to a virtual scholarly consensus that, with the exception of perhaps a handful of texts, Paul uses "Christ" with only referential value, as a proper name and no more.

Some dissenting voices, however, have begun to be heard. These scholars point out that Paul only twice, in Rom 16:18 and Col 3:24, combines "Christ" and "Lord" without further titles — as we would expect him to do if "Christ" were, indeed, no more than a proper name. They also point to texts in which "Christ" does appear to have titular value. Rom 9:5, where Paul lists "the Christ" among the blessings God gave Israel, is the clearest. But there are a number of other such texts, such as Rom 15:3, 7, 8; 1 Cor 1:3; 10:4; 12:12. Furthermore, it must be questioned whether a Jew like Paul, who had been converted to a new movement whose distinguishing claim was that God's promised Messiah was none other than Jesus of Nazareth, crucified by the Romans, could ever have fully discarded the rich Jewish associations of the word.

We need, therefore, to establish a middle ground. Indeed, Paul rarely uses "Christ" to communicate a theological point to his mainly Gentile audiences. Furthermore, he appears to use the word usually without giving much thought to its significance. But there still clings to the word in Paul's letters, more clearly in some texts than others, an allusion to the Old Testament and Jewish background against which Jesus must be understood (see Witherington, "Christology," 98).

Son of God

Paul refers to Jesus as God's Son relatively infrequently — only fifteen times in the early letters we are considering. But the title is more important than simple frequency would imply, for it occurs in several pivotal texts. In Romans, for instance, Paul's opening statement regarding the content of his gospel has to do with God's Son — who was revealed in his earthly state as the Davidic Messiah, "Son of David," but appointed through his resurrection as "Son of God in power" (1:3-4). Christ, Paul implies, has always existed as God's Son, but the resurrection has elevated him to a new status in which he has the power to dispense salvation to the world (cf. also 1:9, 16). And similar key introductory identifications of Christ as "his [God's] Son" or "Son of God" occur in 1 Cor 1:9; 2 Cor 1:19; Gal 1:16; and 1 Thess 1:10 — all of which indicate that for Paul, Jesus' identity as Son of God was integral to the gospel.

The title "Son of God" is not unambiguously attested as a Messianic title in Judaism. There are a few texts, however, which suggest that the title might have been used, through application of Old Testament texts such as 2 Sam 7:14, of the Messiah (see especially 4QFlor 1.10-12; also 4Q246). Perhaps more relevant to Paul's usage is Old Testament and Jewish use of "son" to denote an especially close relationship between individuals or between the nation Israel and God.

But Paul goes even further than these analogies, implying that Jesus stands in a unique relationship to the Father. This is suggested both by the "sending" passages in Rom 8:3 and Gal 4:4 (as noted above) and by the attribution to the Son of divine titles and functions in such passages as 1 Cor

15:28 and 1 Thess 1:10. And Paul's preservation of Jesus' distinctive address to God as *Abba*, "Father," in Rom 8:15 and Gal 4:6 moves in the same direction. Therefore, while the title in itself does not connote deity, it does serve to identify Jesus with God the Father in a relationship that has no precedent and no parallel.

Lord

If "Christ" is Paul's most common designation of Jesus, "Lord" is his most important. He uses the title less frequently than "Christ," but not by much. It occurs 180 times in the letters we are considering. Of course, not all these refer to Jesus. At least sixteen refer to Yahweh in Old Testament quotations and references to the Old Testament. And another ten or so may be debated. But this leaves at least 150 that refer to Jesus, which is an impressive number.

Paul uses the title in various combinations with "Jesus" and/or "Christ," but he more often uses it on its own. The importance of the title in Paul's letters can be gauged from such texts as Rom 10:9, where the confession "Jesus is Lord" summarizes Christian commitment (see also Rom 14:9; 1 Cor 12:3). As could be guessed from its frequency, the title is used in a wide variety of contexts. But Paul uses it especially often in two situations: (1) when he is instructing Christians about the conduct expected of them as those who claim Christ as their "master," and (2) when he describes Jesus' present reign and future coming in glory. In Galatians, for instance, where these events are not prominent, "Lord" occurs only four times, whereas Paul uses it twenty-two times in each of the Thessalonian letters.

Scholars in the "history of religions" school of interpretation, seeking to uncover a clear line of development in New Testament christology, claimed that the title "Lord" first emerged in the Greek-speaking Gentile churches, the Christians having taken the title from the Hellenistic cults and applied it to Jesus, the object of worship in the new Christian cult (e.g., W. Bousset, *Kyrios Christos* [Nashville: Abingdon, 1970], 121-52). That this context might help explain Paul's usage is evident from 1 Cor 8:5-6, where Paul contrasts the "one Lord, Jesus Christ" with the many other "lords" of the Greco-Roman world.

But evidence for a much earlier application of the title to Jesus is overwhelming. Particularly striking is the preservation in 1 Cor 16:22 of the Aramaic prayer *Marana tha*, "Our Lord, come!" — or possibly this should be read as a declaration: *Maran atha*, "Our Lord *has* come." However the Aramaic expression is understood, it seems evident that the title "Lord" was applied to Jesus by Aramaic-speaking Christians long before Paul — in fact, the title seems to go back to the earliest days of the Christian movement. And if we seek a Jewish background for the title, the use among Greek-speaking Jews of *kyrios* for Yahweh in the Old Testament emerges as the most likely candidate.

This background receives some degree of confirmation from Paul himself. For in at least four places he implicitly identifies the Lord in Old Testament quotations with Christ: in Rom 10:13 (Joel 2:32), in 1 Cor 1:31 and 2 Cor 10:17 (Jer 9:23-24), and in 2 Thess 1:8-10 (Isa 2:10, 19, 21). Furthermore, in a similar development, he replaces Yahweh with Christ in the common Old Testament eschatological formula "the Day of the Lord" in 1 Thess 5:2; 2 Thess 2:2; 1 Cor 1:8; 5:5; and 2 Cor 1:14. And throughout his letters he presumes that it is the Lord Christ whom believers are to obey and to whom they are accountable.

It may be said, therefore, that in all likelihood Paul and other early Christians called Jesus "Lord" because they viewed him as functioning for them as Yahweh did for the people of God in the Old Testament. But how far did Paul take this functional overlap between Jesus and God? This is the question we will consider in dealing with the title "God."

God

When we consider "God" as a christological title in the early Pauline letters, two issues arise. First, does Paul attribute to Christ functions and honors that are unique to God? The answer to this question is an unqualified "yes."

Some of the key points have already been noted above. But to those can be added the evidence from Paul's early letters that he and other Christians prayed to Jesus (e.g., 1 Cor 1:2; 16:22; 2 Cor 12:8; 1 Thess 3:11-13; 2 Thess 2:16) and worshiped him (e.g., 1 Cor 12:3). Furthermore, Paul puts Jesus in the role of eschatological judge (e.g., 2 Cor 5:10; 2 Thess 2:7-9). Especially impressive is 1 Cor 8:6: "For us there is but one God, the Father, from whom all things came and for whom we live; and there is but one Lord, Je-

sus Christ, through whom all things came and through whom we live."
Here, combined with an explicit reassertion of Jewish monotheism, we
find Christ given the title "Lord" and associated with God in the work of
creation and providence.

Equally telling, though somewhat more indirect, are the ways in
which Paul develops an implicit binitarianism in the way he associates Jesus with God. The "wish prayers" in his salutations always include Jesus
with God — as, for example, 2 Cor 1:2: "Grace and peace to you from God
our Father and the Lord Jesus Christ." Likewise, he can shift from phrases
such as "the gospel of God" to "the gospel of Christ" without comment (cf.
1 Thess 2:2, 8, 9 with 3:2). And in a few passages an implicit trinitarianism is
also discernible (e.g., Rom 8:1-11; 2 Cor 13:13).

The second issue is this: Does Paul ever go so far as actually to call Jesus "God" in these early letters? Here Rom 9:5 is the one text to consider.
After listing in vv. 4-5a the blessings and privileges that God has conferred
on Israel and concluding that list in v. 5b with reference to God's blessing
of his people with "the Christ" (*ho Christos*, i.e., "the Messiah"), he then
adds a doxology or further blessing: "the one who is over all, God, forever
blessed." The question, which our earliest manuscripts do not answer, is
one of punctuation: Should we place a period after "the Christ," in which
case praise is offered to God the Father? Or, should the punctuation mark
be a comma, in which case the word of praise would apply to the Messiah?
Considerations of both context and style point to the latter alternative.
And so we should probably translate: "Christ, who is supreme over all as
God blessed forever" (see Harris, *Jesus as God,* 143-72).

With the application of the title "God" to Jesus, we reach the high
point of Paul's christology in his early letters. The use of the title for Jesus
should not surprise us. For Paul, with his Jewish training, could hardly ascribe divine functions to Jesus without implying or presupposing his divine identity. But the question still persists: How could Paul call Jesus God
and at the same time preserve his bedrock belief in monotheism? And that
is a major and complex question.

Some scholars have suggested that certain Jewish intermediary figures, such as Wisdom and the Word, may have paved the way for the early
Christian ascription of deity to Jesus. Richard Bauckham, however, is right
to question this approach. As he argues, it fails to do justice to the overwhelming emphasis in Judaism on the absolute distinction between God
and the rest of creation. Nor does the association of Jesus with "semi-

divine" figures such as Wisdom do justice to the high claim Paul makes for Christ. Rather, as Bauckham aptly argues, Paul includes Jesus in the "divine identity," and so transforms Jewish monotheism into christological monotheism (see Bauckham, *God Crucified,* especially 16-42; see also pp. 148-66 above).

SELECTED BIBLIOGRAPHY

Bauckham, Richard. *God Crucified: Monotheism and Christology in the New Testament.* Grand Rapids: Eerdmans, 1998.

Byrne, Brendan. "Christ's Pre-existence in Pauline Soteriology," *Theological Studies* 58 (1997) 308-30.

Dunn, James D. G. *Christology in the Making: A New Testament Inquiry into the Origins of the Doctrine of the Incarnation.* Philadelphia: Westminster, 1980.

————. *The Theology of Paul the Apostle.* Grand Rapids: Eerdmans, 1998.

Furnish, Victor Paul. *Jesus According to Paul.* Cambridge: Cambridge University Press, 1993.

Harris, Murray J. *Jesus as God: The New Testament Use of* Theos *in Reference to Jesus.* Grand Rapids: Baker, 1992.

Hengel, Martin. "Christological Titles in Early Christianity," in *The Messiah: Developments in Earliest Judaism and Christianity,* ed. J. H. Charlesworth. Minneapolis: Fortress, 1992, 425-48.

————. *The Son of God: The Origin of Christology and the History of Jewish-Hellenistic Religions.* Philadelphia: Fortress, 1976.

Hurtado, Larry W. *One God, One Lord: Early Christian Devotion and Ancient Jewish Monotheism.* Philadelphia: Fortress, 1988.

————. "Lord" and "Son of God," in *Dictionary of Paul and His Letters,* ed. G. F. Hawthorne, R. P. Martin, and D. G. Reid. Downers Grove: InterVarsity, 1993, 560-69 and 900-906.

Jonge, Marinus de. *Christology in Context: The Earliest Christian Response to Jesus.* Philadelphia: Westminster, 1988.

Keck, Leander E. "Toward the Renewal of New Testament Christology," *NTS* 32 (1986) 362-77.

Kim, Seyoon. *The Origin of Paul's Gospel.* Tübingen: Mohr-Siebeck; Grand Rapids: Eerdmans, 1981.

Matera, Frank J. *New Testament Christology.* Louisville: Westminster/John Knox, 1999.

Ridderbos, Herman. *Paul: An Outline of His Theology.* Grand Rapids: Eerdmans, 1975.

Witherington, Ben, III. "Christ" and "Christology," in *Dictionary of Paul and His Letters,* ed. G. F. Hawthorne, R. P. Martin, and D. G. Reid. Downers Grove: InterVarsity, 1993, 95-115.

Wright, N. Thomas. *The Climax of the Covenant: Christ and the Law in Pauline Theology.* Minneapolis: Fortress, 1991.

CHAPTER 9

The Christology of the Prison Epistles

Ralph P. Martin

In Paul's thought and theology, knowledge about Christ's person is bound up with an understanding of his saving work. So we must approach our task with Melanchthon's dictum in mind: "To know Christ is to know his benefits" — to which Melanchthon adds, "not to reflect upon his natures and the modes of his incarnation" (*Loci communes* [1521], trans. in the *Library of Christian Classics* 19.21-22).

A further necessary preparation for our present enterprise is to set the Prison Epistles in their historical contexts. For Paul's theology is always to be understood as a transcript of his ministry as pastor-teacher. And it is in light of the community needs he was addressing that we should seek his understanding of the role accorded to the Lord of the church as well as the cosmos. We aim, therefore, to take seriously in our study of Pauline christology the interaction of *coherence* (i.e., the convictional center of the apostle's thought) and *contingency* (i.e., the pastoral and theological problems that arose in the congregational life of his churches), as far as these may be known.

The letters in question purport to have been written by "Paul the prisoner." Their author repeatedly alludes to his imprisonment, his chains, and the circumstances of his being detained. There is no certainty, however, as to the precise location of that imprisonment — or even if it is the same imprisonment for the composition of Philippians (1:7, 12-17, 30) and the writing of Colossians and Philemon (Col 1:24; 2:1; 4:18; Phlm 1, 23). Philippians is more specific and circumstantial, suggesting that Paul was facing a death sentence with his life in the balance (2:17). Ephesians, on the other hand, may use the idea of "Paul the prisoner" (3:1; 6:20) as a rhetorical device to highlight the role of Paul as a faithful martyr — if, indeed, that document is the product of a disciple of Paul who sought to reinforce his master's teaching after his demise. And the same rhetorical ploy has been suggested for "Paul's" reference to his "chains" in Col 4:18 — if that letter, too, is to be seen as a testamentary appeal to Paul's noble example as a suffering apostle. Conceivably, such a life setting could very well have a bearing on our understanding of the christology of Colossians and Ephesians.

1. Philippians

Philippians is a friendship letter addressed to believers in the Roman colony of Philippi in Macedonia. A close bond of affection and loyalty had united the apostle and the Philippian Christians since the church's founding (cf. Acts 16:12-40; Phil 1:7; 4:1). Evidence for this comes partly from the way he pays tribute to the Philippians for their gifts of money in support of his ministry (2:25-30; 4:10-20; perhaps also 1:3) and partly from the warm terms of endearment he uses in writing (e.g., 4:1).

At a deeper level, however, Paul addresses problems that the Philippians were facing. These consisted of external pressures from a hostile society (1:27-30; 2:15), and internal issues arising within the congregation's life, where self-seeking and criticism were causing disunion and there was a mood of habitual complaining about its lot as an afflicted church (2:1-4, 14-15). Possibly this spirit of divisiveness related not only to believers having to endure hardships, which some were finding hard to explain (as implied in 1:29-30), but also reflected discontent with Paul himself as a suffering apostle, whose absence some could not understand (as implied in 1:26).

Here we touch on a key idea of the entire letter. For what Paul presents is a theodicy, or an explanation of God's working, to justify both his readers' persecution and his own suffering. He presents his case by means of an explication of the person and work of Christ that links both their afflictions and his (and his colleagues') trials with the obedience of the church's Lord, who passed through earthly sufferings to vindication as cosmic Ruler.

In so doing, Paul gives a paradigm of the biblical principle that God will bring his faithful ones through trial to ultimate victory. He does this by focusing on the "Christ hymn" of 2:6-11, which is at the heart of the letter in every way. In what follows, therefore, we will trace the impact of this hymn throughout all the chapters of the letter, thereby highlighting in the process the coherence of the letter as a whole.

The Story of Christ: Lordship as Ethical Impetus

In view of the external and internal threats facing the congregation, Paul calls its members to steadfastness and courage (1:27; 4:1) and to unity "in the Lord" (2:1-4; 4:2). These virtues are linked to humility and self-disregard. Paul is not simply handing out bromides to faltering faith. Nor is he calling for oneness on purely prudential grounds. Rather, his rationale is given on the basis of God's sovereign control, and his call to unity rests on a theology of what life in Christ should mean. The key is a selfless regard for others and an active desire for a neighbor's well-being, which prefers another's good rather than one's own. This is part of Paul's *koinōnia* ethics, in which believers are viewed as "members of one body." So we should regard Paul's use of the hymn in 2:6-11 less as a call to imitate humble love, as seen in the incarnate and glorified Lord, and more as a way of expressing what "life in Christ" means and how it sets a pattern to which his converts should conform their corporate life.

The introductory verse to the hymn, 2:5, with its elliptical syntax and need to supply a second verb, should be rendered: "Let this way of life be yours, such as you have in Christ Jesus." It is a call for members of Christ's community to live under Christ's lordship. The ethical admonitions of 2:1-4 prepare the readers for what is to come, just as 2:12, which follows the hymn, enforces the exhortation: "As you have always obeyed [the call to your Christian identity as those confessing Jesus Christ as Lord], so apply the message [of the quoted passage in vv. 6-11] to your well-being, expressed as *sōtēria* [salvation], as God's people."

The noble verses in 2:6-11 almost baffle analysis. This is what might be expected once it is recognized, as most do, that this passage is poetic, imaginative, and quite possibly liturgical in form and setting. Being replete with non-Pauline and rare idioms, it is rightly considered an early Christian hymn that Paul has inserted into his letter.

As to its sequence, the hymn flows in a logical and progressive measure. It sets out the "road" that Christ Jesus took from God's eternal presence, which he enjoyed "in the beginning" (v. 6), to his ultimate glory alongside God's throne, which he now shares. That is, it sets out a narrative whose central features consist of incarnation (v. 7), humble obedience to death (v. 8), and exaltation (vv. 9-11). Evocative metaphors are drawn from the Old Testament, chiefly Adam, who aspired to be "like God" (Gen 3:5), the Suffering Servant of Isa 53:12, who "poured out" his life in death, and the vindicated king-Messiah of Ps 110:1, who is now elevated to co-regency with Israel's covenant God and seated at God's "right hand" — with all hostile powers brought to subservience and acknowledgment of his authority (cf. Isa 45:23). Hence the hymn's center of gravity is the confession by all cosmic forces that "Jesus Christ is *Lord*," which is the very name of God himself (Yahweh) and whose Greek equivalent *kyrios* denotes the right to rule.

As Paul utilized this confessional material of poetic couplets and stanzas — perhaps enriching an original version to bring out the emphases that he wished to highlight — he evidently did so with a single purpose in view. Clearly, his quoting of the hymn was meant to enforce an ethical appeal. Opinion, however, is sharply divided regarding the ground of this appeal.

In a traditional reading of the text, the hymn sets out the example of the humble Christ as a model to rebuke pride and point the way to true selflessness. Paul is faced with a proud and wayward congregation (2:1-4, 14; 4:2). So his call to humility is reinforced by this recital of the path of lowly condescension that was taken by the Lord (2:8). On such a view, v. 5 is understood to be exhorting: "Act as he acted, and resemble the one who revealed God as self-giving, humble love." On this reading of the text and its setting, the hymn reminds readers how gracious God is and elevates Christ's example *ad imitandum* by spurring the readers to follow his steps.

In several places elsewhere, however, I have taken issue with this popular view. Here it will be sufficient simply to restate how Paul's adopting of the cosmic lordship of Christ is a better guide to how the hymn functions in the pastoral context of the Philippian letter. And as a simplified caption under which the hymn may, in our view, be more adequately viewed, we give it the title "Living under Christ's Lordship."

The following three exegetical pointers may here be offered in support:

(1) As noted above, v. 5 is more convincingly understood as saying "Act as it befits those who are in Christ Jesus." The formula "in Christ Jesus" is Paul's shorthand expression for what it means to be incorporated into the community that owes its first allegiance to the church's Lord (1:27).

(2) The structure of the hymn, which is set in a succession of couplets with *parallelismus membrorum* being the key poetic feature, confirms how the flow of the hymn, which sets out the odyssey of Christ, moves to its climax in the second stanza — with the first stanza setting the stage for the great reversal at v. 9:

Stanza I (vv. 6-8)

[It is he] who was in the form of God,
Yet he did not regard it as a prize to be equal with God,

But he emptied himself,
Being born in human likeness.

And disclosing himself in human appearance,
He humbled himself, becoming obedient to death
  [even death on a cross].

Stanza II (vv. 9-11)

So therefore God highly exalted him,
And engraced him with the name high above all names

That at the name of Jesus,
Every knee should bow

And every tongue acknowledge
That "Jesus Christ is Lord"
  [to the glory of God the Father].

(3) Only on such a basis that makes *the obedience of Christ* the key to Stanza I and *the lordship of Christ* the culmination of the saga in Stanza II can we give true weight to Paul's appeal in v. 12, where his exhortation is to "obey the obedient one." It is to Christ's "way" that believers are summoned to conform; and it is his authority, which was achieved as God's vindication of the road he was willing to take from heavenly glory to the ignominy of death, that provides the ground plan for their life in Christ. It is this life, with its behavior patterns spelled out negatively in 2:1-4, that re-

ceives the approbation of God — just as Christ's lowly abasement in obedience in vv. 6-8 was rewarded by the eschatological endorsement in vv. 9-11. This latter theme will be worked out in 3:20, 21, which we will consider later when we set out Paul's cosmic christology in a wider frame.

The Story Illustrated: Lordship as a Way of Life

The finale of the hymn, as found in Stanza II, declares the sole lordship of Christ as victor over all alien powers. This would give believers at Philippi the courage they needed to live in a none-too-friendly society (2:15), for it proclaimed that the Lord to whom they address their encomium of praise is *Christus Victor.* It is a lesson not to be lost on a company of men and women living in a Roman colony (Acts 16:12-40), whose "life in the city" has already been mentioned and who have been given the clarion call: "Whatever happens, live your life in a manner worthy of the gospel of Christ" (1:27).

Christ's lordship would also be a powerful incentive to living together in unity and love, since Christ came to his throne only along a road of self-giving sacrifice and service. He refused to use his "right" within the divine life as a means of "exploiting" that privilege (v. 6, NRSV). Rather, he surrendered his claims and chose "equality with God" as a gift of grace (v. 9). In any community of people called into being by such an act of divine-human condescension, the only appropriate way of life is obedience to the servant-king. So the Philippians should proceed to move from their hymn-singing to repairing human relationships — which activity is exhorted in v. 12: "Work out your own salvation."

Their life together in fellowship with the once-crucified Lord should be the antidote to questioning about their lot as sufferers (2:14). (Paul will return to this point later in 3:10, using language of conforming to the suffering Lord, and in 3:20-21, pointing on to the ultimate conforming to the glorified body of Christ at the *parousia.*) To drive home the thrust of this appeal, which is securely rooted in his christology of cosmic lordship, Paul goes on to show how "living under the authority" of Christ the Lord is to be understood by reference to a set of human models — himself (2:17; 3:8-21) and Timothy and Epaphroditus (2:9-30).

Links between the hymn's language and Paul's autobiographical statements in the letter have often been noted. His life is being "poured out" (2:17), just like that of the suffering servant (2:7; cf. Isa 53:12). His reflection on his ambition to reach out to grasp the prize (3:12-13) runs parallel to the idiom used in 2:6-8. The heavenly Christ always had a place in the life of the Father-God as his "form" (2:6), yet was also presented with the possibility of snatching "equality with God" by seizure or exploitation — as an athlete or swimmer might leap off a springboard and use that start to his or her own advantage. But Christ, the hymn reports, did not aspire to gain lordship in this way. Yet Paul wants to respond to the call to go forward (3:14). So the parallel, which is suggested by the common Greek verb "to reckon" in both 2:6 and 3:7-8, is not exact.

Nor is the parallelism that is often adduced between 2:6-11 and 3:20-21 exactly appropriate. The hymnic conclusion, indeed, brought the obedient Christ to a dignity that was conferred on him as a gracious act (2:9), which installed him as sovereign Lord. But while the hope of resurrection and final conformity to Christ's likeness (3:21) are part of God's saving design (1:10; 2:16), there is no confusion in Paul's thought between the Savior (3:20) and the saved (3:21). Nor is there any hint of Christians being finally rewarded for their meekness and selfless regard for others, which are called for in 2:1-4. Such a prudential motive — which is called by some commentators "eschatological reward" or "vindication" (e.g., Fee, *Philippians,* 44), that is, "Be humble now, so that you may share in Christ's otherworldly glory and office" — is explicitly denied in 2:4: "Don't look to your own interests."

More to the point is Paul's eagerness to be obedient at any cost — even his willingness to meet a martyr's fate. Only in such an understanding of being "in Christ" lies the secret of "partnership" (*koinōnia,* a key term in the letter) with Christ's sufferings and conformity to Christ's pattern of dying to live (3:10-11). Conformity to Christ's sufferings and pattern of dying to live, however, is always with the promise of resurrection as a final, yet to be realized, goal (3:11; cf. 4:5, "the Lord is near," which may include the prayer call of 1 Cor 16:22, *Marana tha,* "Our Lord, come!" as a desire for the *parousia*).

Two colleagues of Paul, both known to the Philippians, are also brought forward in the letter to illustrate the "story of Christ" epitomized in 2:6-11. In particular, Timothy's "worth" in Christian ministry (2:22) and Epaphroditus's courage in a near-death trauma (2:27) contribute to Paul's argument.

Timothy was described in the letter's prescript as a "servant" *(doulos)* of Christ Jesus (1:1), just as Jesus in the hymn is identified as having taken the rank of a "servant" (2:7). And Timothy is said to have played the part of a servant *(edouleusen)* as one bound to the apostle in filial relationship (2:22). His sterling character is praised in 2:20 as unrivaled among Paul's coworkers — with the term *isopsychos,* "of like soul" or "mind," recalling *isa theō,* "like God," in 2:6. Clearly, Paul's language is designed to portray his colleague as one who has lived out the Christ model.

But such modeling of Christ is even more pronounced in the case of Epaphroditus, who is praised as Paul's kinsman in the faith and as engaged in the same conflict as Paul (1:30) as a fellow struggler (2:25-30). Moreover, his sickness brought him to death's door (2:27, 30). "Close to death" (v. 30, NRSV) renders *mechri thanatou* — which is the exact phrasing of the hymn at 2:8.

Again, however, the reference is not precise. For Epaphroditus did not die, whereas Christ's obedience did lead to his death on the cross. But the point is that Epaphroditus exhibited the same spirit of sacrifice in loyalty to the Pauline mission, as one whose life was "in Christ Jesus" (2:5). And the wording of 2:30 — "he came close to death for the work of Christ, risking his life to make up for those services that you could not give me" — would not be lost on the self-seeking Philippians, who are charged in 2:1-4 to renounce their "individual interests" *(ta heautōn).*

These three examples are given to believers who were indeed "seeking their own interests" *(ta heautōn zētousin),* as the sad complaint of 2:21 characterizes them. All three would be to believers at Philippi powerful reminders of Christian leaders whose "life under Christ's lordship" made them conformable to a pattern of service, sacrifice, and, above all, obedience. Thus Paul exhorts his readers: "Brothers and sisters, join in imitating me, and observe those who live according to the example you have in us" (3:17) — spelling that out in terms of what "you have learned and received and heard and seen in me," with the promise that "the God of peace will be with you."

Summation

The christology of Philippians is focused in a noble depiction of the *cosmic* Lord in the Christ hymn of 2:6-11, with the hymn reflecting a double sense in the use of the adjective. For his becoming human has its frontispiece in his life with God and his sharing the divine "image," "glory," and "rank" of God (2:6, *en morphē*). Thereafter, following the story of his condescension and obedience to death, he is lifted to the status of lordship in a cosmic setting where all spiritual powers acknowledge his authority (2:11; cf. Rev 5:13; Ignatius, *Trallians* 9:1).

Paul's citation of the hymn serves to summon his readers to live out their citizen life (1:27) as "in Christ" (2:5) and to yield to Christ the Lord their allegiance as they submit to his lordship (2:12). So cosmic christology is not mere speculative theory but is turned to moral exhortation — a call that is reinforced and illustrated by three human leaders who model what life in Christ is and should be.

2. Colossians

In Colossians Paul rejoices over the ready welcome that the believers in Colossae have given to the message of his colleague, Epaphras, who has brought them "the word of truth" (1:5). Part of their response was to "receive Christ Jesus the Lord" (2:6) and "come to fullness of life in him" (2:10). More specifically, they understood the meaning of the grace of God (1:6-7) — as Epaphras's preaching announced to them the availability of God's offer to include them, along with other Gentiles, within the scope of his mercy (1:27). As a consequence of their understanding of and response to this "mystery" (1:26-27), they have entered a new humanity in which all religious disadvantages and racial distinctions are done away with (3:10-11), into the heritage of God's ancient and covenant people as his elect ones (3:12; cf. 1:26; 2:13). And they have come to share in the inheritance of the family of God, a company embracing both humans and angels (1:12; possibly also 1:26).

They have been rescued from the dark domain of evil powers and brought over to the kingdom of Christ (1:13). Included in that transference, these men and women have come to know the freedom of deliverance from evil, because their sins have been forgiven (1:14; 3:13) and they have been reconciled to God (1:22). God has graciously accepted them as pardoned sinners (2:13) and removed every impediment to their restoration to his favor (2:14). In particular, the demonic powers of angels and spiritual beings, which held their lives captive in a web of superstitious dread, were compelled to relinquish their grip. For God in Christ, who was their liberator, has broken the power of these malign spiritual forces at the cross of Christ — where Christ won a resounding victory over them at a time when it seemed he was their helpless prey (2:14, 15). These observations set the stage for Paul's cosmic christology in this letter.

But we need also to consider Paul's cosmic *soteriology* in this letter. For in that death of Jesus Christ, these Colossian believers died to the "elemental spirits of the universe" (2:20). And in his resurrection triumph over these spirits, they, too, have a share (3:1) — releasing them from the enslavements and inhibitions they have previously known as pagan Gentiles in a society where demons and taboos keep people in a twilight of fear and uncertainty. Formerly they have lived as "belonging to the world" (2:20), doomed under God's righteous sentence (3:6-7), and prisoners to evil passions and practices, which have their origin in a mind at enmity with God (1:21). Now, however, they have experienced divine forgiveness, which cut off the entail of the past and gave them a fresh start, and a moral transformation, which is likened to the imparting of a new nature (3:9-10). This is both God's gift and an expression of his character as demonstrated in Christ (3:10-11).

The dramatic "moment" when this life-changing transference took place is located in an act of renunciation, which is described as "putting off the body of flesh in the circumcision of Christ" (2:11; cf. 3:9). In the next breath, Paul proceeds to talk about baptism with its symbolic actions of burial and being raised out of the water (2:12). Then, as though to show that these actions have their counterpart in religious experience, he applies these baptismal motifs to the acts of God — who both passed the sentence of death on transgressors and vivified the Colossian believers in a spiritual renewal, so that they were lifted out of the realm of death into new life (2:13). Divine condemnation is obliterated and Christians are brought by this faith response in baptism to a new relationship with God and a new standing before him in the new "Adam" (3:10).

From this cursory survey of the letter to the Colossians, we can appreciate how the main lines of Paul's description of new life in the cosmic events of Christ's incarnation, death, and victory are drawn. Our purpose in what follows is to examine two central passages of the letter, 1:15-23 and 2:13-15, with a view to setting them against the backdrop of their historical and theological contexts.

Study of Col 1:15-20 has reached a fairly settled consensus, especially regarding its hymnic genre and form. There is less agreement, however, on matters regarding the background and meaning of this hymn. And even more problematic is the suggestion that Paul redacted an independently existing hymn that was originally written as an aretalogy in praise of the cosmic Lord. Two concerns have dominated current study: (1) the endeavor to set the text into a versified pattern that would be as nearly symmetrical as possible and (2) an interest in isolating a pre-Pauline hymn that Paul took over and adapted for his use in Colossians.

As for the structure of the original pre-Pauline hymn, we suggest the following:

Strophe I (vv. 15-16)
He is the image of the invisible God, the firstborn of all creation;
For in him all things were created in heaven and on earth.
All things were created through him and for him.

This first strophe hails the cosmic Christ as the Lord of creation. He is the one who is uniquely related to God as his manifest presence *(eikōn)*. He holds primacy over all the orders of creation. He stands over against God's handiwork as the agent through whom all the forces of the universe came into being. Indeed, he is creation's sovereign Lord. He is also the rightful "soul" or sphere in which the world exists and he is the one who guides its destiny.

Strophe II (vv. 17-18a)
He is before all things
And in him all things hold together;
He is the head of the body.

The first line of this second strophe partly recapitulates the previous strophe with its emphasis on Christ's preexistent activity. Then the hymn's thought proceeds with the assertion that the same cosmic Lord is the unifying principle that establishes the unity of the cosmos and holds the particles of matter together. This is the sense of the verb "hold together" *(sunestēken)*. As the center around which all things revolve and which gives coherence to the whole creation, he is the head or ruler of the cosmic body.

Strophe III (vv. 18b-20)
He is the beginning, the firstborn from the dead,

For in him all the fullness of God was pleased to dwell;
And through him to reconcile to himself all things.

The final strophe celebrates the triumph of the cosmic Lord who embodies the divine fullness *(to plērōma)*. God's plan is executed through him who, as the risen one, marks a new beginning of world history. He also effects God's design to bring the universe into harmony with the divine purpose of reconciliation.

Certain parts of Col 1:15-20 have been omitted in this reconstruction. By these omissions it is possible to secure a hymn of noticeable symmetry — with each stanza consisting in Greek of three lines and with a discernible rhythmic pattern, which is partly accounted for by the use of special rhetorical devices. If this schematic reconstruction is soundly based, we should be able to see whether Paul had a special reason for inserting extra phrases, the "omissions," into this extant piece of Christian liturgy. The hymn was conceivably used at baptism to celebrate Christ as cosmic Lord and the giver of new life to the world. Paul's emendations were made not by striking out offending parts, but by juxtaposing corrective lines or sentences, which we can detect by how they break the poetic structure of the piece as a whole.

Of all the possible Pauline additions, our attention is concentrated on two verses. In v. 18a he has added, in a way whose grammatical form clearly betrays the fact that it was an afterthought, "the church" to the affirmation "He is the head of the body." This suggestion is no speculation, since we have in 1:24 an illustration of the way Paul would normally write the phrase: "his body, that is, the church" — which is quite different in 1:18. Obviously, "the church" in verse 18a is an explanatory addendum. But it has dramatically altered the meaning of the entire sentence and all that follows. In its original form the line declared that Christ was the head of the body of the universe, but Paul has turned this cosmological statement into an ecclesiological and eschatological statement.

A more significant addition, however, is to be found in the interpretive clause of v. 20c: "making peace by the blood of his cross." The effect of this addendum is again to transform radically the meaning of Christ's work of reconciliation. For in its original form, the cosmic theology of the hymn would have proclaimed a universal harmony because of the creator's work in Christ — contrary to then current Greek thought, which proclaimed that the body of the universe was ruled by Zeus or Logos (see

E. Schweizer, "σῶμα," *TDNT* 7.1037). But Paul felt compelled, it seems, to modify this emphasis and recast the original statement to be an assertion of Christ's lordship in the church.

Evidently, Paul could not leave the Hellenistic idea untouched. He had to insure a fuller understanding of reconciliation as a soteriological reality by relating it closely to the death of Christ on the cross. Only in this way could he insist that redemption comes, not in knowing the cosmic secrets of the universe or by indulging in speculation, but by forgiveness of sins (1:14). And that forgiveness, made possible by the costly death of Jesus as a historical event, is mediated to men and women who are consciously committed to the lordship of Jesus Christ.

As Paul reworked and enlarged the original Christian hymn, it became not just a statement about God's control of the cosmos but a personal confession that believers in Jesus belong to his kingdom and under his rule (1:13). This was the point and purpose of Paul's citation of the hymn, introduced as it is by a description of the way in which his readers became members of Christ's body, the church. And at the close of the hymn, Paul adds a final interpretative comment to make certain that its revised meaning will not be lost.

Reconciliation for Paul is not a cosmic miracle that merely changed the state of the universe outside humankind. By inserting "making peace" *(eirēnopoiēsas,* v. 20) — which is unique in the apostle's writings and is marked by a certain syntactical awkwardness in the verse itself — Paul has ensured that the moral transformation of "the reconciliation of all things" will not be overlooked. Implicit in his addition of the line "making peace by the blood of his cross" are the several ways in which Paul achieves this objective.

First, he has shown that reconciliation is primarily concerned with the restoration of relationships. Accepting the premise that the earlier hymn was an existing part of Christian tradition, as seems likely, it declares that Christ is the restorer of the universe to its true harmony. Paul, however, goes on to insist that speculative interest is not enough to match a moral problem. This is why he can move directly from quoting the hymn, which in its earlier form seems not to have contained a single personal reference, to an application of what the hymn teaches — at least in its expanded form. The link between 1:15-20 and 1:21-23 is close-knit, with the personal pronoun "and you" of v. 21 and the verb "he has now reconciled" of v. 22 standing in emphatic positions in their respective clauses. So having shown how the scope of Christ's work reaches every part of creation, he now applies this teaching in 1:21-23 to his readers.

The second way in which the meaning of "reconciliation" in v. 20 is sharply defined by Paul's theology of the cross is more obviously polemical and designed to answer the needs of the Colossian church. Part of the teaching being challenged in this letter was, it seems, a promise that salvation could be enjoyed "instantly" — that is, with an immediate offer of immortality and very little said by way of the ethical demands of the new life.

But for Paul, such a statement of Christ's relation to the powers was not adequate. For him, as his discussion of Christ's triumph over the powers in 2:13-15 makes clear, these cosmic forces are not simply neutral agencies that need to find their true place in the hierarchy over which Christ presides. Their bid for human allegiance shows that they are rebel forces — and that it is necessary that their hostility should be drawn out and neutralized. So Paul expounds the need for their rebellion to be put down and for peace to be restored in a universe that is at odds with its creator.

Moreover, the creator of a moral world cannot deal with rebel spirits with a wave of the hand. In some way they have to be exposed, with their evil intentions brought out into the open and their claim to human obedience answered. Only then will there be true reconciliation as these usurping powers are called to a trial of strength and shown to be weak and impotent (cf. Gal 4:8-9). That engagement, for Paul, took place at the cross, where the issue of God versus the powers was joined. And peace is now proclaimed throughout the whole universe because of what Christ did both in his submission to the evil spirits and in his triumph over them.

So the emphasis that Paul makes in 1:20c is clear: reconciliation is not secured easily. It "does not work," to quote Eduard Schweizer, "like, to use a Gnostic image, a magnet put up in heaven and drawing those who are brought into its magnetic field irresistibly after it. The effect of Christ's death is the effect of a deed of love bringing its fruit in a human life which is touched by it" (*The Church as the Body of Christ* [Richmond: John Knox, 1964], 70).

New Life in Christ and the Hymn of the Savior (2:13-15)

Col 2:13-15 forms a compact section in which Paul is applying the acts of God to his readers' situation. One dominant act was God's appointment of his Son as "head of all rule and authority" (2:10) — that is, over the elemental spirits of the universe.

The structure of 2:13-15 reflects the same poetic features as 1:15-20. Moreover, it is possible to detect a Pauline insertion that interrupts the flow of the text in v. 14, where *tois dogmasin* (NRSV "with its legal demands") is an awkward pendant and occurs disconnectedly in the middle of the sentence. In addition, the following phrase *ho ēn hypenantion hēmin*, "which was inimical to us" (it is not represented in most modern translations), complicates the meaning and has been regarded as tautologous in view of the preceding *kath' hēmōn* ("against us"), which is descriptive of *to cheirographon* (NRSV "the record"). It is plausible to suggest that these two phrases are insertions by Paul himself, which were added to clarify the special sense in which he wishes *to cheirographon* to be understood.

There is also the problem of knowing exactly the point at which the hypothetical "hymn" begins. We are inclined to treat the participial clause "who forgave us all our trespasses" in v. 13 as Paul's climactic and triumphant declaration, which appears at the close of his recital of the benefits conferred by the gospel message, since he identifies himself ("*us* all") with his erstwhile Gentile readers ("*you* . . . were dead in the uncircumcision of your flesh"). This would be in keeping with his consistent stress on forgiveness in the letter (cf. 1:14; 3:13) and would give some justification for the quoted passage that follows directly.

The key lines of the original pre-Pauline hymn may be set out as follows:

Stanza I (v. 14)
Who canceled the bond of debt which stood against us,
And he removed it,
Nailing it to the cross.

These lines explore the rationale of Christ's forgiveness. He is the one who confers the blessing of pardon, as explicitly mentioned in 3:13: "As the Lord (Christ) forgave you. . . ." The problem posed by the "certificate of indebtedness" *(to cheirographon)*, which was inimical to human hopes of restoration to God, is met by what Christ did. For he wiped the record clear *(exaleiphein)* of the list of human transgressions and then took that discharged document and affixed it to his cross.

207

Stanza II (v. 15)
Who divested himself of the principalities and powers;
He made a public display of them,
Triumphing over them in it [i.e., the cross].

This is a highly dramatic and picturesque account of the historical events of Good Friday. We modern interpreters may find it hard to relate to such imagery, but Paul's first readers probably understood it — as seems evident by the way in which he proceeds to apply this teaching to their new life.

All that Christ did, both in his submission to death and in his overcoming of his foes, has personal and experiential relevance in the light of 3:9-10: "seeing that you have put off the old nature . . . and have put on the new nature." The Christians' "putting off" exactly matches in cognate fashion Christ's "putting off," and so points back to 2:11. For when the Lord consented to yield to the regime of the astral powers and then to triumph over them, Christians, too, were involved in that representative act — and by their faith union with him, as expressed in baptism, were united with him in his death and victory.

The result is clear: You died with Christ from being under the control of the elemental spirits of the universe (2:20). They are now an enemy that brings accusations and indictments against you in vain. For they have done their worst to Christ and have been foiled.

Paul finally drives home the point: Therefore do not allow any teacher to encroach on the life of your congregation and carry you away as a prize of war (2:8). You are assured by Christ's victory that he has "reconciled" — that is, drawn the hostility of — these malign spirits. And the sure token of that victory is the new life that the Colossians already have as men and women risen with Christ and part of the heavenly world (1:12-14; 3:1-4). Specifically, their sins are forgiven and no accusing angel can bring charges against them (as in Rom 8:33-39, especially vv. 38-39). Cosmic reconciliation, therefore, is certified by the knowledge and assurance of divine forgiveness.

3. Philemon

Though the shortest of Paul's surviving letters is addressed to an individual, Philemon, a slave owner in the Colossian church, it was evidently intended for the wider audience of the infant congregation where it would be read out (cf. v. 2; see also the greetings of vv. 23-24) — all of which gives a social frame of reference to Paul's passionate plea for the release of the slave Onesimus, who returned to Colossae presumably with this letter.

Koinōnia *Ethics in Societal Dimension*

The christology of the letter to Philemon is implied rather than expressly stated. For if the companion letter to the Colossians has as its ruling theme reconciliation achieved by the cosmic Lord, this letter shows how reconciliation has a horizontal and societal dimension. It is a paradigm of reconciliation in action as Paul brings together the runaway slave Onesimus, who has offended his master or was merely opportunistic (depending on how vv. 18-19 are construed), and his master Philemon, who is to treat him "no longer as a slave, but more than a slave, as a beloved brother" in the family of God. And in v. 21 Paul hints that this reception may well include his freedom.

The apostle's ground of appeal is partnership — *koinōnia*, in fact, is the key word in the letter — that is based on mutual love and has its reality as "life in Christ" (see T. Preiss, *Life in Christ* [London: SCM, 1954]). The outworking of life "in Christ" is carefully considered in the letter.

Paul's Request on Behalf of Onesimus

Philemon is prompted to the Christian course of action by Paul's letter — which is tender in its appeal (v. 14) yet firm in its insistence that there is in the situation a right thing to do (v. 8). Paul, Philemon, and Onesimus are each left to discover the will of God on the principle of "for love's sake" (v. 9) and "the good that is ours in Christ" (v. 6). What looks like a motive of Stoic self-interest (v. 8, "do what is required" or "fitting") is quickly modified by the acknowledgment of the lordship of Christ (v. 5), who reconciled his people to God (as implied in v. 19). "For love's sake" is the guiding axiom, uniting both the Christian's desire to please God in all that he or she does and the source of gratitude we all share for what has been achieved for our redemption (i.e., brought from slavery to freedom, as expounded in Romans 6) and reconciliation (as expressed in personal terms in Col 3:13).

Paul is the Christian apostle bound by cords of love to both parties. And he is seen as exercising a reconciling or intercessory ministry — not here in public proclamation (2 Cor 5:18-21), but by representing each person in encounter with the other. He touches both lives, and so brings them together into a relationship where each individual finds a place in God's family and fellowship.

The letter thus sheds light on practical Christianity at work in uniting those separated by social divisions. It is a theme that will be worked out more elaborately in Eph 2:11-22, where the christological underpinnings are more obvious.

4. Ephesians

Classifying Ephesians as an epistolary catechism or an exalted prose-poem dedicated to the theme of "Christ in his church" helps us to approach the letter and its historical situation in a new light. The author breaks into elevated meditation — especially in chs. 1–3 — on the great themes that fill his mind: (1) God's purpose in Christ, (2) God's fullness in Christ, (3) Christ's fullness in the church, which is his body, and (4) the church's exaltation to share Christ's present glory. Concepts like these lift the writer on to a plane of rapture and contemplation.

The language used in the letter is particularly significant. Most noticeable is the profusion of rare terms in the letter — a total of eighty-two words not found either in Paul's other letters or in the rest of the New Testament. Also obvious are the parallelisms in thought and sentence construction, the piling up of synonymous words (e.g., 1:19), a fondness for relative pronouns (e.g., 1:3-14, which is one connected sentence!), and the preposition "in," which is used in an exceptional way. All these characteristics are part of a style that is like that used in early Christian liturgy, where words are chosen not only to convey meaning but to communicate feeling and create a worshipful atmosphere.

The Setting of Ephesians

Understanding Ephesians as a transcript of early Christian praise offered to "Christ exalted in the cosmos and the church" has an immediate consequence, for it sets the document in a later period of church history. The church is becoming increasingly ecumenical and accepted as a social institution in the world. The vision of an immediate and dramatic "second coming" of Christ is fading as the church becomes more and more convinced of its place in history and adjusts to its destiny on earth where its future lies. Indeed, our writer can see the church under a double aspect: it is already exalted with its Lord (1:22; 2:5-6; 5:27), yet it lives an empirical existence on earth and faces trials (6:10-12). There are continuing struggles with moral issues (4:17-32; 5:6). But for the church of Ephesians, which is thought of as universal and transcendental, nothing can dissolve the unity it has with its now glorified head (1:22-23; 4:15-16; 5:30).

The new slant put on Paul's teaching in this letter is to be seen in several ways. First, it needs to be recognized that the engagement between Paul as champion of Gentile liberty in Christ and the "Judaizers" who insisted on the necessity of circumcision for his converts is now over and done with. The separation of Christianity and Judaism is recognized. And Jewish Christianity has passed into history as a once-posed threat to Paul's Gentile converts that has no continuing relevance for the audience of the Ephesian letter.

A first reading of Eph 2:11, where Gentile Christians are reminded that they were called "the uncircumcision" by those who are called "the circumcision," seems to contradict this statement. But it is instructive to examine the word for "Gentiles" *(ethnē)* in the letter. For in his earlier letters Paul uses the term ordinarily of Gentiles in the sense of "non-Jews," but in Ephesians it carries a more negative or pejorative flavor — that is, "non-Christians" (3:6; 4:17) or those called "the rest of humankind" (2:3). "Having no hope and without God in the world" (2:12) fits the Gentile world exactly. When the term is intended to mean "non-Jews," the writer adds the phrase "in the flesh" *(ethnē en sarki),* or "Gentiles *physically."* A telltale expression like this suggests a certain distance in time from the Jewish and/or Judaizing controversies of Paul's active ministry — a distance indicated by the text of 2:11, where the readers are spoken of as those who were "at one time . . . Gentiles in the flesh, called the uncircumcision." But this word "uncircumcision," like the word "circumcision," is for both the author and his readers an archaic term.

In a church predominantly made up of Gentile Christians, the danger encountered presented a new face. It was not that Gentile believers would succumb to Judaizing practices, such as circumcision (or the items listed in Ignatius, *Magnesians* 8–10). Rather, the threat was that Gentile Christians would want to cast off all association with the Old Testament and disown their origins in Israel's salvation history. This tendency is reflected in Rom 11:17-22. Here in Ephesians it reaches its extreme form.

Gentile Christians need the salutary reminders (1) that "salvation is of the Jews," to borrow a sentence from the Fourth Gospel, and (2) that Paul's "salvation history" theology never displaced the significance of Israel as the people of God, who have now come to full realization in the "one body" of a worldwide church in the author's day. And that reminder is the theme of 2:11-22, where the breaking down of "the dividing wall of hostility" between Jews and Gentiles takes on added significance as a reminiscence (as seems likely) of the destruction of the Jerusalem Temple in 70 CE. For in that historical event, the balustrade separating the Court of the Gentiles from the inner courtyards was destroyed — and in 2:11-22 the writer is pointing out the symbolic meaning of that happening in the light of Christ's death.

Messiah's death destroyed Jewish privileges in principle and hastened the end of temple religion for those Jews who remained unmoved by his death. In other words, the religious "wall of partition" is now broken down and the religious disabilities that excluded Gentiles are now overcome. At the same time, however, the entry of Gentile Christians into their new privilege of access to God by communion and covenant — becoming, in effect, a living temple, "a dwelling place of God in the Spirit" — is a sure sign that Israel's hope is not destroyed but has become fully realized in a new community where Jews and Gentiles embrace one another as "fellow citizens" (2:19). Neither has forfeited its identity, but both have experienced their separate identities transcended by and subsumed into a new and higher identity: "one new humanity in place of the two, thus making peace" (2:15).

Paul's apostolic ministry, which was often regarded in the early church as disputable and frequently needed to be vigorously defended during his active lifetime, is here in Ephesians viewed in retrospect (cf. 3:1-13). Nothing is clearer in the apostolic record than the constant struggles that Paul had in order to maintain the validity of his call to apostleship and the credibility of his vocation as "the apostle to the Gentiles" (see especially 2 Corinthians 10–13). But Ephesians sets Paul's apostleship apart in a way that defies challenge.

The shift is greater than simply the distinction often noted between

1 Cor 3:10-15 and Eph 2:20; 3:5. For Eph 2:20 — depending somewhat, of course, on whether it should be read "the foundation laid by apostles and prophets" or "the foundation consisting of apostles and prophets" — envisages the foundation of the church, "the household of God," as the work of a corporate group, "apostles and prophets," to whom was given peculiar insight into "the mystery of Christ" (3:4). Thus Paul's apostolate is held up to veneration in a way that seems to reflect a wistful looking back at the leaders of the primitive church as they were later seen as a specific number and as the guarantors of the new society that rests on their witness — which is exactly how they are pictured in Rev 21:14: "the wall of the city has twelve foundations, and on them are the twelve names of the twelve apostles of the Lamb."

The Purpose of Ephesians Seen in Its Chief Christological Emphases

We may well imagine what prompted this manifesto when we study the chief emphases of the epistle itself. Two such emphases are (1) that the call of the Christian life is to the highest levels of morality, both personal and social (4:17; 5:3, 5, 12), and (2) that Gentile believers, who enjoy rich privileges as members of the "one body in Christ," can never deny the Jewish heritage of the gospel without severing that gospel from its historical roots.

The Gentile Christians seem to have been adopting an easygoing moral code based on a perverted understanding of Paul's teaching (cf. Rom. 6:1-12). At the same time, they were boasting of their supposed independence from Israel, intolerant of their Jewish fellow believers and forgetful of the Jewish past of salvation history (cf. Romans 11).

Hence the epistle's insistence that the messianic hope meets all the needs of its Gentile readers (2:11-13; 3:6). Though they were converted to Christ later in time than their Jewish fellow believers (1:12-13), they are in no way inferior on that account. Rather, the privilege they now have binds them indissolubly to their Jewish counterparts in the family of faith — since both Gentile believers and Jewish believers share in the Holy Spirit of messianic promise (1:13; 4:30).

Ephesians effectively checks these two wrongheaded notions of moral laxity and independence from Israel by displaying the true meaning of Christ's relationship to the church. And herein lies the letter's distinctive christology. The chief christological emphases are: (1) that Christ is the church's head and Lord (1:20-23; 4:15), so requiring loyal obedience and service — or, to change the metaphor somewhat, Christ is the bridegroom, seeking a pure bride (5:22-33); and (2) that Christ is both Israel's Messiah and the Gentiles' hope, so uniting in himself a new people, both Jews and Gentiles (3:6).

To be sure, these christological emphases are not altogether unique to Ephesians. It may be appropriately argued that a Pauline disciple has faithfully conveyed the substance of his master's teaching. But much of the epistle takes on an added significance if we view it as a magnificent statement of the theme "Christ-in-his-church," yet one that is presented and applied in such a fashion that non-Pauline ideas and wrong ethical conclusions are rebutted.

The Central Ideas of the Letter:
Blending Christology and Ecclesiology

As a document addressed to a perilous situation, Ephesians is full of instruction of great importance. The author is gripped by what is virtually a single theme that runs like a thread through his treatise. He marvels, as a true disciple and follower of the great apostle in whose name he writes, at the grace of God that has brought into being a united church. In this Christian society, Jews and Gentiles find their true place (2:11-22). The unity of this universal society, which is nothing less than Christ's body (1:23; 3:6; 4:4; 5:30), is his great concern (4:3-5).

The author starts from the premise of the "one new person" (2:15) in which a new humanity has been created by God through Christ's reconciling work on the cross (2:16). By his achievement in relating humankind as sinners to God, Christ has brought Jews and Gentiles into God's family (1:5; 2:19; 4:6; 5:1) as children of the one Father. The coming into existence of this one family, where all barriers of race, culture, and social status are broken down, is the wonder that fills his vision. The earlier Pauline teaching of Gal 3:28-29 and 1 Cor 12:12-13 is now filled out, extended, and its lessons drawn and applied.

There is a new slant put on the apostolic teaching, however, which marks a novel phase of development in the doctrine of Christ and the church. One factor is the way in which Christ and his church are regarded as a single entity. The head-body metaphor, which is familiar to us from the earlier Pauline letters, takes on a new dimension in that the head becomes inseparable from the body. In 1 Corinthians 12, Paul insisted on the indivisibility of the body, which is made up of many members (cf. Rom 12:4-5). But in Ephesians the head and the body are inextricably united and interdependent (see especially 1:22-23; 4:15-16; 5:29-30).

Another important statement about the church's nature, stemming from the exaltation of its cosmic Lord, comes in attributing to it a sort of transcendental status. The church shares the heavenly life of its exalted Lord even now in this age (1:22; 2:6; 5:27). The distinctive features of the church in this epistle are akin to those classically stated in the creed: "I believe in one holy, catholic, and apostolic church." Thus there is in this epistle a timeless, idealistic quality about the church's life, which says more about what people ought to be than what they actually are in this present world.

Yet this epistle knows that the church lives an empirical life in this world and that its readers face pressing dangers. They are counseled against allowing their pre-Christian moral standards to decide and control their present conduct (4:17-24). They are put on their guard against pagan teachers who would undermine the Christian ethic they accepted as part of their new life in Christ (5:3-6). Baptism is appealed to as a dramatic summons to rouse from moral stupor and a call to walk in the light of holy living (5:14).

The seductions of those who were leading the readers astray with empty words (5:6) and causing them to be tossed about by crafty teachings (4:14) suggest the presence of a type of "gnosticizing" teaching. Basic to the Gnostic worldview was a dualism that drove a wedge between God and creation and regarded the latter as alien to God. It insinuated that men and women could safely ignore the claims of morality and — in a strange paradox, with both elements being attested in second-century Gnosticism — taught that people should either indulge their physical appetites without restraint or treat their bodily instincts with contempt. Thus both libertinism and asceticism erupted as logical consequences of the principle that God is remote from matter and unconcerned about what men and women do with their physical life.

Because of such teachings, the writer is moved to give warnings against a cluster of evil practices (5:3, 5, 12) and to argue for resistance to the pull of degrading influences (2:3). He is concerned to defend the value and dignity of marriage (5:22-33) against those who, from false ascetic motives (cf. 1 Corinthians 7; 1 Tim 4:3), would depreciate the marital state. But his real answer to these notions and practices is to deny outright the dualistic basis of the false teaching.

This denial is carried through by an emphatic statement of the church's heavenly origin and its earthly existence. The incarnation of Christ and the elevation of redeemed humanity are two powerful facts to which the author appeals for his conclusion that heaven and earth have been brought together into harmony (1:10). Furthermore, the "gnosticizing" tenet that humankind is held in the grip of a relentless and pitiless fate is effectively challenged and overthrown. For the eternal purpose of God embraces all spiritual beings and cosmic powers — that is, the "aeons" — that people of the first century feared most (3:11).

It was the divine plan that these spiritual beings, which Greek astral religion thought of as holding human lives in thrall, should lose their hold on men and women (3:9-10). God achieved that liberation by raising his Son from death's domain and placing under his feet the entire universe — including all spiritual and cosmic agencies (1:19-23). He has also exalted the church above these powers, and so lifted Christians beyond the range of cosmic tyranny and bad religion (1:22; 2:1-10; 5:8, 14, 27).

Christ's victory through God, who raised him from death, is at the very heart of the christology of Ephesians. Yet the question presses: How do believers come to share in this conquest over evil powers? The answer is that in baptism they (1) "put off" the old nature (4:22-24), and so die to the rule of these malevolent powers (Col. 2:20), and (2) "put on" the new humanity with its corresponding Christ-like qualities. The baptismal chant of 5:14 — "Sleeper, awake! Rise from the dead, and Christ will shine on you!" — is the hinge on which the author's addresses to his readers to be renewed in the image of the new Adam (4:17-24) and his practical and hortatory counsels turn. The experience of baptism, as spelled out in 5:26 (a "cleansing with the washing of water by the word"), marks the start of a new life of holiness to which this epistle summons its readers.

Ephesians, however, warns those who have started their new life of holiness to shun the specious tendencies of "gnosticizing" libertinism with its disparagement of the body. And it calls on them to stand bravely against the evil powers that are ranged against them (6:10-18). These evil powers are potentially defeated foes of the church. But victory will come only as

Christians are diligent in the use of the armor that God has provided and prove the reality of their conversion and baptism by standing firm in the Lord. The eschatology, which in other places looks to be totally fulfilled in Christ's ascension and enthronement, here makes room for an element of a "not yet completed" dimension.

Summation

Ephesians builds on the cardinal doctrine of the one true God who is all-powerful and all-wise and who "in Christ" has a loving design for the world. Christians, who share the risen life of Christ, are raised above the pitiless control of cosmic forces that would treat humans as mere playthings of "fate" and "luck." Equally, they are lifted to a higher plane of noble living that opposes all that is sensual and debasing. The conflict they engage in is a sign of the reality of their new life, which is based on the conquest of Christ and begun in their own experience by conversion and baptism.

The church is the historical witness to God's renewing purpose. Originally centered on Israel, a nation elect for the sake of humankind, that purpose now embraces Gentiles. Jews and Gentiles now find their focal point of harmony and understanding in the creation of a new society, "one new person" (2:15), which is neither Jew nor Greek but Christian (cf. Lincoln, *Ephesians*, 143-44).

Here in the Ephesian letter is the articulation and extension of Paul's thought in 1 Cor 10:32. Here also is to be found the foundation of the later Christian claim that the church forms a "third race" of human beings who, being reconciled to God through Christ, are united in a new way to realize a new society of men and women and to be a microcosm of God's ultimate design for a broken and sinful race.

SELECTED BIBLIOGRAPHY

General

Karris, Robert J. *A Symphony of New Testament Hymns: Commentary on Phil 2:5-11, Col 1:15-20, Eph 2:14-16, 1 Tim 3:16, Tit 3:4-7, 1 Pet 3:18-22, and 2 Tim 2:11-13.* Collegeville: Liturgical, 1966.

Philippians

Bockmuehl, Markus. *The Epistle to the Philippians.* Peabody: Hendrickson, 1998.

Fee, Gordon D. *Paul's Letter to the Philippians.* Grand Rapids: Eerdmans, 1995.

Martin, Ralph P. *Carmen Christi: Philippians 2.5-11 in Recent Interpretation and in the Setting of Early Christian Worship.* Cambridge: Cambridge University Press, 1967; Grand Rapids: Eerdmans, 1983[2]; retitled *A Hymn of Christ*, Downers Grove: InterVarsity, 1997[3].

Martin, Ralph P., and B. J. Dodd. *Where Christianity Began: Essays on Philippians 2.* Louisville: Westminster/John Knox, 1998.

Witherington, Ben, III. *Friendship and Finances in Philippi.* Valley Forge: Trinity Press International, 1994.

Colossians and Philemon

Barth, Markus, and H. Blanke. *Philemon.* Grand Rapids: Eerdmans, 2000.

Dunn, James D. G. *The Epistles to the Colossians and Philemon.* Grand Rapids: Eerdmans, 1996.

Martin, Ralph P. *Colossians: The Church's Lord and the Christian's Liberty.* Exeter: Paternoster; Grand Rapids: Zondervan, 1972; reprint Eugene: Wipf and Stock, 2000.

O'Brien, Peter T. *Colossians and Philemon.* Waco: Word, 1982.

Schweizer, Eduard. *The Letter to the Colossians.* Minneapolis: Augsburg, 1982.

Wright, N. Thomas. "Χριστός as 'Messiah' in Paul: Philemon 6," in *The Climax of the Covenant.* Minneapolis: Fortress, 1992.

Ephesians

Best, Ernest. *Ephesians.* Edinburgh: Clark, 1998.

Lincoln, Andrew T. *Ephesians.* Waco: Word, 1990.

Martin, Ralph P. *Reconciliation: A Study of Paul's Theology.* London: Marshall, Morgan and Scott; Atlanta: John Knox, 1981; reprint Eugene: Wipf and Stock, 1997.

CHAPTER 10

Christology in the Letters to Timothy and Titus

PHILIP H. TOWNER

Past studies of the letters to Timothy and Titus have returned various verdicts concerning their character and relationship to "Pauline" theology. Comparisons of their contents with those of the undisputed letters — particularly with the christology of Paul's major letters, which are often viewed as exhibiting a rather complete symmetry on the subject — have been a mainstay of scholarship, with disparities between these two sets of letters usually highlighted. And conclusions about the sources of their theology — that is, whether Johannine, pre-Pauline, reworked Pauline, Jesus *logia*, rabbinic speculation, or some combination — have generally measured their distance from Paul as well.

Hans Windisch in 1935 discerned a pre-Pauline hue to the material, and suggested that, in the main, the author bypassed Pauline categories in the construction of an adoptionist christology based on Synoptic and other early Christian traditions (see his "Zur Christologie der Pastoralbriefe"). Many scholars have concurred — though, of course, with various adjustments — and so have laid stress on the non-Pauline character of the writer's sources and his subsequent christology. Hanna Stettler's 1998 study, in fact, which argues that the author of these letters was most influenced by the Son of Man tradition as it appears in the Gospel tradition, is not unlike Windisch's. Others, however, have followed Martin Dibelius, who asserted that the christology of the Pastoral Epistles is totally eclectic, unoriginal, and without unity (cf. Dibelius and Conzelmann, *Pastoral Epistles,* especially 8 and 10).

But the scholarly response that Dibelius eventually provoked seems, of late, to have found a better path. For more nuanced interpretations of the letters have regarded the author as an interpreter of Paul (and other materials) who sought to present a "Paul" adjusted for a new theological, cultural, and linguistic situation (e.g., Hasler, "Epiphanie und Christologie in den Pastoralbriefe"; Donelson, *Pseudepigraphy and Ethical Argument in the Pastoral Epistles;* Oberlinner, *Titusbrief;* and Läger, *Christologie der Pastoralbriefe*). And most scholars today, whatever their views of authorship, emphasize the vitality, distinctiveness, and unity of the christology of the Pastoral Epistles, though many points are still in dispute.

While real gains have been made — particularly with respect to the themes of epiphany, savior and salvation, the Greek ethical perspective, and the social setting of the letters — the consensus view of the Pastoral Epistles as "pseudepigrapha" (i.e., written in the name of Paul by a later Pauline disciple, in accord with "widely accepted practice") has kept the investigation of these letters on a narrow, one-way track. The views of this approach need not here be rehearsed. It is necessary to point out, however, that some have recognized that the assumptions and methodology of this approach — whether a consensus view or not — are neither airtight nor completely compelling (cf. Marshall, *Pastoral Epistles,* 79-92; Johnson, *Letters to Timothy,* 55-90). As a consequence, reopened questions and a renewed evaluation of the data have led Marshall to opt for something closer to Paul, which he calls "allonymity" (*Pastoral Epistles,* 83-84), and have caused Johnson to redouble his efforts to understand these letters within the historical Pauline framework (*Letters to Timothy,* 91-99). I simply want to use the room created by the present state of uncertainty to treat the letters as substantially historical and to address one particular methodological mistake of the consensus view.

One of the most disadvantageous features of the current scholarly consensus is the assumption that these three letters constitute one three-part corpus. There are, of course, reasons to think that they are related (see Marshall, *Pastoral Epistles,* 1-2; Oberlinner, *Erster Timotheusbrief,* xxii-xxiii). But their relationship, I believe, has been over-read by scholars to the point where the features of the letters that argue for their individuality — including their respective treatments of christology — have been suppressed.

The two letters to Timothy and the one letter to Titus purport to be separate letters written to Pauline coworkers. The letters identified as 1 Timothy and Titus contain elements of the ancient type of document called *mandata principiis* — that is, a memorandum from a ruler to a newly commissioned delegate *and* to the community to which he was dispatched, and so a blend of private and public discourse (cf. Johnson, *Letters to Timothy,* 137-42). 2 Timothy is a parenetic-protreptic letter, which incorporates example, traditional parenesis, brief admonitions, and sections of polemic (Johnson, 320-24). Features that form these letters into a cluster (cf. the clustered materials of Ephesians-Colossians, 1-2 Thessalonians, 1-2 Corinthians, and Romans-Galatians) should not be ignored, but neither should they be allowed to obscure or distort the individual messages. In what follows, therefore, we will consider both the features that unite and the factors that are distinctive in these three letters.

1. Common Christological Features and the Search for a Christological Center

Christological meaning does not reside simply in titles or names apart from their respective contexts. But while contextual considerations will be important in our separate treatments of each of the Pastoral Epistles, it is necessary first to lay out the raw materials that appear in all three letters and to highlight their common christological features.

Common Titles and Names

The use of titles and names in the Pastoral Epistles other than "Savior" exhibits little thematic stress. "Christ Jesus" occurs twenty-five times, whereas on six occasions the order is "Jesus Christ" — which variation seems to reflect no particular pattern. "Lord" accompanies "Christ Jesus" three times (1 Tim 1:2, 12; 2 Tim 1:2) and "Jesus Christ" twice (1 Tim 6:3, 14) and occurs independently as a designation for Christ fourteen times. It is not apparent that "Christ Jesus," "Jesus Christ," and "Christ" have lost any of their "Pauline" theological significance, and the occurrence of these appellations in soteriological texts bears this out (cf. 1 Tim 1:15, 16; 2:5; 2 Tim 1:9-10; 2:8; Tit 2:13; 3:6).

Furthermore, that Christ is "Lord" has reference in the Pastoral Epistles to both his resurrection and his exaltation. Appeals are directed to the Lord for mercy and blessing (2 Tim 1:16, 18; 2:7; 4:22) and for vindication

(2 Tim 4:14); the Lord's claim on the church is the framework for matters concerning church and mission (1 Tim 6:3, 14; 2 Tim 1:8; 4:8); and Christ is to be "Lord" and "Judge" at his second coming (2 Tim 1:16, 18; 4:1, 8; cf. 1 Tim 6:14; 2 Tim 2:12). However, neither Adam christology, nor "Jesus" independently, nor the title "Son of God" occurs in these letters. Once Jesus is simply designated "the Christ" (1 Tim 5:11).

With the discovery that the author was a creative theologian (*contra* Dibelius and Conzelmann, *Pastoral Epistles*, 9), two features have been typically thought to hold the clue to the coherence or unity of the christology of the Pastoral Epistles: (1) the depiction of Christ as Savior and (2) the epiphany concept. These macro-features, however, always have to be held in tension with the micro-themes and concerns of the individual letters themselves. Nonetheless, as overarching christological features that are common to all three letters, their presence and significance must first be considered — after which we will then explore the unique ways in which each letter develops these interrelated thoughts.

But even more basic than these features is the need to recognize that all the theological elements of these letters serve the broader theme of "salvation in the present age." It is this dominant story that the various kerygmatic statements in all three letters seek to retell (see Towner, *Goal of Our Instruction*, 75-119; Marshall, *Pastoral Epistles*, 291-92; Matera, *New Testament Christology*, 158-59). Their retelling is noticeably Hellenistic in form. More importantly, their retelling seems to have been motivated by a combination of such overlapping concerns as (1) combating false teaching, (2) safeguarding the Pauline gospel, and (3) continuing the Christian mission after Paul's death. The reality of salvation is coupled in these letters with a call for a distinctively Christian response that is both ethical and an expression of true faith. And within each letter christology serves the broader theme of salvation in the present age, taking the shape required by the specific historical and literary situation.

Common Use of "Savior"

"Savior" *(sōtēr)* was already a well-known appellation of Yahweh in the Septuagint, where the exodus was the archetypal salvation event. In New Testament usage, "Savior" depicts God as the Savior of the world through the gift of his Son. Use of the title for Christ, however, was slow to develop and is limited to the later Pauline writings (Phil 3:20; Eph 5:23; 2 Tim 1:10; Tit 1:4; 2:13; 3:6), Luke's two volumes (Luke 2:11; Acts 5:31; 13:23), John's writings (John 4:42; 1 John 4:14), and 2 Pet 1:1.

Perhaps use of "Savior" in the Roman imperial cult for the deified emperor delayed application of the term to Christ. It may finally have been used of Christ (1) because of an increased drawing of meaning from their biblical tradition by believers in Christ and (2) in response to the escalating influence of the stories, symbols, and expectations of the imperial religion on the church and culture. Given this environment of Old Testament rootage and the use of "Savior" language for Hellenistic kings, heroes, and gods, we should not imagine that Christians simply co-opted such politically loaded language as a matter of convenience. Rather, the title seems to have been chosen deliberately to make a point.

In the Pastoral Epistles, God and Christ are both designated "Savior" — and sometimes in close proximity (see especially Tit 1:3-4; 2:10 and 13; 3:4 and 6). Five of six occurrences depict God as "Savior" in the sense of being the architect and initiator of the salvation plan (1 Tim 2:3; 4:10; Tit 1:3; 2:10; 3:4; cf. 1 Tim 1:1). Christ as "Savior" is the means by which this plan is implemented in history (2 Tim 1:10; Tit 3:6; cf. 1:4) and fulfilled at the end (Tit 2:13). 1 Timothy, however, does not use "Savior" for Christ, which cautions against overplaying its role in establishing "the coherence" of christology in these letters.

Yet activities associated with "Savior" are implicit in the use of the *sōzō* word group and other theological formulations of the Christ event in 1 Timothy — for example, the "faithful saying" of 1:15: "Christ Jesus came into the world to save sinners." So the concept seems to be latent in the letter. Suppression of the title itself in 1 Timothy may have resulted from reticence to make the claims that were associated with it in the ancient world — or perhaps it was simply the author's choice to emphasize certain other features of christology in that particular letter (as will be detailed below).

Common Epiphany Motif

Recent scholars have spoken of an "epiphany christology" in the Pastoral Epistles, though there is a wide variation among their interpretations. Victor Hasler, who in 1977 was the first to develop the theme, detected in "epiphany" a retreat from Paul's apocalyptic outlook and new interest in

God's transcendence and the complete futurity of salvation. Lorenz Oberlinner in 1980 argued that the concept shifted the focus in eschatology from the *parousia* to the presence of salvation in the world. Neither view, however, is entirely in line with the eschatology of these letters (cf. Towner, *Goal of Our Instruction*, 66-71; Marshall, *Pastoral Epistles*, 293-96). More helpfully, Andrew Lau in 1996 concluded that the concept represents a reconfiguration of traditional christology for a Greek audience rather than a Hellenizing departure from it.

Both the noun *epiphaneia* (1 Tim 6:14; 2 Tim 1:10; 4:1, 8; Tit 2:13; cf. 2 Thess 2:8) and the verb *epiphainō* (Tit 2:11; 3:4 in the aorist) refer to an "appearance." In Hellenistic religious discourse, these terms were used of the appearance of a god (e.g., Athena) on behalf of his or her worshipers and so paralleled the concept of "savior." The emphasis in the term on divine assistance made it an effective device to explore the Christian belief that God's salvation had intervened in history in a person — sometimes highlighting the movement from invisibility to visibility. The Septuagint and Hellenistic Judaism used the concept of epiphany to retell the stories of Yahweh's interventions in the world, thereby providing some precedent for its later Christian use (see Lau, *Manifest in Flesh*, 179-223).

The "epiphany" motif in the Pastoral Epistles has two foci. The one that is most clearly demarcated is the future appearance of Christ (1 Tim 6:14; 2 Tim 4:1, 8; Tit 2:13), where *epiphaneia* is effectively synonymous with *parousia* ("coming," "presence"). But when *epiphaneia* is used of the historical appearance of Christ as Savior (2 Tim 1:10), the phrase "through the gospel" suspends closure of the "epiphany" and allows consideration of its extension into — and effects on — present human life (cf. Tit 1:2-3). The use of the verb with reference to appearances of God's grace in Tit 2:11 and 3:4, which are descriptive references to the Christ event, is similar.

Does this mean, as Howard Marshall argues, that "the past epiphany is not restricted to the actual historical event of the life of Jesus but encompasses the ongoing effects that are brought about by the gospel . . . [that is] one epiphany inaugurated by the coming of Jesus and continuing throughout present and future time" (Marshall, *Pastoral Epistles*, 295; cf. Oberlinner, *Titusbrief,* 156-57; Läger, *Christologie der Pastoralbriefe,* 111-19)? Or is it that this formative epiphany in some sense recurs in the proclamation of the gospel? In either case, it is important to see that references to the past epiphany of Christ serve as a focus for reflection on the event's salvific effects in human culture. Tit 2:11 and 3:4, in context, refer obliquely to the Christ event in order to view it from both theological and ethical perspectives. In any case, as I see it, the relationships are threefold: (1) God's grace *has appeared* in the epiphany of his Son; (2) it *is being revealed* in and through the church's proclamation of the gospel; and (3) it *will be revealed* finally and ultimately in the future epiphany of the Lord.

Preexistence, which is an attribute of deity, probably attaches to the epiphany concept as used of Christ in the Pastoral Epistles. It represents a christological "experiment" in which Paul explores the link between God's salvation plan and its manifestation in and through a preexistent Savior, the Messiah (2 Tim 1:9-10; cf. 1 Tim 1:15; see Lau, *Manifest in Flesh*, 279). And in combination with the accumulation of epithets and activities formerly associated with Yahweh — Savior, Judge, and Lord — and offering of doxological praise (2 Tim 4:18b), the epiphany motif expresses a christology that encompasses deity.

Epiphany christology reconceptualizes the relation between eschatology and ethics. For by establishing with a single word that the past historical "epiphany" introduces salvation and the future "epiphany" completes it, the present age between these poles — which is a temporal tension that is so important in these letters — comes fully under the influence of "epiphany." This is especially noticeable in Tit 2:11-14 and 3:4-7. And the role of proclamation as influencing the present age in 2 Tim 1:10 and Titus 1:3 strikes a similar note.

What motivated the choice of this motif? Undoubtedly, as with the title "Savior," epiphany language must have been deliberately chosen to engage the dominant religious-political discourse of the day and to force a rethinking of these categories by the proclamation of God's story in Hellenistic dress. Perhaps the challenge posed by co-opting such religious-political language should be considered profound enough. But it also needs to be recognized that the use of "epiphany" with reference to the past human experience of Christ (cf. 2 Tim 1:10) sharpens the subversive point. For the term called to mind divine power and divine intervention — both in secular Greek thought and in the religious sensibilities of Second Temple Judaism (cf. 1 Chron 17:21 LXX; 2 Macc 2:21-23; 3:24-28; 5:2-4; 12:22; 14:15; 15:27; Josephus, *Antiquities* 9.53-60; see further Lau, *Manifest in Flesh*, 182-225). In the epiphany of Jesus Christ, however, divine power and presence are disguised in the forms of human weakness, suffering, and death (cf., e.g., Paul's experiences recounted in 2 Corinthians 10–12). The allusion in the Pastoral Epistles to preexistence only heightens the paradox.

"Epiphany," therefore, is not just catchy language. Rather, it seeks to retell the gospel in a most thought-provoking way.

Summation

Christology in the letters to Timothy and Titus is oriented, in somewhat varying degrees, around the dual themes of "Savior" and "epiphany." The visibility or grip of these themes, however, varies as the letters are read individually and as other goals decide the extent to which christology is served by these themes in each letter. The best illustration of this is 1 Timothy's non-use of "Savior" for Christ and its limitation of "epiphany" language to only one occurrence (see below). The decision to adapt this religiously-politically loaded language for Christian proclamation reveals the intention of each of the letters, to one degree or another, to take the dialogue with the culture of the day to another level, as we will see in the following three sections of this article.

2. The Man Christ Jesus:
The Shape of Christology in 1 Timothy

The occasion and genre of 1 Timothy determine, in large measure, the shape of the letter's christology. There is broad agreement that Paul's chief concerns here were (1) to allay the opposition and (2) to restore church leadership. The opponents were anti-Pauline with a Jewish or Judaizing element (1:7). Their type of *gnōsis* ("knowledge") included ascetic renunciation of the world (4:3-4), and their scriptural exegesis was speculative. The community itself was experiencing social instability, as the teaching regarding women and slaves suggests. But the relation of that instability to the issues raised by the opposition is unclear.

The usual explanation for these features has been, and still is, to refer in some manner to Gnosticism. But the situations of the churches at Corinth and Colossae provide better points of comparison (see Johnson, *Letters to Timothy*, 144-45; Towner, *Goal of Our Instruction*, 33-36). Of the aberrant theology, we know only that the opponents sought to distance themselves from the world. Perhaps their view of salvation was elitist and over-realized. Or, perhaps it was simply that their ethical outworking of the faith encouraged disengagement from life in the world. Other christological emphases in the letter may combat specific distortions of belief, though such matters are somewhat uncertain. But what seems certain, as we will highlight below, is that the christological presentation of 1 Timothy supports engagement in the world.

As Luke Johnson demonstrates (*Letters to Timothy*, 147-54), the theological perspective of 1 Timothy is that of *oikonomia theou* ("God's ordering of reality"), with the appropriate response to this being human "faithfulness" (1:4). The "household" language of the letter indicates that Paul addressed his readers in the understanding, which was common to that culture, that social structure — beginning with the "household" and expanding outward to include civic, political, and religious life — was continuous with the divine will.

Leaving aside the question of how far he accepts the status quo, it is clear that Paul regards the social structure as continuous with God's ordering. The heretics, however, stand in opposition to this ordering, as 1:4 announces from the outset. From here, the description of the church as "the household of God" (3:15) unfolds. And on this basis, the christology of the letter is used to affirm the relevance of salvation and ministry within human society.

The "Saying" of 1:15

The first extensive christological reflection in 1 Timothy comes at 1:15: "The word is trustworthy and worthy of all acceptance, that Christ Jesus came into the world to save sinners — among whom I am the foremost." Located after Paul's first engagement with the false teachers (1:3-10) — and as a reflection of "the gospel" (1:11) and his own experience of mercy and calling (1:12-16) — the saying illustrates his gospel in polemical contrast with that of the false teachers.

First it needs to be noted that this "faithful" or "trustworthy" saying, "that Christ Jesus came into the world to save sinners," combines at least two strands of tradition. Johannine theology seems to have been fond of speaking of Jesus as "coming into the world" (John 9:39; 11:27; 16:28), but the salvific purpose of that "coming" is never explicitly attached to the Johannine statements. Luke speaks of the Son of Man coming to save sinners (cf. Luke 19:10), but there is no reference in that statement to his "coming into the world." Paul's weaving of these traditional strands, however, exceeds both traditions in placing the saving work of Christ Jesus into historical relief as a divine work carried out in the human context.

A second point to note is that while the preexistence of Christ, and hence the divine origin of salvation, is implicit in 1:15, the weight of the saying that "Christ Jesus came into the world to save sinners" is on the humanity of Jesus and its significance. As elsewhere in Paul, this statement telescopes the whole earthly experience of Jesus into the event of his coming (cf. Gal 4:4-5; Rom 8:3-4). Furthermore, the location "into the world" (i.e., the world in need of God) and the declared target of his "coming" (i.e., "to save sinners") disclose the relevance of this tradition for the present church.

The ongoing relevance and authority of this saying are highlighted by Paul's application of its contents to himself. For his apostleship and experience of God's mercy (cf. 1:12-14) are fruits of the work of the Messiah, who lived as a human — and the fact of the Messiah's humanness, Paul insists, must remain central to an understanding of the gospel. Paul's own experience is drawn on to assure Timothy of Christ's human relevance. So whatever else christology might mean, it certainly requires that the ministry of the Christian gospel be carried out in the present sinful world, and it expects that salvation will have its effect in changing this world from within.

This opening christological statement, therefore, combines traditional elements that affirm (1) the humanity of Christ and (2) salvation as its corollary. Paul's own experience illustrates the linkage. Salvation is a present reality. But it is a salvation that is anchored in the humanity of God's Messiah — with that humanity actually making the difference "for those who will believe for eternal life" (1:16; cf. 1:1).

2:5-6

The second christological statement of 1 Timothy appears at 2:5-6: "There is one God; there is one mediator between God and humankind, the man Christ Jesus, who gave himself a ransom for all." This statement also occurs within a broader, carefully constructed discourse about salvation (2:1-7), with the notion of the universality of salvation being central to the argument of the discourse (note the repetition of "all" in vv. 1, 2, 4, and 6). Thus prayer is to be offered for "all people" (v. 1) and for the conditions in which Christian testimony can be most effectively given in society (v. 2) — with such an extensive scope of salvation being supported by God's will to save all people (v. 4). For whatever reasons, however, whether heresy, elitism, or neglect, the teaching that God "desires everyone to be saved and to come to the knowledge of the truth" (v. 4) requires substantiation (note the connecting "for" in v. 5a). So Paul crafts an appropriate theological response out of traditional materials in 2:5-6.

The affirmation "there is one God" (v. 5a) reformulates Deut 6:4, the beginning of the *Shema*. The unity of God, as in Rom 3:29-30 (cf. also 1 Cor 8:4-6; Gal 3:20; Eph 4:5-6), substantiates the claim (v. 4) that God's will to save extends to all people. At this point, christology takes over and the universal claim is attached to a very particular person. "One mediator" accomplishes the universal plan of the one God. Through him, God and people enter into a covenant relationship and people receive the gift that God desires to give.

A "mediator" *(mesitēs)* was a go-between or negotiator who brought two parties together. In the Old Testament the term was used of how God relates to people (Job 9:33 LXX; cf. *Testament of Dan* 6:2). In the New Testament Christ is sometimes referred to as the mediator of a "new" or "better" covenant, the antitype of Moses (Heb 8:6; 9:15; 12:24). The only use of the concept in the undisputed letters of Paul is to be found in Gal 3:19-20, where it serves to place the reception of the Law at a certain distance from God.

Here in 1 Tim 2:5, however, "one mediator" is placed in immediate juxtaposition to "one God," thereby setting up a striking paradox. For "one God" signals universal access to salvation, but "one mediator" narrows that access to a single means. There is nothing in the term *mesitēs* itself to suggest equivalence with God — though, of course, in this formulation it carries a positive connotation. At most, if covenant ideas are present, Jesus occupies a position like that of Moses between God and people. Thus, rather than suggesting equivalence, the thrust of the statement is to locate Jesus' mediatorship precisely in his humanity, with the phrase "the *man* Christ Jesus" defining "mediator."

This unusual use of *anthrōpos* ("man") for Jesus has been traced to (1) Pauline Adam christology (cf. Rom 5:15, "the one man Jesus Christ") or (2) the Son of Man tradition, which is seen to lie behind the words "who gave himself a ransom for all" (cf. Mark 10:45). But neither source fully explains the statement, and there are better antecedents. Within the undisputed letters of Paul, a broader theme — to which Paul's Adam discourse in Rom 5:12-21 possibly belongs — connects Christ's humanity with his death (cf. Gal 4:4-5; Rom 8:3; Phil 2:7-8). Also somewhere behind *anthrōpos* as a christological designation might be the association within developing Jewish messianism of the emergence of "a man to rule the nations" (Num 24:7-8) and Yahweh's sending of "a man who will save" (Isa 19:20; see Horbury, *Jewish Messianism*, 44-45). In any case, the emphasis on "the *man* Christ Jesus" is the high point of this traditional piece (for further discussion, see Towner, *Goal of Our Instruction*, 54-57). And the placement of the *anthrōpos* designation between "one mediator" and "who gave himself a ransom for all" seems intended to locate the mediating activity of Christ Jesus specifically in his humanity. What Jesus did to execute God's universal will to save, therefore, he did as a human being in full solidarity with the human condition.

The argument concludes in the retelling of the tradition of Jesus' self-giving in v. 6, "who gave himself a ransom for all." These words access the Jesus tradition either directly (cf. Mark 10:45) or by way of Pauline adaptation (cf. Gal 1:4; 2:20; Eph 5:2; also Tit 2:14). Coinciding with the universal thrust of this passage, the Pauline preference to apply the work of Christ to "us" is shifted to "all" — as is also inherent in the use of "many" in the Jesus tradition. The means of mediation is Jesus' willing giving of his own life as a "ransom" (*antilytron;* Mark 10:45 has *lytron* and Rom 3:24 and 8:23 have *apolytrōsis,* but the same sense of giving oneself as a ransom payment to secure the release of enslaved humans is present). Finally, in all of this, Jesus' status as a human representative of humans (*hyper,* "in behalf of") stands out. Here the circle that began with universality has run its course through particularity to arrive again at universality: what he has done he has done "for all."

Christology in this statement finds expression at a very human level. While nothing of the higher elements of christology are necessarily sacrificed, for all that is implicit remains, the formulation establishes clearly the necessity of Christ's complete participation in humanity in order to accomplish the work of mediation that was intrinsic to God's universal salvation plan. It is this full participation in the human experience that makes representation and meaningful self-sacrifice possible — which is an important Pauline theme (see especially Rom 5:12-21). And it is as a human, not as an object of belief, that Jesus is the mediator of salvation to all (see Johnson, *Letters to Timothy,* 197).

The Christ Hymn of 3:16

The center point of 1 Timothy is the Christ hymn at 3:16:

> Who was manifested in flesh,
>> vindicated in [the] Spirit,
>> seen by angels;
> Proclaimed among the nations,
>> believed in throughout the world,
>> taken up in glory.

This hymn provides the theological conclusion to the important summarizing section of 3:14-16, where Paul pauses to remind Timothy of his travel plans and places this teaching within the larger framework of the "household of God" (3:15; cf. 1:4). The hymn offers a confessional reflection on "the mystery of godliness" that amounts to a christological interpretation of the essence of Christian existence. For in the Pastoral Epistles, (1) the term "godliness" *(eusebeia)* characterizes Christian existence as the interplay of genuine faith in God and obedient response in life (cf. Towner, *Goal of Our Instruction,* 147-52; Marshall, *Pastoral Epistles,* 135-44), and (2) "mystery" *(mystērion)* is to be read as "the revelation of the mystery" — that is, "confessedly great is [the unveiling of] the mystery of godliness." It is the story of this "mystery" that interests us.

Complementing the theme of Christ's humanity, which is developed in the immediate context, the first line of the hymn begins with a statement of Jesus' entrance into the human sphere: "Who was manifested *(ephanerōthē)* in flesh" — which, by the use of the verb *phaneroō* ("reveal," "make known"), employs language suited to the "mystery" theme (cf. Col 1:26) and coincides with an epiphany scheme. The humanity of Christ is the means by which God's salvation mystery is revealed. The term "in flesh" *(en sarki),* which indicates sphere or mode, refers to the whole of Jesus' earthly existence and its culmination in human death (cf. Rom 8:3; Phil 2:7-8).

The next two lines of the hymn affirm Christ's vindication in response to his earthly ministry. "Vindicated in [the] Spirit" suggests his resurrection from the dead (cf. Rom 1:4; 1 Cor 2:1-10; Phil 2:5-11). Together, "flesh" and "spirit" identify Jesus' two-stage manner of existence. Although the Spirit was fully present in his ministry prior to his death, the resurrection marked Christ's entrance into the supernatural domain characterized by the Spirit's activity and presence (Fowl, *Story of Christ*, 159-62; Towner, *Goal of Our Instruction*, 90-93). Christ's vindication was also celebrated by the rich tradition of his resurrection appearance before angelic powers (cf. Phil 2:9-11; Eph 1:21; Heb 1:3-4; 1 Pet 3:22; Rev 5:8-14). Consequently, the Christ hymn expands on the statements of 1:15 and 2:5-6, showing that the meaning of Jesus' full humanity lies not simply in his experience of weakness and suffering, essential as these were, but also in the vindication and full empowerment of eternal life in the Spirit that resurrection brings.

Lines four and five ("proclaimed among the nations, believed in throughout the world") regard Christ more obliquely as the content of the gospel. The focus shifts to the effects of this mystery among humanity. Again, as in 1:15 and 2:5-6, the humanity of Christ is central in the gospel and the gospel is universal in scope. In preaching, the church takes up its role in continuing the revelation of God's plan. Christ's human life, death, and resurrection fulfill God's plan to save the nations, and the plan has already begun to achieve universal success. Christology, therefore, leads to missiology.

The hymn ends on the note of Christ's exaltation: "He was taken up in glory *(anelēmphthē en doxē)*." The language alludes to Christ's ascension (cf. Mark 16:19; Luke 24:51; Acts 1:2, 11, 22). But the symbolic value of the event predominates, for it represents the exaltation of Christ to God's right hand. Yet this particular view of exaltation — that is, through the lens of the ascension — reinforces the link between the vindicated humanity of Jesus and his present exalted status.

Christology, therefore, binds Christian existence and mission inextricably to the humanity of Christ. Furthermore, it is the vindicated humanity of Christ that is highlighted in the focus of 1 Timothy on the church's present situation, for that is what supplies hope and motivation for the struggles of the Christian faith.

6:13-14

Paul gives a last glimpse of the humanity of Christ alongside a reference to his future epiphany in 6:13-14:

> In the presence of God, the one who gives life to all things, and of Christ Jesus, who in his testimony before Pontius Pilate made the good confes-

sion, I charge you to keep the commandment without spot or blame until the manifestation of our Lord Jesus Christ.

To charge Timothy "in the presence of God and Christ" is not unusual. What is striking is that Paul characterizes God as "the one who gives life" (i.e., resurrects) and speaks of the resurrected and exalted Christ as having, in his human weakness, "made the good confession before Pontius Pilate" (cf. 2 Tim 4:1). The parenetic application is obvious. The text's focus on Christ's human testimony "then" illustrates the necessity of Timothy's faithful testimony "now." The full story of Christ's vindication, as in the Chr hymn of 3:16, provides a motivational backdrop (cf. 6:12, "take hold of eternal life"), but the primary reflection is on the humanity of Christ.

The time of judgment and reward is indicated by the explicit reference to "the manifestation *(epiphaneia)* of our Lord Jesus Christ" in 6:14. Here the future appearance of Christ, which will come about at "the right time" as determined by God (6:15a; cf. also 2:6; 2 Tim 1:9-10; Tit 1:3), represents the boundary of faithfulness and the time of reward. So Paul's charge to Timothy to be faithful, after the model of the human Christ, extends to the *parousia*.

This final christological statement sheds light on the practical implications of the humanity of Christ. Something about the heresy confronted in 1 Timothy — its theology, eschatology, christology, ethics, or whatever — had shifted the balance decisively away from thinking about engagement with the world. Thus the "trustworthy saying" of 1:15 links salvation to Christ's incarnation and extends its relevance into the present via Paul's paradigmatic role. Likewise, the statement of 2:5-6 identifies and interprets Jesus' mediatorial ministry precisely with his humanity, and makes this feature the linchpin in the process by which God's universal salvation can actually reach out to all people; while the Christ hymn of 3:16 explains that Christ's full human experience, including his resurrection and vindication, is to be considered the "fleshly" unveiling of Christian existence — that is, "godliness" *(eusebeia)* — and that his experience determines the church's message and hope. And so in this final christological statement in 6:13-14, mission faithfulness is grounded in Christ's human sign of faithfulness — that is, in his testimony before Pontius Pilate of loyalty to God, which ultimately ended his life and launched the church's mission.

In Christ's humanity, therefore, God's salvation plan and the Christian life are grounded. But the necessity of the final manifestation or epiphany of the vindicated one establishes the tenuous stance of the Christian in the present age.

3. Our Great God and Savior, Jesus Christ: The Shape of Christology in Titus

Christology in the letter to Titus takes a different stance and strikes a different balance than in 1 Timothy. The letter was written specifically and intentionally, not just notionally, to Titus against the background of a nascent Pauline church that had spread to various cities on the island of Crete and was in many ways experiencing stress, frustration, and some uncertainty of commitment — particularly as it sought to be Christian in a rude social and non-ethical environment, for which Crete was infamous, and in the face of a growing anti-Pauline movement (see Kidd, "Titus as Apologia").

Paul initiates a discourse on two intersecting levels, engaging both the Cretan story (cf. 1:12) and an opposition that embodied the deception for which Cretan mythology was well-known (Kidd, "Titus as Apologia"). Thus in 1:2, at the very outset of the letter, he anchors the hope of his gospel in the God who "does not lie." This emphasis on a truthful God is in pointed contrast to Zeus of the Cretan tales, who, though held to be the epitome of virtue, did, in fact, lie to have sexual relations with a human woman, taking the human form of her husband.

Moreover, in the context of the Cretan religious challenge to Olympian traditionalists (i.e., the Cretan claim that Zeus was born and died on the island of Crete), the tendency to portray Zeus as one who received divine status in return for his benefactions to humans suggests an upside-down approach to "theology" at the popular level, which would have inevitably forced a collision between the Christian gospel and Cretan mythology. Paul does not avoid this collision. Rather, playing down the human features of Christ — which are emphasized, as we have seen above, in 1 Tim 1:15; 2:5; 3:16; 6:13-14 — he declares in this letter to Titus that Christ (1) came among humans from above, and (2) conferred gifts (salvation, a life of virtue) as a deity, not as a human who for his benefaction is accorded divine status.

The Pairings of God and Christ as Savior

The first theological section of Titus comes in the salutation of 1:1-4. The main goal is to lay the salvation-historical framework of "promise and fulfillment," within which may be seen the gospel — that is, the appearance of Christ in history, which is referred to obliquely as "his [God's] word" — and Paul's authoritative link to it. But the letter's unique christological theme is also introduced in the successive references to God and Christ as "Savior" in 1:3 and 4; 2:10 and 13; and 3:4 and 6: "God our Savior . . . Christ Jesus our Savior." The equivalence or sharing of status signaled by these pairings is more pronounced than in the letters to Timothy. And its significance will become clear in what follows.

2:11-14

The next christological reflection occurs in 2:11-14:

> For the grace of God has appeared *(epephanē)*, bringing salvation to all, training us to renounce impiety and worldly passions, and in the present age to live lives that are self-controlled, upright, and godly while we wait for the blessed hope and the manifestation *(epiphaneia)* of the glory of our great God and Savior, Jesus Christ. He it is who gave himself for us that he might redeem us from all iniquity and purify for himself a people of his own who are zealous for good deeds.

This passage follows an extended parenetic section that instructs household members to live respectably in their various positions. The degree to which this teaching is situated in the culture is clear from the Greek ethical language that it uses. What prompted the teaching was probably the disruption caused by the opponents, who were "upsetting whole households" and "teaching for sordid gain" (1:11).

With the reference to "God our Savior" in 2:10b, the transition is made from ethics to theology. The theological material that follows in 2:11-14 grounds the reshaped household code. And within the "Savior" and "epiphany" emphases of the three Pastoral Epistles, the christology in this passage reaches the highest point in the letter. For one epiphany in history has communicated a new way of salvation-life in the world (vv. 11-12) that the second epiphany will fulfill (vv. 13-14). Christ is the source of present Christian existence and hope for its completion.

In dialogue with current beliefs and symbols, Paul tells here a Christian epiphany story to rival those of the culture. His verbal thrust and parry is evident from his references to "epiphany" and the gifts of "grace" and "salvation," which were often associated with gods and kings. And the opening oblique reference to Christ's advent as the epiphany of "God's grace, bringing salvation" brings the christological discussion within the framework of the cultural story. Furthermore, Paul exegetes the Christ event in terms of the Hellenistic concept of "education in culture" *(paideia)*, describing the effects of this epiphany, in opposition to the Cretan stereotype, in terms of a "Christian civilization" where the cardinal virtues can indeed be realized (2:12).

Also to be noted is the fact that the Cretan cultural story is thoroughly subverted when 2:13 is reached. For the description of another epiphany, the Christian object of hope, while it starts on the typical theme of the appearances or epiphanies of Hellenistic kings, gods, and Roman emperors — using the expression "our great God and Savior" — defiantly ignores those claims and inserts the name "Jesus Christ."

But does 2:13 refer to the epiphany of one person ("of our great God and Savior, Jesus Christ") or two ("of our great God and of our savior Jesus Christ")? The rarity of divine appellations for Christ in the New Testament perhaps favors the latter. But Paul may have committed himself to the former in Rom 9:5 (cf. 2 Pet 1:1), and Col 1:19 pursues a similar line. And a number of other factors favor a single christological reference: (1) "God and Savior" was a widely used title that generally referred to a single deity; (2) a single definite article governs the two titles "God and Savior"; (3) "epiphany" is used only of Christ in these letters; and (4) a future coming of the Father in association with the End is unprecedented. It seems most reasonable, therefore, that the reference here is to the future "epiphany" of "our God and Savior, Jesus Christ."

The theme of Christ's sharing of the status of Savior in 1:3-4, which is present also in the pairing of 2:10 and 13, invites this extraordinary climax. But this sharing between God and Jesus Christ, together with the divine transfer of their activities, reaches critical mass here in 2:11-14. We are familiar with the statement that describes the Savior as the one "who gave himself for us" (cf. 1 Tim 2:6; Gal 1:4; Eph 5:2). But the intertextual echoes in the purpose statements of 2:14 — which recall statements in Deut 7:6;

14:2; Exod 19:5; and Ezek 37:23 — suggest that Christ is here understood to have done the work of Yahweh in producing a unique "people for his own possession." And this christological development, which urges a refinement of monotheism, is easily accommodated in the epiphany concept, which is used of Christ as the appearance of God in both human history and the future *parousia* (cf. Lau, *Manifest in Flesh*).

Christology in 2:11-14, therefore, sharply challenges the Cretan lie and its corollary tale of Zeus's rise from humanity to deity. Human salvation is equated with the epiphany of Jesus Christ, who was already before his manifestation God and Savior. True civilized culture emerges from Christ's first historical appearance (vv. 11-12) and will be completed in the future epiphany of the divine Savior (vv. 13-14).

3:4-6

Titus 3:1-2 considers Christians as participants in society. The traditional call to recognize political authorities (cf. Rom 13:1-7; 1 Pet 2:13-17) is here expanded to address the public image of the church among all people. Christian behavior is then urged in 3:4-6 because of (1) "the appearance" of "the goodness and loving kindness of God our Savior" (v. 4), (2) salvation as the new Christian reality, which has come about by God's mercy, "the washing of regeneration," and "renewal by the Holy Spirit" (v. 5), and (3) the work of "Jesus Christ our Savior" (v. 6). All of this has introduced a change from the old patterns of normal living (v. 3) to the new patterns of those who are "heirs according to the hope of eternal life" (vv. 7-8).

Using the same strategy as in 2:11, Paul in 3:4 considers the Christ event obliquely as "the appearance" of God's kindness and love for people. These qualities, communicated to people, are just what is needed to live peaceably in the world. The Cretan way of living is thus rejected. And "epiphany" in this text gradually assumes its christological shape as salvation is declared to be "through Jesus Christ our Savior" (3:6).

God and Christ in this passage again share the title "Savior." Building on 2:11-14, the epiphany concept depicts Christ's historical entrance into the world as that of the arrival of the Benefactor-God in order to save his people. Titus, therefore, projects a christology that shares the savior/salvation and epiphany motifs of the letters to Timothy. But within that framework, Paul elevates the depiction of Christ in this letter, portraying him as

Savior and God — no doubt to sharpen his gospel's penetration into Cretan culture.

4. Jesus Christ Raised from the Dead, Paradigm of Suffering and Vindication: The Shape of Christology in 2 Timothy

2 Timothy brings the Pauline story to a conclusion (see Towner, "The Portrait of Paul"). Paul's situation (4:6-8, 16-18) and Timothy's need set both the tone of the letter and the purposes for its christological reflections. For Paul, imprisoned at Rome, the end is in sight. Somber notes intermingle with a strong expectancy of vindication. Timothy's dwindling courage and lagging commitment stand in tension with Paul's call on him to succeed him. For this parenetic letter calls on Timothy to imitate Paul's experiences and hope. And in so doing, it reflects on the resurrection of Christ to a degree that goes beyond what appears in 1 Timothy or Titus.

The Kerygma in 1:9-10

The dual themes of suffering and mission open the letter. Timothy is instructed to revive his gift and his calling, and so to take his stand, in Paul's absence, in suffering for the same gospel that brought suffering to Paul (1:6-8). Mention at the end of 1:8 of the "power of God" that is to enable Timothy — that is, the indwelling Spirit — leads to a theological discussion in 1:9-10 of the gospel for which Paul suffers.

This kerygmatic passage in 1:9-10 follows a revelatory "once hidden, now revealed" pattern in detailing the movement of salvation from its inception in the will of God to its execution in history (cf. Rom 16:25-26; also Tit 1:1-3), with the emphasis falling on the present time of the church. Christ Jesus is the pivotal figure in this drama: "[God] saved us and called us with a holy calling, not according to our works, but according to his purpose and grace, which was given to us in Christ Jesus before the ages" (v. 9). "In Christ Jesus" is typically the sphere of existence in which the blessings of fellowship with Christ are experienced (cf. 1:1, 13; 2:1; 2:10; 3:12, 15; 1 Tim 1:14; 3:13).

As the thought turns in 1:10 to the "manifestation" of God's grace that has "now been revealed," several things need to be noted. First, the means of manifesting God's grace was the event of Christ's historical epiphany as Savior (cf. Tit 2:11; 3:4). This is the only use of the noun *epiphaneia* for the incarnation, and its meaning stretches to include the whole earthly experience of Jesus. A second matter to note is that, although the sharing of status between Christ and God is close to emerging in the statement "[God] saved us . . . according to grace . . . through the epiphany of our Savior Jesus Christ," christology in 2 Timothy seeks another level. The suffering and resurrection of the Savior are central, and the appearance of Christ in history is viewed from the perspective of the results achieved by his suffering and resurrection.

Negatively, Christ is credited with "having abolished death" (*katargēsantos ton thanaton,* 1:10). The allusion is to his death as the instrument of death's annihilation (Rom 6:6, 10; 14:8-9; 2 Cor 4:10; 1 Thess 5:10; see also Heb 2:14). But the accent falls on the positive result: Christ's resurrection has "brought to light life and immortality." "Having brought to light" (*phōtisantos*) forges the link between this singular revelatory and eschatological event of the Savior's resurrection and the promise of eternal life inherent in the gospel (cf. 1 Cor 15:12-23, 53-54; cf. Acts 2:27-31). Paul's christological interest throughout 2 Timothy hovers at this intersection of the Savior's life and death, where the door to eternal life has been opened.

A third matter worthy of note in 1:10 is that the historical "epiphany" of God's grace entails a surprise, for included in it are suffering and death. A non-Christian would scarcely think of the life, suffering, and death of Jesus Christ in terms of a divine "epiphany," for the elements of weakness and shame strike a discordant note (cf. 1:8, 12). The divine and powerful effects of the cross are true enough and tangible enough to qualify for "epiphany" status. But these realities are evident only to faith. For those outside the Christian faith or who would challenge the place of suffering within the faith, this use of the epiphany concept turns common notions inside out and makes a radical claim for the Christian gospel. Indeed, God's grace is powerfully embodied in Christ's death and resurrection; the divine epiphany is expressed in and through utter human frailty. This is a paradox that faith alone resolves.

Finally, christology returns to parenesis at the end of 1:10 in the phrase "through the gospel." Here Paul drives home the point that the results of the Savior's epiphany, his death and resurrection, are effective in the world by means of the proclamation of the Christian gospel — which may very well be seen as an ongoing epiphany. Either cowardice on the part of Timothy or neglect on the part of misguided opponents in the communities can halt the revelatory process, but neither suffering nor death poses a threat to the gospel itself.

2:8-13

Christology again supports parenesis in 2:8-13. Paul's main concern throughout this second letter is not to reiterate the Christian message, but to call on Timothy to live as Paul himself (and Jesus) did. Nonetheless, it is the gospel that explains the logic of his exhortations. So in 2:8-10 he (1) asks Timothy to "remember Jesus Christ, raised from the dead, descended from David," (2) declares this to be "my gospel," (3) links his own sufferings with the suffering of Jesus, and (4) involves Timothy throughout in the process.

Paul's depiction of Jesus is primary. As a retelling of the gospel, the formulaic words "Jesus Christ, raised from the dead, descended from David" leave much implicit. "According to my gospel" (cf. 2 Tim 1:11; 1 Tim 1:11) underlines the statement's authenticity — partly with polemical intention (cf. 2 Tim 2:18), but mainly as an endorsement of its apostolic origin (cf. Rom 2:16; 16:25). The resurrection of Jesus Christ is declared to be central to the gospel (cf. 1 Cor 15:4, 12, 13, 14, 16; 2 Cor 5:15).

Jesus' descent from David (literally, "from the seed of David") is also a stock element within the gospel tradition (cf. Rom 1:3; John 7:42). And although this statement implies incarnation (cf. Gal. 4:4), it goes beyond that to indicate the conviction that Jesus is Messiah (cf. John 7:42). Scholars have often discerned in the formulation "raised from the dead, descended from David [or 'from the seed of David')" reflections of a two-stage christology that distinguishes rigidly between Jesus' earthly status and his exaltation (e.g., Dibelius and Conzelmann, *Pastoral Epistles*, 108). But the two parts of the formula should be seen as a unity: Jesus' messianic identity involves both his descent from David and his resurrection, as in Rom 1:3-4, which most scholars argue stands somehow behind this text. But a comparison of the two texts suggests that here Paul has intentionally inverted the two dimensions of Christ's existence to emphasize the thought of resurrection.

The parenetic function of 2:8-13 implies Paul's reason for this emphasis. The passage recommends a course of action and supports such action by appealing to two models, first Jesus and then Paul himself. And the faithful saying that closes this section in vv. 11-13 reminds Timothy of the promises associated with the eschatological future — that is, that death with Christ will mean life with Christ and faithful endurance now will mean sharing in his reign then. In the saying, the resurrection of Jesus is the fundamental source of hope. For resurrection calls to mind not only the thoughts of Jesus' suffering and crucifixion, but also his ultimate vindication and victory over death.

At the same time, Paul's emphasis on the resurrection seems also to be aimed at deconstructing his opponents' teaching that "the resurrection has already taken place" (2:18), which would make nonsense of any current suffering. The focus of faith is on the present reality that Jesus "has been raised" — with the perfect participle *egēgermenon* highlighting both the past and ongoing relevance of the event. And it is this fact that supports faith in situations of suffering and galvanizes a believer's hope in the future resurrection.

The traditional saying ("the saying is trustworthy") in 2:11-13 is both supportive and illustrative of the command "remember" given earlier in v. 8. Christology runs throughout this piece, developing first the thought of sharing in Christ's victory and rule, and then going on to a consideration of his faithfulness and role as judge.

The first line of this "trustworthy" saying takes the reader into the mysterious territory of "dying and rising" with Christ: "If we died with [him], we will also live with [him]" — though here the promise is totally eschatological (cf. Rom 6:8). The line explains the "remember" in 2:8 by identifying participation in Christ's resurrection and vindication as the reward for faithful suffering. Martyrdom is not specifically exalted, though the earlier metaphor of "dying and rising with" applies equally and ultimately to literal death and resurrection. Christ's own experience assures the certainty of eschatological vindication.

The second line ("if we endure . . ") explores the same reality from another perspective. "Endure" links the action called for to the pattern established by Paul (cf. v. 10). But this time reward for faithfulness in ministry — "we will also reign with [him]" — taps into the well-known theme of participation in Christ's eschatological rule as king and judge (cf. Matt 19:28; 1 Cor 4:8; 6:2-3; Rev 1:6; 3:21; 5:10; 20:4, 6; 22:5). The future timeframe in this line confirms the future horizon in the promise of life in line 1.

In the final two lines, the image of Christ as the eschatological judge reinforces a warning: "If we deny him, he will also deny us; if we are faithless, he remains faithful, for he cannot deny himself." With the defection of most of Paul's former colleagues in mind (cf. 1:15; 4:10, 16), the certainty and severity of judgment are highlighted. Words from the Jesus tradition preserved in Matt 10:33 certainly lie behind this statement. The enigmatic last line, "for he cannot deny himself," either deepens the warning or tempers it with a hint of mercy in response to human weakness (see Matera, *New Testament Christology*, 168). In either case, the specter of future judgment remains.

4:1, 8, and 14

The christological statements in 4:1, 8, and 14 develop the eschatological dimensions of Judge (vv. 1, 8, 14), King (v. 1), and Lord (vv. 8, 14). In all these roles, transference or sharing of divine prerogative between God and Christ Jesus is noticeable. The Old Testament pattern for Yahweh as judge is transferred by Paul to Christ (note the echo of Ps 61:13 LXX in 2 Tim 4:14), as is also the right to rule as King and Lord.

Furthermore, it needs to be noted that these dimensions of christology are specifically linked to the future epiphany of Christ (4:1, 8). Thus, while there is motivational value in the thought of a future judgment (2:12-13), this future event — in keeping with the theme developed from the beginning of the letter — also symbolizes vindication and completion "for all those who have loved his epiphany" (4:8). For enemies of the gospel, however, Christ's future epiphany will be a time of judgment and retribution (4:14).

In these closing verses of ch. 4, then, Paul depicts the resurrected Lord in his most exalted stations — as Judge, King, and Lord. The final focus on the eschatological event suits the thrust of 2 Timothy, which closes the Pauline story. Paul's suffering for the gospel will end in his death, and thus, for obvious reasons, eschatological vindication looms large in his thinking. But Christ in his past epiphany has established the pattern that Paul follows. So Christ's historical resurrection and vindication substantiates Paul's hope for resurrection and vindication. 2 Timothy calls on Paul's young colleague to see himself as following in the same pattern. For the continuation of the gospel ministry, which reveals these truths, is a continuation of suffering, death, and vindication. The conclusion of the salvation that Christ effected and of the gospel ministry that Paul and his colleagues have been engaged in will be the final appearance of Christ as Judge, King, and Lord.

5. Conclusion

Within the broad framework of the "epiphany" and "Savior" concepts, each of these letters shapes christology for its own purpose. This should not really surprise us. But the tendency to read these letters as a single corpus has limited the degree to which they have been allowed to tell their separate stories.

1 Timothy reflects a decided emphasis on the humanity of Christ. Titus explores in greater depth the co-equal status of God and Christ. 2 Timothy brings the promises of resurrection and vindication, as well as the eschatological functions of Christ, to bear on the harsh realities of suffering and death that confronted Timothy and challenged his faithful endurance. In each case, the interplay of christology and ethical parenesis underscores the present relevance of the salvation associated with the Christ event. The "two epiphanies" logic of the letters leaves the time in-between as the age in which faith is to bear fruit — in ministry, in godliness, and in suffering — until Christ's second appearance brings about the final consummation. Greek categories of "epiphany" and "savior," together with exploitation of the Cretan myth, allow Paul to so fashion christology that it co-opts and subverts certain dominant symbols, making the sharp point of the gospel more keenly felt.

The degree to which Savior and epiphany concepts unify the christology of these letters remains in need of careful articulation. On the one hand, both concepts are only minimally present in 1 Timothy, where the focus is on the humanity of Christ. On the other hand, even with such concepts being present, Titus and 2 Timothy fashion christology into shapes that are as distinctive from one another as they are from 1 Timothy. The choice to use these concepts, therefore, whether because of the Greek backgrounds of Timothy and Titus and of the churches in view, because of the spread and increased influence of the Roman Imperial cult and the desire that the gospel penetrate the cultural-religious-political milieu to a new depth, or because of some combination of these factors, represents something of a new step in christological experimentation, which was somehow pertinent to the writing of these three distinct letters.

One could overplay the search for connections with the christology of other Pauline letters — though I have often played down these connections in the interest of reading the letters individually. On the other hand, one could underplay such connections. Personally, I prefer to regard the epiphany/Savior framework of the Pastoral Epistles as a christological feature that links these three letters loosely into a distinctive cluster — much as can be found, though by reference to other features, among the other epistolary clusters that comprise the canonical Pauline corpus.

SELECTED BIBLIOGRAPHY

Dibelius, Martin, and Hans Conzelmann. *The Pastoral Epistles.* Philadelphia: Fortress, 1972.

Donelson, Lewis R. *Pseudepigraphy and Ethical Argument in the Pastoral Epistles.* Tübingen: Mohr-Siebeck, 1986.

Fowl, Stephen E. *The Story of Christ in the Ethics of Paul.* Sheffield: JSOT, 1990.

Hasler, Victor. "Epiphanie und Christologie in den Pastoralbriefe," *TZ* 33 (1977) 193-209.

Horbury, William. *Jewish Messianism and the Cult of Christ.* London: SCM, 1998.

Johnson, Luke Timothy. *The First and Second Letters to Timothy.* New York: Doubleday, 2001.

Kidd, Reggie McReynolds. "Titus as Apologia: Grace for Liars, Beasts, Bellies," *HBT* 21 (1999) 185-209.

Läger, Karoline. *Die Christologie der Pastoralbriefe.* Münster: Lit, 1996.

Lau, Andrew Y. *Manifest in Flesh: The Epiphany Christology of the Pastoral Epistles.* Tübingen: Mohr-Siebeck, 1996.

Marshall, I. Howard. *A Critical and Exegetical Commentary on the Pastoral Epistles.* Edinburgh: Clark, 1999.

Matera, Frank J. *New Testament Christology.* Louisville: Westminster/John Knox, 1999.

Oberlinner, Lorenz. *Die Pastoralbriefe. Erster Timotheusbrief.* Freiburg: Herder, 1994.

———. *Die Pastoralbriefe. Titusbrief.* Freiburg: Herder, 1996, especially 143-59.

Stettler, Hanna. *Die Christologie der Pastoralbriefe.* Tübingen: Mohr-Siebeck, 1998.

Towner, Philip H. *The Goal of Our Instruction: The Structure of Theology and Ethics in the Pastoral Epistles.* Sheffield: Sheffield Academic, 1989.

———. "The Portrait of Paul and the Theology of 2 Timothy: The Closing Chapter of the Pauline Story," *HBT* 21 (1999) 151-70.

Windisch, Hans. "Zur Christologie der Pastoralbriefe," *ZNW* 34 (1935) 213-38.

IV. HEBREWS, CATHOLIC EPISTLES, AND APOCALYPSE

CHAPTER 11

The Son of God as Unique High Priest: The Christology of the Epistle to the Hebrews

DONALD A. HAGNER

Uncertainties abound concerning the New Testament writing we call "The Epistle to the Hebrews." We know neither who wrote it nor to whom it was written — nor, in fact, exactly when or where it was written. Some dispute whether it was written to Jewish Christians at all, concluding that the document was wrongly designated "to the Hebrews." And although it ends like a letter, it lacks altogether the opening of the standard Hellenistic letter found in the Pauline letters. It embodies a mixed literary genre, but is perhaps best described as a carefully crafted treatise-like hortatory sermon.

Scholars have appealed, among other things, to Gnosticism, Philo, Greek dualism, the Dead Sea Scrolls, and Jewish mysticism to explain the distinctive thought-world of Hebrews, particularly its imagery of heavenly archetypes and earthly copies. The structure of the document, with its alternating sections of discourse and exhortation, has long bewildered commentators. And the christological hermeneutic used in the interpretation of the Old Testament is also challenging.

We do know, however, that the community to which Hebrews was written faced a serious crisis that made them contemplate turning away from their Christian faith. The main purpose of the document is to present reasons that such thinking should be far from the readers' minds. It does this mainly by setting forth the incomparable superiority and hence finality of God's work in Jesus Christ. The argument of the book, therefore, is in essence christological. It is because of the identity and the atoning work of Christ that Christianity is absolute in character and universal in scope. Thus, as is so often the case in the New Testament, the practical needs of an immediate and particular situation have called forth a magisterial statement of enormous theological weight and significance that takes us far beyond its original starting point.

Christology in Hebrews, as throughout the New Testament, consists in the identity of Jesus bound together with what he does. Very simply, *it is because of who Christ is that he can do what he does.* The unique emphases of the christology of Hebrews can be best appreciated by examining this connection between the person and work of Christ. To that must only be added the practical significance of this christology for believers.

Hebrews is filled with close, rational argumentation. Its logic runs, in brief, like this: Because of his deity and humanity, Jesus Christ is both Son of God and high priest and therefore is able to make a single offering for sin that is fully efficacious for all time. In what follows, we will take up the individual features of this statement to see how skillfully the author supports them. In so doing we will (1) trace out the logic of his main arguments and (2) highlight how he enriches his presentation with the numerous titles by which he refers to Christ.

1. The Deity of Christ

It is no accident that Hebrews begins with its emphatic Son of God christology. The majestic opening statement is important in establishing the basic premise for the entire book: "In many and various ways God spoke of old to our fathers by the prophets; but in these last days he has spoken to us by a Son" (1:1-2a). Affirming all that God spoke to Israel in the past, our author at the same time contrasts it to the definitive word, which God has now spoken in his Son.

Son/Son of God as the Central Christological Designation

The Son may be spoken of as God's definitive self-revelation. With the coming of the Son, a major turning point in the history of salvation has been reached. This is the most basic element of our author's christology. All else flows from or is significantly related to Jesus as the Son of God.

Only because the Son is the definitive word spoken by God can all that the author has to say about salvation become a possibility at all. This is the closest our author comes to a "word of God" christology, though that precise designation does not occur in Hebrews. ("The word of God" in 4:12 refers not to Jesus but to the voice of God.) The unqualified title "Son" occurs again in 3:6, where Jesus the Son is contrasted to Moses the servant — with Jesus "counted worthy of as much more glory than Moses as the builder of a house has more honor than the house." "Son" occurs also in 5:8 and 7:28. The full title "the Son of God" occurs in 4:14; 6:6; 7:3; and 10:29. This title is clearly the central christological designation of Hebrews. Surprisingly, our author refers to Christ as "the Lord" *(ho kyrios)* only three times (2:3; 7:14; 13:20).

The Descriptive Clauses in 1:2b-3

The content of the title "Son" or "Son of God" at the beginning of Hebrews is immediately filled in by the seven descriptive clauses of 1:2b-3, six of which underline the Son's unique relationship with God. These verses, especially v. 3, may well derive from a hymnic or liturgical tradition.

In the first two clauses, Christ is put at both the end and the beginning of time: he is "appointed the heir of all things" and is the one "through whom God created the world [literally 'the ages']." The role of the Son in creation is unmistakably parallel to that of Wisdom in Jewish tradition (cf. Prov 8:27-30; Wis 9:2, 9). The preexistence and eternality of the Son are here presupposed (cf. 1:8; 5:6; 6:20; 7:17, 21, 24, 28; 13:8).

Clauses three and four underline the closest possible association between the person of Christ and God: Christ in his being "reflects the glory [more properly, the 'radiance' or 'effulgence'] of God," like bright rays in relation to the sun (cf. Wis 7:25-26), and "bears the very stamp of his [God's] nature," like a coin in relation to a die. That is, he is the exact representation of God. The fifth clause also predicates deity of the Son in its assertion that the Son "upholds the universe by his word of power."

The sixth clause is exceptional among the seven because it refers less to who the Son is than to what he has done. In this one case alone, the accomplishment of "purification for sins," the work of the Son can be compared to that of other human beings, namely the priests of the temple. The author will later, however, devote a great deal of space to the contrast between the ongoing and inadequate work of Israel's priests and the final, fully sufficient work of the Son. But that it is the Son who "made purification for sins" indicates from the outset the importance of the vital relation between his sonship and his priesthood — which we will focus on later. That the priestly work of the Son involves his sacrificial death will become the focus of Hebrews.

The seventh clause speaks of Christ's ascension to the right hand of God: "he sat down at the right hand of the Majesty on high." That he "sat down" indicates the finality of his work of atonement. His position at God's right hand is consonant with the statements made about the Son in the previous clauses. Here we have the first allusion in Hebrews to Ps 110:1, an absolutely key text for our author: "The LORD said to my lord, 'Sit at my right hand until I make your enemies your footstool.'" Ps 110:1 is explicitly cited in 1:13 and 10:12-13. It is alluded to here and in 8:1 and 12:2 (see also 4:14; 7:26).

The ascension, and not the resurrection (which is mentioned only in 13:20), is the focus of the author. The ascension of the Son to God's right hand, of course, presupposes Christ's resurrection. So, having accomplished his earthly work, Christ has "passed through the heavens" (4:14) and sits as coregent at God's right hand.

The Old Testament Quotations in 1:5-13

The remainder of ch. 1 is taken up with an argument that is based on Old Testament quotations and concerns the superiority of Christ to the angels. That superiority depends on the divine sonship of Christ.

The first quotation makes this point explicitly: "You are my Son; today I have begotten you" (Ps 2:7, quoted again in 5:5). The second quotation also emphasizes the divine sonship of Jesus and alludes to him as the promised descendant of David: "I will be to him a Father and he will be to me a Son" (2 Sam 7:14; 1 Chron 17:13). The Davidic sonship of Jesus is closely related to his identity as Messiah — a point that is also made clear in Hebrews, as we will see. The third quotation, "Let all God's angels worship him" (Deut 32:43 LXX; Ps 97:7), is introduced with "when he brings his firstborn *(ton prōtotokon)* into the world," a clear allusion to the unique Son.

The fourth quotation is from Ps 45:6-7:

Your throne, O God, is forever and ever,
   and the righteous scepter is the scepter of your kingdom.
You have loved righteousness and hated wickedness;
   therefore God, your God, has anointed you with the oil of gladness
      beyond your companions.

This is introduced with "but of the Son he says." The opening words of the quotation are somewhat ambiguous, for it is possible to translate "your throne" as a predicate nominative, resulting in the strange statement "God is your throne forever and ever." The other, more appealing, possibility is to take "God" *(theos)* as vocative: "Your throne, O God, is forever and ever." In the latter case, we are confronted with the oddity of God addressing another as "God." But given what our author has already explicitly said of the Son — and implicitly of his preexistence and deity — it is not difficult to believe that in applying the passage to Christ, the Son of God, he could understand the Son as the one addressed by the vocative "O God." We thus have here a striking statement concerning the deity of Christ. The application of Ps 45:6-7 to Christ, the anointed one, accords particularly well with the statement about anointing at the close of the quotation: "therefore God, your God, has anointed you with the oil of gladness beyond your companions."

The fifth quotation is from Ps 102:25-27:

In the beginning, Lord, you founded the earth,
   and the heavens are the work of your hands;
they will perish, but you remain;
   they will all wear out like clothing;
like a cloak you will roll them up,
   and like clothing they will be changed.
But you are the same,
   and your years will never end.

This quotation is also used to speak of the deity of the Son. And with the vocative "Lord" *(kyrie),* the role of the Son in creation, which was earlier highlighted in 1:2, leads to an affirmation of the Son's continuance, in contrast to what has been created.

Summation

In the opening chapter of Hebrews we have one of the strongest affirmations of the deity of Jesus Christ to be found in the New Testament. The passage stands with the prologue to the Fourth Gospel and the Christ hymns of Phil 2:6-11 and Col 1:15-20 as the high points of New Testament christology. The stress on the deity of the Son at the beginning of Hebrews serves immediately to demonstrate the superiority of the Son over the angels. But as we proceed through Hebrews, it becomes evident that it serves other purposes that are even more significant. For the deity of the Son is used to show the superiority of Christ to Moses in ch. 3, and eventually the superiority of the New Covenant to the Old Covenant in ch. 8. More important for the writer of Hebrews than all these, however, the deity of the Son finds its climax in the fully effective atoning work of the Son, who acts in the capacity of a unique high priest — which is something, as we will see, that becomes possible only because of his identity as the Son of God.

2. The Humanity of Christ

It is remarkable that the two New Testament writings that most stress the deity of Christ, the Fourth Gospel and the Epistle to the Hebrews, are at the same time the most emphatic about his full humanity. Thus while Hebrews 1 is a resounding statement about the deity of the Son, Hebrews 2 stresses with equal vigor the humanity of the Son. The humanity of the Son, of course, constitutes a potential problem for the author's argument concerning the superiority of the Son to the angels, since it is clear that angels are by their nature superior to human beings. But our author is able to turn this seeming difficulty to his advantage.

The Quotation of Ps 8:5-7

Interpreters disagree concerning the intention of the quotation of Ps 8:5-7 in 2:6-8. It is clear enough that the psalmist speaks of human beings in general, as represented by Adam in particular, when he says: "You have made them a little lower than the angels." It is human beings who are little in comparison to the heavenly beings created by God. So the Psalm says that human beings are little in comparison to the heavenly beings created by God. Yet, paradoxically, human beings are also "crowned . . . with glory and honor" and have "everything in subjection under [their] feet," which is an allusion to the creation story but also something the author of Hebrews recognizes as still a future hope rather than a present reality. Hebrew *'lhym* can be translated "God," "heavenly beings," or "angels," but the Septuagint and Heb 2:7 both have *angelous,* "angels."

It is very difficult, however, to resist the idea that the author of Hebrews also takes the passage to refer to Jesus — indeed, to Jesus as the archetypal human. There are at least three reasons for thinking this. The first is that the last line of the quotation, "putting everything in subjection to him," corresponds to the last line of one of the most important texts for our author, Ps 110:1: "Sit at my right hand until I make your enemies a stool for your feet." Indeed, this correspondence may well have suggested Psalm 8 to the author. So if Ps 110:1 refers to Christ, so too does Ps 8:7.

A second reason for thinking that the author of Hebrews viewed Ps 8:5-7 as referring to Jesus arises from the temporal sequence in the middle of the quotation. The sequence of being "for a little while lower than the angels" and then "crowned . . . with glory and honor" fits the author's view of Christ — who in the incarnation was made "for a little while lower than the angels" and in his exaltation to God's right hand (cf. 1:3, 13, again from the related text Ps 110:1) was "crowned . . . with glory and honor."

And a third reason for so thinking is that the words "son of man," which in the quotation are synonymous with "man," would probably have suggested Jesus to the author. To be sure, the author of Hebrews does not use the title "Son of man" elsewhere to refer to Christ. Nor did the early church. But he would almost certainly have known from the church's oral tradition that Jesus had referred to himself with just that title.

The midrashic exposition of Ps 8:5-7 in Heb 2:8-9 leaves no doubt that our author understood the quotation as applying to Christ. For in 2:8 he observes, "As it is, we do not yet see everything in subjection to him" — thereby bringing to mind again the "until" in the last line of Ps 110:1, "until I make your enemies a stool for your feet." Then he immediately adds in 2:9, "But we see Jesus, who for a little while was made lower than the angels, crowned with glory and honor because of the suffering of death, so that by the grace of God he might taste death for every one." The word order in 2:9 is particularly revealing. Between the definite article *(ton)* that begins the verse and its noun "Jesus" *(Iēsoun),* the words from Ps 8:6, "for a little while was made lower than the angels," are repeated. From this juxta-position of clauses and ideas it seems evident that the author of Hebrews was thinking of Jesus when he says "who for a little while was made lower than the angels." And almost directly following are the words "crowned with glory and honor," which are also applied to Jesus.

Jesus as the Archēgos of Salvation

Although the humanity of Jesus entailed a temporary inferiority to the an-gels, it made possible his substitutionary death — that is, "that by the grace of God he might taste death for every one" (2:9) — and so enabled him to become "the pioneer of their salvation" (2:10). The title *archēgos* in 2:10, which can be translated equally well as "pioneer," "originator," "author," "founder," or "pathbreaker," is used again in connection with the humanity of Jesus in 12:2. There he is described as "the pioneer/founder *(archēgos)* and perfecter *(teleiōtēs)* of our faith, who . . . endured the cross."

The same conjunction of the humanity and the saving death of Jesus is made again in 5:9, "Being made perfect [by his obedience to the call to suffer death], he became the source *(aitios)* of eternal salvation to all who obey him" (5:9). This is what our author indicates, as well, in discussing Je-sus' humanity in 2:14-15: "He partook of the same nature [i.e., 'flesh and blood'] so that through death he might destroy him who has the power of death, that is, the devil, and deliver all those who through fear of death were subject to lifelong bondage."

The Quotation of Ps 40:7-9

A further remarkable passage concerning the humanity of Christ is found in the quotation of Ps 40:7-9 (according to the Septuagint) in 10:5-9. Christ is taken to be the speaker of the following words:

> Sacrifices and offerings you have not desired, but a body you have pre-pared for me. . . . Then I said "Lo, I have come to do thy will, O God," as it is written of me in the roll of the book.

(The Hebrew text has for the second clause "ears you have dug for me," which was taken by the Septuagint translators as an allusion to God forming the body of Adam out of clay as a sculptor might, digging out the ears before breathing life into him.) In his typical midrashic commentary, the author of Hebrews remarks: "He abolishes the first [i.e., sacrifices and offerings, burnt offerings and sin offerings] in order to establish the second [i.e., God's will]. And by that will we have been sanctified through the offering of the body of Jesus Christ once for all" (10:9-10).

A body, therefore, was "prepared for" Christ so that he might do the will of God in his obedient death on the cross. So here, again, we see that the primary purpose of the Son of God taking on humanity was for the sake of his unique sacrificial death. This is why for our author Jesus is "the apostle and high priest of our confession" — the one sent by God in order to accomplish atonement, and so the one who is central to the faith we confess.

Summation

The necessity of the death of the Son of God explains the reason for his coming in the garb of full humanity. The goal is the deliverance of men and women from sin. So our author writes in 2:17: "Therefore he had to be made like his brethren in every respect, so that he might become a merciful and faithful high priest in the service of God, to make expiation for the sins of the people." The same association of ideas occurs in 10:19-20 where the author refers to the confidence we can have to draw near to God "since we have confidence to enter the sanctuary by the blood of Jesus, by the new and living way which he opened up for us through the curtain, that is, through his flesh."

3. Jesus as High Priest

With the establishment of both the deity and the humanity of Christ, the author is now in a position to emphasize the most distinctive aspect of his christology, namely, the priestly identity and function of Jesus. In the New Testament only Hebrews refers to Jesus as high priest, applying the title to Christ no less than ten times: Jesus is the high priest of the order of Melchizedek (5:6, 10; 6:20), "the apostle and high priest of our confession" (3:1), the high priest who accomplishes atonement (2:17; 7:26; 8:1), the "high priest of the good things that have come" (9:11), and the high priest who is able to help us in our weaknesses (4:14-15). Parallel is the reference to "a great priest over the house of God" in 10:21.

The Representative Functions of a High Priest

A priest represents humans to God, functioning on their behalf. We are given virtually a textbook definition in 5:1: "Every high priest chosen from among humans is appointed to act on behalf of humans in relation to God." A priest must therefore be human. "Therefore," our author says regarding Jesus, "he had to be made like his brethren in every respect, so that he might become a merciful and faithful high priest in the service of God" (2:17).

A high priest is "in the service of God" on behalf of needy humans. The main duty of a priest, of course, is "to offer gifts and sacrifices for sins" (5:1). An ordinary priest "is bound to offer sacrifice for his own sins as well as for those of the people" (5:3; cf. 9:7). In this regard, however, the parallel breaks down. For since Christ was "without sin" (4:15), "he has no need, like those high priests, to offer sacrifices daily, first for his own sins and then for those of the people" (7:27).

The Problem of Jesus as High Priest and Its Resolution

But there is a problem here. Our author has begun talking about Jesus as a priest — as, indeed, a high priest (he makes no distinction between the titles) — without any apparent justification. Jesus was not of the tribe of Levi but of the tribe of Judah. And, as our author himself points out, "in connection with that tribe Moses said nothing about priests" (7:14). In his answer to this dilemma the author makes perhaps his greatest contribution to the collection of writings that would become the New Testament: the identification of Christ as a high priest of the unique order of Melchizedek.

Let us trace out the logic of this argument. Our author first introduces the idea that Jesus is our high priest as early as 2:17. He does the same in 3:1; 4:14-15; and 5:5-6a — the latter reference to Jesus as "high priest" and "priest forever" coming just before he quotes in 5:6b what will become the key passage in his argument, Ps 110:4: "You are a priest forever after the order of Melchizedek." This verse is again referred to in 5:10, where, after indicating that through his suffering Jesus "became the source of eternal salvation to all who obey him," he adds the words "being designated by God a high priest after the order of Melchizedek." This is followed immediately in 5:11 by the comment "About this we have much to say which is hard to explain." Then after a characteristic digression, the author returns to the subject in 6:20, "Jesus has gone as a forerunner *(prodromos)* on our behalf [into the inner shrine behind the curtain], having become a high priest forever after the order of Melchizedek." And finally in 7:1-28 our author spells out his argument in considerable detail.

But how the author's reasoning works is already evident from 5:5-6. There, before he quotes Ps 110:4, he quotes Ps 2:7:

> So also Christ did not exalt himself to be made a high priest, but was appointed by him who said to him, "You are my Son, today I have begotten you" [Ps 2:7]; as he says also in another place, "You are a priest forever, after the order of Melchizedek" [Ps 110:4].

The starting point, as at the beginning of Hebrews, is the identity of Jesus as the unique Son of God (1:2, 5). But this Son, as seen in the citation of Ps 110:1 in 1:13, is also the one who is invited to sit at God's right hand: "The LORD says to my lord, 'Sit at my right hand until I make your enemies your footstool'" (cf. also 8:1; 10:12-13; 12:2). Since, therefore, Ps 110:1 refers to the exaltation of Christ, the words spoken in Ps 110:4 also apply to him — that is, Christ is the one who is declared "a priest forever according to the order of Melchizedek." The identity of Christ as high priest is inseparable from — indeed, depends on — his divine sonship. Thus it is his divine sonship that qualifies Christ to be the high priest referred to in Ps 110:4.

Summation

Scholars debate whether our author is responsible for this creative connection of texts in defense and exposition of Jesus as high priest or it had already been made by Christians before him. We cannot know for certain, but we do know that we encounter it first from his hand. Although "high priest" and "priest" are not used of Jesus in other New Testament writings, it is clear that the idea that Christ functions as a priest is not uncommon — as, for example, in the very assertion that Christ provides the atonement for our sins. But while the idea might have been common among the early Christians, our author's application of the title to Christ is unique in the New Testament.

4. Christ as High Priest of the Order of Melchizedek

The author's argument concerning the derivation of Christ's high priesthood from Melchizedek begins in earnest in ch. 7. There he recounts the story of Abraham meeting Melchizedek and offering him a tenth of the spoils from his recent victory (7:1-2a). He points out how in several interesting respects Melchizedek resembles the Son of God (7:2b-3) — in particular, that he is "without father, mother, or genealogy and has neither beginning of days nor end of life, but . . . continues a priest forever" (7:3).

This does not mean that Melchizedek was a pre-incarnate appearance of Christ to Abraham. Opposition to this popular conclusion can already be found in Epiphanius (55.1.8) in the fourth century. The author of Hebrews points, rather, to the interesting coincidence (but surely a divinely intended one!) that very strangely, in contrast to what is usually the case for kings and high priests, we have record of neither lineage, birth, nor death of this Melchizedek, despite the fact that he was both a king and a priest. It is as though he comes out of nowhere and continues forever.

Since Melchizedek blessed Abraham, he is superior to Abraham (7:4-8) — and thus, in effect, to Levi, "who was still in the loins of his ancestor" (7:9-10). Melchizedek was a priest of God Most High (*'ēl 'elyôn*) long before Levi and Aaron. And in this way also it is clearly implied that the priesthood of Melchizedek is superior to the Levitic priesthood. For, our author asks in 7:11, "if perfection had been attainable through the Levitic priesthood . . . what further need would there have been for another priest to arise after the order of Melchizedek, rather than one named after the order of Aaron?"

This brings the author directly to the inadequacy of the old temple cultus and underlines the revolutionary character of what he affirms: "For where there is a change in the priesthood, there is necessarily a change in the law as well" (7:12). Indeed, as we will see, such is the immense significance of the work of Christ that our author regards the Old Covenant as not merely deeply affected, but as outmoded and passé.

After citing the key text of Ps 110:4 once again in 7:17 (note also the allusion in 7:15), the author notes that "a former commandment is set aside because of its weakness and uselessness, for the Law made nothing perfect" (7:18-19a) — that is, the Law brought nothing to completion or fulfillment. The immediate point is that Ps 110:4 qualifies Christ to be a priest, even humanity's high priest, which would otherwise have been an impossibility since Christ was not of the tribe of Levi. And on the basis of this change in the Law and Christ's priesthood "according to the order of Melchizedek," our author does not shrink from drawing out the wider implications of Jesus' work as humanity's superior high priest, as we will see in what follows.

5. The Offering of Jesus the High Priest

Quite remarkably, then, a man born of the tribe of Judah qualifies to be a priest — indeed, a high priest. Furthermore, his single definitive offering at once fulfills the offerings of the Levitic priesthood and brings them to their goal and end. But most remarkable of all is that this high priest brings as an offering not the blood of animals but his own blood. This means that *priest and offering have become one and the same!* The author comes to his central argument in chs. 9–10, where he draws out in considerable detail the parallels between the sacrificial cultus of the Levitic priesthood and the sacrifice of Christ.

The Sacrifice of Christ vis-à-vis the Levitic Sacrifices

As the Aaronic high priest went into the Holy of Holies once a year with the blood of animal sacrifices to make atonement for the sins of the people, Christ, too, "entered once for all into the Holy Place, taking not the blood of goats and calves but his own blood, thus securing an eternal redemption" (9:12). Later in the same chapter we have this restatement, with the contrast to the sacrificial ritual of the tabernacle/Temple still in mind, of the unique character of Christ's work: "But as it is, he has appeared once for all at the end of the age to put away sin by the sacrifice of himself" (9:26; cf. 7:27). And in 10:10: "And by that will [i.e., God's will, mentioned in 10:7, 9; cf. Ps

40:9(8)] we have been sanctified through the offering of the body [i.e., the body mentioned in 10:5; cf. Ps 40:7(6)] of Jesus Christ once for all" (cf. 10:12). Although chs. 9 and 10 constitute the heart of Hebrews, the atonement for sins is already indicated as the purpose of the Son in 2:17 (cf. 1:3).

This is the appropriate point to discuss briefly the author's use of "Christ," that is, "Messiah." Although it is clear that our author regards Jesus as the Messiah, it is not so clear exactly which of the twelve occurrences of *Christos* have the title "Messiah" in mind rather than simply "Christ" as a proper name. It would seem that the title is in view in passages such as 3:14; 6:1; and 11:26. Especially interesting for us are 3:6, which links "Messiah" with "Son," and such passages as 5:5; 9:11, 24-25 and 28, which associate "Messiah" with "High Priest." This association points clearly to the close relation our author sees between the designation "Messiah" and the sacrificial death of Jesus. It would seem perfectly acceptable, therefore, to translate 9:14 as a reference to "the blood of the Messiah." For the reality of God sending not a triumphant, kingly Messiah but one whose mission involved his atoning death is grasped unhesitatingly here.

The Heavenly Sanctuary vis-à-vis the Earthly Tabernacle

When our author compares the earthly tabernacle with the true heavenly sanctuary and notes that Christ offered his blood there (9:11-12, 24), it is very unlikely that he has in mind an actual structure where atonement is accomplished by the offering of the blood of Christ after Christ's ascension into heaven. The famous dualism of Hebrews is better understood as temporal in character — that is, between preparatory anticipation and finality in linear time — rather than vertical, as in Platonic dualism. In the present instance we have our author's way of speaking typologically of the final, definitive character of the death of Christ on the cross. It was there and then on the cross that atonement was made. The temple cultus anticipated the fulfillment encountered in Christ's death on the cross.

This is also true of the description of Christ as "such a high priest, one who is seated at the right hand of the throne of the Majesty in heaven, a minister in the sanctuary and the true tent which is set up not by man but by the Lord" (8:1-2). The contrast is not between ideal and actual but between the initial, preparatory, and imperfect, on the one hand, and the final, efficacious, and perfect, on the other.

Summation

It is worth emphasizing once again the crucial importance of both the deity and the humanity of Christ to his work as high priest. For to act as a priest, he must be human — just as to present himself as an offering through his sacrificial death he must be human. Yet, on the other hand, to be a priest "forever, after the order of Melchizedek" (5:6; 6:20), he must be divine — the unique Son who exists through all time, who "holds his priesthood permanently, because he continues forever" (7:24). Only through this mysterious reality, so central to our author's perspective, can Christ become the "guarantor of a better covenant" (7:22).

6. Jesus as Mediator of the New Covenant

It is the divine sonship and priesthood of Jesus, which we have so far focused on, that makes possible his definitive and finally efficacious sacrificial work. This, in turn, brings us to the reality of the dawning of a new age that is emphasized in the author's realized eschatology (see 1:2; 6:5; 9:11; and especially 12:22-24). A statement that could be used as virtually a summary of Hebrews is found in 9:26: "But as it is, he has appeared once for all at the end of the age to put away sin by the sacrifice of himself." It should perhaps not be surprising that the finality of Christ's work has significant consequences for the status of what is now to be regarded as the Old Covenant.

The Quotation of Jer 31:31-34 and Its Implications

It is particularly noteworthy that although our author writes to Jews, he, more than any other New Testament writer, bravely affirms the discontinuity necessitated by the arrival of the New Covenant. The challenge is eased considerably by the fact that the quotation of Jer 31:31-34 in Heb 8:8-12 already suggests that the new that is to come will supersede the old. Thus the Old Covenant itself anticipates that something new and better is on the horizon. In this way, it is shown to be temporary and by implication faulty too: "For if that first covenant had been faultless, there would have been no occasion for a second" (8:7).

To be sure, the Jeremiah quotation is introduced with "he finds fault with them" (8:8a), that is, with the people, rather than the Old Covenant itself. Nevertheless, the old was ineffective and hence must pass away. And it is this point that the author makes after the quotation from Jeremiah: "In speaking of a new covenant, he treats the first as obsolete. And what is becoming obsolete and growing old is ready to vanish away" (8:13). If the author were writing these words after the destruction of the Second Temple in 70 CE, it is very difficult to believe that he could have resisted referring to that event here.

The Inauguration of the New Covenant

What brings the Old Covenant to its climax and inaugurates the New Covenant is the atoning death of Christ. This is what enables the fulfillment of the promise in the final words of the Jeremiah quotation: "For I will be merciful toward their iniquities, and I will remember their sins no more" (as quoted in Heb 8:12). Christ as Son of God and High Priest, therefore, becomes the Mediator of the New Covenant. The connection between the death of Christ as high priest and his designation as "the mediator of a new covenant" (9:15) is clear from the immediately preceding context (vv. 11-14). That connection is also apparent in the other occurrence of the designation (12:24), where it is paralleled with the "sprinkled blood that speaks more graciously than the blood of Abel." Similarly, it is with the high priestly ministry of Christ in mind that the author writes in 8:6 that "Christ has obtained a ministry which is as much more excellent than the old as the covenant he mediates is better, since it is enacted on better promises."

In his midrashic exposition of Ps. 110:4, where the reference to the Melchizedekian priesthood is introduced with "The Lord has sworn and will not change his mind," our author notes that the commission of Christ as priest "was not without an oath" (7:20). This observation shows the superiority of his priesthood to the Levitic priesthood. But more importantly, our author goes on to observe that "this makes Jesus the surety of a better covenant" (7:22).

Closely allied to the stress on the New Covenant as "a better covenant" (7:22 and 8:6) are the references to "better" promises (8:6), a "better" hope (7:19), a "better" country (11:16), a "better" life (11:35, cf. 40), and a "better possession and an abiding one" (10:34). These references are a part of the larger argument of the author concerning the superiority of the new to the old.

7. The Great Shepherd of the Sheep

The christology of Hebrews is not speculative or abstract. The author is not concerned with ontological questions, although there are clearly onto-logical implications in what he has to say about Christ. He does not write a treatise describing the nature and person of Christ. Rather, as we noted at the outset, the author has the most pragmatic of concerns before him and writes primarily to address the situation and needs of the readers. His greatest concern is that his readers become aware of and take advantage of the resources offered by Christ and his work.

The Great Shepherd Motif

One important resource, referred to in the letter's concluding benediction, is that of Jesus as "the great shepherd of the sheep" (13:20). This striking and familiar metaphor is rich with obvious christological content. In Ezek 34:15 it is God who is the shepherd: "I myself will be the shepherd of my sheep, and I will make them lie down, says the Lord God." "Son of David" christology also comes to mind a few lines later in Ezek 34:23: "my servant David will be their shepherd." In using this metaphor, our author un-doubtedly intends to highlight for his readers the work of the exalted Jesus in providing security and caring for the welfare of his flock (cf. Zech 10:3: "for the Lord of hosts cares for his flock").

The Practical Significance of the Shepherd's Care for His Flock

This brings us finally to the author's christology considered from the standpoint of its practical significance for the Christian life. He is able to draw much meaning for the believer from the deity and humanity of Christ. As we have seen, it is the deity and humanity of Christ that qualify him to be a unique high priest.

The humanity of Christ has much to offer. Our author writes,

"Therefore he had to be made like his brethren in every respect, so that he might become a merciful and faithful high priest in the service of God" (2:17). The immediate purpose of the humanity of Jesus is "to make expiation for the sins of the people."

But another advantage that Christ's humanity and expiatory sufferings afford the readers is quickly added: "For because he himself has suffered and been tempted, he is able to help those who are tempted" (2:18). Because the divine Christ was fully human, he is intimately acquainted with human need. We find the same emphasis in 4:15: "We have not a high priest who is unable to sympathize with our weaknesses, but one who in every respect has been tested as we are, yet without sin." The practical consequence of this is that we are enabled to "draw near to the throne of grace, that we may receive mercy and find grace to help in time of need" (4:16). We have as our own priest, therefore, one who fully understands us and is able to help us in our weakness. In whatever testing comes to believers, Christ our high priest is ready to provide help.

The deity of Christ as the unique Son of God also provides a resource to believers. Jesus became a priest "not according to a legal requirement concerning bodily descent, but by the power of an indestructible life" (7:16). So he is a priest forever "because he continues forever" and "consequently is able for all time to save those who draw near to God through him, since he always lives to make intercession for them" (7:24-25). We have a priest whose existence will never end and who intercedes in unending prayer to his Father on our behalf. Our high priest represents us to God in unceasing petition.

Turning to the atoning work of our high priest on the cross and its effective and finally decisive character, we see how our author finds practical significance here, too, for the life of the individual Christian. This is a theme of the greatest significance in Hebrews. Christ is the "pioneer of salvation" (2:10). The atoning work of Christ the high priest provides forgiveness of sins (2:17; 9:14) and a cleansed conscience (9:14; 10:22), thereby enabling us to "draw near" to the very presence of God and there to receive "mercy and grace" (4:16). It gives the Christian unhindered access to the presence of God — that is, in worship and prayer. Furthermore, because of what Christ accomplished on the cross, we are able to "hold fast" to what we believe — even under the most adverse circumstances. Faithfulness, therefore, becomes a possibility for us because of the security that is ours through the work of Christ (cf. 6:18-19).

Summation

Hebrews provides an account of the work of Christ that brings with it the resources necessary to "run with perseverance the race marked out for us" (12:1). This we are called to do, not by looking to the "great cloud of witnesses" of ch. 11, but rather by fixing "our eyes on Jesus, the pioneer/founder and perfecter of our faith" (12:2). Jesus by his work not only provides the possibility and means for Christian living, he is also himself the perfect example and model of living the life of persevering faith and obedience. Just as their Lord did, Christians are called to give their faith substance by acting boldly and confidently as they count on the reality of the unseen and as they are motivated by the unseen heavenly and better country (11:14, 16) — indeed, the city of God (11:10; 13:14). This is the point of the call to the Jewish Christian readers to "go forth to him outside the camp" (13:13) in their willingness to suffer abuse and rejection.

Conclusion

The christology of Hebrews clearly constitutes one of the high peaks of the entire New Testament. We encounter here at the climax of the story of salvation a three-stage christology that is reminiscent of the Christ hymn in Phil 2:6-11 — that is, one that includes preexistence, incarnation, and exaltation. We encounter one who is fully God but also fully flesh and blood. Furthermore, we encounter one who has ascended to the right hand of God, where he sits enthroned until that future time when all will be put beneath his feet.

At the heart of Hebrews are the identity and work of Christ as high priest. As the Son of God who sits at God's right hand (Ps 110:1), he has become a priest forever according to the order of Melchizedek (Ps 110:4). This unique priesthood of Christ depends on both his deity and his humanity. The results, as we have seen, are of the greatest consequence. The work of this high priest is fully efficacious. His own atoning death makes possible once for all the forgiveness of sins and the cleansing of the conscience of the believer. It thus serves as the fulfilling goal and end of the Old Covenant as well as the inauguration of the New Covenant, of which Jesus remains the guarantor.

What is of the utmost importance, however, is what this christology means for believers in Jesus — in particular, the abundant resources that it provides for believers, both then and today, in their immediate situations of need. For it is above all the purpose of "the great shepherd of the sheep" (13:20) to provide for his flock. That provision begins with the accomplishment of atonement and its results, the forgiveness of sins. This is what provides boldness of access into the very presence of God. And with the work of Christ on the cross comes the abundant fruit of the New Covenant: sanctification, assurance, the gifts of realized eschatology, and the experience of Sabbath rest.

To sustain them in their need, believers can rely on the ongoing intercession of their high priest, who has also experienced testing and who provides a model of faith and fidelity for them. Above all, it is a vision of the Christ that the readers need — a vision of one who is the Son of God, the pioneer of their salvation, their high priest and apostle, the forerunner into the inner shrine, the guarantee of a better covenant, a minister in the true sanctuary, the mediator of a new covenant, the great priest, the pioneer/founder and perfecter of faith, the constant intercessor, and the one who remains always the great shepherd of the sheep.

Those who have fixed their eyes on this Christ cannot contemplate the abandonment of their faith. No matter what they are called to face, no matter what circumstances they may find themselves in, Christ is of definitive and final importance. They will find in him all the resources they need to persevere in their Christian faith. He is the one who will sustain them and bring them to the inheritance that awaits them. The Epistle to the Hebrews presents a christology that showers abundant benefits on those who believe.

SELECTED BIBLIOGRAPHY

Anderson, Hugh. "The Jewish Antecedents of the Christology in Hebrews," in *The Messiah: Developments in Earliest Judaism and Christianity,* ed. J. H. Charlesworth. Minneapolis: Fortress, 1992, 512-35.

Barrett, C. K. "The Christology of Hebrews," in *Who Do You Say That I Am? Essays on Christology* (Festschrift for J. D. Kingsbury), ed. M. A. Powell and D. R. Bauer. Louisville: Westminster/John Knox, 1999, 110-27.

Caird, George B. "Son by Appointment," in *The New Testament Age: Essays in Honor of Bo Reicke,* 2 vols., ed. W. C. Weinrich. Macon: Mercer University Press, 1984, 1.73-81.

Flusser, David. "Messianology and Christology in the Epistle to the Hebrews," in *Judaism and the Origins of Christianity*. Jerusalem: Magnes, 1988, 246-79.

Hagner, Donald A. *Hebrews*. San Francisco: Harper and Row, 1983; Peabody: Hendrickson, 1990.

———. *Encountering the Epistle to the Hebrews*. Grand Rapids: Baker, 2001.

Harris, Murray J. *Jesus as God: The New Testament Use of* Theos *in Reference to Jesus*. Grand Rapids: Baker, 1992, 205-27.

Hughes, Philip E. "The Christology of Hebrews," *Southwestern Journal of Theology* 28 (1985) 19-27.

Humphrey, J. F. "The Christology of Hebrews," *London Quarterly and Holborn Review* 45 (1945) 427-32.

Hurst, Lincoln D. *The Epistle to the Hebrews: Its Background of Thought*. Cambridge: Cambridge University Press, 1990.

Longenecker, Richard N. "The Melchizedek Argument of Hebrews: A Study in the Development and Circumstantial Expression of New Testament Thought," in *Unity and Diversity in New Testament Theology: Essays in Honor of George E. Ladd,* ed. R. A. Guelich. Grand Rapids: Eerdmans, 1978, 161-85.

Mealand, David L. "The Christology of Hebrews," *Modern Churchman* 22 (1979) 180-87.

Parsons, Mikeal C. "Son and High Priest: A Study in the Christology of Hebrews," *Evangelical Quarterly* 60 (1988) 195-216.

Powell, D. L. "Christ as High Priest in the Epistle to the Hebrews," in *Studia Evangelica 7*, ed. E. A. Livingstone. Berlin: Akademie, 1982, 387-99.

Vos, Geerhardus. *The Teaching of the Epistle to the Hebrews,* ed. and rev. by J. G. Vos. Grand Rapids: Eerdmans, 1956.

CHAPTER 12

Catholic Christologies in the Catholic Epistles

J. Ramsey Michaels

The "catholic" or "general" epistles toward the end of the New Testament are called that because most of them claim to be intended for either a very wide or an undefined audience. Thus their salutations include the following destinations: "to the twelve tribes in the Diaspora" (Jas 1:1); "to God's elect strangers of the Diaspora in Pontus, Galatia, Cappadocia, Asia, and Bithynia" (1 Pet 1:1); "to those who have received a faith as precious as ours" (2 Pet 1:1); "to you, so that you may have fellowship with us" (1 John 1:3); and "to those who are called, beloved in God the Father and kept safe for Jesus Christ" (Jude 1). 2 and 3 John have more specific audiences in view: "to the elect lady and her children" and "to my dear friend Gaius." But they are classed as "catholic" epistles by virtue of their association with 1 John.

What has "catholicity" to do with christology? Do these letters share a common christology based on a consensus among Christian churches in the first or early second centuries? Should we expect from them a "high" christology — that is, a relatively "orthodox" one by the standards of later orthodoxy? What do these several letters have in common christologically, and how do they differ?

Reference to the "Catholic Epistles" in my title is, of course, somewhat problematic, and not just because of the danger of confusing "catholic" with "Roman Catholic." It is problematic because it may imply more unity or consensus in these writings than actually exists. Moreover, the phrase "catholic christologies" is, admittedly, an oxymoron. For if a christology is truly "catholic" — or, as the adjective primarily connotes, "universal" — it is by definition singular and not plural. But I will use the plural simply in order to look at these "catholic" letters one by one, and so seek to discern what kind of christology emerges from each, before comparing them. Except for dealing with Jude immediately after 2 Peter and before 1 John, I will follow the canonical order.

1. Christology in James

The canon dictates that we start with the letter of James. Yet James is the last place one might expect an essay on christology to begin. Conventional wisdom decrees that James has no christology. Martin Luther's words have echoed through the centuries:

> In fine, Saint John's Gospel and his first epistle, Saint Paul's epistles, especially those to the Romans, Galatians, Ephesians, and Saint Peter's first epistle — these are the books which show thee Christ, and teach thee everything that is needful and blessed for thee to know, even though thou never see or hear any other book or doctrine. Therefore is Saint James's epistle a right strawy epistle *(eyn rechte stroern Epistel)* in comparison with them, for it has no gospel character to it (from the Introduction to Luther's 1522 New Testament, trans. in Ropes, *James*, 106).

Especially telling is the wedge that Luther has driven between James and its two companions, "Saint John's first epistle" and "Saint Peter's first epistle." The other two "show thee Christ," but James does not.

Is this a fair assessment? My answer used to be, "The distinctly Christian element in James rests not upon theological affirmations *about* Jesus Christ (e.g., the cross or the resurrection), but upon the words or teachings *of* Jesus himself as James had received them" (see my "James — The Royal Law" in *The New Testament Speaks*, 328). While I would not have admitted it, I was in effect agreeing with Luther that James has no christology. Now, however, I am not so sure.

Clearly, James does put much emphasis on certain sayings of Jesus without attributing them to Jesus — for example, on love of God and neighbor and "lead us not into temptation." In fact, James mentions Jesus only twice in the entire letter, in 1:1 and 2:1. Nevertheless, instead of complaining that there are only two such explicit instances, the better procedure is to look at the two references to Jesus more closely. And what stands out is that in each of them Jesus is called "the Lord Jesus Christ."

The Road Not Taken

A word first needs to be said, however, about "the road not taken." For it is tempting to capitalize on the recent popularity of "Wisdom christology" in, say, the Gospel of John and then look for Wisdom christology also in James. Indeed, this short letter accents divine wisdom — even more than John's Gospel does. God's wisdom, in contrast to "earthly," "natural," or "demonic" wisdom (3:15), comes "from above" (3:15, 17), like every other "good and perfect gift" (1:17). God gives wisdom generously to everyone who asks (1:5). Wisdom is an attribute of God and is God's gift — it is, if you like, "the Lord's" gift (1:7).

But wisdom is not "the Lord." Wisdom is traditionally feminine, whereas "the Lord" is resolutely masculine. James has a Wisdom theology but not a Wisdom christology. If we would find christology, we must look for "the Lord." And "the Lord" in the letter of James is Jesus.

1:1 and Related Verses

The reference to "the Lord Jesus Christ" in 1:1 is almost obligatory, given the standard format of New Testament correspondence. Paul consistently identifies himself in relation to "Jesus Christ" — whether as "apostle" or "servant" or both — and wishes grace and peace for his readers from "God the Father and the Lord Jesus Christ." James similarly identifies himself at the opening of his letter as "a servant of God and of the Lord Jesus Christ" (cf. Tit 1:1, "a servant of God and an apostle of Jesus Christ"). If we read James as a Jewish Christian document, as it appears to be, we might expect "Jesus the Christ" or "Jesus the Messiah." But, in fact, we find "the Lord Jesus Christ," just as in Paul.

"Jesus Christ" is a name and "Lord" is his title, thereby signaling a christology every bit as "high" (if we may use that term) as Paul's. "Lord" (*kyrios*) is nothing less than the God of Israel, the covenant "Lord" of the Septuagint (LXX) and the Hebrew Bible. "Servant" (*doulos*) and "Lord" are correlative terms. While the author has been traditionally known as "the brother of the Lord," he introduces himself instead as "a servant of the Lord Jesus Christ" — thereby identifying himself as a Christian and a worshiper of Jesus, just like his readers, but also, at the same time, as an authority figure in the Christian community.

Moreover, the titles "God" and "Lord" are grammatically coordinate in James's greeting in a way that they are not in Paul's. For James, unlike Paul, does not identify "God" as "Father" in distinction from Jesus. Rather, his greeting allows for other translations that would explicitly identify Jesus as God — such as, "James, a servant of God, *even* the Lord Jesus Christ" or "James, a servant of Jesus Christ, *who is* God and Lord." These renderings, which take the Greek conjunction *kai* to be explicative here, fly in the face of conventional wisdom about James — for James has traditionally been thought to be a very early Christian writing, and giving Jesus the title "God" sounds like a late development. Moreover, James is viewed as representing Jewish Christianity, which has usually been seen as accenting Jesus' humanity more than his deity. So while the common translation, which separates "God" and "Lord" by the conjunction *kai*, is admittedly more probable, James's sentence structure presents us with an immediate ambiguity at the beginning of his letter — an ambiguity that seems to exhibit an almost childlike willingness to speak of God and Jesus interchangeably.

This tendency is also characteristic of the other so-called Catholic Letters, in which it is often not possible to distinguish statements about God from statements about Jesus. The difficulty of determining the antecedents of pronouns will haunt us not only in James but throughout most of these other letters as well. For example, within three verses in James it is "God" (1:5) and "the Lord" (1:7) who answer prayer. Is James referring to the Father, to Jesus, or to both? Again, in James it is God who promises the kingdom as an inheritance "to those who love him" (2:5). But who promised "the crown of life to those who love him" (1:12)? Was it God or Jesus (cf. Rev 2:10)? Various manuscripts try to make it specific, using either "the Lord" (the majority of later manuscripts) or "God" (the Latin Vulgate and others). But the earliest and most reliable manuscripts leave it ambiguous.

"God" and "Lord" are used almost interchangeably throughout James. The author can equate "God" and "Father" (1:27), and two chapters later "Lord" and "Father" (3:9). But when he does so, it is in reference to God as the Father of Christian believers (1:17-18), and not specifically as the Father of Jesus Christ. As for Jesus, he is called "Lord" — and, as we have seen, possibly "God" — but never God's "Son." James in his naïveté never explores the relationship between God and Jesus. In fact, he makes no real distinction between them. Both are "Lord" — and the reader cannot help but wonder if perhaps both are "God."

2:1 *and Related Verses*

James makes his second and last explicit reference to Jesus by name in 2:1: "My brothers, do not show favoritism, you who hold the faith of our Lord Jesus Christ of glory." "Of glory" *(tēs doxēs)* is probably used adjectivally, so that we should translate "our glorious Lord." Just as the salutation in 1:1 defined the author's identity as a Christian believer, these words in 2:1 define the people to whom he writes as a Christian community. "The faith" — that is, the body of common tradition centering on "our glorious Lord Jesus Christ" — is what unites them to James and to each other.

The opening paragraph about favoritism in ch. 2 is framed by references to "our Lord Jesus Christ" (v. 1) and to the rich who "blaspheme the good name pronounced over you" (v. 7). Quite clearly, the "good name" is "the name of the Lord" (cf. Hermas, *Similitudes* 8.6.4), specifically "the Lord Jesus Christ." The opposite of showing favoritism is fulfilling "the royal law" as found in Scripture, "You shall love your neighbor as yourself" (v. 8). The poor are those who love God (v. 5). And love of God finds its inevitable sequel in love of neighbor and love for the poor. This is to James the "royal law" (v. 8) or what he has called earlier "the perfect law of liberty" (1:25). But, again, there is an ambiguity. Whose law is it? Who is the Lawgiver? Is it God or "the Lord Jesus Christ"?

Later in ch. 4 James mentions "the Lawgiver" *(nomothetēs),* who is also "the Judge" *(kritēs):* "There is one Lawgiver and Judge, who is able to save and to destroy. So who are you to judge your neighbor?" (v. 12). He might have added "one Teacher" — in view of his warning in 3:1, "Let not many of you become teachers," and in agreement with Jesus' words in Matt 23:8, "for one is your teacher, and you are all brothers." In ch. 5 James identifies the "one Judge" as "the Lord." First he tells his readers to "be patient until the *parousia* of the Lord" (v. 7) and to "strengthen your hearts, for the *parousia* of the Lord is near" (v. 8). Then he reminds them not to "groan against each other, that you be not judged, for look, the Judge stands at the door" (v. 9). Clearly, "the Judge" is "the Lord" who comes at "the *parousia*"

— not the Father, but "the Lord Jesus Christ" (cf. 1 Cor 15:23; 1 Thess 2:19, 3:13, 4:15; 5:23; 2 Thess 2:1, 8; see also Matt 24:3, 27, 37).

James then immediately goes on to mention the prophets, who "spoke in the name of the Lord" (5:10) — suggesting by adding this to what precedes that "the Lord" in whose name they spoke was none other than "the Lord" who will come at the *parousia*, "the Lord Jesus Christ," and that "the name of the Lord" in which they spoke was none other than "the good name pronounced over you" (cf. 2:7). Likewise, referring to the story of Job's endurance, he speaks of "the purpose of the Lord" and of how "the Lord is compassionate and merciful" (5:11b). Furthermore, he tells his readers that, just as the prophets spoke "in the name of the Lord," those who are sick are to call for the elders of the congregation to anoint them with oil "in the name of the Lord" (v. 14; cf. again 2:7) — for when he hears the prayer for the sick person, "the Lord will raise him up" (v. 15), for it is "the Lord" who answers prayer (as in 1:7).

In each of these instances, "the Lord" could be either "the Lord God" of Israel or "the Lord Jesus Christ." The accent on the *parousia* argues strongly for the latter. In the end, however, it makes no real difference. James does not intend that we sort out his uses of "Lord" — assigning some to God and others to Jesus. To James, "the Lord" of the Hebrew Bible and "the Lord Jesus Christ" are one and the same. He has no interest in distinguishing between them as "Father" and "Son," only in recognizing and honoring one "Lord" and "God."

Jesus' Death on the Cross and his Resurrection

As for Jesus' death on the cross and his resurrection, neither is explicit in James. The resurrection of Jesus, however, is implicit in the title "Lord" (cf. Acts 2:36; Rom 10:9) and in the hope of "the Lord's" *parousia* (cf. 1 Cor 15:23; 1 Thess 4:14-15). Quite possibly the resurrection is what James means by the Lord's "glory" (2:1; cf. 1 Pet 1:21).

James had opportunity to speak of the cross of Jesus in connection with Abraham's sacrifice of Isaac (2:21), but he did not do so. Instead, he highlighted Abraham's obedience to God and good works. So it is fair to assume that if he had mentioned Jesus' death at all, he would have emphasized not so much its redemptive power as the obedience it represented (cf. Phil 2:8; Heb 10:8-10).

James may, however, have thought of Jesus as "the Righteous One" condemned and killed by "the rich" (5:6; cf. Acts 3:14; *Barnabas* 6.7). If the last line of 5:6 is to be read as a statement, then the accent would be on the utter helplessness of Jesus before his accusers and murderers: "You have condemned, you have killed the Righteous One, and he does not resist you." But when read as a question, it hints at vindication: "You have condemned, you have killed the Righteous One. Does he not resist you?" Read in this way, the pronouncement echoes the Scripture quoted a chapter earlier: "God resists the proud, but gives grace to the humble" (4:6, quoting Prov 3:34 LXX). There, God is said to "resist" *(antitassetai)* the cruel oppressor; here in 5:6 "the Righteous One" himself does so, perhaps as risen "Lord" or "God."

This is as close as James ever comes to a theology of the cross. There is no doubt that he articulates the notion that God will vindicate the righteous (cf. 4:6, 10). But whether he applies this principle specifically to Jesus and his sufferings remains an open question (see, for example, Wis 2:10-20, where christological-sounding language is applied freely to the experiences of the righteous in general).

Nonetheless, even without a theology of atonement, James exhibits a high christology in the very context of promising vindication to God's people. For after repeatedly accenting "God" — as in "God resists the proud" (4:6), "submit yourselves to God" (4:7), and "draw near to God" (4:8) — he concludes with "bow down before *the Lord,* and he will lift you up" (4:10). Typically for James, "God" and "the Lord" are interchangeable. Here, as much as anywhere, is the heart of James's letter: "The Lord" exalts those who worship him. Who is "the Lord" if not "the Lord Jesus Christ"?

2. Christology in 1 Peter

Luther's inclusion of 1 Peter among "the books which show thee Christ" cannot be faulted. This does not mean that 1 Peter has a "higher" christology than James, only that its christology is richer and more fully developed.

The Context of God the Father's Supremacy

1 Peter begins with a formulation that could be read as trinitarian: "According to the foreknowledge of God the Father, consecrated by the Spirit

for obedience and for sprinkling with the blood of Jesus Christ" (1:2). "Jesus Christ" is here still a name and his title is still "Lord" (v. 3). But Peter explicitly distinguishes him from "God," who is not only "Father" (v. 2) but, as in Paul's letters, specifically "Father of our Lord Jesus Christ" (v. 3). And, in contrast to James, Peter identifies the Father alone as the Judge (1:17) — even as Jesus himself did in his ministry on earth (cf. 2:23; 4:5).

"The high status of Christ," as Larry Hurtado puts it, "is set within God the Father's supremacy" ("Christology," 173). This can be seen by a quick scan of 1 Peter: God the Father has given us new birth "through the resurrection of Jesus Christ from the dead" (1:3); our faith and hope are "in God, who raised Jesus from the dead and gave him glory" (1:21); Jesus is "the living Stone" because he is "in God's sight choice and precious" (2:4); and the "spiritual sacrifices" that believers offer are "acceptable to God through Jesus Christ" (2:5). Furthermore, Christians are called to "do the will of God" and to carry out their respective ministries as "good stewards of God's diversified grace" (2:15; 4:2, 19); those who speak must do so as if speaking "the oracles of God," those who minister "as out of the strength that God supplies, so that in everything God may be glorified through Jesus Christ" (4:10-11); and Christians are exhorted to "humble yourselves under the mighty hand of God" (5:6), who is the "God of all grace," the one who called us to "his eternal glory in Christ Jesus" (5:10). All, in fact, is from God, yet all is "through Jesus Christ" (2:5; 4:11), "through the resurrection of Jesus Christ" (1:3; 3:21), or "in Christ Jesus" (5:10). So without once using "Son" or "Son of God" for Jesus, Peter develops the relationship between Jesus and God to a degree that James never attempted.

The Interchangeability of Father and Son

None of this, however, prevents Peter from ascribing "power forever" to God (5:10-11) and "glory and power forever and ever" to Jesus Christ (4:11). Father and Son are interchangeably the objects of Christian worship, as in James. At times Peter exhibits the same ambiguity about antecedents that we find in James. Christians are born anew by "the word *(logos)* of the living and enduring God" (1:23), which is defined by a quotation from Isa 40:6-8 as "the announcement *(rhēma)* of the Lord" that "endures forever" — that is, the preaching of Jesus during his ministry on earth. This "announcement" the author defines, in turn, as "the gospel that was proclaimed to you" (v. 25) — that is, the church's proclamation about Jesus of Nazareth. Continuing this thought, he urges his readers, like "newborn babies," to "long for that pure spiritual milk by which to grow up to salvation, now that you have tasted that the Lord is good" (*chrēstos ho kyrios,* 2:2-3). The wordplay is striking: to taste that "the Lord is good" *(chrēstos)* is to taste, or learn by experience, that "the Lord is Christ" *(Christos).* The pun, in fact, was so noticeable that a few Greek manuscripts (including the third- or fourth-century Bodmer Papyrus p[72] and the ninth-century uncial codices K and L) had to spoil it by inserting "Christ" explicitly into the text.

A few verses later, in 2:13-17, Peter reminds his readers of their civic obligations and urges them to "defer to every human creature," specifically the emperor and government officials — with all these exhortations being included in v. 13 under the heading "for the sake of the Lord" (*dia ton kyrion;* cf. Col 3:18, 20, 23; Eph 5:22; 6:1). Again, "the Lord" is Jesus. Peter has in mind the example of Jesus in facing hostile authorities, slander, and persecution (cf. 2:21-23). And still later, in 3:15-16, he urges believers, when they face similar situations, to "revere in your hearts the Lord Christ" *(kyrion ton Christon),* so that "when you are accused, those who denounce your good conduct in Christ may be put to shame."

The clear identification of "the Lord" as "Christ" in 3:15 sheds light on Peter's quotation of Ps 34:15-16a in 3:12: "The eyes of the Lord are on the righteous, and his ears to their prayer; but the face of the Lord is against those who do evil." To Peter, "the Lord" in the psalmist's affirmation is Jesus. The text does not simply describe how the God of the Hebrew Bible viewed the righteous and the wicked long ago. Rather, it describes how "the Lord Jesus Christ" sees them in Peter's own day.

Peter also knows that the "spirit of Christ" was in the prophets and spoke through them, testifying to "the sufferings destined for Christ and the glories to follow" (1:11). And in contrast to James, 1 Peter shows precise knowledge about those "sufferings" and "glories," referring to them in 4:13 and 5:1 as the sufferings and glories of "the Christ" (i.e., "the Messiah" or "Anointed"). James hinted at Jesus' vindication. Peter proclaims it explicitly: Jesus was "put to death in the flesh," but "made alive in the spirit" (3:18); and he "went to heaven, with angels, authorities, and powers subject to him" (3:22). James called Jesus "Lord." Peter explains how he became "Lord." And instead of calling him "God," Peter places him "at the right hand of God" (3:22), ruling over God's creation.

The Relationship between Jesus Christ and the Readers

Peter also goes well beyond James in developing the relationship between Jesus Christ and the readers of the letter. They are introduced as a covenant people, who were consecrated, like Israel of old, for "obedience and sprinkling with the blood of Jesus Christ" (1:2; cf. Exod 24:3-8). Peter reminds them that they were redeemed "not with corruptible things like silver and gold, but with Christ's precious blood, as of a faultless and flawless lamb" (1:18-19). Like James (cf. 2:21), Peter seems to know the story of how God told Abraham to sacrifice Isaac his son on the altar. But that story tells him of more than Abraham's faith and good works. "God himself will provide the lamb," Abraham had said (Gen 22:8). And, according to Peter, God's Lamb, who was "foreknown *(proegnōsmenou)* before the creation of the world," has now "appeared *(phanerōthentos)* at the last of the ages for your sake" (1:20).

Like the "Lamb of God" in John 1:29, Jesus is not a passive victim in 1 Peter. Rather, he is an active Redeemer, who "carried our sins in his body to the tree, so that having parted with those sins, we might live for what is right" (2:24). If not quite the fully developed high priest of the letter to the Hebrews, Jesus in 1 Peter has by his death not only atoned for sin but also done away with it once and for all, so that his followers can "live out their remaining time in the flesh no longer impelled by human desires but motivated by the will of God" (4:2).

At the same time, Peter knows full well that having "appeared" once for our salvation (1:20), the Redeemer disappeared again. And he candidly acknowledges Christ's absence, or rather his invisibility: "You have never seen him, but you love him. Even now, without seeing, you believe in him" (1:8). Peter's christology, therefore, is focused on the future, with the object of his hope expressed not as "the coming *(parousia)* of the Lord," as in James, but as "the revelation *(apokalypsis)* of Jesus Christ" (1:7, 13), or of his "glory" (4:13; 5:1).

Jesus in 1 Peter is already vindicated. His very absence or invisibility proves his vindication, for he has "gone into heaven and is at the right hand of God" (3:22). "Glory" *(doxa)* is his already (1:21). It only needs to be made visible for all the world to see. "Salvation" *(sōtēria)*, therefore, is "ready to be revealed at the last day" (1:5). And when it is revealed, it will mean "inexpressible and glorious joy" for those who love and believe in Jesus (1:8-9; 4:13). For he who disappeared will "appear" again as "chief shepherd" — and not only believers in general, but elders and pastors like Peter himself, will receive their "unfading crown of glory" (5:4).

Yet this "indestructible, incorruptible, and unfading inheritance, reserved in heaven for you" (1:4) is not something for which Christian believers simply watch and wait. Rather, it stands at the end of an active life of faithfulness (1:9). "Salvation" is that toward which believers "grow" (2:2) and on which they are "built" (2:5) — with both of these metaphors expressing vibrant activity.

Jesus as the Model for Christian Behavior

Drawing on the Gospel tradition for the notion of discipleship, Peter appeals to the human Jesus as the model for Christian behavior. Jesus was sinless, not in a theoretical or abstract way, but concretely in that he did not sin by speaking deceit (2:22) or trade insults with those who slandered and ridiculed him. He did not curse his enemies or consign them to hell, but left them to the righteous judgment of God (2:23). Peter invites his readers to follow in Jesus' footsteps (2:21). And he extends this path of discipleship even beyond the cross, calling on them to share in Jesus' victory over death and unclean spirits (3:18-22) and to join him at last in heaven (see Michaels, "Going to Heaven with Jesus," 260-61).

Jesus is not simply one who comes to us, but one toward whom we come (2:4). Our coming is first in conversion and baptism, then in a life-long process of becoming "a spiritual house for a holy priesthood" (2:5) — "a people destined for vindication" and for the "marvelous light" (2:9) or "eternal glory" (5:10) to which he summons us.

Summation

The author of 1 Peter develops these christological themes in a manner appropriate to his identification of himself as "Peter, apostle of Jesus Christ" (1:1). His designation of Jesus as a "living Stone, rejected by humans but in God's sight choice and precious" (2:4), recalls Jesus' own quotation of Ps 118:22 to the religious authorities of his day at Jerusalem: "The stone that the builder rejected is made the head of the corner" (Mark 12:10 par.). Apparently more important to the author, however, is the fact that Jesus' citation of Ps 118:22 hints at Peter's own identity as both (1) a "rock" on which Jesus promised to build a new community (cf. Matt 16:18) and (2) a "scandal" to Jesus because of his unbelief (cf. Matt 16:23; see 1 Pet 2:8: "a rock of scandal").

Another image appears in 2:25, "You were going astray like sheep, but now you have returned to the shepherd and guardian of your souls." This recalls Jesus' prediction of his own death and the scattering of his disciples, "I will strike the Shepherd, and the sheep will be scattered" (Mark 14:27, citing Zech 13:7) — with the accompanying promise, "After I am raised up, I will lead you into Galilee" (Mark 14:28). Peter, it is recorded, heard these words and protested, "Even if they are all scandalized, I will not be" (Mark 14:29). But the words came true. And now writing to a scattered flock, designated "exiles of the Dispersion" (1:1), he reminds them that no matter how far geographically they may be scattered, they have "returned to the Shepherd and Guardian of [their] souls" (2:25) — thereby fulfilling Jesus' promise.

In another Gospel account, the resurrected Jesus, the "True and Good Shepherd" (cf. John 10:1-18), invited Peter three times to "Feed my sheep" (John 21:15-17). And now in 1 Peter he undertakes to do just that, all the while recognizing the authority of the "Chief Shepherd" (5:1-4).

Christology in 1 Peter is the key not only to individual salvation but also to life in community. Christian believers are "living stones," who replicate in their own experiences and behavior the life of the "living Stone" on whom they are built. They, too, are "rejected by humans," but are "in God's sight choice and precious" (2:4). By trusting in Christ as their Lord (cf. 3:15), they "will never be put to shame" (2:6; cf. 3:16).

Luther was right. 1 Peter, like certain of Paul's letters, does, indeed, "show Christ" and teach us what we need to know about christology, even if we "never see or hear any other book or doctrine." Contrary to Luther, James "shows Christ" as well, but not to the same extent.

3. Christology in 2 Peter

The author of 2 Peter identifies himself not simply as "Peter" but as "Symeon Peter" (cf. Acts 15:14, where he is just "Symeon") and describes himself as "a servant and apostle of Jesus Christ." He writes "to those who have received a faith as precious as ours, through the righteousness of our

God and Savior Jesus Christ" (1:1, NRSV). As in James, there is in this translation of v. 1 a certain ambiguity. For Peter's words could be read, "in the righteousness of our God and Jesus Christ [our] Savior" — thereby distinguishing between "our God" and "Jesus Christ our Savior." But this is somewhat unlikely. Rather, it is fair to say that Jesus is called "God" more unequivocally in 2 Pet 1:1b than in the salutation of Jas 1:1 — even though the very next verse distinguishes just as clearly as James between God and Jesus: "Grace to you and peace be multiplied in the knowledge of God and of Jesus our Lord" (1:2).

Furthermore, the word order of 1:3-4 suggests that "Jesus our Lord" is the subject of these next two verses as well. For these verses speak of "his [i.e., Jesus'] divine power *(dynamis)*" that has "given us the things needed for life and godliness through the knowledge of him [i.e., God] who called us by his [i.e., God's] own glory and virtue" (v. 3). Thus "Jesus our Lord" is the one *through whom* we learn, and God is the One *about whom* we learn. So for this author, calling Jesus "God" does not in the least interfere with distinguishing between God and Jesus when the sense demands it. "Through these things," Peter continues, "he [i.e., Jesus] has given us his precious and very great promises, so that through them you might become partakers of the divine nature" (v. 4).

The christology of 2 Peter, therefore, centers on revelation. Jesus Christ gives believers in him "knowledge" (*epignōsis*, vv. 2, 3, 8; *gnōsis*, vv. 5, 6) — whether of Jesus himself or of God. And such knowledge produces in Christian believers all the other virtues necessary to the Christian life (1:5-8). Jesus is repeatedly identified in this letter as either "our Lord Jesus Christ" (1:8, 14, 16) or "our Lord and Savior Jesus Christ" (1:11; 2:20, 3:18) — or as simply "Lord and Savior" (3:2).

The author of 2 Peter draws on the Gospel tradition to reflect on the relationship between "our Lord Jesus Christ" (1:16) and "God the Father" (1:17). Speaking as "Symeon Peter" (1:1), and consequently as an "eyewitness" (1:16), he describes a scene on "the holy mountain" (1:18) that would have been recognizable to readers of the Gospels as the Transfiguration, when Jesus took Peter, James, and John to a "high mountain" and was "transfigured before them" (cf. Mark 9:2-10 par.). The author constructs a kind of midrash or interpretive reflection on this incident, using it as evidence of Jesus' "power," of which he has already spoken (1:3), and the reality of Jesus' future "coming" or *parousia*, of which he will speak later (3:4, 12). Implicitly it testifies as well to "the eternal kingdom of our Lord and

Savior Jesus Christ" (1:11), which the Lord's power and coming will bring in.

The midrash seems to encompass not just the Transfiguration story itself, but also the promise of Jesus that precedes it in Mark's Gospel: "Truly I tell you, there are some standing here who will not taste death until they see the kingdom of God come with power" (Mark 9:1). Remembering this statement as one of the "precious and very great promises" that Jesus made (cf. 1:4), Peter — or someone writing in his name — reflects on it in light of Peter's own death (cf. 1:13-15). Will Peter himself "taste death" before seeing "the kingdom of God come with power"? Not at all, for he has witnessed the "power" and "coming" of Christ, with all the "honor and glory" and "majesty" that go with it (1:16-17), and he wants to assure his readers that his eyewitness testimony is reliable.

The voice at the Transfiguration said: "This is my beloved Son, in whom I am well pleased!" (Matt 17:5). All the Gospel accounts add the command "listen to him" *(akouete autou)*. And Peter assures the readers that, indeed, "we heard *(hēmeis ēkousamen)* this voice from heaven, for we were with him on the holy mountain" (1:18). Consequently, "we [that is, Peter and the other apostles] have the prophetic word more fully confirmed" (1:19). So because they have "heard" Jesus, the apostles are now the custodians of the prophetic traditions represented by Moses and Elijah (cf. Mark 9:4). Together, "the words spoken before by the holy prophets" and "the Lord and Savior's commandment through your apostles" (3:2) comprise the "present truth" in which the readers of the letter now stand (1:12), and of which Peter urgently reminds them (1:12-13, 3:1).

Revelation, according to 2 Peter, comes from the Father through the Son. Its content is the Son's "divine power" (1:3, 16), and the "coming" *(parousia)* of his "eternal kingdom" (1:11). These things are emphasized in 2 Peter because they are in danger of attack from those who will deny Christ, "the Master who bought them" (2:1), and reject his promises.

This reference to being "bought" by "the Master" (2:1) is the only place where 2 Peter speaks of redemption through Jesus' death, for this is not the main point at issue. Rather, false teachers will ask, "Where is the promise of his coming?" — complaining that "ever since the fathers fell asleep, everything continues as it was from the time the world began" (3:4). The implication is that Peter's "Lord Jesus Christ" is powerless, therefore that there will be no parousia or final judgment on sin. Appealing to the example of the flood in Noah's time, Peter replies that by the same word that created them "the present heavens and earth are reserved for fire, kept until the day of judgment and destruction of the godless" (3:7). And he warns the scoffers not to mistake the forbearance or long-suffering of "the Lord" for weakness.

Forbearance is characteristic of a sovereign "Lord" *(kyrios)* or "Master" *(despotēs,* cf. 2:1), not of some weak or ineffective king. Judgment is delayed not because the Judge is powerless, but because he is merciful. Forbearance or long-suffering gives opportunity for repentance and salvation (3:9, 15), but it does not make the judgment any less certain. Peter assumes that his readers "already know this" (3:17). Even though scoffers have deliberately "forgotten" it (3:5), he writes to make sure that believers in Jesus do not "forget" (3:8).

As the custodian of saving "knowledge," Peter is aware that those who "have escaped the world's corruption through the knowledge *(epignōsis)* of our Lord and Savior Jesus Christ, but are entangled in it again, are worse off in the end than at the beginning" (2:20). Better not to have known the way of righteousness than to know it and turn away (2:21-22). Consequently, Peter's last word, which summarizes his whole letter, is the exhortation: "Grow in the grace and knowledge *(gnōsis)* of our Lord and Savior Jesus Christ" (3:18a; cf. 1:5-8) — to which is appended the doxology: "To him be glory, both now and forever. Amen" (3:18b).

4. Christology in Jude

The very short letter of Jude is a stepchild of both James and 2 Peter. Tradition has it that James and Jude were two of the brothers of Jesus named in the Gospels of Mark and Matthew (along with "Joseph" or "Joses" and "Simon"; Mark 6:3; Matt 13:55). But James, as we have seen, identified himself not as "a brother" but as "a servant of the Lord Jesus Christ." And Jude follows suit, calling himself "a servant of Jesus Christ," while in the same breath "the brother of James" (v. 1) — thereby calling attention, by bypassing the title "brother of the Lord," to his status as "a servant of Jesus Christ."

Jude says that he intended at first to write a letter about "our common salvation" (v. 3) — a letter, we can imagine, that might have looked something like 1 Peter (cf. 1 Pet 1:5, 9) or, perhaps, the first chapter of 2 Peter (cf. 2 Pet 1:3-11). But a crisis came up. So instead of explaining or meditating on the "common salvation," or "the faith once delivered to the saints" (v. 3; cf. Jas 2:1, "the faith of our glorious Lord Jesus Christ"), which would have been for the general edification of his readers, Jude felt compelled to defend "the faith" against a very specific threat.

The threat evidently centered on ethics and christology. Certain "godless ones" have "slipped in among you," Jude writes, "perverting the grace of God into [an excuse for] immorality, and denying our only Master *(despotēs)* and Lord *(kyrios)* Jesus Christ" (v. 4). Here Jude begins to show his kinship to 2 Peter (cf. 2 Pet 2:1). But it is unclear who these "godless ones" were. Likewise unclear is how many congregations were threatened by their "godless" activities (cf. v. 15). Was Jude referring to a problem in the congregation from which he wrote (wherever that may have been) or to one or more problems in the congregations to which he wrote? Or did he view the teaching of these "godless ones" as a threat to all Christian congregations everywhere? Nothing in the letter specifies the location of his intended audience.

In any event, Jude appeals to the general principle that he who "saves" *(sōsas)* his people also "destroys" *(apōlesen)* those who are unfaithful (v. 5). And having earlier made the point that the condemnation of these intruders was "written long ago" (v. 4), he then gives three examples of divine retribution, not in chronological order: (1) the destruction of the unbelieving Israelites in the desert after their deliverance from Egypt (v. 5; cf. Num 14:26-38; 1 Cor 10:5-11; Heb 3:16-19), (2) the imprisonment in darkness and chains of the angels who left their proper dwellings (v. 6; cf. Gen 6:1-4; 2 Pet 2:4), and (3) the punishment of Sodom and Gomorrah by fire for their sexual immorality (v. 7; cf. Gen 19:4-25).

Who executed these swift and terrible judgments? The manuscripts differ widely and dramatically — though all of them echo in some fashion the preceding phrase, "our Lord Jesus Christ" (v. 4). The majority of later Greek manuscripts, as well as some earlier ones, read simply "the Lord" *(kyrios)*. But several important witnesses (B, A, 33, and the Latin Vulgate) read "Jesus" *(Iēsous)*, while a very few have "God" *(theos)*, and one early papyrus (p[72]) has "God Christ" *(theos Christos)*. Most English translations prefer "the Lord," probably on the theory that some scribes found it ambiguous and tried to resolve the ambiguity by attempting to explain more precisely who "the Lord" was (see Bauckham, *Jude,* 43). But, in actuality, Jude's use of "the Lord" in vv. 5-7 is not really so ambiguous in light of his clear identification of "our Lord and Master" as "Jesus

Christ" in v. 4. And many interpreters, if not most, who accept the reading "the Lord" nevertheless identify "the Lord" in Jude's mind as Jesus Christ (Bauckham, 49).

Certainly "Jesus" is a more difficult reading. The editors of the UBS *Greek New Testament* called it "difficult to the point of impossibility," and so adopted "the Lord" (though with a "D" rating). Bruce Metzger and Allen Wikgren, however, issued a dissent in favor of "Jesus" as the original reading, calling it "the best attested reading among Greek and versional witnesses" (Metzger, *Textual Commentary,* 726). It is uncommon for New Testament writers to find Jesus so explicitly in the Old Testament. And when they do (as in John 12:41 and 1 Cor 10:4, 9), the human name "Jesus" is not used. Some interpreters, therefore, have proposed that "Jesus" here refers to Joshua (*Iēsous* being the Greek equivalent of the Hebrew name Joshua; cf. Heb 4:8). Joshua in Num 14:38 is mentioned by name in the biblical account as one of only two survivors of the destruction in the desert. But there is no way that Joshua can be seen as the author of this destruction — much less of judgments on the fallen angels (v. 6) or on Sodom and Gomorrah (v. 7) centuries earlier.

Rather, "Jesus" — or possibly "the Lord," understood as Jesus — is the implied subject of all three incidents of divine judgment to which Jude refers. "Jesus" is most likely the original reading. He, too, is most likely "the Lord" in whose name Michael the archangel rebuked the devil (v. 9), as well as "the Lord" who, according to Enoch, "has come with tens of thousands of his holy ones to judge everyone, and to convict all the godless of all their godless acts which they have godlessly committed, and of all the harsh words that godless sinners have spoken against him" (vv. 14-15; see Hurtado, "Christology," 175).

Jude's intent is not so much to introduce the preexistence of Jesus as a theological doctrine as simply to accent continuity (Bauckham, *Jude,* 49). The same "Lord Jesus Christ" who "saved his people" in the past has done so again, for Jude's readers shared a "common salvation" (vv. 3, 5). The same "Jesus" who "destroyed the unfaithful" in the desert and judged fallen angels and the people of Sodom and Gomorrah would "judge the godless" again, for Enoch, "the seventh generation from Adam," had prophesied ages ago that he would (v. 14). Much more recently, "the apostles of our Lord Jesus Christ" had confirmed that "in the last times there will be scoffers following their own godless desires" (v. 18; cf. 2 Pet 3:2), and Jude claims that these predictions have come true (v. 19).

In his response, Jude even hints at a sort of rudimentary doctrine of the trinity, calling on his readers not only to "build yourselves on your most holy faith" (cf. v. 3, "the faith once delivered to the saints"), but also to "pray in the Holy Spirit" (v. 20), to "keep yourselves in the love of God," and to "wait for the mercy of our Lord Jesus Christ for eternal life" (v. 21). The end of the letter reinforces the beginning, for those "who are beloved in God the Father" and are "kept safe for Jesus Christ" (v. 1) are to keep themselves "in the love of God" and await his mercy and the eternal life it brings (v. 21).

Jude's final benediction in vv. 24-25 places his high christology, which focuses on "Jesus," within the larger framework of the worship of God. Thus he writes: "To him who is able to guard you from falling, and to present you before his glory faultless and with joy, to the only God our Savior, through Jesus Christ our Lord, be glory, majesty, power, and authority before all ages, now, and through all the ages. Amen."

5. Christology in 1, 2, and 3 John

The three so-called letters of John are unique in the New Testament. Canonically, they are placed among the general or catholic letters. Yet two of them, 2 and 3 John, are not "general," "catholic," or "universal," for they are addressed to specific individuals or congregations; and the other, 1 John, is not a letter, but a short theological tract. Furthermore, they have little in common with the other Catholic Letters. Unlike 1 Peter, which echoes James's reference to a "Diaspora" (1 Pet 1:1; cf. Jas 1:1), unlike 2 Peter, which calls itself "second" (3:1) in relation to 1 Peter, and unlike Jude, which is an apparent stepchild to both James and 2 Peter, these writings are stepchildren of something else entirely — that is, of the Gospel of John.

Where, then, do 1, 2, and 3 John belong in this volume? Are they "Johannine" or are they "catholic"? Aside from the canon, all that links them to the other writings discussed here is their traditional attribution to "John" (identified only as "the Elder" in 2 John 1 and 3 John 1), who, along with "James" and "Cephas," that is, Peter (Gal 2:9), divided up the world for mission with Paul and Barnabas in much the same way that later tradition divided up the Christian canon. While the Gospel of John is one of the most powerful — if not the most powerful — New Testament witness to christology, perhaps it is best to free the stepchildren from the domineering parent and let them speak with their own voices. Their placement in the canon near the end of the so-called "Catholic Epistles" allows them to do just that.

The most striking difference in christology between the "letters of John" and the rest of the Catholic Letters is the absence of the title "Lord," and consequently of the phrase "the Lord Jesus Christ." Jesus is "Lord" even in the Gospel of John (cf. 13:13; 20:28), but not here. This could be attributable in part to the fact that 1 John, not being a letter, lacks the almost obligatory use of the title at the beginning. Yet 2 John, which is a letter, has "Son of the Father" (v. 2) where we might have expected "Lord," and 3 John, also a letter, never mentions Jesus' name at all. 1 John begins by referring to Jesus metaphorically as "Life" (1:1-2) or "eternal Life" (1:2).

A reader coming to 1 John fresh from reading John's Gospel will be tricked by the opening words, "concerning the word of Life" (1:1). The opening lines of John's Gospel — "In the beginning was the Word, and the Word was with God, and the Word was God" (1:1) — might lead one to expect that in 1 John, as well, "the Word" *(logos)* will be the operative title for Jesus. At the end of v. 1, the reader wants to capitalize "Word" and leave "life" lower case: "the Word of life." But in context, it has to be the other way around, with "Life" *(hē zōē)* capitalized and "word" left lower case: "the word of Life." This is evident from the verse that immediately follows: "And the Life [not 'the Word'] appeared, and we have seen and testify and announce to you that eternal Life which was with the Father and appeared to us" (1:2). Just as "the Word" in John's Gospel was "with God" *(pros ton theon),* so "eternal Life" here was "with the Father" *(pros ton patera).*

The natural companion of "the Father" is "the Son," suggesting already a close identification between "Life" or "eternal Life" and "the Son." This identification will finally become explicit near the end of 1 John: "And this is the testimony, that God has given us eternal life, and this life is in his Son. Whoever has the Son has life; whoever does not have the Son does not have life" (5:11-12). It is an identification made also in the Fourth Gospel: "Whoever believes in the Son has eternal life, but whoever disobeys the Son shall not see life, but the wrath of God remains on him" (John 3:36).

Christology asks "Who is Jesus Christ?" a question that can be asked in one of two ways: either "Who is Jesus Christ in relation to God?" or "Who is Jesus Christ to us?" The other Catholic Letters concentrated attention largely on the second question, answering "He is Lord" — even occasionally, perhaps, "He is God." 1 John answers both questions: in relation to God, Jesus Christ is "the Son" (as he is in 1 Pet 1:3 and implicitly in 2 Pet 1:17); in relation to us, he is "Life" or "eternal Life," for life is his promise and his gift to us (cf. 1 John 2:25). This author could easily have joined with Paul in saying, "When Christ appears, who is your life, then you too will appear with him in glory" (Col 3:4; cf. 1 John 3:2).

Early on, 1 John temporarily drops "eternal Life" as a metaphor for Jesus, and begins to speak straightforwardly of the Father and the Son: "our communion is with the Father, and with his Son Jesus Christ" (1:3); "the blood of Jesus his Son cleanses us from all sin" (1:7). Yet despite a clear distinction between Father and Son, 1 John exhibits, at times, the same ambiguity about antecedents that we find in the other Catholic Letters. "If we confess our sins," the author writes, "he is faithful and righteous *(pistos kai dikaios)* to forgive us our sins and cleanse us from all unrighteousness" (1:9). Who is "faithful and righteous"? "If we say we have not sinned, we make him a liar, and his word is not in us" (1:10). Whom do we "make a liar," the Father or the Son? Probably the Son, who is referred to at the beginning of ch. 2 as our "advocate with the Father" and identified as "Jesus Christ the righteous" (2:1).

The phrase "with the Father" *(pros ton patera)* recalls "the eternal Life" that was "with the Father" *(pros ton patera,* 1:2), and "righteous" *(dikaios)* echoes "faithful and righteous" *(pistos kai dikaios,* 1:9). If "the blood of Jesus . . . cleanses us from all sin" (1:7), then it is Jesus, presumably, who "cleanses us from all unrighteousness" (1:9). That Jesus is quite likely the antecedent of all the third person pronouns (i.e., "him" and "his") in 2:1-6 becomes clear when the author writes, "Whoever claims to remain in him ought to walk as he walked" (2:6, referring to Jesus' life on earth). Just as clearly the Father is meant in the repeated phrase "him who is from the beginning" in 2:13-14. But for whose "name's sake" are our sins forgiven (2:12)? Who promised us eternal life (2:25)? From whom do we receive an "anointing," and in whom do we "abide" or remain (2:27, 28)? When we are said to be "born of him" (2:29), does that mean God or Jesus? And when it is said that "the world does not know us because it did not know him" (3:1), is that referring to knowledge of the Father or of the Son?

We could go on and on. Robert Law, for one, was willing to read all these examples christologically — that is, as the product of "a state of mind to which, although the mists of time have gathered around the image of the historical Jesus, He is still the ever-present living personality." Law illustrated his point as follows: "As in old-style Scottish parlance, a wife would speak of her husband, present or departed, as 'himself'; so with the Apostle it is needless to say who 'He' is. There is but one 'He'" (Law, *Tests of Life*, 89-90). But it really does not matter which is intended, whether Father or Son, for in 1 John the Father acts in and through the Son and in no other way. They are as interchangeable in 1 John as in the other Catholic Letters. The author of 1 John even makes this interchangeability explicit in 2:22-23: "Who is the liar, except the one who denies that Jesus is the Christ? This is the antichrist, who denies the Father and the Son. No one who denies the Son has the Father; whoever acknowledges the Son has the Father also."

1 John, unlike James, 2 Peter, and Jude, uses "the Christ" *(ho Christos)* as a title for Jesus (here in 2:22 and 5:1; see also 2 John 9) alongside "Jesus Christ" as a proper name. Only 1 Peter among the other Catholic Letters does this (1 Pet 4:13; 5:1), probably in order to accent biblical prophecy. But in 1 John, believing in Jesus as "the Christ" is the touchstone of Christian faith. No one who denies it can truly claim to believe in God. Another way of saying "Jesus is the Christ" is to say "Jesus Christ has come in the flesh" (1 John 4:2). "By this you know the Spirit of God: every spirit that acknowledges that Jesus Christ has come in the flesh is of God, and every spirit that does not acknowledge Jesus is not of God but of the antichrist, which you have heard is coming and is now already in the world" (4:2-3). For Jesus to "come in the flesh" is what the Gospel of John calls "coming into the world" (cf. John 11:27, 12:46, 16:28, 18:37; see also 1:9, 3:19, 6:14). The author will explain it further later on as "Jesus Christ having come by water and blood, not in the water alone, but in the water and in the blood" (1 John 5:6) — probably referring first to the water of Jesus' baptism and then to the water and blood from his side at his crucifixion (cf. John 19:34).

If the presupposition of 1 John's christology is that Jesus is God's Son and therefore divine, its heart and core is that he truly came into this world, was born as a real human being, and died a fully human — and bloody — death for our sins (cf. 2:2; 4:10). And this is the touchstone in 2 John as well, where those who "do not acknowledge the coming of Jesus Christ in the flesh" are labeled "the deceiver and the antichrist" (v. 7). In 2 John, in fact, this "teaching of the Christ" (v. 9) becomes the test of Christian fellowship, to the extent that "if anyone comes to you and does not bring this teaching, do not receive him into your home or give him greeting. Whoever greets him shares in his evil work" (vv. 10-11; see also Polycarp, *Philippians* 7:1).

Christology in 1 John, however, is more than a way of screening out heretics. It is, above all, the evidence of God's love, and consequently, as we have seen, the source of "life" for those who believe. "In this, God's love is revealed among us, that God sent his one and only Son into the world that we might live through him. In this is love, not that we have loved God, but that he loved us and sent his Son as an atoning sacrifice for our sins" (4:9-10). Like 2 Pet 1:16-17, the author of 1 John identifies Jesus as God's Son on the basis of God's own testimony, whether at his baptism or his Transfiguration: "If we receive the testimony of humans, the testimony of God is greater, for this is the testimony of God that he testified concerning his Son. He who believes in God's Son has the testimony in himself; he who does not believe God has made him a liar, for he has not believed in the testimony that God testified concerning his Son" (5:9-10).

This is where the author concludes that "eternal Life" is in the Son, so that "whoever has the Son has Life; whoever does not have the Son does not have life" (5:11-12). He writes to assure those who "believe in the name of the Son of God" that they have not only "eternal life" (5:13), but also the confidence of answered prayer (5:14-17). And he also assures them, as those "born of God," that Jesus, as the one who has "come in the flesh," is "born of God" too, and that he will keep them from the Evil One (5:18; cf. John 17:15).

Like Luther, the author of 1 John sees a "world with devils filled, threatening to undo us" — a world in the grip of the Evil One (5:19). Probably with a Gentile readership in view, he holds out to his readers "the True One" *(ho alēthinos)* in contrast to all the false gods of the Greco-Roman world: "We know that the Son of God has come, and he has given us a mind to know the True One, and we are in the True One, in his Son Jesus Christ. He is the true God and eternal life" (5:20). Here once again the distinction between Jesus and God disappears, even as Jesus is identified as the Son.

1 John ends as it began. At the beginning "the life appeared . . . that eternal life that was with the Father and appeared to us" (1:2); and here at the end attention centers on "the True One" and "his Son Jesus Christ," defined as "the true God" and "eternal Life" (see also 5:20; John 17:3). Christology in 1 John, therefore, rests on (1) what Jesus means to God, and (2) what Jesus means to us. To God he is Son because he reveals God. To us he is Life because he gives life. Any god not revealed in Jesus the Son is no god but an idol, and the way of idols is the way of death. "Children," the author concludes, "guard yourselves from the idols" (5:21).

6. Conclusion

Reduced to simplest terms, the christologies of James, 1 Peter, 2 Peter, and Jude center on Jesus Christ as "Lord," accenting Jesus' authority over us by virtue of his resurrection and our baptism, and including our accountability to him at his future "revelation" *(apokalypsis)* or "coming" *(parousia).* These are the basic elements of our "common salvation" (Jude 3). Of these, James, 2 Peter, and Jude are content to speak of God and Jesus almost interchangeably.

1 Peter, however, takes christology to another level, as does 1 John. These two letters agree that Jesus Christ both "appeared" once (1 Pet 1:20; 1 John 3:5, 8) and will "appear" again (1 Pet 5:4; 1 John 3:2). 1 Peter explores the relationship between "the Lord Jesus Christ" and the God of Israel by placing the work of Jesus within the larger framework of the plan of God, but without distinguishing between the two as "the Father" and "the Son." 1 John, taking its cue from John's Gospel, defines the relationship as "Father" and "Son," further explained as "the true God" and "eternal Life."

Taken together, the seven "Catholic Letters" teach us that Jesus Christ is both our "Lord" for whom we live and our "Life" by whom we live.

SELECTED BIBLIOGRAPHY

Achtemeier, Paul J. *1 Peter.* Minneapolis: Fortress, 1996.

Bauckham, Richard. *Jude, 2 Peter.* Waco: Word, 1983.

Davids, Peter H. *The Epistle of James.* Grand Rapids: Eerdmans, 1982.

Hurtado, Larry W. "Christology," in *Dictionary of the Later New Testament and Its Development,* ed. R. P. Martin and P. H. Davids. Downers Grove: InterVarsity, 1997, 170-84.

Law, Robert. *The Tests of Life: A Study of the First Epistle of St. John.* Edinburgh: Clark, 1914.

Mayor, Joseph B. *The Epistle of St. James.* London: Macmillan, 1892; 1913 rev. ed.; reprint Grand Rapids: Baker, 1978.

Metzger, Bruce M. *A Textual Commentary on the Greek New Testament.* London/ New York: United Bible Societies, 1971; corrected edition 1975.

Michaels, J. Ramsey. "James — The Royal Law," in *The New Testament Speaks,* ed. Glenn W. Barker, William L. Lane, and J. Ramsey Michaels. New York: Harper and Row, 1969, 325-35.

———. *1 Peter.* Waco: Word, 1988.

————. "Going to Heaven with Jesus: From 1 Peter to *Pilgrim's Progress,*" in *Patterns of Discipleship in the New Testament* (McMaster New Testament Studies 1), ed. R. N. Longenecker. Grand Rapids: Eerdmans, 1996, 248-68.

Newman, Carey C. "Righteousness," in *Dictionary of the Later New Testament and Its Development*, ed. R. P. Martin and P. H. Davids. Downers Grove: InterVarsity, 1997, 1053-59.

Painter, John. *Just James: The Brother of Jesus in History and Tradition.* Columbia: University of South Carolina Press, 1997.

Ropes, James H. *A Critical and Exegetical Commentary on the Epistle of St. James.* Edinburgh: Clark, 1916.

Wall, Robert W. "James, Letter of," in *Dictionary of the Later New Testament and Its Development*, ed. R. P. Martin and P. H. Davids. Downers Grove: InterVarsity, 1997, 545-61.

Webb, Robert L. "Jude," in *Dictionary of the Later New Testament and Its Development*, ed. R. P. Martin and P. H. Davids. Downers Grove: InterVarsity, 1997, 611-21.

Witherington, Ben, III. "Lord," in *Dictionary of the Later New Testament and Its Development*, ed. R. P. Martin and P. H. Davids. Downers Grove: InterVarsity, 1997, 667-78.

CHAPTER 13

Stories of Jesus in the Apocalypse of John

David E. Aune

In looking to the Apocalypse of John for an answer to the question "Who is Jesus Christ?" the problem is how to begin. Since this is a chapter and not a book, it is necessary to find a manageable way to deal with a potentially expansive subject. Inasmuch as the Apocalypse, like the Gospels and Acts, consists primarily of narrative discourse with a heavy blend of description, I will discuss the christology of the Apocalypse from the methodological standpoint of narrative theology.

Theological claims are intentionally embedded in the narratives and descriptions of the Apocalypse, as they are in the Gospels and Acts. But stories and descriptions cannot easily be translated into ideas — nor is that translation necessarily desirable. The meaning of a concrete event, whether in history or in story, is the series of events with which it is causally related, not a supposedly "deeper" allegorical or symbolic reading of the events, characters, and actions that constitute a realistic narrative.

The christological debates of the fourth and fifth centuries centered on metaphysical issues and dealt with such ontological categories as the nature, substance, and being of Christ. There was, however, little focus on the work of Christ during this period. Yet it was precisely the work of Christ that was the primary concern of the New Testament authors. While the christological doctrines that emerged from the fourth and fifth centuries have largely determined the perspective from which the church reads the Bible today (cf. Lindbeck, *The Nature of Doctrine,* 74), ontological categories of nature, substance, and being are more at home in exposition and dialogue than in either narration or description. Unless we wish to turn the Gospels and the Apocalypse into something they are not, it is simply not acceptable to sever meaning from the mutual implications of events in the order of their narration.

1. The Literary Character of the Apocalypse

Before proceeding further, it is appropriate at this point to present a brief overview of the literary character of the Apocalypse. The author has imposed an artificial literary unity on his work by presenting the whole as a single, extensive vision report, which is introduced in 1:9 and concludes somewhat uncertainly at 22:20. But the external narrative unity provided by this overarching vision report does not guarantee the unity of the constitutive episodes. Furthermore, this lengthy vision report is framed as a letter with an epistolary prescript (1:4-5a) and a concluding grace benediction (22:21). This does not mean, despite recent arguments to the contrary, that the material framed by these formal epistolary elements is epistolary in character. This letter framework is further subordinated to a meta-textual introduction (1:1-3), which can be called "meta" because it self-consciously refers to the text that follows, much as a title is prefixed or suffixed to a literary work. The introductory paragraph in 1:1-3, which has no analogies in ancient letters, is an innovation by the author that overrides the formal epistolary features and signals to the reader that what follows is to be understood as a vision narrative rather than a letter.

2. The Uses of Discourse in the Apocalypse

Progression and cohesion are the most basic rhetorical features of both written texts and oral traditions. The focus in this article is on the first two of the four basic types of progression or discourse used in written texts: narrative, description, exposition, and dialogue. Though the Apocalypse of John is dominated by narrative discourse, the main feature of which is temporal progression, it is quite different from the type of narrative discourse that characterizes the Gospels and Acts. Most scholars now recognize that, despite certain distinctive features, the Gospels are basically similar in literary form to Hellenistic biographical literature, while Acts (or Luke-Acts) has close affinities to Hellenistic historiography. The Apocalypse of John, on the other hand, is associated with the apocalypse genre of early Jewish and early Christian revelatory literature. Since types of discourse, with some limits, typically cross generic boundaries, it is not surprising that the narrative discourse functions in a markedly different way in the Apocalypse than it does in the Gospels and Acts.

Narrative Discourse

Four major characteristics of narrative discourse in apocalypses in general and in the Apocalypse of John in particular distinguish the narrative discourse of the Apocalypse from that of the Gospels and Acts. First and most importantly, the Johannine Apocalypse narrates a "Master Story" or "Grand Narrative" into which believers can read their own stories in a way analogous to how many during the past hundred and fifty years have inscribed their own stories into such seductive Master Stories as Marxism, Darwinism, and Freudianism.

The Master Story reflected in the Apocalypse is actually a mythically formulated account of two different and conflicting sets of stories: (1) the story of the People of God, that is, the followers of Jesus Christ, which is paired with (2) the story of the Evil Kingdom, that is, the Roman Empire and those under its domination. Both stories are set in the natural world. The Master Story of the Apocalypse is generated by the conflict between these two rival stories, which are significant primarily because they mask a paired opposing set of supernatural stories of cosmic significance — the conflict between the story of God and Jesus and the story of Satan. *This* Master Story, like all other stories, has a plot that focuses on the resolution of the conflict. And in this case, the conflict is resolved with the ultimate triumph of God, with Jesus and the followers of Jesus being triumphant over Satan and the people of the Roman Empire who blindly and obstinately follow him.

The Master Story of the Apocalypse of John is a Christian rewriting of an early Jewish Master Story typically found in many Jewish apocalypses — a story unapologetically utopian and intended by its authors to be received as the true story of the world. But this Christian Master Story is larger, longer, and stronger than the individual stories of those followers of Jesus who first heard it read aloud in worship. For it not only includes everything but also tells the hearers who they are while assuring them that things cannot fail to turn out better. The dramatic (or melodramatic) character of the Apocalypse invites its hearers to identify themselves in the story and, in so doing, to subordinate their own stories to that of the Master Story. The appropriate term for moving from a failed Master Story (the story of the Roman Empire and those under its domination) to a new Master Story (the story of the victory of God through Jesus Christ), or for subordinating one's own story to the latter Master Story, is "conversion."

A second characteristic of narrative discourse in the Apocalypse of John is that its narrative sequences or episodes, while exhibiting internal progression, are often not temporally linked — which is a feature unlike most other narrative genres. For example, the *dramatis personae* in the story of the Woman, the Child, and the Dragon in 12:1-17, except for the Dragon, are found nowhere else in the book, and the story itself is connected only tenuously with the story of the Beast from the Sea and the Beast from the Land that follows in ch. 13. Furthermore, the rather nightmarish tale of the enslavement of a willing world by the two beasts in ch. 13 is suspended by an enigmatic conclusion in which the riddle of the mysterious number of the beast is posed but not answered (13:18). The threads of this interrupted narrative are eventually picked up again and finally brought to a conclusion when the rider on the white horse captures the two beasts (after ch. 13 the second beast is called the false prophet), consigns them to the lake of fire, and slaughters the armies of the kings of the earth (19:11-21). Thus while some of the narrative episodes in the Apocalypse appear to be *disjecta membra,* they are all explicitly or implicitly woven into the Master Story. They are all there for a reason.

Third, like all stories, the Gospels, Acts, and the Apocalypse each have a beginning, a middle, and an end. While the story world of the Gospels and Acts is set in the *past,* the story world of the Apocalypse of John is set primarily in the *future.* However, paradoxically, the canonical and ecclesial setting of the Gospels means that even though the story of Jesus has a literary "end" in each of them (the empty tomb in Mark, the resurrection appearance of Jesus to the eleven in Matthew, the ascension of Jesus in Luke, and the resurrection appearances in John), each Gospel, nevertheless, remains open and is perpetuated in the story of the people of God or the church — a story that continues to be shaped by the story of Jesus. This means that the Gospels, too, function as a Master Story, since whatever narrative gaps they have are filled in by the people of God who read them in public worship in the context of the overarching Master Story they already know and own.

While the future is normally considered open, since the possibilities it holds out have yet to be realized (though here "openness" is admittedly a modern conception), the future in the Apocalypse of John is essentially closed, for it concludes with a vision of the final triumph of God — with Jesus forever united with the people of God in the New Jerusalem in a renovated heaven and earth. We are told how the Master Story ends, even though its ending lies in the future. There is an important sense in which the Apocalypse is the appropriate work to conclude the Christian canon, for it is the only biblical book that draws everything to a final and decisive conclusion.

A fourth characteristic of the narrative discourse of the Johannine Apocalypse, like that of apocalypses in general, is that its narratives are "mythical narratives" — that is, highly symbolic and imaginative stories placed in settings in heaven or in the future or both, which the living have not yet experienced — whereas those of the Gospels and Acts are what can be designated "realistic narrative" — that is, history-like and set in a recognizable, real world. Since the visions of the Apocalypse are not set in the real world, it is, of course, less tempting to read them (as many have) as history written in advance. "Realistic narrative" carries no hidden meaning, but simply means what it says. Events in "realistic narrative" are not interchangeable symbols. One of the central characteristics of "mythical narrative," however, is precisely the fact that events are interchangeable symbols, and the narrative embodies a subtext encoded in story form. This subtext is the Master Story.

Because realistic narrative, though found throughout the Bible, is not the only type of discourse in Scripture, Hans Frei and others might be faulted for ignoring the other main forms of biblical discourse — that is, for being reductionistic by limiting all forms of discourse to narrative, and even for ignoring other types of narrative such as that found in apocalypses. Like the realistic narrative of the Gospels, the Apocalypse of John cannot be reduced to ideas or timeless truths, but rather must be read in terms of its more basic narrative — that is, its implied Master Story. Yet since even descriptive discourse in the Apocalypse presupposes the basic realistic narrative of the Master Story (as we will see below), Frei is certainly correct to identify realistic narrative as the hermeneutically significant key to understanding the Bible.

Descriptive Discourse

Like most narrative genres, the Apocalypse of John uses other types of discourse in subordinate ways. One of the more important of these is description, which is a type of discourse that is organized spatially in apocalypses, usually from the point of view of the revealer or the visionary. Description is a central feature of most apocalypses, for visual aspects of revelatory experience can be imagined by the hearer only through verbally communicated word-pictures.

Relatively long descriptive passages occur in the Johannine Apocalypse with some frequency — as in 1:12-16; 4:2-11; 7:9-12; 9:7-11; 10:1-3; 15:5-8; 17:3-6; 19:11-16; 21:10–22:5, along with other shorter passages too numerous to mention. The symbolic character of descriptive discourse more frequently than not presupposes a story that is already known to the hearers or that can be appropriately understood only within the context of a story already known. When John looks toward the throne of God, for example, he sees "a Lamb standing as though slain, with seven horns and seven eyes" (5:6) — a cluster of symbols obviously representing the story of the death, resurrection, and cosmic sovereignty of Jesus Christ.

Two of the more extended descriptive passages of the Apocalypse focus on Jesus Christ, but these passages could hardly differ from each other more than they do. The first is the description of the one like a son of man in 1:12-16, the second, that of the rider on the white horse in 19:11-16. Despite their differences, both descriptive passages make sense within the context of the Master Story known to the hearers, but not with each other.

Expository Discourse

The Apocalypse of John also contains some rather lengthy passages of expository discourse, primarily at the beginning of the book in 1:1-3, 4-5a, 5b-8 and 2:1–3:22. But here also the exposition makes sense only in light of a story already known to the hearers. Progression in expository discourse is based primarily on various types of logical progressions that link a series of statements, questions, or commands together. Expository discourse is concentrated in the New Testament in the letters. But these often have also a dialogical character, as, for example, when Paul or the author of James makes use of a diatribe style. Dialogical progression is primarily marked by questions and answers, as well as by affirmations and negations. There are, to be sure, also a few quasi-dialogical passages in the Apocalypse, as in 7:13-17; 17:6b-18; and 22:8-17 — though this type of discourse is more common in Jewish apocalypses that feature an *angelus interpres* in dialogue with the visionary, a literary device that is all but absent from the Johannine Apocalypse.

3. Opening Gambits

The Title (1:1-3)

The first thing that the first hearers of the Apocalypse of John heard on the occasion of its inaugural reading was the title and a beatitude, which were bundled together in a short metatextual unit of expository discourse found in 1:1-3. While this is a rich and complex text, my present concern is only with the christological signals that this passage might have sent to the original hearers and how it might have prepared them for what follows.

The name "Jesus Christ" occurs twice in this title. Thereafter in the book it appears only in the epistolary prescript that immediately follows in 1:5. "Jesus Christ" in all three references is a proper name for that Jesus who is the object of Christian faith, with no hint that the designation "Christ" may have gained currency earlier as a messianic title predicated of Jesus in confessional contexts, i.e., "Jesus is the Christ," meaning "Jesus is the Messiah" (John 11:27; 20:31; Acts 17:3; 1 John 2:22; 5:1). "Jesus Christ" as a proper name is a characteristic usage of Paul (the author of the earliest extant Christian works), who never uses the term "Christ" (i.e., "Messiah") as a predicate of "Jesus." All three references to "Jesus Christ" in the Apocalypse link him closely with God, as the following discussion will indicate.

The title "the Christ" or "the Messiah" occurs four times in the body of the Apocalypse: in 11:15; 12:10; and 20:4, 6. It always occurs with reference to the exalted Jesus, always with the definite article (and so should be translated "the Messiah"), and always closely linked with the cognate Greek terms for "kingdom" and "to reign," three times in tandem with names for God (11:15; 12:10; 20:6), twice in hymnic contexts (11:15; 12:10), and once in a beatitude (20:6). This leaves a single instance where "the Christ" occurs in a narrative context (20:4: "they came to life and reigned with the Messiah a thousand years"). Three of the four contexts in which "the Messiah" is used (11:15; 12:10; 20:6) suggest that the final victory of God is realizable only by and with Jesus Christ.

The first three words in 1:1 can be translated "This is a revelation from Jesus Christ," a phrase that characterizes the entire Apocalypse of John as divine in origin. This revelation is further described as having been given to Jesus Christ by God to disclose to God's servants those end-time events which will shortly occur. The Lamb's reception of the sealed scroll from the one seated on the throne in 5:7 is certainly an appropriate dramatization of this opening clause in the Apocalypse.

That God imparted this revelation exclusively to Jesus Christ has several implications. First, Jesus Christ is not a figure of the past alone but also, and more importantly, a figure of the present. This point is reinforced by the vision of one like a son of man in 1:9-20. Second, Jesus Christ functions as the sole mediator of divine revelation. He functions, as it were, as the Director of Communications for the heavenly court. He is also, after God himself, the central divine actor in the Master Story that follows, though he appears in a number of guises and with a number of aliases — all of which transparently refer to Jesus Christ for those believing hearers who have subscribed to the Master Story.

According to 1:2, John testifies to "the word of God and the testimony borne by Jesus Christ." This phrase can also be translated "the word of God, that is, the testimony borne by Jesus," thus referring to a single message. If I have correctly construed the linking "and" as epexegetic or explanatory, then "the word of God," which is a widely used Old Testament term for divine revelation, is equated with "the testimony borne by Jesus." Understood in this way, this clause is another way of saying that God has given the revelation to Jesus Christ, and "the testimony borne by Jesus Christ" is precisely that of the revelation transmitted to John — that is, the contents of the Apocalypse, as the qualifying phrase "whatever he saw" indicates.

The Epistolary Salutation (1:4-5a)

In the expository salutation of the epistolary prescript in 1:4-5a, John greets the churches in Asia with "grace and peace" from God (using the very special designation "the One who is and was and who will come"), from the seven spirits before the throne, and "from Jesus Christ, the faithful witness, the firstborn from the dead and the ruler of the kings of the earth." Again, God and Jesus Christ are closely linked, separated by the reference to the seven spirits before the throne (apparently the seven archangels). This epistolary salutation has close links with those used by Paul, though the sources of grace and peace for him are typically limited to "God the Father and the Lord Jesus Christ" (cf. Rom 1:7; 1 Cor 1:3; 2 Cor 1:2; Gal 1:3; Phil 1:2; Phlm 3), with no intervening reference to any other supernatural being or beings.

Each element of an epistolary prescript was typically susceptible to expansion (cf. the close parallel to Rev 1:4-5a in Gal 1:4). Here the name "Jesus Christ" in the salutation is expanded by three appositional phrases: "the faithful witness, the firstborn from the dead, and the ruler of the kings of the earth." Though the author is still using expository discourse, these three phrases are a succinct way of summarizing the distinctive events in the story of Jesus. "The faithful witness" refers to his death (which was preceded by his testimony before hostile leaders); "the firstborn from the dead" refers to his resurrection; and "the ruler of the kings of the earth" refers to the certainty of his future cosmic triumph over all opposition when he truly becomes "King of kings and Lord of lords" (17:14; 19:16). These three events are simply placed in sequential order with no indication of a causal relationship, though a narrative is clearly implied. The content of this part of the epistolary prescript can be summarized in this way: death of Christ + resurrection of Christ + sovereignty of Christ (the + indicating that the events are placed in sequential order with no indication of causal relationships).

The Doxology (1:5b-6)

The epistolary prescript in 1:4-5a is closely followed by a doxology, which is a pattern also found in Gal 1:5. While early Christian doxologies were almost exclusively addressed to God, this one is exceptional in that it is directed to Christ (the doxology in 5:13 is directed to both God and Christ). It is, therefore, a liturgical or quasi-liturgical witness to the phenomenon of the worship of Jesus, as Richard Bauckham has rightly emphasized. Though Jesus is not explicitly named, the content makes it certain that it is directed to Jesus Christ:

> To the one who loved us
>> and freed us from our sins by his blood,
> and made us a kingdom,
>> priests to his God and Father,
> To him is the glory and power for ever. Amen.

Here the author abruptly switches from expository to narrative discourse, for this doxology is essentially a narrative centering on two significant episodes in the story of Jesus: *Christ's liberating death* has brought about *the formation of a liberated people.* Yet a closer examination of the doxology suggests that this schema can be expanded with the addition of two actions: (1) *Christ's anticipatory love for his people* has brought about (2) *Christ's liberating death,* which has brought about (3) *the formation of a liberated people* and (4) *the worship of God.* The phrase "the one who loved us" is striking, for it refers to the motivation of the historical Jesus to sacrifice his life on behalf of others.

The doxology of 1:5b-6, therefore, incorporates one of the few references to the historical Jesus found in the Apocalypse. It is also one of a number of formulaic passages in the New Testament that coordinate Jesus' love (reflecting the motivation for his voluntary death) with his death — as in Gal 2:20, "who loved me and gave himself for me," where Christ's self-giving love is personalized by Paul who regards himself (and no doubt others like him) as the object of the voluntary death of Jesus Christ (cf. also Eph 5:2, 25). Emphasis on the voluntary, sacrificial nature of the death of Christ and the salvific benefits of that death were central features of early Christian catechesis (cf. Mark 10:45 = Matt 20:28; John 10:11; Gal 1:4; 1 Tim 2:6; 1 John 3:16). The doxology in Rev 1:5b-6 is similar to the hymn-like statement in Tit 2:13-14, though "love" is substituted for "gave": "Jesus Christ, who gave himself for us to redeem us from all iniquity and to purify for himself a people of his own who are zealous for good deeds."

4. The Lamb in Revelation 4:1–8:1

Rev 4:1–8:1 is a narrative unit that consists of a lengthy heavenly throne room scene in two parts (4:1-11 and 5:1-14), followed by a narrative of the breaking of the seven seals by the Lamb and the resultant plagues that afflict the people of the world (6:1-17, 8:1). The Lamb dominates the entire narrative unit even when he does not appear to be present. This narrative is "interrupted" in a puzzling way between the breaking of the sixth and seventh seals by a two-part vision: the sealing of the 144,000 on earth (7:1-8), followed by the heavenly throne room and the innumerable host worshiping God (7:9-17).

The Heavenly Throne Room (4:1-11)

The vision of the heavenly throne room in ch. 4, apart from a brief narrative setting in v. 1, consists almost entirely of descriptive discourse. The One seated on the throne is described as appearing like jasper and carnelian, while a rainbow, which looks like an emerald, surrounds the throne — from which come thunder, lightning, and strange noises. All these symbols are attempts to capture the majesty and power of God, who is further described as surrounded by seven torches of fire (i.e., the seven spirits of God), four living creatures, and twenty-four elders, all engaged in unending worship. While a first reading of ch. 4 turns up no reference to Jesus, this will have to be revised in light of ch. 5.

The Investiture of the Lamb (5:1-14)

The essentially static scene of ch. 4 becomes the prelude to the brief dramatic episode in ch. 5, the quest for one who is worthy to unseal a mysterious scroll (vv. 1-6) and the subsequent investiture of the Lamb (vv. 7-14).

The chapter begins with a close-up shot of a single object in the right hand of God, a mysterious scroll sealed with seven seals. An angelic herald of the heavenly court asks if anyone is worthy to open this scroll, but no one can be found throughout the entire cosmos. This fruitless cosmic search is obviously staged to emphasize the unique qualifications of the Lamb. John himself weeps that no one worthy can be found, but is comforted by one of the twenty-four elders, who declares that the lion of the tribe of Judah, the root of David, has conquered and is therefore qualified to break the seals and open the scroll (v. 5).

Looking more closely, John sees, between the throne of God and the four living creatures and the twenty-four elders, "a Lamb, standing as though slain, with seven horns and seven eyes, which are the seven spirits of God sent out to all the earth" (v. 6). As soon as the seven spirits of God are mentioned, we realize that the Lamb was present in the heavenly throne room all along, though initially unrecognized. In 4:5, "the seven torches of fire" are interpreted as "the seven spirits of God," just as the seven eyes of the Lamb are interpreted as "the seven spirits of God sent out to all the earth" (5:6). The seven torches of fire are the seven eyes of the Lamb.

John has juxtaposed two symbolic descriptions in 5:5-6, each representing a widely known story. The initial description of the Lamb identifies him with traditional language as the Messiah, who must be of Davidic ancestry and whose main function is to liberate Israel from Gentile oppressors (v. 5). Yet this messianic figure is reinterpreted through his depiction as a slain, yet living Lamb, with seven horns and seven eyes. This somewhat grotesque imagery succinctly summarizes a competing story, the story of Jesus who, though he has all the qualifications of the Messiah of Jewish expectation, has conquered through death, yet lives. The narrative implied in this second symbolic description can be summarized in this way: *Death of the Lamb* (which signals conquest) + *Resurrection of the Lamb*. This reflects the simplest theological abbreviation of the significance of the mission of Jesus Christ: the temporal juxtaposition of the motifs of the fact of the death of Jesus and the fact that God raised him from the dead (cf. Acts 3:15; 4:10; 5:30; 10:39-40; 13:28-30; Rom 4:24; 1 Cor 15:3-4).

The scene of the investiture of the Lamb in vv. 7-14 begins with his reception of the sealed scroll from the hand of God, but is thereafter dominated by a profound and complex scene of worship in which the Lamb is extolled with a hymn of praise. This antiphonal hymn consists of the basic two actions in the story celebrated in the doxology of 1:5b-6 — that is, the liberating death of Jesus and the formation of a new people constituted by those who were liberated (the italicized words below are repeated in the passage quoted in v. 13):

> You are worthy to receive the book
> and to open its seals,
> because you were slain
> and you redeemed for God by your death
> people from every tribe and tongue and people and nation,
> and made them for our God a kingdom and priests. (5:9-10)
> Worthy is the Lamb who was slain

> to receive *power* and wealth and wisdom and might
> and *honor* and *glory* and *praise.* (5:12)

The underlying narrative events expressed in this hymn are: (1) *the redemptive death of the Lamb,* which has brought about (2) *the formation of a redeemed people for God* and (3) *the worship of the sovereign Lamb.* The absence of a reference to the resurrection of Jesus is striking, and requires further explanation.

God is depicted in this entire throne room scene as a remarkably passive figure, despite the awesome power and majesty attributed to him. The Lamb's reception of the sealed scroll from the right hand of God surely places him in an obviously subordinate position to God — though, at the same time, God is apparently unable to act (or, perhaps better, chooses not to act) apart from the mediation of the Lamb. Thus, just as 1:1-2 makes it clear that Jesus Christ is the exclusive transmitter of divine revelation to the servants of God in the world, so chs. 4-5 make it clear that he is also, under the metaphor of the Lamb, the exclusive agent of God, the only one who is in a position to see God's intentions realized in the world.

Those who hear the hymn of praise in 5:9-10, 12 would instantly recall the earlier hymn sung in praise of God in 4:11 (the common terms of adoration shared by these hymns are italicized):

> Worthy are you, our Lord and God,
> to receive *glory* and *honor* and *power,*
> because you created all things,
> and by your will they existed, yes, were created.

God is honored primarily for his creative work, while Jesus Christ, as the Lamb, is celebrated for his redemptive death and his establishment of the church.

This juxtaposition of (1) the creative activity of God, (2) the redemptive death of Christ, and (3) the establishment of the new people of God is precisely the pattern of the hymn to Christ in Col 1:15-20 — where the first stanza (vv. 15-17) describes Christ's role as the image of the invisible God, the firstborn of all creation, and the agent through which God created the cosmos, and the second stanza (vv. 18-20) centers on Christ as the founder of the church, on him whose death became the basis for reconciling humankind with God:

He is the head of the body, the church;
> he is the beginning, the firstborn from the dead,
>> so that in everything he might be preeminent.
> For in him all the fullness of God was pleased to dwell,
>> and through him to reconcile to himself all things,
> whether on earth or in heaven,
>> making peace by the blood of his cross.

If the hearers failed to catch the significance of the parallel hymns to God and to Christ in 4:11 and 5:9-10, 12, the author gives them a final chance with a doxology jointly addressed to God and the Lamb (v. 13, again italicizing the terms of adoration shared with the previous passages quoted above):

> To the One who sits on the throne and to the Lamb
>> be *praise* and *honor* and *glory* and *power* forever.

This joint doxology is a powerful statement of the unique relationship between the One seated on the throne and Jesus Christ.

What does the scroll sealed with seven seals symbolize? There have been a variety of answers to this question, none of which have commanded general agreement. At a basic level, the scroll must represent the will or intention of God for the world — and that intention, at least in its initial phase, is dramatized in the story of the breaking of the seven seals. The author provides a clue at the conclusion of the catastrophes inflicted on the world with the breaking of the seventh seal, when he has the people of the earth implore the mountains and rocks to hide them "from the One who sits on the throne and from the wrath of the Lamb, because the great day of his wrath has come" (6:16-17). Those who are being punished know the program — that it is none other than God himself who is inflicting divine punishment on them, with the Lamb acting as his exclusive agent.

The Lamb Breaks the Seven Seals (6:1-17; 8:1)

We must now turn to the narrative of the breaking of the seven seals by the Lamb described in 6:1-17 and 8:1. This entire section consists of seven brief narratives, each initiated by the Lamb's serial breaking of the seven seals.

This is obviously part of a literary pattern, which serves as the means for introducing the particular effects associated with each seal.

The breaking of the first seal is introduced with the phrase, "Then I saw when the Lamb broke the first of the seven seals" (6:1). But thereafter the Lamb is represented simply by the third person singular verb "he broke" (6:3, 5, 7, 9, 12; 8:1). This failure to remind the readers of the subject of "break" is particularly striking in 8:1, which follows the extended "interruption" of 7:1-17. But much more than a formal literary pattern is involved here, for central to the narrative theology of the Apocalypse is the sovereign will of God mediated to the world by Jesus Christ, who, through his role in breaking each of the seven seals, functions as the agent of God in punishing a disobedient world.

The first four seals constitute a group in which each of the four living creatures calls forth a cavalier who visits a particular type of destruction and devastation on the earth (6:1-8). This series of four divine judgments is relieved by the breaking of the fifth seal, which shifts the focus from plagues inflicted on the wicked to the righteous who were slain for their fidelity to the word of God and who now cry out to God for vengeance (6:9-11). If the earliest hearers of the Apocalypse identified themselves with anyone in this melodramatic narrative of the seven seals, it would have been with these martyrs rather than with those afflicted by the waves of plagues sent by God to punish wickedness. In fact, the author gives the hearers little choice in the matter. None of them would want to experience the terrible plagues by which God punished the ungodly. Yet the only other option is to identify with the *martyrs,* not, more comfortably, with ordinary Christians who survive. The author, in effect, is using a literary strategy to push their commitment to God and to Jesus to the point that they identify themselves with those willing to lay down their lives for their faith.

The opening of the sixth seal (6:12-17) initiates a series of earthquakes and cosmic catastrophes that terrifies the people of the earth, who try to flee from the calamities that have overtaken them. Together they cry to the mountains and the rocks (6:16-17): "Fall on us and hide us from the One who sits on the throne and from the wrath of the Lamb, because the great day of his wrath has come, and who is able to withstand it?" Here the author uses the collective voice of the people of the world in a short expository passage to reiterate succinctly to the hearers what they already know: that God has initiated payback time and that the Lamb is his exclusive agent in mediating that plan in the world.

Focus on the People of God (7:1-17)

The position and meaning of the interjected vision in ch. 7 has been a perennial problem for interpreters. For many, it provides an answer to the plaintive cry of those doomed to experience divine punishment in 6:17: Who can stand before the wrath of God and the Lamb? Vv. 1-8 are set on earth and focus on the sealing of the 144,000 — which surely represents salvation in one form or other, despite arguments over the identity of the 144,000. Vv. 9-17 are set in heaven and focus on the innumerable host who have come out of the great tribulation — a group which surely represents the saved. The hearers of the Apocalypse could easily have identified themselves with either group — with the 144,000 because they are still in the world or with the innumerable host because, though they are dead (many, if not all of them, having been victims of violence), they have experienced the ultimate salvation, which is the object of hope for all of God's people.

The Lamb, who figures prominently as the agent of God in the narrative throughout 5:1–8:1, is mentioned three times in the second half of this interruption (7:9-17). The first is in the cry of victory addressed to God and the Lamb in v. 10: "Victory belongs to our God who sits on the throne, and to the Lamb." This *Siegesruf* ("cry of victory") constitutes a proleptic celebration of the cosmic victory of both God and the Lamb. Both are mentioned because such a victory is not possible apart from the role played by the Lamb.

The second mention of the Lamb is in the speech of the *senior interpres*, who tells the seer that the innumerable multitude consists of those "who came from the great tribulation; they washed their robes and made them white in the blood of the Lamb" (v. 14). The Great Tribulation is one of the plotted eschatological events that, together with other historical and eschatological events, form part of the Master Story that is never fully articulated but expressed tantalizingly in bits and pieces throughout the Apocalypse. This reference to the liberating effects of the death of Christ has already been mentioned in the doxology in 1:5b-6 and in the hymn of praise to the Lamb in 5:9-10, 12.

The third reference to the Lamb is in the conclusion of the heavenly elder's speech, where he tells John that "the Lamb in the midst of the throne will be their shepherd, and he will lead them to springs of living water" (v. 17). The dual focus on the foundation of the new people of God based on the liberating death of Jesus has already been referred to in 1:5b-6 and 5:9-10, 12. The presence of the Lamb with his redeemed people is further dramatized in 14:1-5, where the seer describes a vision of the 144,000, each with the names of the Lamb and his Father inscribed on their foreheads. The language of discipleship familiar from the Gospels is evoked in 14:4: "It is these who follow the Lamb wherever he goes; these have been redeemed from humanity, servants devoted to God and the Lamb."

Thus each of the three references to the Lamb in 7:9-17 evokes a different phase of the Master Story. The first speaks of the Lamb sharing the cosmic victory with God (v. 10); the second highlights the death of the Lamb, which provides the basis for the victory (v. 14); and the third portrays the Lamb as the center of a redeemed people (v. 17).

To this point in 4:1–8:1, the emphasis has been on judgment rather than salvation — though the hymn of praise sung by the heavenly chorus in 5:9-10, 12 emphasizes the liberation of people by the death of the Lamb and the complementary foundation of a new people of God. The presentation of white robes to the souls under the altar also represents salvation for the faithful martyrs. Just as the Lamb by his liberating death has created a new people constituted by those who are his obedient followers, so his death has also qualified him to function as God's agent in the destruction of those who are disobedient. Salvation is, of course, more pleasant to contemplate than judgment. But while a preoccupation with the latter is certainly theologically unfashionable, both are part of the biblical depiction of the role of Jesus Christ.

5. Stories Implied in Descriptions

Despite the dominance of narrative discourse in the Apocalypse of John, there are (as we have seen) some relatively long descriptive passages. Two of these are descriptions of Jesus Christ in the context of symbolic visions. Though he is not explicitly named in either, his identity is not in doubt. The descriptive sections in both passages introduce larger textual units that conclude with relatively extensive sections of narrative discourse. The heavily symbolic and mythic character of these descriptive passages suggests that they are founded on narratives already known to the hearers.

One Like a Son of Man (1:9-20)

The first of the two long descriptive passages is the vision of "the One like a Son of Man" in 1:9-20, which begins with a lengthy description in vv. 12-16. Part of the material of this passage is repeated and augmented by the exalted Christ in the introductory sections to each of the seven proclamations in 2:1, 8, 12, 18; 3:1, 7, 14. The following chart sets out a translation of the descriptive section of 1:12-19 in the left column and parallels that appear in the introductions to the seven proclamations in chs. 2–3 in the right column. The *italicized* words and phrases are not found in the other column, while the underlined words and phrases are common to both columns.

1:12-19	chs. 2–3
12 Then I turned to see the voice speaking to me. Upon turning around I saw <u>seven golden menorahs,</u> 13 <u>and in the midst of the menorahs,</u>	2:1 Thus says the one . . . who walks <u>in the midst of the seven golden menorahs.</u>
one like a son of man [Dan 7:13; 10:16] *wearing a long robe and with a golden sash encircling his chest* [Dan 10:5]. 14 *His head, that is, his white hair, was like white wool, like snow* [Dan 7:9],	
	2:18 Thus says *the Son of God*
and <u>his eyes were like a flame of fire</u> [cf. Dan 10:6c],	<u>whose eyes are like a flame of fire</u>
15 and <u>his feet were like bronze</u> [Dan 10:6d] *when smelted in a furnace, and his voice was like the sound of cascading water* [Dan 10:6e].	and <u>his feet as burnished bronze.</u>
	2:1 Thus says the one
16 <u>In his right hand he had seven stars,</u>	who holds <u>the seven stars in his right hand.</u>
	3:1 Thus says the one who has *the seven spirits of God, namely the seven stars.*

and a <u>sharp double-edged sword projecting from his mouth,</u>	2:12 Thus says the one with the <u>sharp double-edged sword.</u> [Cf. 2:16, I will come to you soon and war against them with <u>the sword of my mouth.</u>]
and *his face was like the sun shining in full strength* [cf. Dan 10:6b]. 17 And when I saw him, I fell at his feet as though dead, and he placed his right hand upon me, saying: "Stop being afraid.	
I am <u>the First and the Last</u>, 18 *even the Living One,* and <u>I was dead, but behold I now live</u> *for ever and ever,*	2:8 Thus says <u>the First and the Last,</u> <u>the one who died, but came to life.</u>
and <u>I have the keys</u> *to Death and Hades."*	3:7 Thus says *the Holy One, the True One,* <u>the One who has the key</u> *of David, who opens so that no one can shut, and shuts so that no one can open.*
	3:14 Thus says *the Master Workman, the faithful and true Witness, the Origin of the creation of God.*

It can readily be seen that many features in the description and exposition in 1:9-20 (as italicized) have no counterpart in the christological predications found in the introductions to the seven proclamations. Similarly, there are christological predications in the seven proclamations (as underlined) that have no counterpart in 1:9-20.

Rev 1:9-20 itself is comprised of two units of text: (1) the description of "One like a Son of Man" in vv. 12-16, and (2) an expository speech that includes several striking "I"-predications in vv. 17-20. There is a surprising disjunction between these two sections, for none of the "I" self-predications in the expository section has a counterpart in the descriptive section.

The figure described as "One like a Son of Man" in 1:13 is not further identified, but is called "the Son of God" in the christological predicate in 2:18 — the only occurrence of the title "Son of God" in the Apocalypse. It is striking that the designation "Son of Man" is not repeated in the christological predicates in chs. 2–3, which suggests that the author does not connect the anarthrous phrase "a son of man" with the Son of Man traditions in the Gospels. It is clear that the phrase "One like a Son of Man" is a direct allusion to either Dan 7:13, where "one like a son of man" comes to the Ancient of Days, or Dan 10:16, 18, where the phrase refers to the angelic figure described in Dan 10:5-6. If the former, then the description is apparently dependent on an exegetical tradition of Daniel 7 in which "the Ancient of Days" and "the one like a son of man" are merged into a single figure. This exegetical tradition is represented in the only two extant LXX manuscripts of Daniel (967 and 88), which, translated literally, read Dan 7:13 as follows:

> He came like a son of man
> and like the Ancient of Days was present,
> and those who were near approached him.

Here the two figures are identified in a synonymous couplet. This is one of several instances in the Apocalypse where, under various guises, Jesus Christ is described in language that was normally or appropriately used only of God.

The story implied in the description in 1:9-16 is limited to four features: (1) the designation "One like a Son of Man," (2) the sharp two-edged sword that proceeds from his mouth, (3) the seven golden menorahs, and (4) the seven stars that he holds in his right hand. If the Son of Man designation is intended to remind the hearers of the judgment scene in Dan 7:9-14, this coheres well with the symbol of the two-edged sword proceeding from his mouth — a symbol occurring nowhere else in Daniel, but twice mentioned in connection with the rider on the white horse in Rev 19:15, 21. Here the sword is a metaphor for the tongue, that is, the word of Christ used in reproof and admonition (cf. 4 Ezra 13:10, 37-38; 2 Thess 2:8).

These features combine to highlight Christ's role in the final judgment, a theme that occurs frequently in early Christian literature (Acts 10:42; 17:31; Rom 2:16; 1 Cor 4:4-5; 2 Cor 5:10; 2 Thess 1:7-10; 2 Tim. 4:1; 1 Pet 4:5; 2 *Clement* 1:1; *Barnabas* 5:7; 7:2; 15:5; Polycarp, *Philippians* 2:1; *Diognetus* 7:6; Justin, *Dialogue* 118.1; 132.1). One such version of the role of Christ in the eschatological judgment is that of 2 Cor 5:10: "For we all must appear before the tribunal of Christ, so that everyone might receive what he or she did while living, in proportion to what he or she did, whether good or bad." In Rev 1:9–3:22, however, the judgment of Christ is not directed to human beings in general at the last judgment, but rather toward the Christian communities of Roman Asia in the present.

The seven golden menorahs and the seven stars that the exalted Christ holds in his right hand both represent the seven churches (1:20) and so dramatize the close link between Christ and his people. This is a dramatization of the second part of the two-part story that appeared earlier in the doxology in 1:5b-6, in which the liberating death of Jesus becomes the basis for the creation of a new people of God. And the same two-part story is celebrated, as we have seen, in the hymn of praise to the Lamb in 5:9-10, 12.

Rev 1:9-20 concludes in vv. 17-20 with a brief but complex expository speech of the exalted Christ that contains two statements, each with three motifs. The first is an "I am" *(egō eimi)* predication: "I am the First and the Last, even the *Living* One" (vv. 17b-18a). The second statement shares but a single motif ("Living," "live") with the first: "I was dead, but behold I now *live* forever and ever, and I have the keys to Death and Hades" (v. 18b). Both statements are based, at least in part, on a temporal continuum — which means that they imply a story.

"The First and the Last" is a title that occurs three times in the Apocalypse, always as a self-predication of the exalted Christ (1:17; 2:8; 22:13). It is a clear allusion to the Hebrew text of Isa 44:6b, where it is part of a lengthy speech attributed to God (42:14–44:23) in which, toward the end, God emphasizes his absolute sovereignty. That such a predication is fully appropriate only to the God of Israel complements the blended description of "One like a Son of Man" in Rev 1:13-14 with "the Ancient of Days" in Dan 7:9-13, and so implies some kind of equal status for God and Jesus Christ.

The "and" that introduces the third element, "the Living One," should almost certainly be regarded as epexegetic or explanatory (as we have translated it above), suggesting that "the First and the Last" is also "the Living One." This phrase is probably a *double entendre,* or language that lends itself to more than one meaning, for it calls to mind numerous Old Testament passages that refer to the God of Israel as "the living God" (e.g., Deut 5:26; 1 Sam 17:26; Jer 10:10; Dan 6:27), yet is followed in v. 18 by a reference to the death and resurrection of Jesus, who by virtue of the latter event is truly "the living one." And this is in line with the title "the First and the Last" as a self-predication of the exalted Christ in 1:17 being juxtaposed in 22:13 with two other titles used primarily of God: "the Alpha and the Omega" (cf. 1:8; 21:6) and "the Beginning and the End" (cf. 21:6).

Turning to the second christological statement in 1:17-20, the exalted Jesus is presented in v. 18 as saying: "I was dead, but behold I now live forever and ever, and I have the keys to Death and Hades." The death and resurrection of Jesus Christ constitutes a theological abbreviation of the central story of early Christian faith, the Master Story to which each believer subordinates his or her own individual story. The phrase "I have the keys to Death and Hades" refers to the cosmic sovereignty to which Jesus has attained following the act of God raising him from the dead. All three elements are featured in the brief description of the Lamb in 5:6, which was "standing as though slain, with seven horns and seven eyes, which are the seven spirits of God sent out into all the earth." Here "standing" refers to the fact that he is now living, despite the fact that he was slain. And the "seven eyes," understood as "the seven spirits of God sent out into all the earth," is another symbolic way of emphasizing the sovereignty of Jesus Christ.

The Divine Warrior (19:11-21)

The second extensive description of the exalted Christ in the Apocalypse is found in the vision of the rider on the white horse in 19:11-21, which is widely thought to represent the *parousia* of Christ. Like that of 1:9-20, this vision narrative begins in 19:11-16 with a lengthy descriptive passage and then concludes in vv. 17-21 with a truncated narrative of the defeat and destruction of the beast, the false prophet, and the armies of their allied kings. The following chart sets out a translation of the descriptive section of 19:11-16 with parallels from other passages in the Apocalypse. Close parallels are underlined.

Rev 19:11-16   *Parallels in Revelation*

11 I then saw heaven open, and
behold a white steed, and the
person mounted on it

                            3:14 Thus says the Master

is <u>faithful and true</u>.   Workman, <u>the faithful and true</u>
                            Witness
                            1:5 <u>faithful</u> witness
                            3:7 Thus says the Holy One, <u>the</u>
                            <u>True One</u>,

With justice he judges and wages
war.
12 Now <u>his eyes were like a flame of</u>   1:14b <u>His eyes were like a flame of</u>
<u>fire</u> [Dan 10:6c], and on his head   <u>fire</u>
were many diadems with a name
inscribed that no one knows but he
himself. 13 He was dressed in a
garment stained with blood [Isa
63:1, 3b], and his name was called
the Word of God. 14 The heavenly
armies followed him on white
steeds, wearing white, pure linen.
15 <u>From his mouth projected a</u>   1:16b <u>from his mouth issued a</u>
<u>sharp sword</u> that he might smite the   <u>sharp</u> two-edged <u>sword</u>
nations with it [Isa 11:4],

and <u>he himself will rule them with</u>   12:5 <u>one who is to rule all the</u>
<u>an iron crook</u> [Ps 2:9],   <u>nations with an iron crook</u>
                            2:27 <u>he</u> [the conquering believer]
                            <u>shall rule them with a crook of</u>
                            <u>iron</u>

and he himself will tread   14:19b <u>the great winepress of the</u>
<u>the winepress of the furious wrath</u>   <u>wrath of God</u>
<u>of God the Almighty</u> [Isa 63:3].
16 And he has upon his robe, that is,
upon his thigh, a name inscribed,

	17:14 the Lamb . . . is
"King of kings and Lord of lords."	Lord of lords and King of kings

This text sets out a detailed description of a divine warrior that is heavily dependent on the depiction of God as a warrior in Isa 63:1-3 and owes much to the expansive messianic paraphrasing in the Targums, where the winepress and garments bloodied from battle are metaphors for destruction. The exalted Christ is identified here by three positive designations and one negative one: (1) he is "faithful and true" (v. 11), (2) he has "a name inscribed that no one knows but himself" (v. 12), (3) his name is "the Word of God" (v. 13), and (4) he is called "King of kings and Lord of lords" (v. 16). The adjectives "faithful" and "true" are used of Jesus elsewhere in the Apocalypse (1:5; 3:7, 14). That Jesus has a name known to no one but himself (like the conquering believer in 2:17) is enigmatic, but may allude to the true name of God, unknown to all but himself.

"The Word of God" conveys the idea that the rider on the white horse, alias Jesus Christ, represents the will or intention of God in the world. The three motifs of the Word of God, the sharp sword symbolizing that word, and the death that he meted out, are all juxtaposed in Wis 18:15-16, which suggests that this combination of motifs is traditional:

> Thy all-powerful word leaped from heaven,
> from the royal throne,
> into the midst of the land that was doomed;
> a stern warrior carrying the sharp sword
> of thy authentic command,
> and stood and filled all things with death,
> and touched heaven while standing on the earth.

The narrative of the eschatological battle in 19:17-21 is strangely truncated. Preparations for battle are described (vv. 17-19), and the aftermath of the battle is narrated (vv. 20-21), but there is no explicit detailing of the battle itself. Another text in the Apocalypse that briefly narrates the final eschatological battle, 17:14, exhibits a similar "before and after" pattern: "They [the ten kings who cooperate with the beast] will fight against the Lamb, and the Lamb will conquer them, because he is Lord of lords and King of kings, and those with him are called and elect and faithful." Perhaps the first feature of 17:14 that strikes us when comparing it with 19:11-21 is that there the Lamb is called "Lord of lords and King of kings" whereas in 19:16 the order is reversed. These two texts look like versions of the same eschatological event: the beast and his allies are conquered by a protagonist accompanied by a host. There are also, however, some differences — in particular, the protagonist in 17:14 is the Lamb, whereas the protagonist in 19:11-21 is the divine Warrior. But both are transparent guises for Jesus Christ.

If this episode represents the *parousia,* as most commentators suppose, it is distinctive. For the only motif that it shares with other *parousia* passages in the New Testament and early Christian literature is the heavenly host accompanying the protagonist. Absent are references to the Son of Man figure, his coming with clouds, the sounding of the trumpet, and the gathering of the elect (cf. 1 Thess 4:13-17; 2 Thess 2:1-12; Mark 13:26-27 = Matt 24:30-31; Mark 14:62 = Matt 26:64; Rev 1:7; *Didache* 16:7-8; cf. Matt 25:31-46). The various descriptions of the *parousia* in early Christian literature, however, suggest that it was understood as a polyvalent event that could be recounted in a variety of ways depending on the rhetorical situation, emphasizing either the salvific aspects of the *parousia* or its judgmental aspect. The emphasis on the judgment and destruction of the enemies of God in Rev 19:11-21 is captured by the motto in v. 11: "with justice he judges and wages war." Though no mention is made of the people of God, their situation in the world or their eschatological salvation, it is still possible to regard this as a *parousia* narrative, given the variety of performance variants seen elsewhere.

The description and narrative in 19:11-21 center on one significant eschatological feature that concludes the Master Story of the triumph of Jesus Christ: that he acts as God's agent in his role as the future judge of the world in rebellion against God. So in v. 16, which contains the fourth designation of the exalted Christ in the passage, he is called "King of kings and Lord of lords."

6. Concluding Summary

"Who is Jesus Christ?" is obviously a loaded question, since it already implies an answer. "Is" means that Jesus Christ is a figure not only of the past but also — and more importantly — of the present. The name "Jesus Christ," with its submerged reference to messianic status, is not primarily in the Johannine Apocalypse the name of a historical figure, but of the Lord and Savior of the Christian church — thereby investing him with ultimate religious significance.

It is entirely appropriate, however, for a person of faith to direct the question "Who is Jesus Christ?" to the Apocalypse of John. But as central as Jesus Christ is to faith, faith is a Master Story and such stories do not consist of a single character. While the Master Story is never narrated in a complete form in the Apocalypse, it is the presupposition that underlies the entire narrative. And while I have not presented a complete account of the ways in which the Master Story makes its appearances in the Apocalypse, I have attempted to approach several important textual units from a narrative theological perspective.

Even though Hans Frei's exploration of the identity of Jesus focuses on a theological reading of the Gospels, his conclusions appear equally applicable to our narrative reading of the Apocalypse of John (*Identity of Jesus Christ*, 107):

> Jesus' very identity involves the will and purpose of the Father who sent him. He becomes who he is in the story by consenting to God's intention and by enacting that intention in the midst of the circumstances that devolve around him as the fulfillment of God's purpose.

Though the Apocalypse, unlike the Gospels, does not consist of "realistic narrative," but rather "mythical narrative," the author's dramatization of the role of Jesus Christ in the guise of the Lamb appears to reiterate the story of Jesus as found in the Gospels.

As one might expect, the death and resurrection of Jesus constitute focal events in the Master Story of the Apocalypse (as they do in the Gospels), but are rarely mentioned in isolation from other events. The epistolary salutation refers to Jesus Christ as "the faithful witness," "the firstborn from the dead," and "the ruler of the kings of the earth," which refer to his *death, resurrection*, and *cosmic sovereignty* — with these motifs being juxtaposed but not plotted. A similar series of motifs is found among the self-predications of "the One like a Son of Man." In claiming in 1:17-18 that "I was dead, but behold now I live for ever and ever, and I have the keys to Death and Hades," the pattern of *death + resurrection + cosmic sovereignty* is repeated, though still with no causal links between them. Another pattern of events is referred to in the doxology in 1:5b-6: "To the one who loved us and freed us from our sins by his blood, and made us a kingdom, priests to his God and Father." This is a causal pattern, with Jesus Christ's *atoning death* resulting in *the creation of a people*. The same pattern is evident in the hymn of praise in 5:9-10, 12 as well. And lurking at the edges in the reference to "his God and Father" is a central feature of the Master Story of Jesus in the Apocalypse — that is, his role as the agent of God in carrying out God's intentions in the world — which is developed more fully in 4:1–8:1.

The lengthy narrative unit in 4:1–8:1 centers on the figure of the Lamb. Only the Lamb, as depicted in 5:1–6:17; 8:1, is qualified to act as an agent for God — whose intentions for the world apparently cannot be realized without the mediation of the Lamb. The Lamb "completes" or "complements" God, as it were, in his relation to the cosmos. This suggests a pattern of events different from those summarized above: his *conquering death* entitles him to be *the agent of God's will for the cosmos* and so brings about *the conquest of the enemies of God*.

Two very different descriptions of Jesus Christ are presented in the Apocalypse of John: "One like a Son of Man" in 1:9-20 and "the Divine Warrior" in 19:11-21. Both describe the protagonist in language normally thought appropriate only for God. The "One like a Son of Man" is the present Lord of the church, whose will (which must be understood as the intention of God) is made known through revelation to his servant John for the reproof, admonition, and exhortation of his people in the world. "The Divine Warrior" is the agent of God, the "Word of God" who inflicts punishment on the enemies of God and thereby achieves cosmic sovereignty as "King of kings and Lord of lords." This pattern consists of two elements: *conquest of God's enemies*, which results in *cosmic sovereignty*.

SELECTED BIBLIOGRAPHY

Aune, David E. *Revelation*, 3 vols. Nashville: Nelson, 1997-98.

Barr, David L. *Tales of the End: A Narrative Commentary on the Book of Revelation*. Santa Rosa: Polebridge, 1998.

Bauckham, Richard. *The Theology of the Book of Revelation*. Cambridge: Cambridge University Press, 1993.

Boring, M. Eugene. "Narrative Christology in the Apocalypse," *Catholic Biblical Quarterly* 54 (1992) 702-23.

Frei, Hans. *The Identity of Jesus Christ: The Hermeneutical Bases of Dogmatic Theology*. Philadelphia: Fortress, 1975.

————. *Theology and Narrative: Selected Essays,* ed. G. Hunsinger and W. C. Placher. New York: Oxford University Press, 1993.

Krieg, Robert A. *Story-Shaped Christology: The Roles of Narratives in Identifying Jesus Christ.* New York: Paulist, 1988.

Lindbeck, George. *The Nature of Doctrine: Religion and Theology in a Postliberal Age.* Philadelphia: Westminster, 1984.

Robinson, Robert B. "Narrative Theology and Biblical Theology," in *The Promise and Practice of Biblical Theology,* ed. J. Reumann. Minneapolis: Fortress, 1991, 129-42.

Wolter, Michael. "'Revelation' and 'Story' in Jewish and Christian Apocalyptic," in *Revelation and Story: Narrative Theology and the Centrality of Story,* ed. G. Sauter and J. Barton. Aldershot: Ashgate, 2000, 127-44.

Index of Authors

Index of Authors

Index of Subjects

Index of Subjects

Index of Scripture and Other Ancient References

Index of Scripture and Other Ancient References